MAKING AND MOVING KNOWLEDGE

Making and Moving Knowledge

Interdisciplinary and Community-based Research in a World on the Edge

Edited by

JOHN SUTTON LUTZ AND BARBARA NEIS

McGill-Queen's University Press
Montreal & Kingston • London • Ithaca

© McGill-Queen's University Press 2008

ISBN 978-0-7735-3373-8 (cloth)
ISBN 978-0-7735-3393-6 (paper)

Legal deposit second quarter 2008
Bibliothèque nationale du Québec

Printed in Canada on acid-free paper that is 100% ancient forest free (100% post-consumer recycled), processed chlorine free.

This book has been published with the help of a grant from the Canadian Federation for the Humanities and Social Sciences, through the Aid to Scholarly Publications Programme, using funds provided by the Social Sciences and Humanities Research Council of Canada. Funding has also been received from the Social Sciences and Humanities Research Council of Canada and the Natural Sciences and Engineering Humanities Research Council of Canada and the Natural Sciences and Engineering Research Council of Canada through the Coasts Under Stress Research Project.

McGill-Queen's University Press acknowledges the support of the Canada Council for the Arts for our publishing program. We also acknowledge the financial support of the Government of Canada through the Book Publishing Industry Development Program (BPIDP) for our publishing activities.

Library and Archives Canada Cataloguing in Publication

Moving and making knowledge : interdisciplinary and community-based knowledge for a world on the edge / edited by John Lutz and Barbara Neis.

Includes bibliographical references and index.
ISBN 978-0-7735-3373-8 (bnd)
ISBN 978-0-7735-3393-6 (pbk)

1. Knowledge, Sociology of. 2. Interdisciplinary approach to knowledge. 3. Traditional ecological knowledge. I. Lutz, John S. (John Sutton), 1959– II. Neis, Barbara, 1952–

HM651.M69 2008   306.4'2   C2008-900676-3

Typeset by Jay Tee Graphics Ltd. in 10/13 New Baskerville

Contents

Tables and Figures ix
Foreword by Rosemary Ommer xi

PART ONE   GETTING STARTED

1 Introduction   3
   John Sutton Lutz and Barbara Neis

2 Knowledge, Uncertainty, and Wisdom   20
   Rosemary E. Ommer, Harold Coward, and Christopher C. Parrish

PART TWO   BUILDING AND MOVING KNOWLEDGE WITHIN COMMUNITIES

3 "Ebb and Flow": Transmitting Environmental Knowledge in a Contemporary Aboriginal Community   45
   Nancy J. Turner, Anne Marshall, Judith C. Thompson (Edōsdi), Robin June Hood, Cameron Hill, and Eva-Ann Hill

4 Students as Community Participants: Knowledge through Engagement in the Coastal Context   64
   Carol E. Harris and Sandra L. Umpleby

PART THREE   KNOWLEDGE FLOWS AND BLOCKAGES: FISH HARVESTERS' KNOWLEDGE, SCIENCE, AND MANAGEMENT

5 The Evolving Use of Knowledge Sources in Fisheries Assessment   85
   David C. Schneider, Erin Alcock, and Danny Ings

6 Opening the Black Box: Methods, Procedures, and Challenges in the Historical Reconstruction of Marine Social-ecological Systems 100
Grant Murray, Barbara Neis, David C. Schneider, Danny Ings, Karen Gosse, Jennifer Whalen, and Craig T. Palmer

7 Data Fouling in Newfoundland's Marine Fisheries 121
Kaija I. Metuzals, C. Michael Wernerheim, Richard L. Haedrich, Parzival Copes, and Ann Murrin

PART FOUR   KNOWLEDGE FLOWS, POLICY DEVELOPMENT, AND PRACTICE

8 Knowledge Flows around Youth: What Do They "Know" about Human and Community Health? 139
Anne Marshall, Lois Jackson, Blythe Shepard, Susan Tirone, and Catherine Donovan

9 Promoting, Blocking, and Diverting the Flow of Knowledge: Four Case Studies from Newfoundland and Labrador 155
R. John Gibson, Richard L. Haedrich, John C. Kennedy, Kelly M. Vodden, and C. Michael Wernerheim

10 Knowledge Flows, Conservation Values, and Municipal Wetlands Stewardship 178
Brian McLaren, Tim Hollis, Catherine Roach, Kathleen Blanchard, Eric Chaurette, and Dean Bavington

PART FIVE   MOVING KNOWLEDGE ACROSS DISCIPLINES AND BETWEEN UNIVERSITY AND COMMUNITY

11 Knowledge Movement in Response to Coastal British Columbia Oil and Gas Development: Past, Present, and Future 197
Christopher R. Barnes, Robert H. Dennis, Lorne F. Hammond, Marjorie J. Johns, and Gregory S. Kealey

12 The Process of Large-Scale Interdisciplinary Science: A Reflexive Study 222
Peter Trnka

13 Circularizing Knowledge Flows: Institutional Structures, Policies, and Practices for Community-University Collaborations 245
Kelly Vodden and Kelly Bannister

14 Conclusion: Miles To Go 271
Barbara Neis and John Sutton Lutz

Notes 279
Bibliography 295
Index 329

Tables and Figures

TABLES

6.1 Summary of Different Types of Information and Degree of Reliance (High, Medium, Low) in Each Example   117

7.1 Estimated Crab Discards by Weight and Mesh Size   129

7.2 Summary of Fisheries Violations and Convictions, 1970–93   130

9.1 Promoting, Blocking, and Diverting Knowledge: Case Study Summary   159

13.1 Characteristics of Community-University Partnership Models   262

FIGURES

1.1 Research areas in Newfoundland and Labrador   xv

1.2 Research areas in British Columbia   xvi

3.1 Gitga'at elder Helen Clifton and her granddaughter Janelle Reece pounding *wooks* of dried halibut   47

3.2 Differing spatial and temporal scales of traditional ecological knowledge and Western scientific knowledge   48

3.3 Gitga'at elder Archie Dundas harvesting the inner bark of silver fir (*Abies amabilis*)   57

5.1 Shift in sources of information in Eastern Canadian snow crab fisheries   90

5.2 Shift in sources of information in selected Canadian herring fisheries   94

6.1 Changes in vessel length, distance travelled, and cod landings for one respondent   109

6.2 Space and time scales of knowledge gathering and assembly (A) by computational model in fisheries research; (B) for a community of people engaged in fishing   110

6.3 Cod migration patterns described by respondents on the Great Northern Peninsula and the Strait of Belle Isle   112

6.4 Knowledge assembly and flow through participatory action research   118

9.1 Locations of the case studies in Newfoundland and Labrador   158

9.2 The loss and remediation of the trophy trout fishery at Indian Bay   161

9.3 The importance of interactions between local ecological knowledge and scientific knowledge, and co-operation between the various authorities   170

10.1 Knowledge flow in (A) Traditional resource conservation programs in Canada, and (B) Municipal Wetlands Stewardship (MWS) programs   181

11.1 Dispersed impact of knowledge movement   199

11.2 Participants and patterns of knowledge flow   200

11.3 Components of learning and knowledge bundles   200

11.4 Time slice of knowledge flow   201

11.5 Shell Canada Ltd, Sedco 135F semi-submersible drilling rig under construction in Victoria, 1966–67   207

Foreword

This volume grows out of the realization developed over many research projects that science is not sufficient if we are to lead lives that are in harmony with our society and our environment. We need better ways of knowing what we are doing and of knowing what to do about the problems that face us in the form of endangered fish stocks, depleted forests, and troubled coastal communities. Coastal people are suffering, and our science does not have all the answers. We need more knowledge, and more different kinds of knowledge, and that knowledge, when it is created, needs pathways, needs to be stored and retrieved, and most of all it needs an audience. We need to understand much more about how knowledge accumulates, moves, and does not move. We need to think about what has to happen to turn knowledge into wise choices.

This book is a rare look at what knowledge is, how different kinds of knowledge are created, and what needs to guide the vital relationship between knowledge creation and its dissemination to a variety of different audiences. It is concerned particularly with social-ecological knowledge systems and the challenges associated with moving knowledge across disciplinary boundaries, within and between knowledge systems, and from people to researchers to policy-makers to students and back to communities, in order to grapple with interactive restructuring and its effect.

The volume grows out of a bold experiment in creating and moving knowledge. Coasts Under Stress was a five-year, completely interdisciplinary (social sciences, humanities, natural and earth sciences, education, and health) project based at the University of Victoria and Memorial University of Newfoundland that examined the ways in which interactive restructuring of society and the environment affected the health of both. We put together natural and social scientists, educators, humanists, and health professionals to consider, in consultation with coastal communities, what was wrong, how it had come about, and what might be done about it. Our results are to be found in numerous journal articles, two films, one book written especially for policymakers, one book written especially for coastal communities, one overview volume, and three thematic collections that looked in depth at some of the important issues we uncovered. Together they show how the various parts of life in coastal communities fit together and how interactive restructuring has generated the risks, threats, and opportunities coastal communities (human and biophysical) confront.

The coastal communities of Canada are important. They not only carry significant parts of our history and culture, but they are also the interface between threatened ecosystems, terrestrial and marine. They are a microcosm of the battle that the world needs to wage against resource degradation, which interacts in powerful ways with society to produce cultural, social, and economic distress and further degradation of the natural environment. In an increasingly urbanized world, we forget what is happening "on the margin," but it is on the margin that the confrontations are most bleak and most apparent, because the scale is small enough and the social and technological buffers slight enough not to blur our vision. Canada's coastal resource communities will either be stewards of the ocean for us in the future or symbols of the way in which a globalized world can – for a short time – engulf small places, small-scale livelihoods, and cultural particularities. Thought about from a longer-term perspective, however, they are the "miner's canary" for a world in which resources are becoming scarcer, environmental degradation more pervasive, and power imbalances more overwhelming.

In addition to this book, a second thematic volume (Sinclair and Ommer 2006) looks at issues of power in a restructured natural and social world and the relationship between interactive restructuring and power, whether as energy (oil and gas, hydro) or as "power over nature constructs" or as power and agency in nature and in human communities. The third volume (Parish et al. 2008) is concerned with the history of health, diet, and nutrition – with a particular focus on the issue of decreasing food security in places where once-stable food webs have suffered radical shock, as have the cultures of human communities that have always been interdependent with now-endangered food sources.

The overview volume (Ommer et al. 2007) was team-written and was, in itself, an experiment in interdisciplinary scholarship in which the team planned the volume, contributed their findings to all the sections (which were then written up by the project director), commented on the manuscript as it evolved, and approved its final shape.

In all our work, by *environmental restructuring* we mean changes in the environment, usually at large scales, that are thought to be caused, at least in part, by such things as environmental damage through pollution or other factors or climate variation. We take *social restructuring* to mean changes in society at a range of scales that result in, for example, changes in community cohesion, social support, health care delivery, or the availability of educational resources. Such changes include industrial restructuring, which deals with changes in patterns of ownership and control and in work environments, and political restructuring, which deals with shifts in policy regimes. We take *health* to be the capacity to cope with stressors. Recognizing that people are part of (not outside) nature, we take s*ocial-ecological* health to be the capacity of the human-natural world nexus to deal resiliently with change and the stress that it brings.

We wish to take this opportunity to thank the Social Sciences and Humanities Research Council of Canada, the Natural Sciences and Engineering Research Council of Canada, Memorial University of Newfoundland, and the University of Victoria for major funding of this work and for ongoing support throughout the lifetime of the project. We owe a debt of gratitude to Yves Mougeot and Katharine Benzekri of SSHRC, along with the various SSHRC officers who assisted us, particularly Jacques Critchely, who got us started; Pierre-Francois LeFol, who was with us in our middle period; and Michele Dupuis, who saw us through to the end. We also wish to express our gratitude to André Isabelle and Anne Alper of NSERC, whose assistance has likewise been invaluable throughout all the years of our work. This project could not have been carried out without a dedicated staff, and we here thank Janet Oliver, Carrie Holcapek, Cathy King, Kari Marks, Angela Drake, and Moira Wainwright for their hard work, constancy, and continued support through thick and thin. We wish also to thank the other universities whose faculty contributed to our work: the University of British Columbia (and, in particular, the Fisheries Centre and the Department of Geography), Dalhousie University, Saint Mary's University, and the University of New Brunswick. Our heartfelt thanks go to our partners and our advisory boards, named on our website (www. coastsunderstress. ca), and to the Centre for Studies in Religion and Society and the Centre for Earth and Ocean Research, both at the University of Victoria, for providing the West Coast part of the team with a home. On the East Coast, Memorial University provided a small building for the use of staff, faculty, and students, while on the West Coast the University of Victoria gave the project director an academic home. We are grateful to both these institutions for their generosity and for their faith in us.

For helping bring this book into being, we particularly wish to thank Janet Oliver for her support and Graeme Brock and Kari Marks for preparing a thorough index. We also want to thank Ron Curtis for his careful and thoughtful copy editing and Joan McGilvray at McGill-Queen's University Press for guiding the book through the publication process.

Rosemary E. Ommer, University of Victoria, March 2008

Figure 1.1 Research areas in Newfoundland and Labrador

Figure 1.2 Research areas in British Columbia

PART ONE
Getting Started

1

Introduction

JOHN SUTTON LUTZ AND BARBARA NEIS

How we turn information into knowledge and knowledge into wisdom is one of the two most pressing questions of our time. How we move knowledge and wisdom to the people who urgently need it is the second. Whether the immediate challenge is global warming, epidemic disease, poverty, environmental degradation, or social fragmentation, our research efforts are all wasted if we cannot devise processes to create and transfer knowledge to policy-makers, interested groups, and ordinary people in a manner that is efficient and understandable.

Whether we look at scientific, policy, or popular literature, the new dominant paradigms point to our world being on the verge of an environmental and social collapse. The most comprehensive recent report, the United Nations-sponsored Millennium Ecosystem Assessment, a product of the work of thousands of scientists in dozens of working groups, warns "that changes being made in ecosystems are increasing the likelihood of nonlinear changes in ecosystems" (MA 2005, 16). In everyday parlance, these scientists are talking of the likelihood of ecological systems hitting critical "tipping points" where change will be catastrophic and irreversible, the so-called "house of cards effect." Social scientists like Jared Diamond and humanist Ronald Wright have demonstrated how societies have historically fallen into knowledge traps, where the mechanisms needed to transmit knowledge and avoid repeating destructive behaviour have failed and empires have fallen.

From all these different points of view contemporary observers make it clear that lack of knowledge is often not the only or the most fundamental problem (Ommer et al. 2007; Diamond 2005, 1997; Wright 2004; Homer-Dixon 2001; Tainter 1988). Rather, in the language of the Millennium Ecosystem Assessment, "there is limited capability of communicating to non-specialists the complexity associated with holistic models and scenarios," especially given the complex, non-linear features, feedbacks, and time lags in most ecosystems (MA 2005, 170). The gap between what people "in the know" *know* and what the public and people in power *know* is huge and often growing. But the problem is even deeper. The Millennium Assessment takes account only of the difficulty of communicating the complexity of ecosystem processes, not social processes and institutional barriers to change and awareness. We do not know enough about interactive processes, particularly interactions between social and environmental change. We do not know how to effectively move knowledge in a way that interconnects communities, governments, businesses, universities, and individuals. Nor do we understand why, even in the face of clear and imminent danger, institutions and people with knowledge will not always act wisely.

One of the most profound awakenings and greatest challenges that the twentieth century left to the twenty-first is the realization of the complex interconnectedness of humans, human health, and knowledge production with the natural and social worlds we inhabit. With this awakening has come disillusionment with the utopian claims of modern science and greater awareness of the inevitable presence of uncertainty, complexity, and dynamism within the social and natural worlds. It has long been acknowledged that research does not directly translate into knowledge, that knowledge does not necessarily, or even often, translate into wisdom. While the application of research to real-world problems can benefit society, it can also contribute to serious, often unintended consequences for people, societies, and physical and biochemical environments. It is becoming increasingly clear that "[i]mperfect knowledge and uncertainties characterize and challenge environmental decision-making and governance at all levels" (Paavola and Adger 2004, 175). How we can maximize the strength of research, refine that into knowledge, distill it into wisdom, and increase the likelihood that our research will benefit wider society and the environment in the short and longer terms must be *the* key issues in a world with scarce research resources and urgent social, scientific, environmental, and health challenges to resolve (SSHRC 2003).

This book arises from and draws on research carried out for the Coasts Under Stress project, a Major Collaborative Research Initiative jointly funded by the Canadian Social Sciences and Humanities Research Council (SSHRC) and the Natural Science and Engineering Research Council (NSERC), to try to address these interconnections.

The central research question in the Coasts Under Stress project asks how industrial, institutional, and social restructuring have interacted with the restructuring of biophysical environments and food webs to affect the health of people, communities, and environments on Canada's East and West Coasts (Dolan et al. 2005). Restructuring implies not only changes to environments, the lives of people, and their communities but also requirements for new knowledge and new institutional structures for knowledge production and transfer. Acknowledgement of these interactive effects of restructuring points to the need for new avenues of research; new types of sources are required, as are many, more inclusive methodologies.

Coastal areas are "frontier societies" in that they are on the edges of the world economy where ongoing events such as resource degradation, in- and out-migration, administrative neglect, and other processes are further contributing to their marginalization and vulnerability (Visser 2004, 25). If coastal communities are on the environmental and economic frontiers their experience is a bellwether for the urban core. As with other parts of the world, coastal areas are grappling with the effects of resource degradation, ecosystem transformation, and resource scarcity. They are diversifying economically and socially and are becoming increasingly complex and dynamic in the sense that they are subject to the influence of lengthening chains of interaction (Kooiman and Bavinck 2005, 13).

Key coastal economic activities such as fisheries, forestry, mining, and tourism are experiencing the effects of the globalization of production, trade, and regulation. The globalization of production relates to the increasing range of activities in these sectors, the globalization of trade refers to the increasing commodification of coastal resources and of the economic lives of coastal peoples; and the globalization of regulatory control refers to "the burgeoning body of rules and guidelines" affecting these sectors at all levels (Kooiman and Bavinck 2005, 13). These transformations of coastal areas have highlighted the shortcomings associated with discipline-based science, as well as command-and-control approaches to resource management and the bodies of knowledge with which they have been associated. Questions about how knowledge is produced and moves, does not move, and should move are fundamental to understanding this and other crises and to developing appropriate responses to those crises.

This volume uses studies of Canada's East and West Coasts to directly address the issues of how knowledge is created, moved, distorted, blocked, and used. The essays in this book take on the challenges of trans-boundary knowledge production and exchange with a focus not only on the boundaries between disciplines but also on those between researchers and communities, within communities, and between research and policy. Environmental, social, and economic change by definition affects how we generate information (for example, by means of markets, new research tools, different pressing questions) and how we transmit it (for example, through schools, government, courts). Research on interactive processes can offer reflections, suggestions, critiques, and concrete tools to communities of learning: schools, universities, researchers, research teams, and funding agencies.

We believe that what we have learned throughout Coasts Under Stress work is relevant to multiple audiences with an interest in knowledge, research, transdisciplinarity, and "outside-the-box" thinking. The project has offered a particular vantage point because points of crisis, such as those evident on Canada's coasts, often reveal underlying problems which are normally hard to discern and usually pass unacknowledged. The research relayed here arises from, and is grounded in, these social-ecological crises; it describes and, in some ways, models institutional structures, formulas, and pathways that affect the generation and effective transmission of knowledge about social-ecological systems.

Our coasts are littoral zones – areas of transition where the edges of the land meet the sea and the air. As worlds on the continental fringes teetering on the edge of social-ecological crisis they are appropriate places to take on the challenges associated with producing and moving transdisciplinary, interdisciplinary, and integrated knowledge production. What are some of those challenges? First, how can we bring knowledge generated by universities and governments together with "traditional" and practical knowledge generated in aboriginal and non-aboriginal communities? Second, how can we get knowledge to move outside the narrow silos of disciplinary understanding when universities are built upon disciplinary divisions, when natural and social scientists and humanists are often trained to specialize and to emphasize the uniqueness of their work relative to that of other disciplines and approaches? Even governments are structured to receive knowledge in discrete and competing ministries of fishery or forestry, of health or environment. The urgent problems of our time are too vast to be taken up by a team comprised exclusively of political scientists, climatologists, physicians, sociologists, or historians. Third, how do we organize "science" so that knowledge can flow, be understood and redeployed in different communities of knowledge: researchers to politicians, to public health programs, and to local communities. In a "knowledge society," how can we ensure that it flows not just in one direction but in a circle, so that it is generated, acknowledged, tested, refined, rethought, and ultimately diffused as wisdom?

There are thirteen essays in this book, but forty authors, from fields as diverse as geoscience and philosophy. This book is an experiment in transdisciplinary team writing. All but one of the chapters was written by trans- or interdisciplinary teams, and each chapter has been reviewed and discussed with the authors of all the other chapters. The key concepts have emerged from this team work. The chapters are theoretical and methodological, as well as applied, since there has been a commitment to knowledge transfer and exchange among researchers and between researchers and members of participating communities, some of whom are co-authors. As a result, the chapters both reflect on *and* model innovative forms of knowledge production and knowledge movement.

Underlying the collection are three key concerns: linking the production and movement of knowledge to power relations; engaging the relationships between knowledge, uncertainty, and scale; and addressing the problems of inter- or transdisciplinarity as an important example of cross-cultural interaction, with all its inherent difficulties in mutual comprehension. These are key and understudied features of knowledge movement, given that "the data and information that are available are generally related to either the characteristics of the ecological system or the characteristics of the social system, not to the all-important interactions between these systems" (MA 2005, 11).

The collection is organized into five parts. Part 1 sets the context for the collection and contains this overview and the contribution "Knowledge, Uncertainty, and Wisdom" by economic historian Rosemary E. Ommer, humanist Harold Coward, and natural scientist Christopher C. Parrish. They explore knowledge production within the natural and social sciences and humanities, distinguishing between facts, information, data, knowledge, and wisdom.

Throughout the book we use the term *information* to refer to data gathered from any source and organized so that it has some relationship to a question or a problem. For our purposes, *knowledge* is the application of critical faculties to information/data to gain understanding, as distinct from opinion. Knowledge may be "theoretical or practical understanding, and familiarity gained by experience" (Fowler and

Fowler 1964). Inherent then, as Ommer et al. tell us, in the definition of knowledge – and without any ranking – are theoretical, practical, and experiential forms, including traditional knowledge. "Knowledge is far more than simple information. It can be regarded as a complex system of learning and understanding, with many different facets and components. It incorporates experiences, skills, and techniques, remembered and accumulated. It embodies perceptions, observations, actions, analyses, conceptual constructs, attitudes, and worldviews" (Turner et al., this volume, chap. 3).

While information can be disembodied, packaged, quantified archived and transmitted, knowledge requires a "knower." Knowledge exists only in a social context, and often, since it has an experiential component, it exists in a place. All knowledge is environmental in that it is constructed and shaped through interactions with particular environments (institutional, built and technological, biochemical, physical). Because it is embodied in people and in particular places and institutions, knowledge, unlike information, is surprisingly difficult to move. (Brown and Duguild 2000).

Since knowledge is the culmination of the effort to conceptualize a problem, the construction of a research method (however simple); the accumulation of information, the discrimination between relevant and irrelevant information, and the application of critical thinking that is culturally bound, it cannot be universally "true". All knowledge is social in that it is "constructed through interactions among individuals" (Longino 1990, 231). It is our overarching assumption that approaching an object, or an event from different locations/standpoints can help us see more clearly the specificity and situatedness of our knowledge and where that of others can help.

Ommer, Coward, and Parrish remind us that because knowledge is socially embedded, it is subject to the observational and other biases associated with a specific society at a specific period of history. They draw particular attention to the challenge of uncertainty and the importance of bi-directional knowledge movement from academic creators to a broad range of users and from other knowledge creators (such as communities) back to the academy. Historically, much energy has been invested in promoting some knowledge forms over others: whether disciplinary rivals, paradigmatic rivals, applied versus basic research, or scientific versus folk and indigenous peoples' knowledge. This has been wasted energy that, given our scarce resources and time, must be redirected to learning from each other.

Part 2, "Building and Moving Knowledge within Communities," recognizes that the most institutionalized of all sites of knowledge transmission, schools and universities, are themselves embedded in a stratigraphy of power (Bourdieu 1996). The chapters focus on building opportunities for intergenerational knowledge transfer (Turner, Marshall, Thompson (Edosdi), Hood, C. Hill, and E. Hill) and on the relationship between restructuring and knowledge production, and flows between schools and larger communities in contemporary British Columbia (Harris and Umpleby).

"'Ebb and Flow': Transmitting Environmental Knowledge in a Contemporary Aboriginal Community" looks at past mechanisms for transmission of ecological knowledge and practices within indigenous communities and ways to adapt these practices within contemporary communities. The authors include university researchers, two local teachers, and a graduate student. They argue that traditional knowledge is a complex system of learning and understanding that is essential to community adaptation and resilience. The chapter uses a case study of a program involving youth and elders designed to promote acquisition and revitalization of traditional knowledge related to the harvesting and processing of food resources within the Gitga'at (Coast Tsimshian) community of Hartley Bay, on the north coast of British Columbia.

In "Students as Community Participants: Knowledge through Engagement in the Coastal Context," Harris and Umpleby focus their attention on the relationship between knowledge and power. All knowledge production and all knowledge exchange (including science) are susceptible to the influence of power. In essence, "[p]ower and knowledge are inextricably intertwined" (Gaventa and Cornwall 2001, 70). Knowledge and research can be seen as resources mobilized in public debates and in decision making more generally. They are also part of agenda-setting processes (the so-called second dimension of power) that influence the issues that make it onto decision-making agendas. Finally knowledge and research can influence power through influencing consciousness – that is, how we see the world and our interests (Gaventa and Cornwall 2001, 71–2). However, this formulation of the relationship between knowledge and power focuses only on "power over" and the repressive potential of power and hence of knowledge. More recent conceptualizations, drawing on the work of Foucault and others, have advocated a broader approach to power with a focus on how power (and knowledge) both delimit and enable action. From this point of view,

[k]nowledge, as much as any resource, determines definitions of what is conceived as important, as possible, for, and by whom. Through access to knowledge, and participation in its production, use and dissemination, actors can affect the boundaries and indeed the conceptualization of the possible. In some situations, the asymmetrical control of knowledge productions of others can severely limit the possibilities which can be either imagined or acted upon; in other situations, agency in the process of knowledge production, or co-production with others, can broaden these boundaries enormously. (Gaventa and Cornwall 2001, 72)

Harris and Umpleby distinguish between knowledge *about* the world acquired through information or facts and knowledge *of* the world gained through engagement. Education is not simply putting students in touch with information; it is also putting them in touch with communities. Using two case studies of student activities in British Columbia schools, they highlight ways teachers and students have found to resist the effects of educational restructuring, including support for megaschools, youth out-migration, the separation of education from communities, and an associated shift in power away from communities and students. In their examples drawn from the schools, students move into their communities and, through engagement, come to embody knowledge *of* and *with* their communities. Like Turner *et al.*, Harris and Umpleby argue that restructuring links between schools, students, and communities has the potential to encourage questioning, support cultural identity, and promote community health and resilience.

Part 3, "Knowledge Flows and Blockages: Fish Harvesters' Knowledge, Science, and Management," contains three chapters about knowledge production and reconstruction, and flows, with a particular focus on changing relationships between different knowledge systems in fisheries (fish harvesters' knowledge, scientific knowledge, and management knowledge). Each chapter explores the relationship between those changes and the wider society, and the challenges, as well as the potential benefits, associated with attempting to combine information from different knowledge systems. Taking as their point of departure inshore fish harvesters' complaints in the 1980s and 1990s that their knowledge and concerns about the health of Newfoundland and Labrador's northern cod stocks were ignored by scientists and managers, biologists Schneider, Alcock, and Ings examine the history of knowledge creation and flow within fisheries science and management in chapter 5. To do this, they reviewed the historical assessment documents for Atlantic cod, developed a model of change in knowledge sources over time, and then tested this model against multiple fisheries for two other species. Overall, they found a similar pattern of knowledge production and transmission for very different fisheries: a movement from an initial reliance on harvester knowledge to knowledge almost exclusively based on expert modelling and large-scale estimates, which has been followed by a fisheries crisis and a move to more hybrid systems, with harvesters' knowledge regaining (at least temporarily) a place in stock assessment and management decisions.

Contemporary thinking supports the view that there is no single, "true" understanding of a particular reality but that there are instead multiple possibilities and areas of focus (Haraway 1991). Now, when so much is at stake, when problems are so large, we must "learn how to learn" across cultural and disciplinary boundaries and imposed hierarchies that have ranked disciplines and scholarly and folk knowledge. Real abstract and practical knowledge lives in communities of scientists and in workers and fishers, hunters and teachers, bureaucrats and youth, as well as in schools, universities, corporations, and government.

Discipline-based knowledge production will tend to mask or misinterpret processes and outcomes associated with interactive effects. Placing our focus on such effects highlights the need to move beyond the status quo within which "[e]nvironmental change and social transformation are mostly analysed in isolation from each other, according to different epistemologies, and approached from different bodies of knowledge" (Visser 2004, 25). Documenting these interactive processes and their effects requires cross-disciplinary and cross-cultural collaborations and, in many cases, the development of new methodologies and new approaches to knowledge production. If the creation of new knowledge is a kind of discovery, the spaces between disciplines and cultures are rich spaces for exploration because, by definition, they are neglected spaces. These intellectual "wild spaces" beyond the cultivated gardens of disciplinary knowledge, where the fisher meets the forest, the scholar meets the storyteller, and the paleogeologist the philosopher, are in today's world very productive places for the discovery of knowledge and the cultivation of wisdom.

How do we learn from knowledge generated in other cultures and contexts (that is, from other disciplines, from vernacular knowledge, and from other forms) when their ways of knowing seem so foreign, so incommensurable, with our own ways of knowing? For working across disciplines, Visser advocates "a concerted interaction between the social sciences and the natural sciences [and, we would add, the health sciences], in which epistemological differences and conceptual incongruences become transparent in order to be overcome" (2004, 27). It is not enough to gather two or three disciplines around a theme; as Roland Barthes has observed, "interdisciplinarity consists of creating a new object that belongs to no one." Visser calls for *transdisciplinarity* rather than *multidisciplinarity* or *interdisciplinarity*, arguing that there is a paradox to transdisciplinary research in that "the more one starts thinking along transdisciplinary lines, the more this trajectory provides an incentive to or even demands that one reconsiders one's own disciplinary assumptions and concepts" (Visser 2004, 27–8). Transdisciplinarity, she argues, invites us to critically examine our own disciplinary assumptions and to reveal, rather than conceal, discontinuities; it aims at "boundary areas" and at discovering "cutting-edge issues" and new research questions that go beyond partner disciplines. Whatever term we choose, the issues she addresses are important to our understanding of making and moving knowledge. The challenges she associates with transdisciplinarity are also evident in efforts to combine insights from vernacular or local or traditional knowledge and science.

In chapter 6 the problem of reconciling apparently incommensurable systems of knowledge is tackled by a transdisciplinary team of researchers from natural resource management, sociology, geography, anthropology, and fisheries biology. "Opening the Black Box: Methods, Procedures, and Challenges in the Historical Reconstruction of Marine Social-ecological Systems" examines information drawn from a range of methodologies and from science and fish harvesters' knowledge. This Newfoundland and Labrador project was designed to collect, analyse, and combine information drawn from fish harvesters' ecological knowledge, historical data on fish landings, and results from research vessel surveys to track social-ecological interactions between fish and fishers over time. Murray, Neis, Schneider, Ings, Gosse, Whalen, and Palmer start from the premise that there are different knowledge systems (local ecological knowledge [LEK], natural sciences, governance, and social sciences) based on different assumptions and observations but that all contain information relevant to understanding the complex and interactive changes in social-ecological systems like coastal communities and linked marine environments. Each type of knowledge is incomplete, falling short of producing a multi-scale picture, but, they propose a methodology to allow the different sources of information to complement one another, helping to make macro-micro and historical linkages more apparent.

In chapter 7, "Data Fouling in Newfoundland's Marine Fisheries," the team of Metuzals, Wernerheim, Haedrich, Copes, and Murrin, consisting of natural scientists and economists, raises the question nobody wants to ask: What if the "scientific data" our decisions are based on is so flawed that it misleads? They argue that this is indeed the case in many fisheries, owing to the serious problem of unreported catch (bycatch, discards, and so forth) and "data fouling," that is, distortion of the information available for stock assessment science and management. Data fouling, they argue, results in stocks appearing healthier than they are, and hence leads to unsustainable quotas and overfishing. Their chapter presents results from a survey of fish harvesters related to unreported catches that they have used as a basis for modelling the scope of data fouling under different scenarios.

Part 4, "Knowledge Flows, Policy Development, and Practice," draws on research conducted on Canada's East and West Coasts. Chapter 8, "Knowledge Flows around Youth: What do They 'Know' about Human and Community Health?" by education researcher Marshall and health sociologist Jackson uses a social-constructivist approach that, as with other contributions, treats knowledge as situated in time, space, and culture. This youth-focused research explores issues related to "knowledge uptake" and the ways youth transitioning into adulthood understand, communicate, and make meaning of knowledge linked to health and well-being in communities that have undergone rapid and multidimensional restructuring in recent years. They note the frequent marginalization of youth in biomedical research on health, arguing that their social location (including their limited power in decision-making processes) means that youth living in coastal communities have a distinct understanding of health. They point to the need for new strategies to understand the real sources of youth knowledge and new pathways to learn from youth. Marshall and Jackson demonstrate how certain knowledges, particularly youth knowledge, are often marginalized by educational and community structures. At the same time, the earlier essays by Turner et al. and Harris and Umpleby show, these structures are not fixed. Schools, universities, and the media can be and have been reorganized and their resources redeployed to critique and reverse the flow of knowledge that was previously dominant.

In "Promoting, Blocking, and Diverting the Flow of Knowledge: Four Case Studies from Newfoundland and Labrador," biologists Gibson and Haedrich join with anthropologist Kennedy, environmental studies specialist Vodden, and economist Wernerheim to present an ideal model for the production and movement of knowledge. They use the model to assess actual patterns of knowledge production and flow in four situations where restructuring posed a threat to natural environments in Newfoundland and Labrador. They open with an exploration of the interaction between knowledge production, social dynamics, and policy outcomes in the Indian Bay watershed area in central Newfoundland. This case study approximates their ideal of an appropriate and effective knowledge flow situation. In the other case studies, including studies of the recent construction of the Labrador Road from Red Bay to Cartwright in southeastern Labrador, a development decision in a watershed area in St John's, and the construction of a hydro dam at Star Lake, knowledge flows were, to varying degrees, less than ideal, with significant consequences for the natural environment.

Chapter 10, "Knowledge Flows, Conservation Values, and Municipal Wetlands Stewardship" is contributed by biologist McLaren, working with geographers, humanists, and others. McLaren, Hollis, Roach, Blanchard, Chaurette, and Bavington use a case study of the Newfoundland and Labrador Municipal Wetland Stewardship Program to explore knowledge and its role in determining and predicting conservation values related to this program. They focus on the often blurred boundaries between "knowledge" and "values" associated with environmental education and conservation programs of this kind. Their examination of the Municipal Wetland Stewardship Program brings to the fore the values and judgments embedded within it. Results from research carried out in four different communities show that people in some communities embraced these values and reinterpreted their surroundings in line with them. Elsewhere, there was a conflict between these values and those of local people, whose traditional knowledge and approaches could provide an alternative approach to promoting conservation through stewardship in the future. When they work, the authors argue, such programs create a structure that permits the capturing of knowledge that is otherwise diffuse and partial, and they can promote voluntary care of the environment (stewardship) through knowledge acquisition, internalization, and a related willingness to work voluntarily for conservation. Such programs also provide a hedge against the problems associated with uncertainty and fallible science that can erode the legitimacy of command-and-control approaches to management.

Part 5, "Moving Knowledge across Disciplines and between University and Community," begins with a contribution co-authored by earth scientists (Barnes and Johns) and historians (Dennis, Hammond, and Kealey). "Knowledge Movement in Response to Coastal British Columbia Oil and Gas Development: Past, Present and Future" (chap. 11) offers a model of knowledge production and flows comprising multiple stakeholders, spatial and temporal dimensions, communications, and other pathways related to knowledge flows and outcomes. The authors' analytical framework also includes the notion of knowledge bundles which tend to expand over time as events unfold and that include ideas, questions, and information. Like McLaren *et al.*, they highlight the importance of values. In the main body of the chapter, Barnes et al. use a discussion of the past, present, and future of oil and gas development in British Columbia to explore two main elements of their model: the relationship between values, knowledge, and policy in the interplay between government and the public (communities), as well as the role of disciplinary values (another type of community value) in the creation and application of scientific knowledge around oil and gas development. Differences in the history of offshore oil and gas development on Canada's East and West Coasts are used to help us understand the relationship between knowledge flows, the impact of the media, and policy outcomes. A history of geoscience contributes to our understanding of the dynamics of knowledge production and communication. The concluding section speaks to contemporary challenges confronting geoscience, arguing for "big science," that is, an "earth system science" that incorporates environmental/human impact studies linking earth, ocean, and atmospheric sciences. It identifies the persistence of disciplinary silos within the earth sciences and between these and the social sciences within universities as a barrier to earth system science. Other barriers to a broadly interdisciplinary earth system science within government and elsewhere are also discussed.

Chapter 12, "The Process of Large-Scale Interdisciplinary Science: A Reflexive Study," written by philosopher Trnka is the only single-authored contribution to this collection. It reports on some of Trnka's research into knowledge production and interactions within Coasts Under Stress, a working example of "big interdisciplinary science" in action. Like Barnes et al., he explores some of the factors that appear to be driving the paradigm shift from individual, disciplinary science to large, interdisciplinary, team-based science. He asks whether this trend to big science is justified in terms of its scientific benefits or whether it is really about something else, including, potentially, the self-aggrandizement of scientists. Drawing on work done in the philosophy and sociology of science, he decides to make the Coasts Under Stress investigators, rather than their science, the focus of his inquiry, using social science tools such as a semi-structured questionnaire. This reflexive piece discusses the research process as much as the research results associated with the Coasts Under Stress project.

Trnka highlights multiple issues related to the definition or understanding of the meaning of "science," disciplinarity, interdisciplinarity, and transdisciplinarity, issues related to the organization and dynamics of the project, as well as issues related to the administrative push versus scientific pull of large projects. The problem of transdisciplinarity and interdisciplinarity is the problem of reconciling different world views. The cultures of the physical scientist, the social scientist, and the humanist or the cultures of the urban bureaucrat and the rural harvester can be as foreign to each other as the culture of the Finnish utopians who settled British Columbia's Malcolm Island in the second decade of the twentieth century was to the culture of the Namgis Aboriginal People on neighbouring Cormorant Island or as the culture of the Labrador Innu was to the American airmen who built the wartime defences at Goose Bay in the 1940s.

Thinking about knowledge production and exchange as a cross-cultural project, we can see some of the obstacles. Each discipline has a different culture of knowledge, proof, and truth, particularly when you cross the divide separating the "hard" sciences from the "soft" social sciences and humanities (Ommer et al., this volume, chap. 2). As Trnka says, each discipline has its own specialized language and words mean one thing in one discipline and something different in another. There are different notions of what constitutes objective and subjective knowledge (Ommer et al., this volume, chap. 2; Ommer et al., 2007). The disciplines have different rituals of communication (historians like books; geologists like articles) and socialization (philosophers like to work alone; biologists in extended laboratory families), different economies ($56.4 million for the University of Saskatchewan's Light Source Project, for example), tools, and hierarchies.

One discipline, among the many, specializes in cross-cultural understanding – anthropology, and more especially ethnography – and there may be ways in which insights ethnographers have gained from studying the movement of meaning across cultures can assist the knowledge project. Another discipline, literary studies, has specialized in how meaning is transformed when words are transmitted. These days, scholars in both fields are drawing on the work of Mikhail Bakhtin, who engaged the problem of communication. His is ultimately a hopeful approach because he suggests that in every attempt at communication, something is transmitted, since it is an attempt to enter the conceptual world of the person/people we want to engage. We want to be understood, and we continually adjust our message until we see signs of comprehension and mutual understanding (Bakhtin 1996; Todorov 1984). In the Coasts Under Stress project natural scientists, humanists, and social scientists met and met and met some more, until such comprehension started to happen. The approach suggests we need to step into transdisciplinary projects as carefully as a Newfoundland ethnographer might step into a Tibetan yurt or a Romany caravan. We must be prepared to engage in the hard work of listening across boundaries and enter into the strangeness on the other side. That is the hard part. But the harder part is trying to step out of our own disciplinary or cultural world view, or put another way, to pull back the blinders just enough to see that they are there.

We return to one of the core issues in moving knowledge in chapter 13, "Circularizing Knowledge Flows: Institutional Structures, Policies, and Practices for Community-University Collaborations," by Vodden and Bannister. Sharing knowledge is an integral and assumed aspect of such partnerships. In their contribution, Vodden and Bannister ask just how effectively knowledge flows between universities and communities. They also try to identify the essential components of reciprocal interchanges, as well as the main barriers to them. They explore these issues by drawing on insights from four case studies of community-university initiatives: studies of the Northern Barkley and Clayoquot Sound region of western Vancouver Island (British Columbia), northern Vancouver Island (British Columbia), the Indian Bay watershed (Newfoundland), and associated field research in the Bras d'Or Lakes watershed of Cape Breton. For each case, they examine the organizational structures, policies, and practices that facilitate or impede reciprocal knowledge exchange. In particular, they examine how knowledge does or does not move between universities and communities and why. Returning to the question of power, they highlight what they consider essential elements in ethical and equitable community-university research partnerships for coastal communities and universities. They conclude that there is a growing collective *will* to attempt to link knowledge systems. They suggest some models and point to the need for more attention to this critical nexus in a desirable circular information flow.

The Coasts Under Stress project attempted to model a circular flow of knowledge, with the Bannister and Vodden work among many projects disseminating results in the communities where research knowledge was first gained, as well as in policy and scholarly forums. We have sought to build into our work multiple occasions and venues for meeting with individuals and groups within coastal communities, in an attempt to verify our findings and to promote a dialogue not only between researchers and those groups but also between sometimes isolated groups within these communities (fishery people and others in coastal communities; students and communities; elders and youth). Finally, we are seeking to create tools and venues for communication, often in the voices of coastal people, of their issues and concerns to policy-makers and the wider community. Of course there are challenges: as a society we have not built the institutional structures to "hear" this kind of knowledge; many of us are highly skilled in one type of communication but need training in the others; communication of results takes as much time and resources as the research, but institutional rewards are seldom allocated to the resources and time needed for dissemination.

Other challenges arise from the fact that moving knowledge is always a mediated process. First, it is moved selectively: the generators, transmitters, and translators always have an agenda. Several essays in this volume show that knowledge is inseparable from values (McLaren et al., chap. 10; Barnes et al., chap. 11). Second, there are unintentional challenges in transmission: what we intend to say, what we say, and what people hear are all different. "Collapse" can mean one thing to a natural scientist and something else to a philosopher, and something else again to a religious fundamentalist, who may see it as both ordained and as a predictable consequence of our behaviour (Marshall et al., chap. 8; Harris and Umpleby, chap. 4). Third, knowledge may be cumulative over certain time scales but not in the long run. Civilizations have been wiped out along with their wisdom, research gets forgotten, legions of researchers charge off into what in the long run proves to be a dead end. Turner *et al.* (chap. 3) give a concrete example of loss of knowledge in contemporary indigenous communities, along with some proposed solutions. Knowledge and wisdom do not accumulate and grow of their own accord. They need to be fostered and archived through the creation, maintenance, and continual recreation of institutional frameworks, pathways, and social conventions. Some of these pathways and institutions are described in the essays by Marshall et al. (chap. 8), Turner et al. (chap. 3), Harris and Umbleby (chap. 4), Trnka (chap. 12), and Mclaren et al. (chap. 10). An index of the democracy of a society is the extent to which there is a diversity of pathways and knowledge is seen as communal property.

This volume ends with a brief conclusion by John S. Lutz, a historian, and Barbara Neis, a sociologist, that synthesizes some of the key issues and findings related to this work, points forward to look at areas for future research, and considers how we turn knowledge into wisdom. Only when we understand that our culture and our knowledge are as peculiar to others as theirs is to us, only when we can see that there are other equally valid but different world views, and only when we acknowledge the relationship between knowledge, social justice, communication, and wisdom can we work across the multiple boundaries that divide us. In a world "on the edge" we urgently need to cross those boundaries to maximize the potential for recovery. This book is proof that it can be done.

2

Knowledge, Uncertainty, and Wisdom

ROSEMARY E. OMMER, HAROLD COWARD,
AND CHRISTOPHER C. PARRISH

> The only wisdom we can hope to acquire
> Is the wisdom of humility: humility is endless
> Eliot 1963, 199

INTRODUCTION

This chapter provides a conceptual framework for thinking about knowledge, uncertainty, and wisdom.[1] Our purpose is to explore the nature of facts, knowledge, wisdom, and uncertainty by examining various kinds of knowledge and the way they move (changing understanding) or are moved to different recipients.[2] Within the context of the ongoing social-ecological restructuring that coastal communities (and many others) have to face, we draw particular attention to the increasingly recognized challenge of "uncertainty" and the need for the transmission of academic knowledge to be bi-directional, from academic creator to other user and from other knowledge creators (such as communities) back to the academy.

Academic knowledge is usually concerned with new understanding created by contemporary disciplinary scholarship, and each discipline – as well as having its own specific areas of study – also has its own statement of method by which it achieves such understanding. Scientific disciplines such as physics, biology, and chemistry follow broadly what is known as "scientific methodology." The humanities (disciplines such as philosophy, history, and literature) follow their own methods which are often quite different from those of science, employing (for example) archival research; close questioning and exploration of the meaning and implications of verbally expressed concepts;[3] other forms of textual interpretation and discussion; the art and discipline of writing prose and poetry; the creation, interpretation, and performance of music; the practice, interpretation, and analysis of the visual arts; and the creation, practice, and interpretation of dance. Social science uses both scientific and humanistic approaches to knowledge. The epigraph to this chapter reminds us, however, that there is no absolute truth, that all understanding is imperfect, that our world is bounded by uncertainty, and that knowledge is socially constructed and temporally fluid, both evolving and depending upon the social context in which it is created.

We start our discussion by distinguishing between the hierarchical levels of human understanding, starting with facts that, when combined to become information, can then be transmuted into knowledge and even wisdom. Facts in research are observations (data) which, along with their interpretations, are always mediated to some degree by context. Facts are not absolute: many people in the eighteenth century, for example, viewed slavery as acceptable and democracy as radical and dangerous That is no longer the case. It *was* a fact that there were plenty of Atlantic cod (*Gadus morhua*) in the ocean, and that is no longer the case (see Murray et al., this volume, chap. 6). Information is a collection of facts, packaged to give a description of something (the Gulf War, for example). Data, as specifically used in scientific inquiry, are demonstrable facts, observations that are presented with a description of methodology that, in theory, allows them to be replicated by others. Generally speaking, a single data point is not of much use to science where context is vital. Data points are interpreted in relationship to each other; research is designed and clusters are interpreted in relation to larger paradigms and theories.[4] Data, then, are considered stable, but not immutable, because a change in paradigm, methodology, and context, and in any identified cluster of data points may produce a change in conclusions and hence in understanding.

To create knowledge is to work with data as described above, testing them until they can become the basis for understanding. Knowledge, then, is not just "ideas" but ideas that, although they have been pondered at length, are still embedded in social institutions, structures, and cultures, and thus subject to the perceptions, misperceptions, limitations of understanding, biases, and ideologies of a specific society at a specific period of history. The *Oxford Dictionary*'s (Fowler and Fowler 1964) definition of knowledge – "theoretical or practical understanding, certain understanding as distinct from opinion, and familiarity gained by experience" – is problematic, since "certain" understanding is still subject to uncertainty, as we have indicated above. Knowledge defined as "familiarity gained by experience" includes what is often called "traditional" or "local" knowledge (see later), which also evolves over time and space and is subject to uncertainty: as when experience fails under new conditions, such as climate change.

Knowledge does not always arise from facts, nor progress through to wisdom, as we shall see. Moreover, all conceptual knowledge, whether scientific or humanistic, falls short of reaching "full truth." "Right" judgment (right for whom?), for example, is based on value judgment, which means that what may be certain for one person or culture may be quite the contrary for another. Uncertainty, therefore, is always present, and it is wise (that is, possessing wisdom) to acknowledge uncertainty and take into account its existence, particularly when dealing with issues that need "right judgment," such as actions whose impact on social-ecological health are not well understood. The example is poignant, because such uncertainty is precisely what it is difficult for decision makers to deal with, given the current institutional structures that support them. Policy-makers are constrained by the requirement to exercise right judgment, to do so *fast*, and also to be able to defend the correctness of their decisions. Hence they will often feel unable to use theoretical knowledge for policy decision making, not only because it takes time to grasp and apply but also because theoretical knowledge offers no certainty, but a closely reasoned argument about the way things probably are.

Finally, wisdom – the capacity (according to the *Oxford Dictionary*) of judging rightly in matters relating to life and conduct – is at the apex of this hierarchy. It requires not only knowledge but reflexive awareness of alternatives or choices, along with awareness of standards as well as context. "Rightly," of course, will vary with culture and ideology and will be influenced by social, institutional, and sometimes also physical environments.

THEORETICAL AND APPLIED KNOWLEDGE

Scientific Knowledge

Science is systematic knowledge increasingly acquired in the context of society, culture, and the economy. It can be either applied or theoretical (pure) – that is, it can derive from understanding gained through the acquisition and analysis of data that are "applied" to real world situations whose effects are assessed on an ongoing basis, or it can be primarily concerned with identifying patterns in observed data and postulating the most probable explanations, which is the task of theory. Once a theory has been tested and "proved" (demonstrated from duplicable empirical evidence), it becomes accepted as fact (actual, rather than probable), subject to the constraints on absolute truth discussed above. As fact, it can then provide a building block towards new theory. That is how knowledge grows.

There is science concerned with society (social science), and there is science concerned with nature and the physical world (natural science). Each has sub-components (life science or institutional studies, for example) and disciplines (chemistry or sociology, for example). Each aims at the rational analysis described above, and the methodologies of science must serve to further this aim (Cooke 1991). Nonetheless, a degree of uncertainty remains in all findings, because they are subject to revision when new data are acquired and/or when a new context for observation and inclusion is provided.[5] Even when accumulated evidence seems to provide overwhelming support for a scientific conclusion, it is never final, never the absolute truth. It will remain open to re-evaluation in the face of new evidence and as new technologies emerge for collecting new evidence or means of analysis. Indeed, since all science is to some degree socially constructed, conclusions will also be re-evaluated from time to time through new perspectives, which may also open up a new series of data collection, an amassing of new evidence, a whole set of new questions.

Natural science theories give insight into natural processes, but they are not, as we have seen, immutable. Indeed, at the leading edges of a field, they are highly uncertain and subject to often-intense debate. Such was the debate between the "steady state" universe theory and the "big bang" theory, which now appears to have been resolved.[6] By the same token, observations may not be comprehensive, not least because observations are technology-dependent: what Ptolemy could not see, Galileo could; what he could not see, Hubble could ... and so on. In terms of ecosystem health, to take an example pertinent to this volume, Department of Fisheries and Oceans Canada (DFO) observations of the health of the Atlantic groundfish stocks in the 1980s are now known to have been subject to inaccuracies that arose from the manner in which data were acquired (Finlayson 1994), being a combination of catch and research trawl data focused on single species rather than the wider picture that would have suggested that there was something wrong at the ecosystem level (Gomes 1994). That is, models can (and often need to) increase in complexity; underlying theories are subject to corrections; and since we can rarely observe all members of a population, we depend on statistics.

Scientists use statistics based on a sample population to say something about an entire group. Depending on the number in the sample, limits of "confidence" or margins of error provide a measure of how likely the results are to be "true" (correct to within a certain range, such as "nineteen times out of twenty"). Statistical methods, founded on probability theory, are used to extract reliable information from incomplete data. However, statistical methods per se cannot prevent mistakes, inaccuracies, faulty reasoning, incorrect conclusions, or even the faulty use of statistics – it is estimated that about half the papers submitted to medical journals are actually based on erroneous statistics (Glantz 1997). We noted above that there were problems with data in the groundfish stock assessments prior to the 1992 collapse. We also note that, for political reasons, when stock assessment science is presented to the larger world, the confidence limits are often removed from the presentation, and we add that environmental degradation tends to be blamed on science, when some of the responsibility lies with managers and communities of users whose practices may distort evidence (see Metuzals et al., this volume, chap. 7) and with managers who do not follow scientific advice.

Errors are present in all measurements. Random errors are irregular and unpredictable, causing data variability (Calcutt and Boddy 1983). Systematic errors affect a sequence of determinations equally. If determinations are made in batches, then a systematic error may result, with every determination made within one particular batch being increased by a fixed amount, while every determination in the following batch might be decreased by some other amount. This is a fixed systematic error rather than a relative systematic error in which all determinations are changed by the same proportion. Gross errors differ from random or systematic errors in that they are rare occurrences that do not fit the usual pattern of errors associated with a particular situation. These various errors cause inaccuracy in scientific data (Keith et al. 1983).

"Accuracy" refers to the correctness of the data, while "precision" refers to dispersion. Accuracy can be difficult to evaluate, although intercomparisons and inter-calibrations can quickly reveal problems. Large-scale multi-institutional studies of the environment have given results that differ by factors of two and sometimes much more (Wangersky 2000). Such differences can be attributed to differences in analytical techniques, sampling procedures, and patchiness within the highly variable natural environment, as is the case with the seabed in the Hecate Strait area, where we are not really certain of the extent and nature of the oil and gas reserves, although our knowledge improves as technology improves (see Barnes et al., this volume, chap. 11; in Ommer et al., 2007, chap. 13). We should use such studies with caution.

Science is thus ongoing, bounded, and multi-faceted, and its relationship to developments in the real world is mediated by, for example, local environments (biophysical and biological agents) as well as human agents: technicians, politicians, industrial actors, and communities. The scientific process ideally involves making hypotheses that are rigorously and repeatedly tested: we should never stop examining our existing scientific knowledge, especially in the light of new observations. This uncertainty in science also applies to our everyday world (*Internet Weekly Report* 2003), where both research and policy implementation are conducted in the context of dynamic, increasingly complex, and increasingly interconnected human societies, and in the context of rapid and often unpredictable environmental change. This means in effect that science rarely provides us with absolute answers, but it can provide calculable probabilities (Nowotny et al. 2001).

Environmental research can be used to provide calculable probabilities for policy-makers, who must take into account any social-ecological interactive effects associated with environmental, policy, and other types of changes. To fail to so do is to incur serious risk. In the environmental field, policy-makers will also receive considerable technical and political input at every level from local to international: the policy-making process itself will influence decision making. The wider work carried out by Coasts Under Stress provides a historical example. We examined non-renewable resource extraction on both coasts (Ommer et al., 2007), investigating the creation, operation, and history of selected mines, including the policies behind them, in Anyox on the West Coast and Tilt Cove on the East (frontispiece). There was little or no scientific environmental assessment work carried out when these mines were opened (1875 in the East, 1912 in the West), but in the last three decades, policy concerns over environmental damage developed, and scientific testing at these sites indicated localized environmental damage around the immediate area surrounding the mines. Concerns about the more distant environment and the surrounding human community, however, were neither taken into account nor seen to be part of the mandate of policy-makers at the time and were therefore not studied. Nonetheless, our research has shown that pollution was more widespread than realized and that the fabric of human society was also damaged by the manner in which the mines operated and were later closed down (Ommer et al., 2007: chap. 5).

Humanistic Knowledge

The humanities offer a variety of approaches to knowledge, but we can differentiate them from the sciences (social and natural) to some degree through an appreciation of the centrality of symbolic thinking to their methodologies, as well as the centrality of the individual observer as unique, and thought, reflection, and observation as embedded in time, place, and person. Of course, symbols are not unique to the humanities. In the form of particular signs, they are used routinely in mathematics and chemistry as a convenient shorthand notation. Beyond arithmetic, they are used to denote shapes, angles, and inequalities in geometry, procedures dealing with variable quantities and their rates of change in calculus, and sets and set operations as illustrated in Venn diagrams. Letter symbols are used to represent the names of elements in the periodic table of the elements and to represent one atom of an element in formulae and equations. In some cases the symbol is related to the Latin name, as in Au for gold (*aurum*).

In the humanities, however, symbolic thinking is often rather different. Basing herself on Ernst Cassirer's *Philosophy of Symbolic Forms* (1965), Susan Langer points out that the data of science function as a sign language to indicate directly the specific object or part of an object being studied. However, the use of symbols in literature or philosophy differs from the use of a sign, in that the purpose of a symbol is not to indicate or announce the physical existence of an object but to point the investigator towards an understanding of the meaning or purpose of the object (1948, 61). That is, the concern of humanistic knowledge is not so much with observed physical existence as with meaning and purpose.

Paul Tillich (1961, 301–21) observes that the first and basic characteristic of a symbol is its figurative quality: it points beyond itself to something else. This means that one's consciousness is drawn not so much to the symbol itself but, rather, to what is symbolized in it. The second characteristic, he says, is its ability to make something that is intrinsically invisible, ideal, or transcendent perceptible and thus to give it a kind of "objectivity." Such perceptibility need not be sensory – it can also be imaginatively conceived, as in poetic symbols. T.S. Eliot, for example, talks about poems as metaphors, in that they can function as an "objective correlative" that moves the initial subject (its motivation, if you will) for a poem to a more universal applicability. The idea of "Divine" as a symbol of ultimate concern in the consciousness of a religious community is another example of this concept-oriented characteristic of symbols. We note that this characteristic is shared by the natural sciences, particularly in such disciplines as mathematics and quantum physics, where, to take one example, the symbol Ω (Omega) stands for the concept "density of stuff in the early universe – matter and energy," much of which we cannot see and which many of us can barely imagine, let alone comprehend (Seife 2003).[7]

Tillich's third characteristic of the symbol is its intrinsic power. This is what distinguishes a symbol from a sign, which in and of itself is impotent. It is, says Tillich, the symbol's most important characteristic and is diagnostic of the distinction between sign and symbol. He points out that words originally had a symbolic character, an inherent power and meaning of their own but that in the course of cultural evolution and as a result of the transition from the mystical to the technical view of the world, words have largely lost their symbolic character. With their intrinsic power lost, words then function merely as signs rather than "living symbols." Such a word is "potency," which has become so sexualized that its original meaning of "being imbued with dynamic power" has been effectively lost. In mathematics, o (zero) is a symbol that we no longer associate with terror, but in much of the early western world, zero was held to be evil – the void. There was no such concept as the void in the Greek world system of Aristotle and Ptolemy, and both Dionysius and Bede had no zero in their calendars (we inherit this as the question of whether the millennium started in 2000 or 2001), while other medieval scholars such as Boethius saw zero as the opposite of God, who cannot do evil but who can do everything – so it had to be evil (Satan)(Seife 2003, 58–61).

The fourth characteristic of the symbol, says Tillich, is its social acceptability. Since a symbol is socially rooted and supported, it is incorrect to say that a thing is first a symbol and then gains acceptance. From the beginning the act by which a symbol is created is a social act –

even though it may first appear in an individual. The individual can devise signs for his or her own private needs, but one person cannot create a symbol. For that to happen, it always has to be recognized as a symbol by a community who agree that they recognize that it stands for something meaningful. For example, a great play is a symbolic form that challenges ordinary views of the world and offers a radically different perspective on society – *King Lear* speaks to the nature of autocratic power, filial love, and the wisdom and follies of old age. One Christian symbol of Christ is "Alpha and Omega" drawn together, signifying deity – prime mover and the end of all things.

The humanities, then, are concerned with the study of symbols (in religion, myth, poem, story, art, music, and so on) as the self-expression of people, communities, nations – humanity. How would this humanistic approach to knowledge deal with such modern scientific and technological issues as mining practices? To take the mine as symbol is to embrace not only the physical structure and the surrounding environment but also the "life meaning" the mine gives (or gave) to its surrounding human community, contextualized within the culture and science of the day. Economic historians, for example, speak about "wheat mining" and "timber mining" as metaphors (symbols) for the concept of mine as destroyer or obliterator. To use them in that way is to understand that policy (in these examples, agricultural and forestry policy) has failed to hold those who own the means of exploitation of the resource responsible for their obligations with respect to employment, to being the economic attractor for home relocation, the provider of community rootedness, and a major driver of social-ecological health and well-being. Should this understanding ever come to be accepted by policy-makers, policy decisions will have to take into account wider issues of concern to both human and environmental communities, such as the capacity for renewal or otherwise of a resource, social dislocations, and social-ecological health.

The social sciences have a "Janus face" when it comes to methodologies, looking both to the natural and earth sciences and to the humanities, using both qualitative and quantitative approaches, depending on need, and also (to some degree) on discipline. As in the other sciences, the social sciences use theory, which may be sustained by measurement (as in much economics) or discursive argument, qualitative comparison and analysis (as in some, but not all) anthropology and sociology), and symbol. There are methodological challenges, of course – the participant observer in sociology and anthropology changes the situation being analysed simply by virtue of observation. As well, much depends on how the observer "sees" and what is chosen for analysis – the dilemma of what to examine and what not to examine, which produces imbalance and imperfect information in all fields of knowledge. Here, "representativeness" and reproducibility may not be the key concern, since the exceptional or the limiting case may be the purpose. As Tillich clearly shows, this is even true in areas such as religion, since doubt is necessary for dynamic faith (Tillich 1958). Within the last quarter-century, the existential movement, the feminist critique, and the deconstruction tradition in Western literature and philosophy have all made clear that humanistic knowledge does not give us "the truth" and that all knowledge must be understood in context. This is also true of temporal context – there is an ongoing need for new plays, poems, and stories that search for and uncover insights in the midst of environmental and social change. Language tires, gets overused, fails to carry the message that is needed:

> Words strain,
> Crack and sometimes break, under the burden,
> Under the tension, slip, slide, perish,
> Decay with imprecision, will not stay in place,
> Will not stay still.
> (Eliot 1963, 194; written in 1935)

In short, the differences between natural or social science knowledge or that of the humanities are not absolute, nor can we ever claim absolute truth in any of them. Nor does interdisciplinarity, however constituted, ensure absolute truth. While we cannot deal with this question in any detail here (there is a vast and growing literature on precisely this topic; see Ommer et al., 2007: chap. 2), we note that interdisciplinary work broadens the inputs to understanding, increases the complexity of that understanding, and generates fuller knowledge of the subject at hand. This is strikingly clear in the work of Coasts Under Stress, where the understanding of, for example, fishing practices on either coast is enriched by the combined thought of marine biologists, sociologists, economists, ethnobotanists, historians, and ethics experts. Even so, there are always gaps in understanding to be acknowledged, elements of uncertainty to be explored, and hence we always need humility – the recognition that we are subject to error.

UNCERTAINTY

Thus far we have argued that for the humanities as well as for the sciences uncertainty is always present. Wrestling with new and escalating uncertainties has been a feature of the late twentieth century and the opening years of this new century. In 1977, John Kenneth Galbraith published *The Age of Uncertainty,* and in 1992, *The Culture of Contentment.* This is a telling juxtaposition. Uncertainty is composed of many things – the collapse of the old world order of two superpowers, the weakening of the welfare state, the strategy of increased flexibility for firms, which has meant decreased flexibility (fewer and fewer available options) for communities (Ommer 2002), and many other uncertainties, such as the growing impact of climate change. However, for the most part, those who are "content" (those who are benefiting from the increasing gap between rich and poor) are not living with the discomfort of uncertainty in their everyday lives and are resisting the broader concerns of climate change, at least insofar as mitigation of greenhouse gases is concerned. At the same time, the increased awareness of uncertainty for some is countered by an increasing faith in technology among others.

The two opposing trends speak to two views of the world, one essentially optimistic about our ability to solve whatever problems confront us and the other deeply troubled by the increasing tensions and uncertainties around an array of issues ranging all the way from environmental and social distress through terrorism to climate change. It is no accident that a recent national bestseller was Thomas Homer-Dixon's (2001) *The Ingenuity Gap: Can We Solve the Problems of the Future?*[8] He suggests that in our swiftly changing world "the growing disparities between those who adapt well and those who don't will hinder our progress towards a shared sense of human community and erode our new global society's stability and prosperity. The next century is likely ... to be a time of fragmentation and turmoil ... of humanity's patent failure to manage its affairs in critical domains," and he notes that "[t]his picture does not correspond to today's received wisdom ... The opinion and commentary ... has lately held a distinctly triumphalist tone" (1–2). Part of the reason for that triumphalist tone is, he suggests, "techno-hubris."

The term "techno-hubris" was coined to warn about the mindset that believes that, regardless of the difficulties we face or create, we can assume that we have, or can create, all the necessary technological skills for resolving the problems that beset the world. That mindset is dangerous for many reasons, not least because it encourages us to feel that we can proceed with new ventures without due caution – to think that (like Icarus in the Greek myth) we can fly without our wing technology failing us. Some people reject the need for the United Nations' precautionary principle to be in effect when dealing with activities that can create environmental damage because, they theorize, we can assume that a technological "fix" will be forthcoming, be it mechanical or biotechnological (as in aquaculture where we are dealing with vast uncertainties). That is why Homer-Dixon is right to conclude that "despite our extraordinary technological and scientific prowess, it's not at all clear that we really know what we are doing ... we may not be ingenious enough to manage our world and prosper in it" (2001, 277).

Theory is not enough: it is always the case that somewhere in theoretical knowledge, no matter how abstract, is a situational component. Take, for example, the creation and use of the floating oil rig Ocean Ranger which was lost with all hands on the Grand Banks of Newfoundland in a February storm in the 1980s. That rig, touted as the biggest and the best in the world, was built and tested for conditions in the Gulf of Mexico – a manifestly different environment from the Grand Banks – and while "theoretically" it was thought to be able to withstand the conditions of the North Atlantic, in practice that proved not to be the case. There is a tragic tension here between oil rig data that fed theory and purported to produce knowledge and the fatal human failure to apply that knowledge with wisdom. Moreover, for a complex of reasons that include disciplinary boundaries, technological advances, and the historical relationship between science, communities of people, and the environment, uncertainty is now even greater than previously realized. Worse, we all too often fail to know what it is that we do not know or to realize that as our technological powers increase, uncertainty escalates and becomes dangerous in contexts where we are approaching the limits of social-ecological systems. New technology is making possible interactions between people and their environments which create cascades of rapid and widening unexpected effects that, in their turn, leave scientists, policy-makers, and others running around after the event trying to sort out the mess. The collapse of the groundfish of the northwest Atlantic is just such a case in point. That is why we need the precautionary principle, which adjures us to proceed with caution – within the limits of what we *know*, not what we theoretically infer, when we are dealing with practices that involve social-ecological health.

Homer-Dixon (2001) argues that "the complexity, unpredictability, and pace of events in our world, and the severity of global environmental stress, are soaring" and that some parts of the world face "a shortfall between their rapidly rising need for ingenuity and their inadequate supply" (see Barnes et al., this volume, chap. 11). Importantly, ingenuity is seen not merely as technological but also as social and managerial, and Homer-Dixon remarks that overconfidence (techno-hubris) that fails to take other forms of knowledge into account is part of the problem (2001, 1–8). So, for example, the complex dynamics of global capitalism treat world economic and development problems as a consequence of inadequate economic demand, and hence strive to raise consumption, which in turn puts more stress on the global ecosystem. That then requires a further techno-fix (aquaculture or science-based agribusiness with genetically modified grains, whose ultimate effects we do not yet have sufficient time-based data to identify) – and so it continues, on and up.

Computers, the web, and other communications innovations in all their dazzling complexity give us ever-increasing opportunities for access to data and to "information," but they do not tell us about context, and so they do not tell us about application. In short, they do not make us wise. Arguably, they may not even make us better informed. Access to huge amounts of often poorly digested or undigested forms of information can easily lead to intellectual overload. The human capacity for taking in information and dealing with it in a highly productive manner at any given time is finite. The scholarly capacity for taking in information and dealing with it productively (that is, producing high-quality reflection, which we used to call wisdom) is likewise limited. The more information one has, the more one has to process, and it has become hard to identify the things we need to read and reflect on without getting bogged down. The challenge is to find out what is appropriate, and that is where overload becomes a handicap in the production and transfer of knowledge. It is important not to assume that because more and easier access to scholarly work is a good thing, even more would be a better thing, and so on incrementally. The opposite is actually the case. We need more time for reflection, especially focused and quality reflection on the problems that beset us and on the knowledge we have with which to deal with them.

This has been a challenge for Coasts Under Stress, as it is for any complex research. In attempting to get close to the lived reality of coastal communities, we have acquired large amounts of information about the vulnerabilities and resilience of coastal peoples and ecosystems, but how we might organize those data into meaningful packages that will be transformative in policy thinking has been a considerable challenge. If we had packaged our findings in the usual kind of way (by resource sector, for example, or by academic discipline), we would merely have offered new detail about coastal communities, but because other writing in this field has not drawn attention in policy circles, to do so seemed pointless. Had we instead just presented that information in all its complexity, we could have ended up mirroring the chaotic nature of the problem, rather than moving towards a solution.

Recent developments in the (theoretical and applied) literature on chaotic systems and complexity and on bringing together the structural and organizational models of natural and social science have proved more helpful. There are several approaches to system complexity. The first is that of self-organization in physical systems, for which the famous model is the sand pile, where the dynamics of landslides are now known to capture the key features of scaling behaviour, which is responsible for such diverse phenomena as earthquakes, El Niño events, and pest outbreaks. This model leads us to anticipate, for example, that climatic fluctuation will increase as the planet warms.

The second approach is that of complex adaptive systems, for which the canonical model is evolution in loosely connected populations of organisms, where small populations allow genetic innovations to take hold in response to local variation and where these innovations may then spread to the species level. Originally the brainchild of C.S. "Buzz" Holling (1973), who created the approach in order to find a better way to think about regime shifts and ecosystem change in the biological sciences, complex adaptive systems theory is now being developed to incorporate social systems analysis as well. The result is a far more flexible response to environmental change,[9] but there remains some concern that the approach may founder on the shoals of social determinism.[10] The third approach examines the reflexive behaviour of symbolic systems, recognizing that knowledge systems, for example, change rapidly to the degree that they seek novelty and resist change to the degree that they are shaped by the interests of a single group. This interplay explains stasis and change, since knowledge systems and governance at large scales differ in fundamental ways from those at small scales (Bak et al. 1988; Levin 1999; Schneider 2001).[11] This insight has proved useful for some parts of our analysis, particularly those presented in this book.

The risk of reductive application of biological models for the analysis of human society is much reduced in recent thinking, particularly by the Resilience Alliance.[12] Their work is devoted to exploring the idea of resilience in both ecosystems and human social systems, using the idea of "coping with surprise," which is another way of thinking about uncertainty, with "surprise" functioning as a symbol for many uncertainties (Quinlan 2003). The challenge implicit in such structural thinking is that there are problems of scale that must then be tackled, since human and biological systems have traditionally been analysed at different geographical and temporal analytical scales. In society, many lessons are to be learned at the community (micro-scale) level and from the past, and not all of this kind of work fits comfortably into the larger-scale modelling (at the broad ecosystem scale and beyond) that predominates in most natural science work (Perry and Ommer 2003). Complex adaptive systems theory recognizes this, and calls it "panarchy," referring to "the cross-scale, interdisciplinary, and dynamic nature of the theory" (Gunderson and Holling 2002, 5).

The work on panarchy to date has been either theoretical or tested and developed at the very micro scale in single case studies. It suggests that complex adaptive systems are dynamic and that restructuring, and adaptation to it, may be most usefully seen not as a problem to be fixed but as a natural part of a dynamic mechanism for handling surprise. The implication is that we need to learn to identify, understand, and encourage such dynamism where we find it. However, there is resistance to nuanced complexity thinking in the policy environment, because there is a serious misfit between that kind of interdisciplinary analysis and bureaucratic structures. Bureaucracies do not yet, for the most part, possess ways of mitigating and monitoring interactive effects, nor do they have the capacity to develop policy frameworks that can promote social-ecological health and involve inter-sectoral (read interdisciplinary) collaboration.

The panarchy approach, however, holds that both change and persistence are required if adaptation is to be successful, and this suggests that there are also benefits to be derived from bureaucratic caution if it does not actually strangle ingenuity. Three kinds of learning – incremental, "lurching," and transforming – are all essential to good management, and for all of us, including slow-moving bureaucracies, two of the big lessons to be learned are that functional diversity is the best response to uncertainty (it builds resilience) and that adaptive management is required if resilience is to be achieved (Gunderson and Holling

2002, 396–7). That is, at least, a more productive and hopeful conclusion than the recent (1999) review by Scoones, which suggested that complexity and uncertainty in social-ecological systems may mean that "prediction, management and control are unlikely, if not impossible" (1999, 479). Were that the case, all that truly interdisciplinary work could do would be to conclude that while recognizing complexity gets us closer to the real world, it also means that not only is there no certainty but, more frighteningly, perhaps even no capacity to manage our destinies.

Rural coastal communities are good places in which to seek understanding of the interaction of human systems with ecosystems at multiple scales. They are complex, yet they are small enough that in-depth field interviews and archival data allow us to reconstruct the interplay of human systems with the natural world's ecosystems of which they are a part and in which human society is embedded. The problems we face in coastal communities and beyond are highly complex, operate at multiple scales, have built up over a long period, and are fostered by often-unconscious mindsets, assumptions (of which techno-hubris is one), and ideologies. Their solution will have to go far beyond mere ingenuity, however defined. Advanced societies such as our own, however, seem unable to be humble, to come to an intelligent understanding of our limits, and to realize that some problems cannot be solved since we do not have ultimate domination over nature. In the final analysis, we are part of nature, part of our environment, and subject to its laws.

We need ingenuity, then, but we need more. We need to progress from the ingenious creation of technology, based on facts and information and turned into technological "know-how" (which is a kind of knowledge), to reflection on what is wrong, what is needed, what is sure, what is unsure, what we do not know, what it would be folly to attempt. We need ethics and values, generally accepted and applied, and we need a deep awareness of our fallibility and the dangerous social-ecological context in which we live. In short, we need humility, not hubris, as our chapter epigraph indicates, if we are to proceed down the far-from-guaranteed path to wisdom.

WISDOM

In this troubled twenty-first century, people search for the sage who will reveal firm ground on which we can stand.[13] The popular idea of wisdom is usefully reflected in the box office triumph *The Lord of the Rings*. Replete with demons, evil, heroes, heroines, and sages (including one who forgets humility and falls from grace), the movie and the book on which it was based portray the sage as Gandalf the Grey, who becomes Gandalf the White. This is a flawed symbol, since true wisdom does not deal in black-and-white but negotiates the nuances of greys. The other problem with Gandalf as (in the movie) the twenty-first century personification of the Mage archetype (a meta-symbol) is that he is possessed of magic, but that is balanced, fortunately and endearingly, by Tolkien's giving him fallibility and fear, which the movie also presents – even the Mage knows and has to deal with uncertainty. This is an important message for our age.

We think it is unwise to define wisdom categorically, for it can have many forms, but we discuss some of the hallmarks by which one can tell if it is present. It manifests its existence in the possession of experience and knowledge, together with the power of applying these critically or practically, resulting in sagacity, prudence, and common sense (Fowler and Fowler 1964, 1499). It also demonstrates the capacity to allow for human error. When experiential and scientific "knowers" encounter each other, for example, differences in the observational basis for those different kinds of knowledge and the cultural processes associated with knowledge production can make it difficult to communicate but can also open up the possibility of both parties gaining some wisdom by seeing the constructed basis of their own knowledge. Taken together, these elements are constitutive of what we call "being wise."

The dictionary definition of wisdom (above) speaks of "right judgment." It is important to remember that what is considered right is, of course, culturally and temporally bounded – thus, what is considered wise will vary among actors and observers. In Eastern philosophy, wisdom is distinguished from theoretical knowledge in that if one aspires to possess wisdom, one's life must bear witness to that aspiration: to qualify, one must practise what one preaches. The Buddha, who lived in an era of major socio-economic restructuring in some ways not unlike our own (Mishra 2004), insisted that even his teachings had to be experienced to be useful. He also crafted a whole approach to life based on the inevitability of uncertainty – groundlessness, the fact that change is the only constant (Armstrong 2000). Wisdom, then, goes beyond information gained through analysis (which transforms it into knowledge) and reflection on the circumstances of the time (this is where right judgment comes in and where ethics and values are essential components of the reflective process), thus moving towards wisdom – the end product of human intelligence. This wisdom, in turn, requires constant reassessment and revision in this uncertain and changing world.

There is, however, no guarantee, as we observed earlier, that wisdom will flow automatically from information or even from knowledge. Knowing lots of things does not invariably make us wise. Today, academics have ever-increasing opportunities for access to information (data), but it is only when we have the time and opportunity for high-quality reflection that we begin to approach scholarly wisdom. We need time if we are to assess new ideas critically and to recognize the inherent uncertainty even of our knowledge, although we need not necessarily reject it, for that would be mere conservatism. Wisdom must involve the critical assessment of new ideas, tradition, and "received wisdom" – all three. To act wisely, then, means several things. It means being unafraid of trying new things when new opportunities or unforeseen exigencies require it, but it also means doing so with the humility of the acknowledged human capacity for error. Therefore, in matters to do with the environment and wherever we know we lack knowledge, it means respecting uncertainty by using the precautionary principle. Moreover, it means reflecting on a range of perspectives and then acting from a position that is not limited to the interests of a single community.

Yet even this may not be enough. We learn from aboriginal traditions about the importance of knowledge handed down by a community's elders. Such understanding has gone through the process of data collection (experience), analysis, and reflection, and it is composed not only of event-specific reflection but of reflection incrementally over the long term on a multitude of such events, reflection handed down through generations.

The end result is a type of wisdom that can speak to the specific but that can also cope with the unexpected because it has been refined through long contemplation of underlying processes. Functional diversity, which took place over an annual seasonal round and is now being "discovered" by the various versions of complexity theory as the most effective way to deal with uncertainty, was standard practice in the multiple renewable-resource use[14] of First Nations and (albeit to a lesser degree) settler communities. In First Nation communities, management was directed by the elders, often with an explicit awareness of sustainability requirements (Turner and Ommer 2004).

First Nations elders exhibit wisdom when they take their traditional and culturally inspired understanding of their own people and the place in which they have lived over innumerable generations – a social-ecological understanding that has co-evolved with the places they have called home over the millennia – and reflect on how that understanding helps now, under conditions of great change, to inform guidelines for social-ecological health. The lessons from such reflection are often passed on through story – the creation of myths that speak to generic principles of good and bad, compassion and arrogance, respect and carelessness. They teach the underlying principles of wise existence through the metaphors of mythology. Thus, for example, Raven is the Trickster in many mythologies, a character who is not only mischievous but also ironic and didactic, the promulgator of uncertainty whose mockery and game playing, properly understood, stimulate the creative element in the human/environment interaction. He is – perhaps like variation in evolution, or like complex adaptive behaviours with their indeterminate outcomes – the personification of "surprise," be that genetic, climatological, economic, political, or even scientific. The social-ecological wisdom of First Nations elders has not been gained overnight, and it has the huge virtue of taking a long-term perspective on important issues of social and environmental health, seeking to ensure that benefits will be bestowed not just on those living in the present but on multiple generations of society. It also understands its limits.

In the Middle Ages and until late in the nineteenth century, secular wisdom was the domain of the university.[15] The university was the place for thinkers; what the academy did was to think – reflect, study, debate, and ponder, and only after all that had been done, actually announce its conclusions. Mostly, the disciplines were humanist in foundation. As science advanced, however, its mode of operation required not only reflection but the activity of getting experiments disseminated so that they could be copied, retested, and then added to the growing body of knowledge – a different process, but one designed to reach the same fundamental goal of understanding. In the sciences, including social science, reflection led to theory, experimentation, observation, and new knowledge. The professional schools, when they became part of the university, added another training dimension, a different process again, while also retaining theory and experiment. Knowledge has moved – and this movement speaks to the evolution of the university as a multi-purpose institution and hence one with multiple goals. The academy has become a complex adaptive system, fraught with uncertainties in its own right. It is, after all, dealing with more and more of the real world.

CONCLUSION

Restructuring has left coastal social-ecological systems around the world with an uncertain future. The work that we have done on the East and West Coasts of Canada has required reflection at many scales and a growing comprehension of the various forms of knowledge with which we have worked both in the team and in the field. We have found wisdom in many of our coastal communities, both First Nations and non-aboriginal, where there has been a history of functional diversity and of formal (First Nations) and informal (non-aboriginal) resource management practices based on generations-deep experience of the local environment.[16] We also found, however, that as renewable resources came under federal jurisdiction, flexibility gave way to "efficient" scientific management practices. Close ties to the ecosystem were lost as the formal collection and dissemination of information about resources shifted to the scientists in government and industry, whose focus was most usually that of a single "commercial" species and not the environment as a whole. Long-term settlement survival was seen as a concern only where such communities had existed prior to the discovery of the resource, as happened with Newfoundland energy and may well happen if the oil and gas resources of the Hecate Strait are accessed (Ommer et al., 2007, chaps. 5, 13). The survival of such places once the resources or markets have gone, however, will have to depend on their capacity to find alternative ways of supporting the residual local economy. In all cases, the track record of modern governmental resource management has been poor, not least because it has lacked the flexibility that is fundamental to adaptation.

We would suggest (based on the work we have done, the theories we have tested and applied, our discussions among ourselves, and our continuing reflection on our own research findings) that management learning is imperative at this stage. We would further suggest that the reintroduction of community economic diversity is something that the state should encourage. This would amount to a policy of "back to the future," a policy that would examine the appropriate scale at which diverse economic functions should occur, reflect on past errors, and learn from them. In the process both the state and communities would have to learn also to take past successful community survival strategies and adapt them for twenty-first-century conditions on Canada's coasts.

It is commonplace these days to speak dismissively of academics as belonging to an ivory tower where research findings take too long to produce and are too esoteric and too remote from the real world to be useful in policy-making. In a world that moves quickly and promotes itself in sound bites and photo ops – the quick hit, the quick explanation, the quick fix – the academy is thought to be too slow, to spend time counting angels dancing on the head of a pin, to be too airy-fairy, and thus to have nothing useful to say to society. Academic reflection, therefore, is viewed with impatience or even contempt, its musings dismissed as appropriate only for exchanges inside the ivory tower, where the elite talk to one another in code. This is deeply unfortunate, for reflection, as well as experience reflected on, are both vital to wisdom. It is also unfair, because the academy is neither static nor unconcerned in its relationship with society. It can and does change (albeit slowly) in the course of maintaining a relationship that has always been complex and frequently combative.

The issue is not that the academy cannot change but that it is not yet clear where the appropriate direction of change lies. The modern academy sits on the horns of a dilemma. If its task is to reflect, it needs time to do that; if its task is to advise society, then it needs to avoid taking too much time doing its reflection, and it needs also to be understandable when it does speak out. Moreover, if it is to be a contributing member of society, then its mandate in society needs to be agreed upon, recognized, and respected for what it is, not dismissed for what it is not. Academics are not consultants providing a quick analysis of a situation within a timeline set by a client.[17] That is valuable work, but it is not the primary function of academics in society. Our function is to create new knowledge, such as that found in this book, and doing so means working with the information, understanding, and knowledge of non-academics as well as the academy.

It is then our task to create theory, test it, and apply it, where appropriate, as part of our mandate to generate new scientific, humanistic, and social understanding. Thereafter, we have to reflect on that knowledge, to seek wisdom, where possible. Only then – but most importantly – do we need to convey that knowledge and wisdom to the wider world of communities and policy-makers and others in the academy and to listen to what is said back, reflecting on it in an iterative bi-directional movement of knowledge and understanding that can give birth to real wisdom. Wisdom is needed by society at all scales ranging from the local to the global, particularly in a world where many quick fixes are sought through the wonders of technology. Society needs places where there is enough time for reflection, for the making of new knowledge, and for the debate, discussion, communication, and concern that, taken together and conducted with humility, might produce wisdom in an age that needs it desperately. It is our hope that the new knowledge produced in Coasts Under Stress will prove useful to the society we seek to serve.

PART TWO

Building and Moving Knowledge within Communities

3

"Ebb and Flow": Transmitting Environmental Knowledge in a Contemporary Aboriginal Community

NANCY J. TURNER, ANNE MARSHALL,
JUDITH C. THOMPSON (EDŌSDI), ROBIN JUNE
HOOD, CAMERON HILL, AND EVA-ANN HILL

INTRODUCTION

It's good to teach them [the Gitga'at children], but you gotta be there to *show* them what the plant's all about.
    Archie Dundas, Gitga'at elder, discussing the Gitga'at Plant Project described in this chapter, June 2004.

Indigenous communities across the world are experiencing the distressing phenomenon of the loss of traditional cultural and environmental knowledge as elders pass away and earlier systems of knowledge transmission lose their relevance. As a result, cultural and linguistic diversity are being lost at an even faster rate than biological diversity. This chapter examines how ecological knowledge and practices have been perpetuated within indigenous communities in the past and how, in a contemporary context, this knowledge can be retained and strengthened within the communities for the benefit of future generations. The Gitga'at (Coast Tsimshian) community of Hartley Bay, on the north coast of British Columbia, presents insights on acquisition and revitalization of traditional ecological knowledge through the ongoing participation of youth with elders and others knowledgeable in the harvesting and processing of traditional food and other resources within Gitga'at territory. A program on learning ethnobotanical knowledge undertaken with the children of Hartley Bay through the school and a film project with Gitga'at elders Chief Johnny Clifton (Wahmoodmx) and Helen Clifton and their family at their traditional spring harvesting camp at K'yel have provided us with opportunities to research new methods of facilitating the transfer of such knowledge within a contemporary context. The lessons we have learned may be more broadly applicable for indigenous societies throughout Canada and other parts of the world that are facing erosion of their traditional knowledge systems. Ultimately, we suggest, it is the knowledge itself that is critical to community adaptation and resilience, and not just the ways in which it is transmitted or learned.

Knowledge is far more than simple information. It can be regarded as a complex system of learning and understanding, with many different facets and components. It incorporates experiences, skills, and techniques, remembered and accumulated. It embodies perceptions, observations, actions, analyses, conceptual constructs, attitudes, and world views. Some might argue that it also pertains to the many ways of conveying and communicating these components to others, as well as to the ways of acquiring and developing them. Recent global recognition (Brundtland 1987) of the particular type of environmental knowledge now known as traditional ecological knowledge (TEK), or simply indigenous knowledge (IK) – the knowledge about local environments held by indigenous and other long-resident peoples – has focused our attention on the significance of this knowledge for the common future of humans everywhere.

Why is TEK so special, and how does it differ from academic knowledge of the type conveyed in standard school curricula? Many definitions of TEK have been offered, but the one from Fikret Berkes' book *Sacred Ecology* (1999, 8) is both complete and concise: "A cumulative body of knowledge, practice, and belief, evolving by adaptive processes and handed down through generations by cultural transmission, about the relationship of living beings (including humans) with one another and with their environment." TEK is knowledge that people have acquired and relied upon for their very survival, for sustainable living in a given place, accessing and utilizing a given suite of resources over long periods of time. The ways in which this knowledge is learned and shared are critical to this endeavor. TEK has been discussed and debated in many other recent publications. In 2000, for example, an entire issue of *Ecological Applications*, a journal of the Ecological Society of America, was devoted to studies and characterizations of different

Figure 3.1 Gitga'at elder Helen Clifton and her granddaughter Jenelle Reece pounding *wooks* of dried halibut together – an excellent example of intergenerational transmission of knowledge and practice.

aspects of TEK (Ford and Martinez 2000). This issue and other overviews (Freeman and Carbyn 1988; Freeman 1992; Johnson 1992; Hunn 1999; Nazarea 1999) provide numerous specific references focusing on traditional knowledge systems.

In terms of understanding environmental dynamics and interrelationships, TEK is particularly important because it is *cumulative* knowledge over a multi-generational time frame, in some cases thousands of

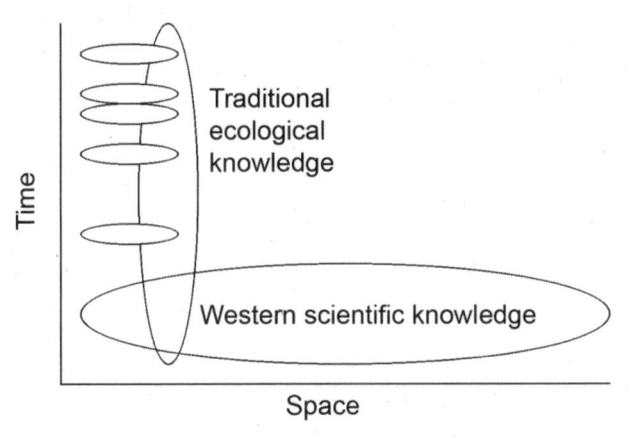

Figure 3.2 Schematic diagram showing the differing scales of traditional ecological knowledge (focused location, long time scale) and Western scientific knowledge (wide geographical extent, relatively short time scale).

years. Many academic disciplines, including Western science, are relatively recent in comparison, and scientific studies focusing on integrated understandings of particular localities across the earth are sporadic at best. In contrast, although the TEK for any group of people may be spatially limited, its continuity and understandings of one location or territory extend back into the past on a more-or-less continuous basis through intergenerational transmission (figures 3.1, 3.2). If the knowledge systems of different indigenous groups, each from their own territories, are superimposed, detailed environmental understandings and observations can be extended over a broad spatial range, as well as into the past. Furthermore, traditional knowledge embodies particular values and beliefs about peoples' relationships with each other and the environment; often there is a concept of kinship with all living things, which is reflected in stories, metaphorical expressions, language and vocabulary, and ceremonies and traditional practices relating to resource harvesting and management (Turner and Atleo 1998; Turner et al. 2001; Umeek 2004). Western academic practitioners, especially in the sciences, would profess that their research is truth-seeking and objective, free of values and biases. This in itself represents a particular world view and set of assumptions and values, but one that tends to distance the human intellect from our biological requirements and to establish a division between humans and other life forms rather than linking them through perceived kinship.

Some of TEK's more practical aspects, however, are similar to those of some of the sciences, including ecology, taxonomy, engineering, and climatology (Corsiglia and Snively 1995). If such knowledge is integrated with scientific knowledge about a particular place, event, or ecological relationship, the results can validate and complement each other, creating a more robust understanding than can be achieved with just one or the other knowledge system alone.

TRADITIONAL ECOLOGICAL KNOWLEDGE TODAY

Traditional ecological knowledge is as important today as it ever was. In all of its forms and iterations around the world it is a critical component of the ethnosphere, as defined by ethnobotanist Wade Davis: "the sum total of all thoughts, beliefs, myths and institutions made manifest today by the myriad cultures of the world" (2001, 8). Since traditional ecological knowledge also embodies the world views and perspectives of human relationships with their environment, it reflects and determines in large measure the ways that people interact with other species, including those that they use as resources. In general, because indigenous peoples regard other species, including trees and other plants, as relatives, such resources are treated with respect and care. This approach is important for all of us in today's world, where environmental deterioration caused by waste, over-harvesting, and careless behaviour towards other species and their habitats is rampant. As Davis emphasizes, however, the ethnosphere is even more vulnerable to erosion and loss than the earth's biosphere. On a global scale, languages and cultural knowledge of indigenous and local peoples are disappearing even faster than species extinctions are occurring, at least in part because traditional knowledge is not being passed on to younger generations.

Ohmagari and Berkes (1997) have identified four elements that work against traditional knowledge acquisition and perpetuation:

- Changes in the educational environment and peer influence,
- Effects of the diminished time available to spend on traditional skills resulting from formal schooling and wage employment,
- Problems related to learning traditional skills at later ages, or delayed transmission, and
- Effects of changes in value systems.

One of the goals of Coasts Under Stress is to assist local communities in the documentation and perpetuation of traditional knowledge and to demonstrate its importance to younger members of the communities. As Gitga'at teachers Cam and Eva-Ann Hill have written (2003), "You would think that growing up in such an isolated First Nations community, such as Hartley Bay ... our youth would be more in-tune with their natural surroundings. This is, however, not the case in certain areas such as botany. The knowledge of plants within Hartley Bay lies with our elderly people. It is up to us, as teachers, to bridge the gap between generations." One of the strategies for bridging the knowledge gap regarding plants and traditional knowledge was to devise a research project for some of the students at the Hartley Bay school that required direct interaction with the knowledgeable elders in the community, and to document its development, implementation, and evaluation through multiple and varied sources of data. Another approach was to produce a film featuring environmental knowledge and cultural perspectives of some of the Gitga'at elders, particularly Chief Johnny Clifton and Helen Clifton, which would serve as a legacy for teaching and reinforcing traditional knowledge and values within the Gitga'at community and beyond.

The Gitga'at: Reinforcing Traditional Knowledge

The Gitga'at are a Coast Tsimshian people whose traditional territory is on the northwest coast of Canada, encompassing a substantial portion of the British Columbia mainland south of the Skeena River, as well as many offshore islands. The main Gitga'at village is Hartley Bay, situated at the confluence of Grenville and Douglas Channels about 140 km (90 miles) south-east of Prince Rupert (see figure 1.2, chap. 1). The Gitga'at are closely related to the neighbouring Tsimshian communities of Lax Kw'alaams, Metlakatla, Kitkatla, Kitselas, Kitsumkalum, and Kitasoo/Xaixais and are also related, but more distantly, to the Nisga'a and Gitxsan Nations. Many Gitga'at people – over half of their population of about 630 – reside outside Hartley Bay, in Prince Rupert or on the southern coast or Vancouver Island, but they still maintain strong ties to their home community and their home territory, on which they have resided for thousands of years.

The Gitga'at are divided into three main clans, Raven, Eagle, and Blackfish, with a few people belonging to the Wolf clan. Marriage is not permitted between members of the same clan, and inheritance of clan membership and title to property and names is matrilineal, through the mother's side of the family. Leadership is through hereditary chiefs and matriarchs, as well as through an elected chief and council.

The forests, rivers, lakes, and ocean of their territory have supported Gitga'at lifeways over thousands of years, providing them with the foods, materials, and medicines they require for health and well-being. Like other coastal peoples, they have been sustained by a diet of seafood, including salmon, halibut and other fish; salmon and herring eggs; oulachen grease; seal; shellfish (e.g., abalone, sea urchin, mussels, cockles, chitons, and crab); and laver seaweed. They have also been sustained by terrestrial food: land mammals, deer, bear, and moose); game birds, ducks and geese, and seabird eggs; and a range of edible plants, including berries, root vegetables, greens, and inner bark of fir and hemlock (Port Simpson Curriculum Committee 1983; Turner and Thompson 2006). Their survival, health, and well-being have been assured by their traditional knowledge of their own territory and of how to access, harvest, and process their resources.

In the past, and in some cases up to the present, learning about cultural traditions has been an ongoing process of observing, listening, practising, and participating in all aspects of daily life through the seasons and the years, in the home and "big house" (feast and ceremonial hall) and out on the land and waters. Traditionally, cultural learning and training start at birth, and even young children are set to undertake tasks that would help them to learn techniques and approaches, as well as giving them self-esteem and cultural identity through their contributions to their family, clan, and community. As in other indigenous societies, TEK is widely held and communicated from parents to children and from elders to other community members in both formal and informal situations, often during the course of applying the knowledge in everyday living (Turner 2003a). By the time the children and youth mature and assume major roles in food provisioning and community leadership, they have both the experience and the confidence to undertake these responsibilities and, in their turn, to take part in instructing and mentoring their own children. For example, many Gitga'at children go out fishing with their parents or grandparents and help in the cutting and smoking of fish. In performing these tasks, they not only learn the specific techniques of fishing and food processing but also learn about the tides and currents and the weather; and they learn how to steer and navigate a canoe or boat, how to sharpen and use a knife, how to maintain a fire for smoking, and all the other details and concepts that are necessary for survival in their home territory. They learn about the habits and identities of the different species of fish, seabirds, seals, sea lions and whales, and the habitats and characteristics of all the other life-forms they encounter. In the course of their learning, they also develop attitudes of respect towards these species and towards each other. All these things they learn are aspects of the Gitga'at traditional knowledge system (Turner and Berkes 2006).

As the elders and teachers attest, however, these circumstances have been changing. Although the Gitga'at still harvest and enjoy their traditional food, many of the younger people today prefer store-bought food, and some of the original foods, especially the wild greens, roots, and inner bark, have been largely forgotten. Many previously used medicines and materials are likewise not well known. Our preliminary studies indicated that at least 90 native plant species, with nearly 170 different uses, are known to one or more Gitga'at elders. However, of these, only about 35 species and 55 uses are widely known within the community (Turner 2003b; Turner and Thompson 2006). Furthermore, some of the foods are no longer available, because of habitat destruction or over-harvesting by outsiders. This situation is worrisome for the elders, because they realize that not only the healthy foods of their ancestors but also the detailed information and skills that go with resource harvesting and processing are disappearing from common knowledge. The late chief Johnny Clifton commented, "We used to be able to gather abalone but we can't. There are none any more." Later, he expressed a concern about loss of critically important knowledge: "My fear is for the children now, not understanding and not knowing how to prepare the food that we gather here [at K'yel, the Gitga'at seaweed camp]. It will be a lost cause if we don't take them down every year, like we do, to try to teach our grandchildren how to prepare the food that we get and we share with everybody that is living in our community." Helen Clifton added, "They [the children] may have to survive one of these days and they're not going to have the food that you could get from a grocery store. They have it all here [at K'yel]; if they learn about it, they can survive. Those are the things that they have to be taught" (Gitga'at Nation and Coasts Under Stress 2003).

New Ways Of Transmitting Knowledge

Many factors have influenced the declining use and knowledge of plants for the Gitga'at. Introduced species and marketed products have replaced many of the native species in peoples' diets and technologies. Residential school programs imposed by the churches and colonial governments and then the requirements of contemporary provincially based school curricula have tended to stress knowledge, practices, and beliefs from outside the Gitga'at culture and in the process have disparaged the value of local knowledge. Further, since much of the original Gitga'at knowledge was embedded within the Sm'algyax language, the traditional understandings and practices have been eroded as this language was replaced by English. Although Gitga'at children have been able to attend school in their own community, as a group they spend significantly less time than previous generations with the elders and other teachers of traditional knowledge. As well as the largely externally based school curriculum, Gitga'at children and youth are increasingly exposed to television programming and printed materials based on dominant Western culture and globalized subject matter.

We felt the school could become an effective agent in providing enhanced opportunities for students to continue learning the important traditional knowledge and skills based on their own home territory, culture, and language and that modern technology, including television, computers, and cameras, could also be recruited to assist in this endeavor. These devices, we reasoned, could serve to perpetuate and rebuild local environmental knowledge and survival skills. While they have been agents of knowledge erosion by providing an overwhelming range of compelling new images and perspectives, in our project these institutions and tools could be transformed and used to a different end.

THE GITGA'AT PLANT PROJECT

The Gitga'at Plant Project was initiated in an attempt to support ways of linking students of the Hartley Bay School with the elders and other Gitga'at holders of traditional ecological knowledge, in order to assist the students in acquiring traditional knowledge about their home territory and, in particular about native plants and the survival skills that accompany such knowledge. A secondary motivation was to help revise the provincially prescribed school science curriculum in order to make science as a subject more accessible and relevant to First Nations students.

In consultation with Gitga'at elders, most notably Chief Johnny Clifton and Helen Clifton, Nancy Turner originally developed a proposal in which "each student would undertake research about a particular indigenous plant that is known to have cultural importance to the Gitga'at and neighbouring people" (Turner et al. 2001). The proposal was submitted to Ernie Hill Jr, principal of the Hartley Bay School and hereditary chief of the Eagle clan, and received his approval as a concept. Concurrently, Judith Thompson, First Nations educator and masters student with Coasts Under Stress, had developed a school curriculum entitled "Traditional Plant Knowledge of the Tsimshian" (Thompson 2003). Drawing on some of the principles in this curriculum, she, together with Cameron Hill, Eva-Ann Hill, and other teachers at the school, refined and began to implement the Gitga'at Plant Project. At the same time, a program was established for evaluating, from the perspectives of the students and Gitga'at community, the effectiveness of the project in achieving the objectives of assisting in the intergenerational transmission of traditional ecological knowledge and enhancing students' learning about research and science.

The project extended from September 2003 to June 2004. The students from grades 9 to 12 worked in pairs to research culturally important plants assigned to them. The assignment was based on the premise that First Nations children need to learn about their own culture and their homelands through the voices of their own people. The students studied the plants using "academic" information found in textbooks and encyclopedias, on the Internet, and in other secondary sources. They also observed the plants directly during field study sessions. Most significantly, however, assisted by their teachers, Principal Ernie Hill, and Vice-principal Lynne Hill, they visited and interviewed Elders in their community, and from these interviews, they learned about the Gitga'at names, uses, and cultural relevance of the plants.

The students learned the Sm'algyax names and characteristics and the medicinal, material, and food uses, as well as the cultural significance of the plants, and were able to explain these to their classmates and community members. They gave presentations of their findings at community gatherings. Posters of the students with their plants and a summary of what they had learned were presented to the elders and others with whom the students consulted, as well as to the other students. A booklet including the students' detailed findings, along with relevant photographs was compiled and presented to the community in recognition of the knowledge and contributions of the elders and other consultants. The students' writings from this project were also incorporated into a more extensive book (Turner and Thompson 2006).

To evaluate the success of the project, interviews with all the participants in the project were conducted, and student learning and perceptions were monitored from ongoing responses to questions and notebook entries, as well as in their final written and oral reports (Thompson 2004). Overall, the effects of the Gitga'at Plant Project were very positive. The students learned a great deal about the plants. For example, one student described the importance of the plant she researched: "I learned that yew wood is just not a plant, it is very important to us First Nations, it is used for cancer, and some people in Hartley Bay have to drink it, it's used for any kind of cancer." Another wrote about salmonberry: "I learned that a lot of people like to eat salmonberries with oolichan grease and sugar or milk and sugar. Salmonberries grow last at Old Town up in the valleys. I also learned that you can eat the sprouts (*ooyʻ*). People really enjoy salmonberry jam at feasts. They never used to use freezers to preserve salmonberries; they would make jam ... Bears and birds really enjoy eating salmonberries."

The benefits of the project, however, went well beyond the specific information the students acquired; students' attitudes and interests were also enhanced. For example, one student commented, "Well, I think it's [the project] pretty cool if you ask me and I hope we can do this again ... And well, I think this book will be cool and maybe our kids can look at this or these books and maybe they'll get to do this experience too and they'll have fun, lots of fun." Another student stated, "This is such a great experience for me. I'm really enjoying this and since we're doing blueberries, it's all good. They're so yummy too. Some things we found out about blueberries were so amazing. I never even knew they can be used as a medicine. I just really like this whole plant project." Yet another student wrote, "But doing this experience is really fun, getting to know what is important to our relatives and what relatives have to use it, it's very interesting."

The students also shared the knowledge they learned with their family, and parents noted positive changes in their children. One mother said that her child had never got into anything at school but now seemed really interested in the plant project. Another parent noticed that her children were "into plants now." Yet another parent wrote, "My son definitely tackles homework assignments in a different way; more methodical." The teachers all spoke or wrote about how culturally significant the project was. A First Nations teacher raised in Hartley Bay wrote, "A whole project done by First Nations, for First Nations, what more could you want? A community like Hartley Bay where all of the plants are from and used by the people here, with input from the people that know and use the plants. The Gitga'at voice shines through our kids in the project." Another teacher who has taught several generations of Gitga'at children stated, "I think that sometimes our students do not see a relationship to the things that they learn in school and their lives as First Nations youth. The Plant Project offered opportunities to exemplify this in a very concrete way." Many adults saw changes in the children's self-esteem, their pride in themselves and their people, and confidence in their new knowledge and wisdom. Most of the elders were very impressed with the way that the students behaved and with the respect that they showed to them, with many expressing a desire to spend more time with students teaching them about their TEK.

The teachers and the elders and others interviewed were also favourably impressed with the project and its outcomes: One teacher stated: "The students' experience with the plant project has been positive on so many levels, from the standpoint of doing research, of sharing knowledge, of marrying the practical experience of fieldwork, to the 'book learning.' They learned to meet deadlines, to write reports, and to express what they were learning in a variety of ways of reporting." The adults were able to identify additional gains, such as pride, respect, and self-confidence. A teacher wrote, "I saw growth in the students. They were shy at first to go out and do the interviews, but they did it, and they seemed to have pride in the results that began to appear." It was also observed that the project "helped the younger generation interact with the older generation and learn more about their culture, which they do not do on their own time or inclination." An elder observed that many of the students were showing interest in their people's knowledge as well as pride in their heritage.

Recommendations for the project were mostly concerned with how it could be expanded: to all the grades in the school; to include more community members; and to extend beyond just learning about the plants to learning about animals, seafood, and other aspects of survival. One teacher noted, "This project could be the beginning of documenting much more of our traditional knowledge of nature." Especially significant was the entreaty from the elders that the students needed to actually go out and participate in harvesting and preparing the plants (see Archie Dundas' words in the epigraph to this chapter). This next step is already starting to be realized. In June 2004, one of the students,

Figure 3.3 Gitga'at elder Archie Dundas demonstrates harvesting the inner bark of silver fir (*Abies amabilis*) for food while Kayla Wilson films this action with a video camera.

with careful instructions from Helen Clifton, harvested devil's club medicine for her and other elders. Archie Dundas and his sister Elizabeth took two of the students, along with us (Nancy Turner and Judith Thompson), out to participate in harvesting the inner bark of silver fir, as well as gathering medicine (figure 3.3). Furthermore, one teacher noticed that more children were out picking berries in the year of the project (2004) than in any other year, and he attributed this to the project itself.

GITGA'ATA SPRING HARVEST: AUDIOVISUAL TEACHINGS IN TRADITIONAL KNOWLEDGE

K'yel (Kiel), on the west coast of Princess Royal Island (Lax'a'lit'aa Koo), has been the main traditional Gitga'at spring harvesting camp for many generations. The late Johnny Clifton, Gitga'at hereditary chief, was born at K'yel during the spring harvest (15 May 1918) almost ninety years ago. Every year, for most of the month of May, the Gitga'at elders and as many family members who are able have travelled to K'yel to harvest edible seaweed (K'yel is also called the Seaweed Camp), to fish for halibut and spring salmon, and to obtain other traditional food such as shellfish and seagull eggs (Turner 2003c; Turner and Clifton 2006). Many people today have jobs they cannot leave, and the children need to be in school at this time, so there are limited opportunities for students and young adults to participate in the K'yel spring harvest. Nevertheless, the K'yel activities remain a time-honoured tradition that brings cohesion to families and communities, provides important opportunities for learning knowledge and skills and interacting with elders, and promotes health and well-being through providing nutritious food, encouraging exercise and a healthy outdoor lifestyle, and reinforcing cultural values.

The idea of producing a film about the harvesting of seaweed and other traditional foods of K'yel developed through conversations with Chief Johnny Clifton, Helen Clifton, and the other elders, who thought that providing a visual context for important teachings about Gitga'at food, territory, and perspectives might be a way to reinforce this knowledge, making it available to the younger community members even after the elders had passed on. Elected chief Pat Sterritt and the Gitga'at Council approved the project, and filming took place in May 2002, with a production crew of two: Robin June Hood and Ben Fox.

The film, produced using collaborative ethnographic filmmaking techniques, follows the daily rhythms of life at K'yel. It "provides a portrait of the ecological knowledge that has underpinned the Gitga'at people's way of life for millennia" (Gitga'at Nation and Coasts Under Stress 2003). Robin and Ben joined the daily work of the spring camp, unobtrusively filming the routines and rhythms of daily life there. The people at the camp were respectfully asked if they would like to contribute their stories, activities, and ideas for the film, and in many cases they reviewed the images and looked through the viewfinder at the shots being filmed. Ben quickly became a friend and companion to Johnny Clifton (who gave him the nickname "Ben Hur"). Johnny became an active participant in directing the form and the content of the film. During his film interviews, he positioned his wife Helen at the door and directed her to keep the usually busy kitchen quiet because he had important stories to tell "that you will remember long after I'm gone."

The filming soon became almost a spontaneous integrated part of camp life, with everyone contributing skills that they wanted to be recorded, such as how to make a medicinal salve or the correct technique for pounding dried halibut. The filming took place along the trails to the other side of camp, in the woods to record medicine being collected, and within the small cabins to record the processes of preparing food and medicine, as well as the laborious techniques for preparing fish for the winter. Although initially the elders and researchers had planned a film about the seaweed harvest, the month of May 2002 was exceptionally rainy, and the seaweed harvest was delayed until June, beyond the period allowed for the filming. The film, therefore, became more a portrait of the spring camp in the rainy month of May and of the teachings of the elders about resource collection activities. Ultimately, the change of the film's focus imposed by the rainy weather allowed it to become an intimate portrait of Johnny Clifton and to convey, in his words, the wisdom of a traditional elder and leader. Using collaborative filmmaking techniques, the film also represented a community development process, with a collective, creative community engagement and remembering practice. The Gitga'at people at the spring camp determined what was important to tell, who should tell it, and where it should be told or filmed. Certain other people, the elders decided, would collect old photographs to be portrayed in the film, and others still would remember, practice, and record important songs for the sound track.

A draft version of the film was shown to Johnny and Helen Clifton and the other Gitga'at elders, who provided important feedback and suggestions which were incorporated into the final version. In June 2003, the film was shown at the official opening of the Gitga'at Cultural Centre at Hartley Bay, named Waaps Wahmoodmx in honour of Johnny Clifton whose Sm'algyax name was Wahmoodmx (see Tirone et al. 2007). The film has also been shown on television and at public viewings on several occasions since then. It is offered for sale through the Gitga'at Nation's development office in Hartley Bay, as well as through a commercial distributor; proceeds from sales go to the Gitga'at Cultural Centre.

In the film the voices of the elders are clear and powerful. Sadly, less than a year after it was shown, in April 2004 Chief Johnny Clifton died at the age of eighty-six after a short illness. Johnny Clifton's passing emphasized, more than any other single event, just how significant and powerful film can be as a medium. Through *Gitga'ata Spring Harvest*, the words of Wahmoodmx, the last of the old-time Tsimshian hereditary chiefs, will be carried, along with the impression of his voice and of his kind, serious, concerned face, on into the future. The images and voices captured in the film not only will inform viewers about specific food-related practices, such as how to hang fish for smoking or how to dry seaweed but also will impart critical perceptions and emotions of pride, resourcefulness, and self-reliance. It is our hope that they will inform, instruct, and inspire new generations of Gitga'at leaders and proponents of resource stewardship and community spirit. These ideas, if taken up, can become a focus for community revitalization and a way to perpetuate a whole lifestyle, a whole approach and attitude to living.

DECOLONIZING METHODOLOGIES

Traditional ecological knowledge systems are critically important as reflections of cultural diversity at a time when knowledge of the environment and the languages that embody it are rapidly succumbing to the onslaught of globalized Western industrialized society. In the not-too-distant past, the predominant view of colonial and post-colonial society was that the knowledge and practices of indigenous peoples were primitive, irrelevant, and useless in a modern context. Today, there is increasing recognition that this was a short-sighted and flawed perception. All over the world, academics – historians, educators, anthropologists, sociologists, ethnobiologists, and others – who have worked with and learned from indigenous and local peoples are stressing the critical importance of these "other ways of knowing." The knowledge these peoples hold and the life-ways that have sustained them in their home places for sometimes thousands of years are now seen as necessary for their survival and cultural identity, as well as for providing critical information in the general struggle to find ways of using our resources without damaging the species and processes on which we humans all rely for our health and well-being. Academic knowledge and ways of imparting information have not been enough to enable us to care for our environments and sustain them over long periods. Furthermore, traditional knowledge may provide keys to adaptation and resilience in the face of major change – economic and environmental restructuring – which we are increasingly confronting as our impacts on the earth expand and magnify. For local communities, the specific knowledge of their own places from their own cultural perspectives may be the only solution for maintaining health and well-being during such restructuring.

In this chapter, we have provided two examples of how traditional ecological knowledge can be perpetuated and reinforced for future generations. Both the Gitga'at Plant Project and the *Gitga'ata Spring*

Harvest film were collaborative projects between the Gitga'at Nation and Coasts Under Stress researchers. These projects were based on community action research methodologies, which are recognized as empowering for both individuals and communities (St Denis 1992; Stringer 1996; Thompson 2004). They represent "an approach to building knowledge that seeks to change the conditions of people's lives, both individually and collectively" (Ristock and Pennell 1996: 1).

Such research is termed "decolonizing" by Linda Tuhiwai Smith, who writes in her book *Decolonizing Methodologies*:

> The implications for indigenous research which have derived from the imperatives inside the struggles of the 1970s seem to be clear and straightforward; the survival of peoples, cultures and languages; the struggle to become self determining, the need to take back control of our own destinies. The acts of reclaiming, reformulating, and reconstituting indigenous cultures and languages have required the mounting of an ambitious research program, one that is very strategic in its purposes and activities and relentless in its pursuit of social justice. Themes such as cultural survival, self-determination, healing, restoration and social justice are engaging researchers and indigenous communities in a diverse array of projects. (1999, 142–3).

Smith describes, using numerous case examples, the characteristics of community-based research guided by and supporting the interests of indigenous communities. The two research projects we describe here fit in a number of ways with the attributes she identifies:

- *Claiming or teaching histories.* In *Gitga'ata Spring Harvest*, Johnny Clifton provided new generations of Tsimshian people with an elder's account of their collective story about the month of May at Kiel. The Gitga'at Plant Project, likewise, incorporated a history of the people, as imparted by the elders to the students.
- *Providing testimonies.* Helen and Johnny Clifton and the other elders featured in the film provided testimonies about traditional resource management practices and the decline of resources due to over-harvesting and mismanagement by others. Personal testimonies about plant food and medicine use and environmental change were an important part of the Gitga'at Plant Project as well.

- *Storytelling and oral Histories.* In oral histories, "the story and the storyteller both serve to connect the past with the future, one generation with the other, the land with the people and the people with the story" (Smith 1999: 145). Film is an excellent method for recording oral histories and stories, especially when the authentic, authoritative voices of the knowledge holders themselves are retained. The stories and oral traditions relating to plants were a strong theme in the Plant Project.
- *Celebrating survival.* Positive reinforcement through sharing and celebrating traditional lifeways was provided in both projects through visual images and demonstrations, as well as through the elders' words on film, and was shared with the students during interviews. Illustrating provisioning activities and emphasizing the proper manner of harvesting and preparing traditional foods and medicines is an effective way to highlight positive aspects of a culture and to celebrate a people's survival.
- *Revitalizing.* Tsimshian culture, language, music, and traditional ways of knowing and teaching, especially about the environment and resources, are endangered on the British Columbia coast. Filmmaking and projects such as the Gitga'at Plant Project can help revitalize these traditions and ensure that they are passed on to the next generations.
- *Sharing.* Smith (1999: 161) explains that "sharing contains views about knowledge being a collective benefit and knowledge being a form of resistance. Sharing is also related to the failure of the education systems to educate indigenous peoples adequately or appropriately. It is a form of oral literacy, which connects with storytelling and formal occasions which feature in indigenous life." Our projects provided a conscious way of both collectively engaging in collaborative research and creating methods for dissemination of the research that are effective and culturally relevant. A film, for example, like a formal oral speech, can be shown at a community gathering and can convey and share meaning at a visceral level, communicating directly to people, just as orators have done for thousands of years. The sharing undertaken by the elders with the students in the Gitga'at Plant Project and the reciprocal sharing of the students and what they had learned with the community were similarly major aspects of our research.

CONCLUSIONS

It was through the inspiration and encouragement of Gitga'at leaders and matriarchs that the plant and film projects were undertaken, and through their guidance that they were successful. Now the models this research provides and the approaches that were used can serve as templates for other projects with the Gitga'at and for other communities aiming to perpetuate and reinforce their traditional and local knowledge.

A number of factors have contributed to the general success of these projects, including the whole-hearted support and assistance of the Gitga'at students, teachers, school administrators, elders and traditional-knowledge holders, and parents. In the Gitga'at Plant Project, it was significant that we worked within the existing educational and curriculum requirements, molding the plant project to fit those requirements and to contribute not only to traditional learning but to the school district's set student learning outcomes for research, science education, and oral and written communication skills. Using the electronic media, web-based research, and tools such as video cameras, the students were able to further their learning on both fronts simultaneously. Similarly, with the *Spring Harvest* video project, the modern communications venue of film served to sustain and support the transmission of ages-old wisdom and knowledge of a particular location and of specific activities that have taken place there for centuries. With "new" devices and institutions being recruited in service of the "very old," we stand the best chance ever of ensuring that the traditional knowledge and the values and concepts embedded within it will retain their vibrancy. Utilizing and adapting to advantage whatever conveyances and technologies present themselves is characteristic of traditional knowledge systems. This is what makes them adaptive and what helps to build resilience in indigenous societies. It is through these means that the messages they hold will be taken up by younger generations and will continue to inform, sustain and support communities into the future.

4

Students as Community Participants: Knowledge through Engagement in the Coastal Context

CAROL E. HARRIS AND SANDRA L. UMPLEBY

INTRODUCTION

Global forces and provincial government policies comprise what Mills (1959) refers to as the "larger issues" embedding BC coastal schools. From these forces flow a host of "local problems" within the field of education, including the creation of mega-school districts, out-migration of students with their families, and reduced funding for schools, particularly for those children deemed to be "at risk"[1] This, in turn, leads to fewer supports for special-needs students, larger class sizes, the intensification of teachers' work (Bromley and Apple 1998; Maxwell 2003; Robinson 2003), and – given the recent re/turn to standardized testing, record keeping, and accountability contracts – increased levels of stress and anxiety among teachers (Maxwell 2003). Despite these challenges, many teachers, administrators and schools continue to provide excellent programs. Several of these recognize and celebrate people and cultures that have previously been marginalized in the dominant Eurocentric setting.

Rural educators contend that the key to healthy communities involves the interaction of young people with other youth and adults (Hunter 2000; Kretzmann and McKnight 1993). "But for this task to be accomplished, *youth must no longer be relegated to the margins of community life*" (Kretzmann and McKnight 1993, 29, our emphasis). Instead, they need to be included in community-wide meetings and training sessions, interviews, site visits, and planning symposia, and, eventually, to become engaged in research, assessment, and planning. Such engagement marks an effort to counteract the tendency noted by Corbett (2007) whereby students "learn to leave." It acquaints them with their own environments and local issues and, in the process, prepares them to participate in and reshape sustainable communities.

Miller (2005) outlines in some detail three approaches to student-inclusive community involvement. The first harkens back to the *school as community centre*. This model can be seen in rural and inner-city "community schools" from Newfoundland to British Columbia (Harris 2002). At present in Canada, these schools house public as well as school libraries, technology laboratories, adult sports events, and other special learning programs to bring parents and other community members into the school – and to save money in communities with declining populations. Miller describes an even wider sharing of resources in rural schools that accommodate, for example, daycare, health screening, and dental-treatment centers, and a greater involvement of teachers as adult educators.

The second approach Miller calls *school-based enterprise*. In this approach, the "emphasis rests on developing entrepreneurial skills whereby students not only identify potential service needs in their rural communities, but actually establish a business to address those needs" (2005). The objective here, rather than providing work experience alone, is to foster in students initiative, imagination, and a sense of belonging. Miller gives examples of a student-initiated shoe repair service, a delicatessen, and a daycare business. While these examples from the United States may not all be legally feasible in Canada, they clearly demonstrate youth-generated enterprise that may find parallels in this nation's coastal settings and exemplify the growing influence of a consumer culture.

Miller's third approach, and the focus of this paper, considers *community as curriculum*. In Miller's examples, students generate knowledge about their communities by assessing people's needs and desires, monitoring environmental and land-use patterns, participating in local arts and culture, and documenting local events and history through interviews and photo essays. The benefits for this kind of outreach are many. Not only do students record important information that might otherwise be lost, but also, as Miller points out, their study of local issues and their involvement in these issues lead students to value their community.

In this chapter, we use case studies of two schools and their outreach to explore questions of school and community interaction. With our main focus on Miller's third approach, our purpose is to understand the possibilities of knowledge flow linking school students with their historical and cultural roots through face-to-face encounters with community members. In documenting these flows, we look not only for what is stated but also for what goes unsaid. It is important to distinguish between knowledge *about* the world gained through an accumulation of facts and knowledge *of* the world acquired through engagement (Ryle 1990). In describing school-community initiatives in an elementary school and a high school on Canada's West Coast, we trace the movement of students into communities as workers and researchers (Miller 2005; Simon 2001). We demonstrate that these students, through engagement, come to embody knowledge *of* and *with* their communities. While learning *of* the world calls for learners' attentiveness and ability to conceptualize (a cognitive pursuit), experience *in* the world engages the learner's senses of touch, sight, and feeling – both as tactility and as emotion (an affective response). These two processes, Ryle reminds us, are intricately interwoven in experience.

The analysis in this chapter blends data from two sources; first, from the experiences of Umpleby, who, as a former principal of the high school and, later, of a largely First Nations elementary school, assumes the role of action researcher or "insider" (Anderson and Jones 2000). Umpleby both creates and uses knowledge in the single setting as "a powerful lever for personal, professional, and organizational transformation" (428). The second data set comes from an empirical study of the high school conducted over a two-year period (2002–4) by Harris. As town demographics change, with professional families leaving this community, many of the remaining Caucasian, Asian, and First Nations students are considered by district personnel to be "at high risk" socially and academically. Sources of information for Harris include classroom-community observations, and in-depth interviews with townspeople, administrators, teachers, support staff, and secondary-level students.

PROGRAMS OF EMBODIED KNOWLEDGE

The Elementary School

Beaver Lodge Elementary School was built in the late sixties, its name being representative of the geographical area and its colonial heritage but also an acknowledgement of the First Nations village just down the road. The school's front door is less than two hundred meters from a beautiful white sand beach overlooking the Queen Charlotte Strait. Because of evergreen copses near the school, black bears pose an occasional safety issue.

For the past few years, the student population has been fairly evenly divided between First Nations and non–First Nations students. This ratio has shifted recently because of the relocation of non-native families to jobs elsewhere. In keeping with the enrolment decline in the rest of the school district, Beaver Lodge has suffered from a severe loss of staff and programs in the past three years. All classrooms are now split-graded, with two classes supporting three grades.

The First Nations Cultural Program was eliminated by the school district in 2002. In response, the band's education coordinator requested and acquired from the federal government a special grant for the academic year 2002–3, making available several thousand dollars for the purpose of sponsoring culturally-focused field trips for all students. Several stimulating activities, such as a feast at the Big House and a dugout canoe trip to an island in the band's traditional territory, permitted knowledge transfer from band members to the school children.

This initiative filled a need. Like other tribes in the geographical area, band members rarely come to the public schools to share their knowledge. The reasons are probably varied and personal and both historical and cultural. Some members, having survived difficult residential school experiences and other social indignities, prefer now to isolate themselves from non-native society. Isolation is possible when one lives "on reserve." Others resist supporting the hegemonic education system, despite their children's involvement. As Mary, a parent and band member points out, however, "Just because I don't come into the school doesn't mean I don't care about my child's education"(personal conversation 2003).

The project reported here was not part of the band initiative, but it did provide the elementary students with an unanticipated opportunity to interact with the First Nations community. It demonstrates not only the potential flow of knowledge from community to school but also knowledge moving from the school to the community.

Our Children Have Shown Us the Way

Early in the school year, a group of intermediate-level students was involved in an interdisciplinary study of the life cycle of the salmon, a topic highly relevant to children of the Pacific Northwest. They spent a morning in November at a fish hatchery while staff were taking eggs from the mature coho females and fertilizing the eggs with milt from the males. The coho had earlier been captured from a nearby river in a helicopter lift.

Hatchery staff explained the process to the students, some of whom helped to carry the big males from their tank to the fertilizing table, where tiny orange coho eggs were cascading into yellow bowls. The children's distress at the slitting of the females' bellies was alleviated somewhat by the knowledge that the bright red females would have died in the wild anyway shortly after depositing their eggs. After all the eggs were stripped, the children were taken to the nursery shed where the eggs were stored on trays. They saw eggs from various local salmon species at differing stages of development. The students' final observations were made at the outdoor tanks, where young salmon of various sizes were kept before being released back into the river. The students begged to be given some coho eggs to take back to the classroom and promised to raise them responsibly. While the hatchery staff did not meet their requests at the time, they did give the students the name of the local Department of Fisheries and Oceans (DFO) education coordinator who could assist them.

Thus, all of the following activities emanated directly from the interests and wishes of the students themselves, an ideal platform upon which to build a meaningful school-community project. But neither they nor the DFO staff could have conceived of the final outcome of the project or of the unanticipated impacts on the community beyond the acknowledged environmental and curricular ones.

Several students volunteered themselves as contacts for Jackie Hildering, the DFO education coordinator. She was delighted with the assistance that they and other students provided – setting up the nursery aquarium in the classroom, organizing the water temperature and feeding charts, and keeping the water clean. Jackie came into the classroom on many occasions to check on the welfare of the growing fry and to offer the students relevant lessons related to salmon, marine environments, and ecology. Their combined efforts were so successful that in April, upon release, forty-seven of the fifty fry were deemed healthy, an almost 100 percent higher survival rate than would have occurred in the wild.

In March, Jackie had looked for a suitable coho stream in the vicinity of the school. The small stream behind the school was a possibility, but it was not suited to coho, although it would have been a meaningful location for the students. She then explored a creek on the adjacent First Nations reserve that proved to be an ideal habitat. She asked for and received permission from the hereditary chief to release the fry there. It was suggested by the chief that a ceremony, to be organized by the First Nations community, should be held at the time of release.

The class project had now grown well beyond the boundaries of the school. As plans advanced, First Nations students in the school were asked by their band members to participate in the release ceremony. Children in the village's band school prepared dances, band office staff acted in a liaison capacity, and one of their members provided food to celebrate the occasion.

On the morning of the release, Jackie, understanding the importance of the attachment that the children felt for the coho fry, carried the pails on the 1.5 kilometre walk with the children from the school to the creek. The heavy burden she carried, with occasional assistance from children, we believe, demonstrated their collective involvement in the project. As the class arrived at the site, they were greeted by a number of other children and adults in full regalia, as well as by drummers, singers, and dancers. Also gathered at the site were interested parents and school community members.

Jackie, who had been involved in a number of salmon fry releases in her career, said that she had never taken part in a release ceremony such as the one that followed. While overwhelmed by the pageantry and involvement of the First Nations community generally, she and the school staff were especially touched by the powerful words spoken by one of the chiefs leading the ceremony: "We have been talking for a lot of years here in the village, about restocking our creek. And that's all we've done – just talk. But now our children have done it for us. They have shown us the way" (Kwakiutl Hereditary Chief, April 2003). Since the event, the children have articulated their belief that in two or three years, coho that they will take or that will be taken by members of their village in the food fishery will be "their" coho.

This past April, in a similar ceremony, the release of 120 coho fry into the creek was similarly blessed. In addition to continued participation by the staff and students of the public school, the band school and adult members working in the band office also care for coho fry from January to April.

From this single example in the elementary school, we go to the secondary school, where the movement from school to community becomes much more complex and multi-faceted.

The Secondary School

The regional high school, Beaver Lodge Secondary School (BLSS),[2] draws students from five elementary schools and two band schools and from several isolated First Nations villages along the coast. Although the enrolment in 2000 was over 550 full-time students, today, with fewer students entering from its feeder schools and a declining town population, the student population has fallen to approximately 400. More than 40 percent of the school's student population is of First Nations heritage.

From the outside, BLSS appears to be a hastily erected series of buildings strung together with no particular purpose or design – like many other educational institutions. One enters the school, however, to see a floor-to-ceiling totem pole of magnificent proportions. Carved by a local First Nations artist over a one-year period and with student apprentices, this pole establishes a statement about First Nations significance and about art, tradition, and culture. Since much of British Columbia highlights its First Nations ancestry for tourist and festive occasions, while continuing policies and practices of dominance and neglect, one might initially be skeptical of this display. Would this symbol of inclusion and respect flow through the rest of the school? And if so, would this ethos point to programs that support – economically, socially, and culturally – both advantaged and disadvantaged students?

Support for First Nations Culture

Our first investigative step, and one that informed each visit to the school, was to see which programs were particularly dedicated to the needs of First Nations students. The most obvious was Marian's Room. Some ten years earlier, the school had been singularly fortunate in obtaining Marian MacKenzie's services as a First Nations counsellor. Marian, who is herself a First Nations person and who prefers to be called by her given name, brought to the school a rich history of social service and work experience in foreign countries, and an MA in educational psychology. On the personal front, she relates warmly with all students and attends carefully to their individual problems. She provides the home to which these students gravitate first thing each morning, return to during the day when they want to make themselves a sandwich, and check out last thing in the evening before boarding the bus. The room, with its native artwork, comfortable sofas, kitchenette, and side rooms for private consultation, provides the emotional and cultural rock for the school's First Nations population.

As Marian often visits the school's three First Nations feeder communities, students from these villages know her well. This leads to their habit in the high school of dropping by her room whenever they wish. Angel and Chrissy, two grade 9 students, talk about how much it means to them to have such a place. As Angel explains, in Marian's room "everyone is welcome." Once a month, Chrissy says, the room "becomes an open house to the entire school. This will be for everyone to come for lunch, and there's one [First Nations] band that will support it each time." During a typical open house, some eighty students and staff share soup and sandwiches, see what is new in the room, perhaps meet a visitor, and chat with one another.

Marian and the First Nations support staff, of whom there are seven in the school, sponsor many educational activities, including crafts and skills such as basket weaving, embroidery, and cooking. Sometimes Marian shows a documentary film of First Nations history or accomplishment, or she introduces the students to one of the elders from a local band. Then there are the talking circles, in which students discuss topics of importance to them, trade points of view, and receive gentle guidance from Marian and other adults who happen to take part.

Various programs contribute to First Nations studies. Some are formal, like that of Mr Picasso, who runs the cultural program, and others are informal, like the drop-in meetings for young parents. Some are led by First Nations teachers or support staff, while others – again as in Mr Picasso's class – are not. There have been many success stories from Mr Picasso's class; Marty's transformation is one of these.

Marty was at one time, according to several staff members, one of the school's most disruptive youth. He readily acknowledges his rebellious past but claims that in his last year at school, he was able to pull himself around. Largely, he said, he did so because of Mr Picasso's demand that he mend his ways or "stop wasting everyone's time," and Mr Picasso's expectation that he "would shape up." At this point, Marty is almost through his second year as a teacher-in-training. He wants to do for other First Nations youth what Mr Picasso and others in the school have done for him.

One of the high points in Mr Picasso's course, and quite possibly the event that turned Marty around, illustrates the movement of students from school to community. Each spring, the First Nations students travel down the Island and to the mainland, visiting several post-secondary institutions along the way. During these visits, students are able to assess each site, both for its academic possibilities and for its cultural affinity. According to Marty, they know their chances of success will be greatly diminished in a context that does not recognize and honour their traditions and history. Marty explained that this trip clarified for him "pretty fast" which universities would *not* be for him and allowed him to "select the one that would."

In addition to Mr Picasso's program, a variety of support classes – some at the school and others in the community – assist students who have trouble bridging the move from their reserves to the high school. The First Nations Support Programme in the high school, for instance, provides an informal "helping" class where students can come in and out as they feel the need for remedial help with their lessons. As an example of movement out of BLSS, Angel told me about the Young Adult Programme on the reserve. This is like the high school program (and is, in fact, administered by BLSS), "but we don't start class down there until nine [o'clock], and [much like Marian's room] this is where we have our own little kitchen and fridge and we can have coffee or hot chocolate."

> RESEARCHER (R): Does this resemble an alternate program where you also do lessons?
> ANGEL: Yeah, it's um, like, well say if you had – like me, I had trouble with my reading so I went down there. And we have these decoding books where we just fit it, like, we can work at our own pace. It only goes up until grade ten, so I was down there working on my grade ten. They helped me with my reading. Like before, I wouldn't even pick up a book and I'm actually reading now.
> R: Good.
> ANGEL: 'Cause, last year [the teacher] let me read a lot. Like, I would be working on it for my English, and I would get marks for it, but I would just sit there and read on the couch and then I was really into reading.

Setting was important for Angel, as it was for her friend Chrissy. In the special, community-based program, they were able to combine new learning with a warm and familiar environment.

Food and its associated celebration provide an essential component of the environment for First Nations students. In addition to visiting the kitchens in Marian's room and the other First Nations meeting places, students at BLSS can come to Ms. Noonan's nutrition classroom for snacks. Sally Noonan sees two groups in her courses, those "who are simply hungry, and those who really want to go on [academically] and are looking at something more than becoming a waitress. But they want to work in the food industry." Although Sally initially observed what she felt were appalling food habits, together with the health problems that accompany them – particularly obesity and diabetes – she notes "positive changes in personal food choices" among those students who continue nutritional studies for several years. She now sees students bringing a "can of soup for lunch, rather than going to the vending machine for a bag of chips and a pop." The very existence of vending machines for junk foods in a high school like BLSS throws light on the intricate intersection of school funding, corporate intrusions into education, and student health.[3]

Each of these programs and supports for First Nations students – Mr Picasso's cultural program, Marian's Room, and other classes such as visual art (omitted from this discussion) that combine academics with a cultural atmosphere – provide an incentive for First Nations students to remain in school but, of greater importance, add to their sense of belonging in an otherwise alien institution. Cultural exploration and accommodation is well under way at BLSS, although most teachers, support workers, and administrators recognize the gaps that remain between a dominantly bureaucratic school system and traditional First Nations communities. Both the present strengths of First Nations programs and an exploration of missing components invite new and proactive explorations of the town and band communities by all students.

The Journalism Program

Journalism at BLSS perhaps best illustrates the outward reach of school to community. All schools require programs that address the needs and interests of students who have been motivated already in their homes and social milieu to achieve academically. Journalism is one such program, boasting numerous awards for journalistic excellence as exemplified in its quarterly newspaper, *The Sounder*, and in its highly creative school yearbook. *The Sounder*, provided freely to the community, covers not only school news but also investigative reporting on items of general interest such as new businesses, tourism, and local history. Occasionally, the paper turns a critical lens on community activity but never without encountering resistance, as illustrated below. The program runs for three years as Journalism 10, 11, and 12, with two preparatory courses at the grade 8 and grade 9 levels. A few students enroll in all these courses, but many more take two or three and then volunteer to work on the paper or the yearbook. Not surprisingly, the volunteer work can be all-consuming, especially for the editors and the teacher, Mr King.

The program prepares students in a wide array of skills. While writing and editing take centre stage, students also learn photography, page layout, and computer skills. Nora, an editor in the 2001–2 year, was one of three editors. When interviewed a year after graduation, Nora spoke about gaining generalizable, as well as specific, skills: "What did I learn? Just about everything. I learned to be efficient, I learned to organize myself, to lead other students – because obviously, as editor, you have to decide on directions and guide others." Nora, like the other two editors, was given the opportunity one summer of producing, from beginning to end, a newspaper called *Island Outlook*. This project is sponsored by Community Futures, an initiative of the federal government for youth in community development. We told Nora that she must have learned a great deal from this experience.

> NORA: Oh, it was great! Before I did the *Island Outlook*, I hadn't really done ads or anything. Like I had seen other people do them, but not myself. I learned to work, not under peers, but under my employers. There were guidelines you had to follow. You had to advertise – not propaganda – but information for the company. And [a page] on what Community Futures does – point out what's relevant to communities.
>
> RESEARCHER: *You* got to be a researcher of sorts?
>
> NORA: For sure. I did interviews over the phone and in person. There was a lot I didn't know about before, about the companies, and the communities.

Nora knew little about writing before she met Mr King and enrolled in journalism. When we talk with her today, her journalistic interests are still focused on the technical aspects of design and layout, although her university majors are English literature, creative writing, and classics.

Mr King tries to plan courses so that students with different strengths will discover their own milieu. Those who find writing difficult, work in the darkroom, on desktop publishing, or on the journalism web site. Some prepare PowerPoint presentations for other classes. Several conduct email correspondence with students in other countries.

Most teenage students, it is widely held, consider their schools to be overly prescriptive in rules, regulations, and curricula. Students at BLSS, being no exception, appreciate the relative freedom offered by their journalism program. Sonja, a former editor, when asked what she would tell a grade 9 student about the advantages of journalism, spoke about the relative independence inherent in getting to choose what you want. "When you are in those younger grades, you don't get to do that very often. [Here] you can do photography. If you enjoy writing, you can do that. We can teach you how to use the Macintosh platform, which will help you if you decide to go on to do something else."

Several related programs extend this feeling of freedom for senior students. One is the one hundred hours of work study, part of a course called Career and Personal Planning (CAPP) and arranged in cooperation with the school's counselling department. Through CAPP, journalism students are placed with professional papers locally and in distant towns and cities. Samantha, who has worked with the local daily paper, spoke of specific links between school interests and those of the community. "Our school body is really involved with MADD [Mothers against Drunk Driving]. And we have quite a few people who go with the RCMP. Probably every month, we have one article mentioning MADD, because [name], who was a graduate here, died – killed by a drunk driver. We've done a lot of stuff with that."

Samantha was also able to identify conceptual links between different school programs. When asked if she saw any connection between visual art and journalism, she said, "With journalism, you are speaking to the public; with art, you can't use words. You have to do an image that is going to indicate something to the person who is looking at it. When you combine the two, it just works together. You have the one big picture. You have the words, you have the picture." Then she added music to the mix, noting the "three different ways of communicating with people – journalism, visual art and music – and it's three different things that add so much colour, and life *to* life."

Samantha saw connections in writing, as well, noting the different styles needed for creative writing and journalism. Her writing teacher, Mr Picasso, whom she sees as both "very open minded" and also "very critical," will "tell you what's not right. The type of writing you do there, is much more, like, your own opinion and how you interpret things. When it comes to journalism, it can't be exactly what you think. The public has to read this, and be able to relate to it. You don't want to write these great big words that people won't understand. You have to walk a fine line. With any newspaper, you have to write so that the general public can comprehend what you're saying." With comments like this, Samantha and the other two editors demonstrate an understanding of interdisciplinarity, as well as personal initiative and a desire to be actively involved in their town. They each appreciate the freedom vested in them by their instructor, Mr King, and the kinds of research required by their various journalistic projects.

Mr King's objectives are to develop in students independent work habits and an ability to think critically. That is not always popular, even with intellectually gifted children, especially when they have realized success in the past through adherence to their textbooks and methods of memorization. "Many of these kids," Mr King claims, "have a hard time when there is not stuff written on the board. With this course, it's 'go find a story.' I am not giving you an assignment and, no, there is no textbook; and, no, there is no test. A lot of them aren't used to that." Nor is critical thinking always popular with the school, he adds, "particularly when students criticize – even in mild terms – actions of teachers or administrators."

An example of investigative journalism, not entirely popular with the town, involved an extensive analysis of students' smoking habits, including the investigation of local stores that sold cigarettes. For this reportage, fourteen-year-old BLSS students visited the stores with money to buy a pack of cigarettes. On their return, they were interviewed regarding their ability to make the illegal purchase and how they were treated when they made their request. As part of their report, *The Sounder* published the names of all the stores that had sold cigarettes to minors and challenged the local police force to act on the information. The police, we understand, did not take up the challenge.

In another controversial instance, student journalists gave the community specific information, derived from an interview with the secretary-treasurer of the school board, about the board's plan to cut field trip funding to schools. Because their methods were ethically sound, the superintendent and board members could not complain when parents called an emergency meeting to publicly contest the issue.

At present, the BLSS program attracts mainly white, middle-class, female students. In the eleven years Mr King has run this program, he's had only "three or four male editors ... and one or two First Nations, but not from the reserve." The young women who stay with journalism tend to excel in their school work and will probably be leaders in their communities and post-secondary institutions. Although some boys and First Nation students join the classes at the earlier levels of schooling, relatively few, apart from the yearbook staff, make it to the final graduation class. We believe that a program such as this, which engages students directly as researchers in their own community, would benefit a broad range of students.

The BLSS journalism program is one of only three similar in British Columbia. Its advantages, from career preparation to critical thinking skills for students, and the benefits to the community of both knowledge flow and perception situate it as a program that merits wide dissemination. Unfortunately, given the mix of the course's limited appeal, dropping enrolments, a province-wide freeze on educational spending and soaring expenses, the continuation of this BLSS program is under threat.

DISCUSSION

Coastal community students require, especially in these turbulent economic times, a voice in the possible futures of their towns. Ideally, they need a safe place from which to challenge the dominant rationality and reflect as a group on the contradictions, problems, and possibilities of their restructured world, in order to envision how it could be different. Our purpose in conducting this study was to understand some mechanisms for the flow of knowledge between students and their communities and, with a detailed description of local contexts, to assess this flow in terms of its potential and actual impact on the health and well-being of one coastal region. In the preceding scenarios, elementary and secondary students moved into their respective communities in ways that engaged them and their constituencies. Together, they constructed knowledge both *about* their environments and also *of* them (Ryle 1990).

The school-community interaction described in these examples has, in our view, beneficial ramifications. The students themselves are engaged in experiential activities beyond the walls of the classroom that help to enhance an appreciation of their own social and cultural heritage and that of others. Portelli and Vibert (2001) refer to this learning strategy as a "curriculum of life, grounded in the immediate daily world of students as well as in the larger social, political contexts of their lives" (63). Many of these students also have the potential of experiencing that nebulous but powerful sense of "place" that connects them to home community and environs. Furthermore, in some cases, they have been able to perceive that they could effect a "change from below" (Ife 2002).

The local communities also benefit from the initiatives of their children. In keeping with the belief that resilient communities require the meaningful involvement of youth (Kretzmann and McKnight 1993; Miller 1995), the people of the town and the neighbouring First Nations villages, by working collaboratively to improve community health and viability, appear to acknowledge and demonstrate the value they place on their children's capabilities and contributions.

The secondary students, through their community outreach, hone skills that are rarely taught in school – those of critical thinking (although students in this case study tended uncritically to accept existing cultural and economic power relations), problem setting and solving, evaluation and synthesis, and useful career skills, as in the example of journalism. These skills may, with or without help from teachers and community members, lead to an enhanced awareness of the local; such awareness may, in turn, begin a process of learning to stay, as opposed to "learning to leave" (Corbett 2007).

With community affirmation, as seen in the story of coho cultivation, elementary school children have the opportunity to feel the sense of self-worth that stems from recognition and a sense of belonging. School becomes less a "prison" (Foucault 1980, 39) and more an opportunity for meaningful engagement with the adults in their lives, thereby shifting somewhat the imbalance of power. Cultural exchange is significant here as non-First Nations students gain an opportunity to appreciate new forms of meaning and First Nations students are able to highlight – and thus construct new appreciation for – their own ways.

Several problems arise, however, in the context of educational restructuring. One is that the almost idyllic example from the elementary school took place, not through the public school system but, rather, through funding from the federal Department of Fisheries and Oceans. Programs of community outreach similar to this are rarely found or are short-lived in the schools of the Coasts Under Stress project. In an inner-city school in Prince Rupert, for instance, Harris observed elementary children, largely of First Nations, move out into the community to share their choral music with parents and senior citizens. The next year, because of funding cuts and program reductions, and despite the expressed appreciation of children and adults alike, the school's music program was eliminated.

With increasingly scarce resources and a ministerial emphasis on accountability by way of standardized testing – "knowledge of" facts, in Ryle's (1990) terms – programs that encourage school-community interaction are declining. Knowledge that is transmitted solely for the purpose of passing examinations tends to be bereft of meaning beyond the immediate context. The accompanying skills of memorization and repetition will not serve students or communities well in socio-economic or political crises that require critical thinking and a healthy imagination. In addition, because of layoffs and contractual obligations related to seniority, teachers are assuming positions without requisite subject discipline qualifications. Students today and in the coming years can neither presume stability of programs nor expect that their teachers will have specialized subject knowledge. At a critical juncture in the health of British Columbia's coastal communities, overextended teachers may not have the support to inspire this generation of students to return their creative energies to their communities.

There are also many attitudinal, structural, and economic barriers to meaningful school-to-community interactions. One of the most subtle and pervasive is the general indifference of adults towards students' capabilities or capacity for knowledge, together with assumptions about its relevance. Even professional teachers, as they prepare to teach new concepts, sometimes neglect to draw on children's experiences and understandings. As children mature, their frustrations stemming from a lack of "voice" and "ear" can lead to alienation and negative social ramifications. Whatever the contributors to drift may be, the fact remains that schools during the latter half of the twentieth century and early twenty-first century, have increasingly become entities unto themselves, as conceptions of teaching and learning are more securely limited "within the perimeters of the school's walls and the textbooks" (Miller 1995, 1).

Numerous structural attempts have been made to rejoin school and community, although these usually involve a unidirectional move from community to institution. For example, many see the legally instituted system of school councils (parent advisory councils (PACs) in British Columbia), with their strictly regulated membership, as an attempt to re-ignite dialogue between communities and their schools.[4] This move, of course, is not new; it is consistent with a long history of home and school activity (or parent teacher associations, in British Columbia) in

Canada (C.E. Harris 1998). The difference today lies in the rationalization of such organizations to include a few "interested" actors in the parent-school community. Associations are no longer invitational to all, or intended as a space for adult learning. The PACs and school planning councils of today have a definite composition, differing from province-to-province, but nevertheless governed by rules and regulations of inclusion and exclusion and enshrined in law. The informal efforts of teachers and students to move from school to community can add a meaningful and inclusive counter-dimension to the mandated requirements.

Another ongoing barrier to authentic school-community links in British Columbia is inherent in the consistent underfunding of education. Coupled with intensified accountability requirements, the debt load passed on by government to districts has resulted in reduced staffing and course offerings in coastal communities, particularly for those curricula that are not easily quantified. Thus, courses such as journalism, media arts (including television production and computer animation) and First Nations cultural programs have become unfortunate casualties of new efficiencies, as have students, many of whom attend their coastal school because of passions for, interest in, and simple comfort in these and other specialty disciplines.

Ironically, it is in these community-oriented subject disciplines that bi-directional knowledge transfer is most likely to occur. A possible solution is to insert a community focus into regular academic curricula (*community as curriculum*), an initiative that would require additional efforts of busy teachers and administrators. This solution could, however, help to ameliorate the malaise in relationships between community members and adolescents generally. In this coastal school district, for example, some efforts are being made to integrate First Nations history, geography, foods and nutrition, and fine arts into provincial curricula. Such strategies may also help to refine graduating students' appreciation of their home community and of the opportunities that lie within.

In addition to attending to the juxtaposition of school and communities, we entered this study with a curiosity about "teaching for democracy" (Portelli and Solomon 2001), through the development of student knowledge about history, cultural traditions, and cooperative learning. Martin (1994) defines two applications of the term "democracy." She contends that "developmental democracy" is achieved when people are "exerters, developers, and enjoyers of their own capacities"

(p. 179), and she contrasts this state favorably with "equilibrium democracy," which merely involves a mechanism for choosing governments. While school-to-community engagement takes time in a world where that commodity is scarce (Bromley and Apple 1998: 138), "developmental democracy" by definition is enhanced by such engagement. Students actively participating in their community's development deepen the meaning of Martin's term.

CONCLUSION

Greater cooperation is needed between school and community – especially within coastal contexts – but cooperation needs to be informed by new lines of political and social engagement. Such engagement has been shown to engender mutual learning and understanding, to break down dichotomies that exist between school and community, and to enhance an appreciation for "place."

An overarching consideration regarding knowledge concerns whose interpretation of everyday reality constitutes knowledge in the first place. The communities of these schools are marked by divisions of class, race, and gender. Students, particularly at the high-school level, can begin the democratic adventure by examining power structures along racial and gendered lines. How are decisions arrived at within the community? Which students have voice in representing the school? Above all hovers the critical question: how can things be arranged differently in school and community?

According to Kretzmann and McKnight (1993), the interactions of youth with adults provide the key to healthy, resilient coastal communities; the knowledge flow from school to community places impetus, power, and responsibility in the hands of students and their teachers. Heretofore, small coastal communities have educated their children by preparing them to leave; the experiments traced in the schools of this study can stimulate the kind of disputed and imaginative knowledge that encourages children to stay.

PART THREE

Knowledge Flows and Blockages: Fish Harvesters' Knowledge, Science, and Management

5

The Evolving Use of Knowledge Sources in Fisheries Assessment

DAVID C. SCHNEIDER, ERIN ALCOCK, AND DANNY INGS

INTRODUCTION

Fisheries management in the twentieth century was shaped by disasters, of which the most prominent have been the collapse and closure of the California sardine (*Sardinops caerulea*) fishery in 1941 (McEvoy 1986) and the collapse and closure of the cod (*Gadus morhua*) fishery in Newfoundland in 1992 (Kurlansky 1997). Among the important lessons learned from the sardine collapse were that sea fisheries are not inexhaustible and that catch per unit effort cannot be used to gauge stock status. Right until the last days of the fishery, sardine boats arrived at the dock loaded to the gunwales (McEvoy 1986). Catch per unit effort had remained high as the stock collapsed, because sardines form into shoals; fishers converge on the remaining shoals until the last shoal is gone.

The Newfoundland cod disaster occurred in very different circumstances, with even greater social impact. It took place in a highly regulated fishery directed toward biologically sustainable rates of removal as estimated by widely accepted methods in population biology. The total allowable catch (TAC) for the fishing banks east of Newfoundland (zone 2J3KL of the North Atlantic Fisheries Organization) was projected for 1987 at 380,000 tonnes (Kirby 1983). By 1986 the TAC had been revised downward to 286,000 tonnes using a conservative management criterion (fishing mortality set at $F = 10\%/\text{year}$) to allow continued growth of the stocks, rather than merely preventing stock or recruitment overfishing. By 1989 it was apparent that the stock was not growing, and TACs were reduced further. The TAC in 1992 was set at 121,000 tonnes, but this was never captured because a moratorium was declared in July of that year. This moratorium was extended to recreational and personal consumption, effectively ending the traditional basis of outport life that had existed over several centuries along the eastern coast of Newfoundland. The moratorium remains in effect today. This disaster occurred in a stock complex that had sustained commercial fishing for five hundred years (Kurlansky 1997) at removal rates on the order of 200,000 tonnes per year.

In 1984 the inshore fishermen of Bonavista, Newfoundland, raised money to send a delegation to Ottawa to warn of impending stock collapse (H. Butler, personal communication). The delegation returned, complaining that their advice was ignored in favour of scientific information. This became a recurring theme in public debate throughout the decade leading up to the closure of the fishery in 1992. A sociological analysis (Finlayson 1994) arrived at a similar conclusion, that the knowledge of fishers had been ignored.

In 1994 an interdisciplinary group consisting of sociologists (B. Neis, L. Felt, P. Sinclair) and fisheries scientists (R. Haedrich, J. Hutchings, D. Schneider) began assembling the local knowledge of fishers in Bonavista and Trinity Bays, Newfoundland (Neis et al. 1996; Murray et al., this volume, chap. 6). The study was driven in part by the public debate over use of fishers' knowledge in managing the resource. Hutchings (1996) listed several ways that local ecological knowledge can be useful in scientific assessments. He argued that local familiarity with the dates and locations for fish catches from fixed gear can indicate seasonal and directional movements of fish populations. Fish harvesters can provide information on aspects of stock structure, including movement patterns, spawning grounds, juvenile habitat, and spatial patterns in fish morphology. Hutchings (1996) also noted that catch rates may mirror local changes in fish abundance. Neis et al. (1996, 1999) showed that local ecological knowledge provides information on stock distinctiveness, fishing efficiency, and catch per unit of effort (CPUE). Vernacular terms collected during the interview process reflect stock structure and dynamics, including direction and timing of movements, seasonal locations, and spawning aggregations. The tracing of career histories of resource users uncovers important and rapidly changing components of fishing efficiency, notably, gear quantity, engine power, trip time, and hold capacity (Neis et al. 1999b). These measures reflect substantial changes in efficiency. They are more informative than counts of boats in size classes, particularly when restrictions on licenses for large boats are imposed to reduce effort, as was the case for the inshore cod fishery. Negative trends in catch per unit of effort on a decadal scale were far more evident from longitudinal information (catch per effort by individual over time) than from aggregate cross-sectional measures (total landings divided by number of boats, in size classes defined by length). In the 1990s stock status advice for cod began including local knowledge (e.g., Neis et al. 1996). This was a change compared to prior cod assessments attended by one of us (D. Schneider).

In this chapter we examine the historical context of this shift toward inclusion of knowledge held by fishers into science-based assessment practice. To do this, we assembled all the assessment documents used each year in the assessment of a fishery. These documents do not, of course, include all the information exchanged at assessment meetings. However, the bulk of the discussion does focus on these documents, which become part of the public record. In a pilot study we focused on cod stocks in eastern Newfoundland, covered in the NAFO geographic divisions 2J, 3K, and 3L, extending from Cape Race to southern Labrador. The results pointed toward a more complex picture than we had anticipated. Using cod, we developed a model of change in knowledge sources over time, which we then tested by examining the documents for crab and herring fisheries.

METHODS

The reconstruction of sources of information in stock assessment for Atlantic snow crab and herring fisheries was from stock assessments, management plans, and other research documents, from which a brief history and a timeline of the main sources of data were constructed. To illustrate the change in flow of information over time, timelines were divided into periods, which were then positioned in a triangular diagram of three axes indicating the relative contributions from science surveys, fishers, and/or economic reports. For example, in the early stages of a fishery, when logbooks are the main source of data, the block of time would be nearest the corner of the triangle labeled fishers.

We used icons to distinguish the different types of input from fish harvesters. The book icon indicates information from logbooks structured by DFO. The microphone icon indicates knowledge from semi-structured interviews (Neis et al. 1999), which allow the resource user to steer the conversation; these provide knowledge of local conditions, comparison of current with past conditions, and other information. The ship icon represents data from scientific surveys. The fish icon represents documents where both fish harvesters and scientists assemble knowledge by working together. The dollar sign indicates that the information is largely economic, such as export data.

RESULTS

Cod fishery in 2J3KL

A review of the stock assessment documents for cod in NAFO division 2J3KL revealed that logbooks were an important component of assessment in the early stages of government efforts to manage that fishery. Logbooks provide local information in a format that is structured by scientists, who then assemble the information. The accuracy of logbook information is often checked by follow-up activities, usually by telephone. There is little or no opportunity for input of knowledge held by fishers. Scientific surveys appear to allow even less input, although from our own experience with a scientific survey for juvenile cod (Schneider et al. 1997) we know that fishers contribute substantially to the initial design of surveys through their knowledge of gear and location.

Based on our review of the documents for the cod fishery, we developed a descriptive model of shifting information sources in science-based fisheries management. During the first phase, scientists gather knowledge of the fishery from fishers informally. During the next phase, scientists gather information from fishers in a structured format, logbooks, which are assembled for use in stock assessments. In lucrative fisheries, where political pressures create additional resources for large-scale surveys, scientists design the field protocol based on knowledge of gear by fishers. In the case of the survey of juvenile cod initiated by Alastair Fleming (Schneider et al. 1997), this phase was important in the first year, 1959, but not afterwards. Science based assessment then changes either in response to what is learned from stock scale surveys or when an established means of assembling knowledge (assessment model) is replaced by another. In the assessment of cod, for example, cohort-based assessment techniques and stratified random surveys replaced yield per recruit models that focus on maximum economic value per fish (Lear and Parsons 1993).

Several factors act to divorce the knowledge systems of scientists from that of fishers. Contributing factors are the following:

1 it is the central tenet of fisheries resource management, as it developed from the work of Hjort in the early twentieth century, that sustainable harvest requires knowledge of change in the size of an entire breeding stock, which cannot be gained from surveys at spatial scales smaller than the stock;
2 scientists know that catch records are fouled by practices such as misreporting (Metuzals et al., this volume, chap. 7) and hence distrust fishermen's input;
3 the management agency may take the view that catch statistics need to be confidential lest they be used for economic gain;
4 bureaucracies become defensive when under siege;
5 institutional policies may not reward public outreach by scientists;
6 scientists are under pressure to discount the uncertainty inherent in fish stock assessment lest their knowledge be discounted to zero; and
7 short-term economic interests can trump the precautionary principle.

For cod, the divorce of science knowledge from that of fishers reached crisis proportions in 1989, when substantial reductions in cod quotas were announced. Collaborative data gathering and knowledge assembly by scientists and fishers began after the closure of the fishery in 1992, with activities such as the sentinel fishery (Lilly et al. 2003).

To evaluate this model of sequential sources of knowledge and shifting patterns of knowledge assembly, we examined stock status reports and historical reviews for all the Atlantic snow crab fisheries (six areas) and all of the Canadian herring fisheries (three areas in the Atlantic, one in the Pacific). We found just over sixty documents, which are reported in detail by Alcock et al. (2003). From that report we have extracted a brief history of each fishery with a narrative of changes in sources of information and events associated with these changes.

Snow Crab (Chionoecetes opilio) Fisheries

The snow crab fishery in Newfoundland began in 1968, with effort confined to deep bays within thirty kilometers of the coast (Taylor et al. 1994). Offshore areas east of the Avalon Peninsula (3L) were first fished in 1978, and as effort increased, so did landings, which peaked

90 Flows and Blockages

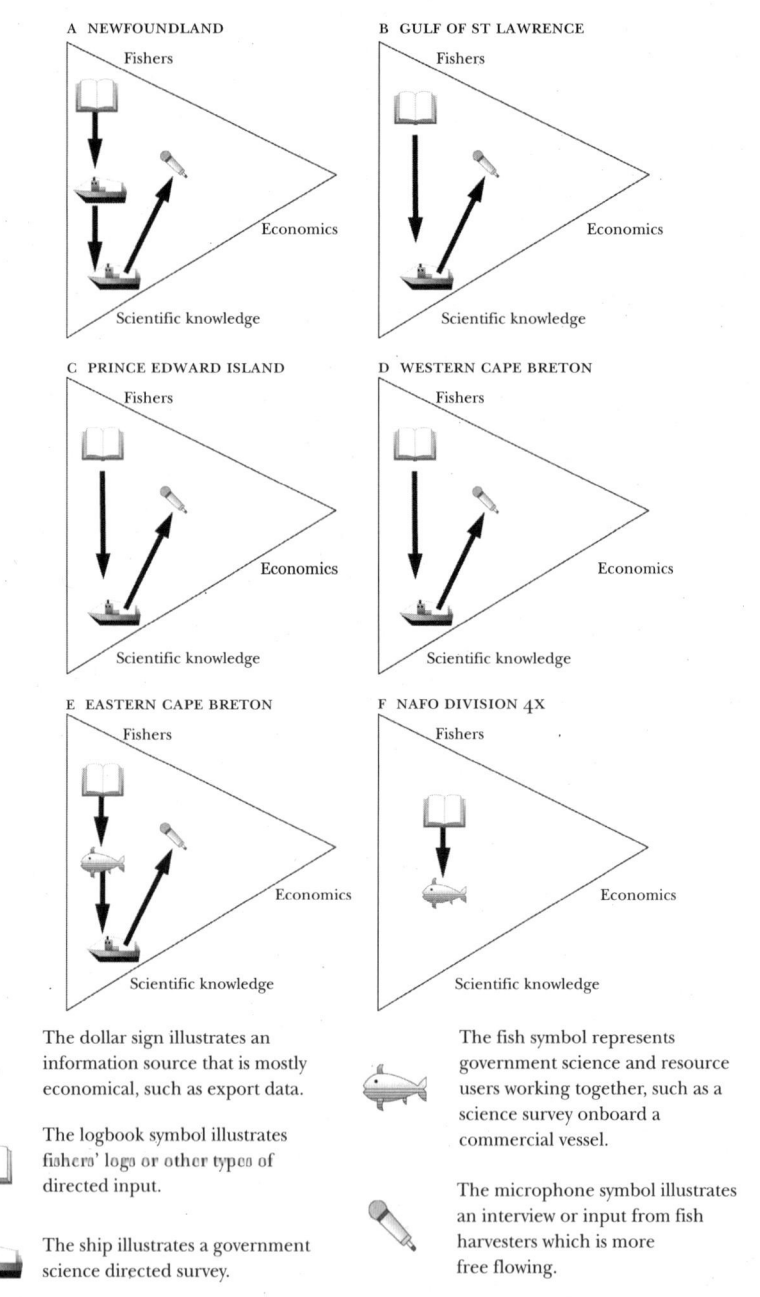

A NEWFOUNDLAND

B GULF OF ST LAWRENCE

C PRINCE EDWARD ISLAND

D WESTERN CAPE BRETON

E EASTERN CAPE BRETON

F NAFO DIVISION 4X

$ The dollar sign illustrates an information source that is mostly economical, such as export data.

The logbook symbol illustrates fishers' logs or other types of directed input.

The ship illustrates a government science directed survey.

The fish symbol represents government science and resource users working together, such as a science survey onboard a commercial vessel.

The microphone symbol illustrates an interview or input from fish harvesters which is more free flowing.

Figure 5.1 Shift in sources of information in Eastern Canadian snow crab fisheries. Images by Gary Tunnell

at 8,609 t in 1981. Landings declined from 1982 to a low of 74 t in 1985, and new areas were added. In 1985, supplementary fisheries for snow crab began in 2J, 3K, and 3PS, to supplement the incomes of groundfish operators (Anonymous 1999a). Snow crab landings were first recorded from the west coast of Newfoundland in 1996, when 1,032 t were reported; 708 t and 720 t were landed in 1997 and 1998 respectively (Taylor and O'Keefe 1999). This west coast fishery ceased one year (1992), owing to high occurrence of soft-shell (molting) crabs (Mallet et al. 1993).

The sources of information for this fishery began with structured logbooks completed by fishers, shifted to a science-based survey, then shifted to a second survey design, which was ultimately replaced by an integrated management plan that assembled information from large scale surveys and the local experience of fishers (figure 5.1A). From the 1970s onward logbooks were submitted by fishers (Taylor and O'Keefe 1989, 1998). In the 1980s scientists carried out inshore trap surveys within bays around the east coast of the island to estimate relative year class strength. Catch per unit effort (CPUE) data and landings were used to calculate exploitation rates (Taylor and O'Keefe 1989) using the Leslie matrix (Leslie and Davis 1939). Trap surveys were then replaced by post-season trawling estimates (Dawe et al. 1999). The introduction of an integrated management plan in 1999 expanded information sources to include dockside monitoring; at-sea observer coverage; and participation by fishers in meetings to develop the plan.

The snow crab fishery of the Gulf of St Lawrence began with exploratory fishing in Nova Scotia in 1965, spreading to Prince Edward Island, New Brunswick, and Quebec in 1966. Landings through the mid-1980s remained above 11,000 t, but with slight drops in 1989 and 1990 to 7,882 t and 6,950 t respectively (Hébert et al. 2000). Landings increased to 19,995 t in 1994, with a low of 11,136 t in 1998. In 1995 two new exploratory zones were added, one in the Laurentian Channel and one in the Magdalen Islands/Cape Breton. Landings in these new zones were moderate, remaining above 150 t in area E (1995–99) and above 250 t in area F (Hébert et al. 2000).

The Atlantic Crab Association (1966–73) and the Gulf Snow Crab Management Advisory Committee (1974–78) imposed few regulations. The Canadian Atlantic Fisheries Scientific Advisory Committee (1978–96) introduced regulations that resulted in protests, demonstrations, plant vandalization, and data fouling practices such as discarding catch at sea and dual record logbooks (Hare and Dunn

1993). Beginning in the 1990s the entire southern Gulf was managed as a single stock (Anonymous 1997). An integrated management plan released in 1997 mandated logbook use, dockside monitoring, a dockside sampling program, and fishery officer surveillance by sea and air.

The sources of information (figure 5.1B and 5.1C) show a pattern similar to that for Newfoundland, except that only one science based survey was used. Logbook-based Leslie analysis was replaced by a post-season bottom trawl survey in 1988 (Loch et al. 1994). In the 1990s interviews were undertaken (Chiasson et al. 1992), and assessment was conducted in collaboration with local fishers, the industry, processors, and government officials (Loch et al. 1994).

The snow crab fishery on Cape Breton is assessed in seven zones, extending from Area 18 in the South-west around to Area 24 in the South-east (Biron et al. 2000b). The fishery began with exploratory surveys concentrated around the north coast of Cape Breton in 1967. Catches off western Cape Breton remained steady near 2,000 t through the late 1980s and all the 1990s (DeGrâce et al. 2000), while landings off eastern Cape Breton varied through the late 1970s at 1,634 t in 1979, dropping to 89 t in 1985, and returning to over 1,500 t in the years since 1991 (Biron et al. 2000b). Western Cape Breton was among the first areas in Atlantic Canada to establish individual quotas (IQs) as a management tool in the early 1980s (Anonymous 1996).

The sources of information in western Cape Breton over time follow the same pattern as those for the Gulf (figure 5.1D). Assessment practice relied initially on logbooks, then on a trawl survey (beginning in 1988), then on integrated management in the 1990s. The sources of information in eastern Cape Breton followed this pattern (figure 5.1E), except that at-sea samples were collected by fishers for a time (Tremblay et al. 1994).

The snow crab fishery off southwestern Nova Scotia lies at the southern limit of this species. The fishery began in 1994, with landings at 130 kg. Landings in the next five years fell as low as 2 t and never rose above 91 t (Biron et al. 2000a). In 1996 fishers began submitting logbooks. In 1999 biologists began working aboard commercial vessels. The source of information thus went from structured logbook data directly to collaborative data collection and exchange of knowledge (figure 5.1F).

Herring (Clupea harengus) Fisheries

The herring fishery on the east coast of Newfoundland has long been a source of bait, with landings reported as far back as 1834. Landings ranged from 8,143 t in 1862 to 76,225 t in 1946 (Hourston and Chaulk 1968). Five herring stock complexes were identified: predominantly spring spawning and distributed along the east coast of Newfoundland (Anonymous 1999b). These stock complexes have supported bait, commercial, and food fisheries. Landings averaged 55,000 t (Anonymous 1984) in the late 1940s, owing to post-World War II food requests from Europe. Through the 1950s and 1960s landings from the East Coast were between 1,000 t and 2,000 t and were mainly used for bait and feed (Winters and Moores 1977). The southeast coast fishery came into prominence during the 1960s, while the northeast coast became prominent in the mid-1970s (Anonymous 1999b). Landings through the 1970s were high (25,000 t) and attributable to a very strong 1968 year class and to the market pressures created by the collapse of stocks in both the North Sea and on the West Coast of Canada (Anonymous 1999b). All Eastern stock areas were closed during the early 1980s owing to poor recruitment after the 1968 year class (Wheeler and Chaulk 1987). These areas reopened in 1986, when a significant 1982 year class became available (Anonymous 1999b). Herring roe on kelp, a significant fishery in British Columbia that serves mainly Asian markets, is at its early stages in Newfoundland, with 200 t available within the current management plan to develop this fishery sector (Anonymous 1999b).

Herring stocks were in practice unregulated through the early 1970s. Quota regulations were placed in northeastern Newfoundland, initially on only a few gear types, then eventually on all gear types in 1980. Southeastern areas had quotas slightly earlier, in 1973. Quotas are now set in six areas ranging from southern Labrador to Fortune Bay (Anonymous 1984, 1999b). A total allowable catch (TAC) is set from biological information, but since the early 1980s the TAC has rarely been met – the fishery is kept at lower levels by weak market demand. In 1995, new entrants were barred from the fishery (Anonymous 1999b).

Figure 5.2A shows the shifts in sources of information for herring stock assessment in eastern Newfoundland. Before 1900, the main source of catch data was data on annual exports compiled in House of Assembly journals. Since 1965, logbook records and processing-plant production data have been readily available, including information on

94   Flows and Blockages

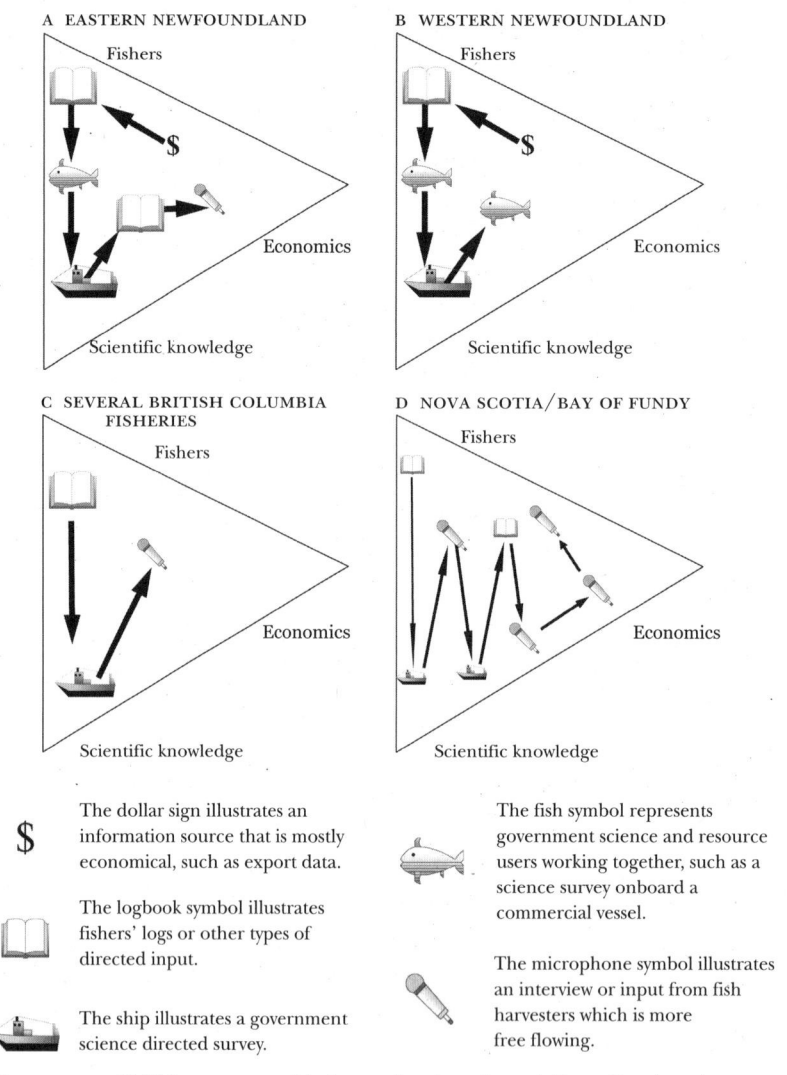

Figure 5.2   Shift in sources of information in selected Canadian herring fisheries. Images by Gary Tunnell

location and time of capture (Hourston and Chaulk 1968). Fishers submitting logs have been provided with a summary of the fishery in their area by personnel of the Pelagic Section of DFO once the data have been coded and analysed (Wheeler et al. 1999). Acoustic survey biomass estimates began in the early 1980s. The index fishers program has been ongoing since 1980, whether the fishery has occurred or not. This program has allowed fishers to gain insight into the role of fisheries biologists; it has provided biologists with knowledge of day-to-day issues of fishers as they pursue their livelihood (Wheeler et al. 1988). The approach has been to add indices, rather than to replace indices, with the result that in the 1990s biological advice rested on two scientific indices of abundance (research gill-net catch rates and acoustic-survey biomass estimates) and three fisher based indices (commercial gill-net catch rates, gill-net fisher observations, and purse-seine fisher observations). An integrated management plan (Anonymous 1999b) provided the resources to undertake collaborative information-gathering activities, including questionnaires in which herring abundance was estimated by the fish harvesters.

The herring fishery of western Newfoundland is divided into two spawning stocks (McQuinn and Lefebvre 1997). In the period 1940–70 landings in the region fluctuated from as high as 80,000 t (Moores and Winters 1984) to as low as 4,000 t (McQuinn and Lefebvre 1995). Total allowable catches have been in effect since 1977, and there have been allocations to the fixed gear and mobile gear sector since 1981. Since 1988, between 90 and 98 percent of the catch has been by purse seine, though approximately 45 percent of the TAC remains allocated for fixed gear. The advised target fishing level was reached only in 1991.

The shift in sources of information for stock assessment in this fishery (figure 5.2B) is similar to that in eastern Newfoundland. Economic data is available before the advent of logbook data collected mainly from index fishers since 1984. Biological samples of the commercial catch were then collected by index fishermen and by at-port samplers. Beginning in 1989, acoustic surveys were carried out in the area, normally in every second year (McQuinn and Lefebvre 1995). In 1995 and in 1997 the acoustic surveys were carried out in close collaboration with the seine fleet from the west coast of Newfoundland (McQuinn et al. 1999).

Pacific herring (*Clupea harengus pallasi*) has been fished off British Columbia since 1877, and a commercial fishery began at the turn of the century. The fishery expanded in the 1930s with demand for dry-salted product. The reduction (meal) fishery began in the 1940s (Anonymous 2001a). The fishery collapsed in the 1960s and was closed in 1967. By the mid-1970s the stock had recovered, and the fishery reopened gradually; a small roe fishery began in 1972, followed by other sectors throughout the 1970s. Quotas were set as far back as the

1930s but were not effective because extensions were nearly always granted (Stocker 1993). Enforceable quotas were first put into place in the region in 1988, but the catch has depended on markets since then (Anonymous 2000).

Figure 5.2C shows the flow of information since 1988, beginning with logbooks, then adding surveys and interviews. By, 1993, assessment was based upon two models (age structure and escapement), which both use data from scientific surveys. The interview data informs the management process, where the coordinator of the herring management working group must seek consensus from all sides of the herring industry before any decisions or recommendations are made (Stocker 1993).

Herrings has served as a convenient source of bait in the cod fishery in the western Atlantic for centuries. A meal industry developed in the 1950s, providing feed for the poultry industry. The roe fishery has been the most important component in recent years (Power and Stephenson 1987). The Scotia Fundy herring fishery is the largest in the western Atlantic; it consists predominantly of purse seiners (Stephenson et al. 1999). Since the early 1960s, landings in the region have been consistently above 100,000 t, with catches peaking in the late 1960s and again in the early 1970s as foreign interest in the area increased (Stephenson et al. 1998). Non-quota catches during this period, before the 200 mile limit was introduced, were often well above 50,000 t (Anonymous 1981). Given the value of the fishery and the mobility of the gear, it is not surprising that management history has been complex, as indicated by a succession of responsible agencies: Ministry task force (1968), Atlantic Herring Coordinator (1969), Atlantic Herring Management Committee (1971), CAFSAC (1977), Small Pelagics Advisory Committees (1981), Monitoring Working Group (1995), Pelagics Research Council (1996), and Scotia-Fundy Fisheries Herring Purse Seine Monitoring Committee (1997). Integrated management plans were introduced in 1997 and again in 1999.

In this region the main source of information used in stock assessment has shifted often (figure 5.2D). Fishers were first admitted as equal partners to the management forum in the early 1970s, when the minister of fisheries invited fishers to take part in developing proposals within the management constraints of the time (Iles 1993). In 1985, a detailed purse seine logbook was introduced and used through 1989. The main use of the logbooks was to track the progress of the fishery, the total catch and effort, but they were also used in documenting the market and fish conditions (Power and Stephenson 1990). A science and technology internship program was created in 1996 to give people in the industry experience with techniques such as sampling, data recording and documentation, tagging, acoustic survey methods, and ecology (Stephenson et al. 1998). In 1997 new license conditions required completion of log records. In 1998, 245 fixed-gear herring fishers were interviewed in person, from 11 Nova Scotia counties, and asked mainly about changes in gear use over time (Clark et al. 1999). Acoustic surveys to assess abundance were completed on commercial vessels; these were occasionally supplemented by research vessels (Anonymous 2001). Through the late 1990s there were workshops where all interested parties could contribute to discussions on conservation and management (Stephenson et al. 1998). Thus, as with the other fisheries, the knowledge was assembled from increasingly diverse sources.

DISCUSSION

The central tenet of science-based fisheries management as it developed in the twentieth century is that sustainable harvest requires knowledge of change in the size of an entire breeding stock. This disconnects the knowledge of scientists, who conduct surveys at the scale of the stock, from the knowledge of resource users, who develop detailed knowledge of local movements, abundance, and habitat use. Science-based assessment came to mean stock scale estimates of change, based where possible on knowledge of cohort sizes from scientific surveys. We examined the degree to which knowledge of stock status used in management relies on scientific surveys. In particular, we looked at the relative contribution of three sources of knowledge (local harvester knowledge, commercial statistics, and stock scale assessment) as a fishery develops. We found that a similar pattern appeared in three very different fisheries. Logbook and landings data are used initially in stock assessment and management. Over time, management advice comes to rely increasingly on stock scale estimates and models. Because fish and fishing effort are spatially heterogeneous, this stock scale knowledge inevitably deviates from local knowledge. This deviation, when accompanied by regulatory limits and rapid innovation to maintain catch rates, results in demands by resource users that their knowledge be included in the assessment process. Local knowledge then regains a place in stock assessment and management decisions. This re-injection of local knowledge typically brings with it a wider variety of topics than the highly structured flow of information via logbook statistics used in the early stages of a fishery. In a mature knowledge network, scientists and resource users collaborate in assembling reports of stock status used in management.

The patterns of knowledge assembly and flow in the case of the cod, crab, and herring fisheries can be interpreted in light of Latour's (1987) actor network concepts, which introduce the dynamics of aligned interests as an explanation of complexity (stasis and rapid change) in knowledge systems. Scientists need information when they "enter" the fishery as providers of advice and so align themselves informally with fishers, who hold practical knowledge of gear, seasonal abundances, and local conditions. These alignments tend to dissolve relative to alignments within the profession of science and within the guild of fishing, each of which has its own dynamics of stasis and change. In science, professional recognition drives the development of new procedures, which are resisted by adherence to the principle of consistency and comparability. The result is stasis punctuated by brief periods of rapid shift to new procedures embedded in a new way of assembling knowledge. Examples are the sudden shift to cohort-based models in the cod fishery and the sudden shift away from Leslie based models in the crab fishery. Similar patterns of stasis and rapid change occurred in the fishery, where traditional knowledge is valued relative to the need to catch fish reliably, while new knowledge and techniques spread rapidly once they are shown to be reliable. Examples in the fishery are the rapid adoption of novel techniques that were initially resisted, such as the cod trap; acoustic detection of fish; and navigation aids such as Loran or satellite navigation.

In the middle to late twentieth century the knowledge systems of scientists and fishers were driven to an increasing degree by internal forces: professionalization in science and commodification in fisheries in industrialized countries. These forces resulted not only in stasis and change within science and within fishing but also in the divergence of knowledge systems developed by scientists from that developed by the fishing guild. In Newfoundland, this divergence was reflected in the fact that scientists did not go out on fishing vessels (some never went to sea at all) and fishers did not go out on research vessels (until recently).

If an alignment of interests drove the divergence of knowledge systems in science and in fishing, what ended the divergence? Within the knowledge system of traditional inshore fishers, the decline in cod became serious by 1984; within the knowledge system of scientists, serious decline became evident by 1987, and within the knowledge system of a vocal minority of highly entrepreneurial fishers there was no decline in abundance. The fish themselves ended the divergence, in that their recruitment and growth rates fell short of the rate of removal, leading to declines that forced the differing assessments of abundance into the open. Within the framework of Latour's actor network concept one might dub the fish actors whose dwindling numbers forced an end to the divergence in knowledge. This salvages the concept at the expense of making the concept so plastic as to explain both everything and nothing.

Alternatively, one can distinguish degrees of empirical content as determinants of outcome. That the earth turns, that smoking causes cancer, and that fish and crabs are depletable resources have higher degrees of empirical content than knowledge to the contrary, knowledge that was once held widely and backed by powerful interests. Within the knowledge system of highly entrepreneurial fishers the concept of fewer fish is superfluous because reduced catch rates have not been experienced; the empirical content of that system is low in that it does not include increases in efficiency (to maintain catch rates), increases in the number of fishers, or failing catch rates of other fishers.

Latour's actor network concepts provide insight into stasis and change in the knowledge systems of both fishers and scientists. The concepts provide considerable insight into the divergence of these knowledge systems. Because Latour's concepts do not recognize differences in empirical content as a determinant of outcome, they do less well in explaining the outcome of divergence in knowledge of cod abundance – the divergence abated when the disappearance of fish forced the closure of the fishery.

Acknowledgements
We thank H. Coward, B. Neis, R. Ommer, and P. Trnka for comments and for challenging us to explain the patterns we observed in knowledge sources in fisheries.

6

Opening the Black Box: Methods, Procedures, and Challenges in the Historical Reconstruction of Marine Social-ecological Systems

GRANT MURRAY, BARBARA NEIS,
DAVID C. SCHNEIDER, DANNY INGS,
KAREN GOSSE, JENNIFER WHALEN,
AND CRAIG T. PALMER

INTRODUCTION

When dealing with issues centred on environmental change or economic development, we are often faced with conflicting information. "Experts" tell us different things, often based on specialized knowledge. A biologist, for example, may tell us that fish stocks are declining, while at the same time a fish harvester may say the stocks are in good shape (or vice versa); an environmentalist tells us that fish farms are destructive, while a community may find them acceptable. As a result, we are often faced with the questions, whom do we believe and, perhaps more importantly, why do we believe them? The claims of different experts can be particularly difficult to assess (or even access) when they are based on different types of knowledge: local observations, scientific sampling or modelling, experience elsewhere, or historical precedents, to name a few. As researchers, we are faced with the underlying issue of how we can compare different types of knowledge that on the face of it appear incommensurable.

This chapter describes the efforts by our research team to address this critical issue as part of our attempt to reconstruct historical changes in the marine social-ecological systems[1] of the northern Gulf of St Lawrence, the Strait of Belle Isle and southeastern Labrador. Focusing specifically on fisheries, we have sought to collect, analyse, and combine information drawn from different knowledge systems in order to track social-ecological interactions over time and compare them and to assess potential consequences for the health of fishery dependent communities, as well as fish and shellfish stocks (Dolan et al. 2005).

Developing a historical perspective on social-ecological system change is an important tool for fisheries-related reflection and discussion. Determining historical stock levels helps to counteract the "shifting baseline syndrome" (Pauly 1995), or the tendency among fishers and scientists to assess current abundance against the abundance they observed when they first entered the field – rather than against earlier (and often higher) levels of abundance. It can also help to highlight key factors that have influenced social-ecological change, paving the way for future-oriented discussion.

Incorporating existing fisheries science data into an environmental history is, however, challenging. One of the key challenges lies in the fact that systematic data related to fisheries are incomplete and/or insufficient: they often consist of scientific time series that are relatively short; they can be based on marked differences in the spatial and temporal scale of the data, and they may not cover the full range of processes involved in social-ecological change.

We address the central theme of this book by describing how we have mobilized and synthesized information derived from different forms of knowledge to carry out a historical reconstruction and discuss how this combination of information might be useful in future approaches. Our research starts from the premise that there are different knowledge systems (local ecological knowledge [LEK], natural sciences, and social sciences) that are based on different assumptions and different kinds of observations, yet contain information relevant to understanding the complex and interactive processes and changes associated with social-ecological system change. We have also begun with the premise that each also falls short of producing a complete, multi-scale picture. In this chapter, we argue that these different sources of information can complement one another and help to make macro/micro level and historical linkages more apparent. While comparing and/or reconciling information derived from these systems can be difficult and while our knowledge of fish and fisheries will always be partial, we further argue that our understanding of fisheries and the social-ecological systems in which they take place broadens as the diversity of sources increases.

Recognizing the value of these different knowledge sources we have combined insights from fish harvesters (LEK) with archival information and offshore research vessel (RV) trawl survey data collected by the Canadian Department of Fisheries and Oceans (DFO). We have systematically assembled and combined information from each of these different knowledge systems, with attention to differences in spatial and temporal scales.

LOCAL ECOLOGICAL KNOWLEDGE – THE "BLACK BOX"

In many cases, LEK has proved the most difficult source of information to reconcile with other sources. While many authors have suggested that LEK can provide a powerful addition to science and management, few have explicitly described how this data might be collected in a rigorous, efficient manner that is sensitive to the epistemological characteristics of this knowledge system – hence the "black box" metaphor used to characterize some LEK research (Holm 2003). Still fewer have described how information derived from this knowledge system might be made commensurable with different kinds of information (derived from different knowledge systems) as diverse as archival, landings, or catch and sampling data.

At the same time, epistemological concerns and a perceived lack of methodological clarity have engendered criticism from some quarters. Two types of critiques of LEK research essentially draw attention to the opacity of the "black-box" process by which LEK moves from local resource users to LEK researchers and then on to other audiences. Anthony Davis and John Wagner (2003), for example, have complained of a lack of methodological rigour within fisheries LEK research, and particularly of a general imprecision in descriptions of the methods used to identify and select local "experts." They argue that this has served to weaken the field and diminish the capacity for comparative studies.

A second type of critique derives from within the sociology of science literature (see Holm 2003; Gray 2002; and Pálsson 2000). Holm (2003), for example, argues that while LEK researchers assert the validity and utility of LEK and claim a sort of epistemological equivalency with traditional science, the *practices* of LEK researchers actually tend to subordinate LEK to traditional science. Holm charges that by "cleaning up" fishers' knowledge, researchers turn fishers ecological knowledge (FEK) into FEK*, a different, filtered, and reduced product that has been "subtly refined" in the hands of researchers.[2] Holm further charges that local-knowledge researchers tend to "mine" only those bits of knowledge that can be properly validated, analysed, or interpreted by more rigorous scientific methods (Holm 2003; see also Neis 2003, response to Holm; Agrawal 1995; Pálsson 2000; Gray 2002; Nadasdy 2006).

Holm makes some valid points. Trying to move FEK from the world of fishing and memories of fish harvesters does involve selecting from a much larger knowledge set and, to some degree, de-contextualizing and de-individualizing that information, freezing it in time and space and interpreting it. Because we are aggregating, greater weight is accorded to consistency, and to make it comparable to other data we are bounding, charting and graphing it. FEK is also being deployed in ways that the originators of the knowledge did not foresee when they accumulated and, to some degree, when they shared this knowledge.

Acknowledging the existence of these transformations, as well as the limits and partiality of FEK is a part of opening the black box. So too is a discussion of a rigorous approach to how these transformations take place (i.e., the collection and comparison of information). In fact, the clarification helps place FEK on a par with other forms of information, scientific and historic, that have undergone somewhat similar transformations (See Holm 1996, 2001; Latour 1987, 2004).

This chapter pays particular attention to the "black box" characterization of FEK, showing that FEK has its own strengths and weaknesses, which can be critically evaluated and compared to historical and contemporary scientific data (with their own strengths and weaknesses) to build a more robust knowledge set and to provide an understanding upon which to build improved stock and harvest management. We begin with a description of the research team that was assembled to analyse the different sources of information. After describing the general strengths and weaknesses of these sources in more detail, we then discuss how we have conceptualized the linkages between them and elaborate on how the notion of *scale* has helped us in that conceptualization. Next, we provide several examples of how we have formed these linkages. We conclude with a discussion of general issues related to mobilizing and linking knowledge from different sources for historical reconstruction and for addressing current science and management issues.

MOVING KNOWLEDGE

We assembled an interdisciplinary team of researchers to gather and analyse the different types of data available for use in our work and to help overcome existing disciplinary boundaries. Social scientists, for example, are relatively familiar with interviewing techniques, some sampling issues, the dynamics of fisheries, local fisheries terminologies, and fishing technologies, but can be less familiar than natural scientists with fisheries ecology, population dynamics, stock assessment science, ecosystem modelling, and so on.

Our interdisciplinary research team had four core researchers experienced in collecting FEK from fishers (a sociologist, two biologists, and an environmental historian) and was supplemented by others, ranging from an anthropologist who had done research in part of the study area to several graduate students (as well as supervisors and committee members) at different points in the study. The collaborations of this research team have led to several independent efforts linked by a common focus on *social-ecological system change* in our study area, but each have generally drawn, to varying degrees, from one or more of the sources of information listed below (see also the specific methodologies as summarized in Whalen 2005 and Gosse 2003).

SOURCES OF KNOWLEDGE

Archival Sources

Archival data were collected on licensing and participation, fleet characteristics, changes in markets, and management trends over time from the libraries and online resources of the DFO in St John's, Newfoundland. We also drew on census data from Statistics Canada. A major component, however, has consisted of landings data compiled by the International Commission of the Northwest Atlantic Fisheries (ICNAF) and its successor, the Northwest Atlantic Fisheries Organization (NAFO). Landings data are quite useful and have been widely used in developing historical perspectives on fisheries. Such data can be used to track broad spatial shifts in fishing effort from one NAFO subdivision to another over time, as well as to track shifts in landings between vessel size and general gear sectors (e.g., offshore/mobile gear versus inshore/fixed gear). They are also effective for demonstrating patterns of ecological intensification or shifting of aggregate effort across species and down trophic levels (see below; see also Murray, et al. 2008; Neis and Kean 2003; Pauly et al. 1998).

However, these NAFO landings data share some of the same shortcomings of many, if not most, fisheries landings data sets. They cannot tell us much about underlying spatial and temporal shifts in effort (or the causal factors behind those shifts) the full range of ecological processes involved (e.g., whether there were changes in the stocks accessed or the size of fish captured) or about possible interactions between the shifts described.[3] Landings data also tend to be sparse or uneven over time, are collected in spatial units that do not always fit with the underlying ecology, do not include information on by-catch or discarding, and are vulnerable to misreporting.

Research Vessel Survey Data:

Like landings data, research vessel (RV) trawl survey data are powerful but limited sources of information. These data provide information on changes in such things as the abundance, distribution, and size of various species over time and sometimes include information on the diets of particular species. RV data provide a randomly placed and hence representative sample of fish densities and distributions for a broad range of species at a particular time of year. RV survey data are extremely valuable but have some limitations from the point of view of ecological history. In Newfoundland, for example, consistent RV data are available only from the 1970s onward and can therefore tell us little about patterns of distribution and abundance before that period – and therefore about the relative abundances and ranges of particular species that might be associated with an ecosystem before the intensive fishing effort of the last several decades. Furthermore, trawl surveys extend only over several weeks at a fixed time of the year (the fall for Newfoundland groundfish) and cannot capture shifts in distribution at other times during the year. In addition, they do not sample many coastal fisheries and critical spawning, nursery, and other habitats. Localized (particularly inshore) fish populations such as the Gilbert Bay "golden cod" are therefore potentially overlooked during RV surveys (see below). These surveys are also not designed to monitor ecosystem change and by themselves are of limited utility in evaluating the potential for recovery of particular populations. Moreover, RV surveys target groundfish and provide only incidental information on benthic organisms that seek shelter in rocks, retreat into the substrate (e.g., sand eels), live in the substrate (benthic infauna), or live in the water column (pelagic fish and invertebrates).

While a good time series of RV data can provide an indication of overall trends in abundance, such data cannot by themselves uncover dynamics, defined as the processes that together augment or diminish stock size. Understanding dynamics requires supplementary information on growth rates, spatial and temporal variation in exploitation rate, and age specific variation in both natural and fishing mortality. For example, high rates of discarding of small fish can lead to the overestimation of stock abundance based on RV data because it causes the amount of fish harvested from a stock to be underestimated. The time series used in assessments also provide little or no information on the interaction of fish populations with the environment (Fischer and Haedrich 2002) or with other species through predation outside the period or area of the survey.

Fish Harvesters' LEK

Fish harvesters and members of their families can develop detailed knowledge about resources and their environments that is sometimes referred to as LEK (Berkes 1993, 1999; Freeman and Carbyn 1988; Johannes 1981; Neis and Felt 2000). As we consider it, LEK includes more than knowledge of the non-human, biophysical environment or a strictly utilitarian set of productive practices. Consistent with the idea of social-ecological systems, we view fishers as embedded in networks that extend well beyond their vessels to include not only the surrounding biophysical environment but also such things as management regulations, kinship ties, peer pressure, social support mechanisms, and the global seafood market (Murray et al. 2006). Fish harvesters' knowledge includes varying degrees of (and sometimes quite profound) understanding of the elements, processes, and interactions within these networks. At the same time it is created and mediated by those networks (Murray et al. 2006; Johnsen 2005).

LEK is largely orally transmitted, and the information it contains is subject to the effects of memory. It is not standardized in terms of measurement frequency, territorial coverage, technology, effort, and expertise (Neis and Kean 2003; Murray et al. 2006). On the other hand, LEK is necessarily subject to empirical ground truthing when poor knowledge reduces success. However, this is probably less true for aspects of LEK not directly related to such practical concerns.[4] LEK is also subject to an additional source of cross-checking, in that commercial harvesters glean knowledge from others. We know little about how this works in particular contexts, and this process of ground truthing and data gleaning clearly differs from the processes of knowledge construction that prevail in the social and natural sciences.

Opening the Black Box: Systematizing LEK

LEK can be documented in a systematic and ethical fashion through involvement of fish harvesters. Below, we provide several examples of how LEK can be aggregated to construct a larger scale, finely textured picture of regional fisheries extending back several decades (Neis, Felt et al. 1999; Neis, Schneider, et al. 1999). The methodology described in this section refers to examples 1 and 2 below, while the specific (though essentially similar) methodology utilized in example 3 is explained in more detail in Whalen, 2005. To varying degrees, out methodological approach is also described elsewhere (Murray et al. 2005, 2006; Murray et al. 2008; Murray et al. accepted)

In collecting fish harvesters' LEK, we opted for interviews rather than participant observation with fish harvesters as recommended by some researchers (e.g., Fischer 2000; Stanley and Rice 2003) because our interest was in historical reconstruction of changes in fish and fisheries more than in assessing in fine detail current events and issues. The large study area also made participant observation for the core research impractical.

Our target population of fishers was distributed throughout the entire study area, with some concentration in areas where fisheries were particularly intensive and were dominated by older (retired and nearly retired) harvesters who could comment on situations and changes taking place over several decades. We were also concerned about having a sample large enough to encompass individual variability along several axes, notably age, gear sector and mobility, experience, local physical and social contextual influences, and individual "truthfulness" and "devotion to observation" (Butler 1983; Neis et al. 1999b; Mailhot 1993; Johannes 1981; Davis and Wagner 2003). We chose a referral process as appropriate because fishers differ in experience and observational tendencies, and information is concentrated among a few individuals, particularly skippers. Furthermore, the referral process often brings with it an implied trust of the interviewers by another fisher. These "local experts"[5] were indicated on two lists composed on our request: one by field representatives of the provincial Department of Fisheries and Aquaculture (DFA) and the second by chairs of local fisheries committees (who are also fish harvesters).

Interviews were semi-structured and guided by an interview schedule that included a short questionnaire focusing on demographic information. This approach allowed us to initially gather a wide range of knowledge and allowed the interviewee to shape the direction of the interview (Neis et al. 1999b). We used nautical charts during the interview to help structure the conversation and to tie observations to places, as appropriate.

Because LEK is largely motivated by fishing success rather than scientific criteria of consistency and generality, it is more difficult to "take out of people" and present to an audience so that it can be digested and understood. In order to compare, contrast, and, where appropriate, combine this information with information from other sources, we need to find or develop some "common ground." We therefore began the process of turning the tapes and maps into formats that could be more easily transported, processed, aggregated, analysed, and combined with other sources of information to address our particular research questions and goals. We first copied our tapes and returned a copy to the fish harvesters who had requested a copy of their interview. Then the audio-cassettes were transcribed,[6] and the contents of the transcripts organized using a combination of Excel, QSR (N6), and MapInfo (GIS) software. Quantitative information, including information on vessel characteristics, gear type and quantity, and catch per unit effort was organized into a spreadsheet (generally Excel). N6 software was used to organize more qualitative information from the interviews. MapInfo (GIS) software was used to organize information captured on nautical charts. These databases were linked using a series of identifying codes.

The process of organizing the data described above served to facilitate analysis by allowing for aggregation along axes we developed. This means that, first, in a spatial sense we were able to aggregate information from fishers from different geographic areas by "pasting together" the highly detailed descriptions of particular areas (e.g., individual fishing grounds) into an overall regional description. Second, we were able to compare/contrast information from fishers about certain events, processes, techniques, and so on, and thereby to get an overall impression of the similarities and differences between the individuals we interviewed. Once individual maps were digitized and the interviews coded,

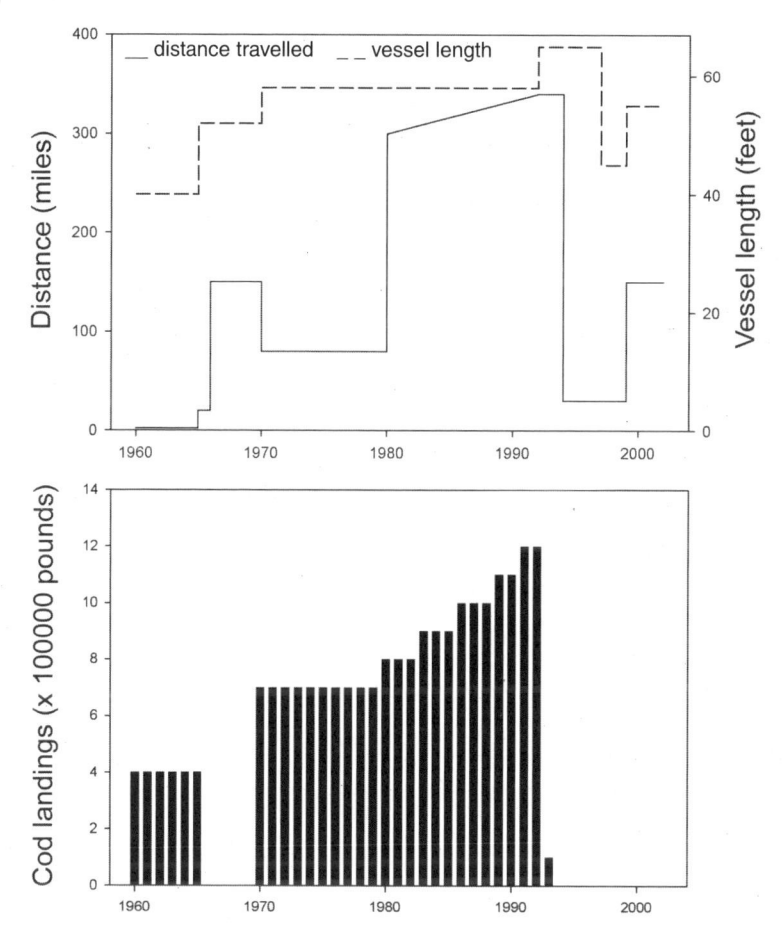

Figure 6.1 Changes in vessel length (one component of effort), distance travelled, and cod landings for one respondent

it was possible to produce aggregate maps showing, for example, information on cod migrations in the transcripts of respondents we interviewed in particular areas, all of the fishing areas, and so on. It was also possible to track spatial shifts in fishing effort, over time within and among interviews (figure 6.1).

THE ISSUE OF SCALE AND THE RISKS OF SCALING UP

Overall, the information contained in each of these types of knowledge is both partial and situated (by "situated" we mean that it is to some

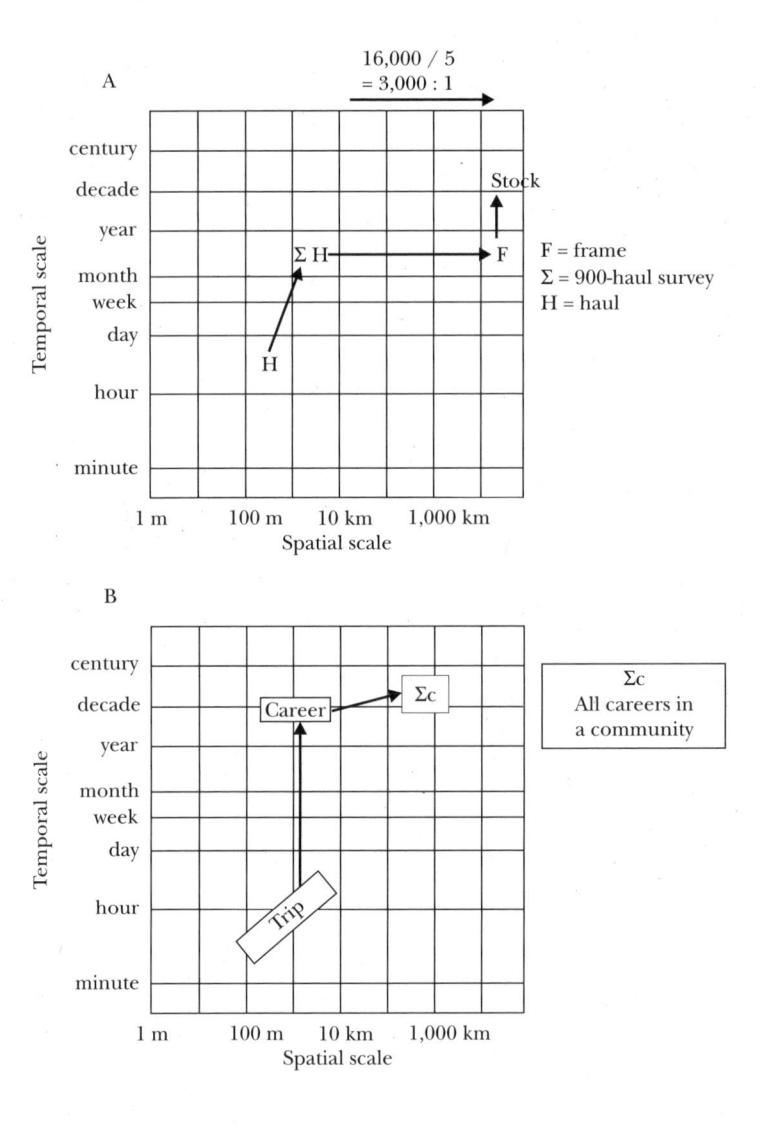

Figure 6.2 The space and time scales of knowledge gathering and assembly (A) by computational model in fisheries research; (B) for a community of people engaged in fishing. Figure 6.2A adapted from figure 17.1 in Vodden, Ommer, and Schneider (2005, 294) With kind permission of Springer Science and Business Media

degree a product of particular times, places, and social-cultural and ecological contexts). In comparing these sources of information, it is helpful to consider the issue of scale. For our purposes we take scale to mean spatial and temporal extent. The "issue" lies in the fact that the scale of measurements (or individual experience) falls well short of the extent of the system we wish to understand.

We can compare the production of knowledge and the scaling issues in reconciling different types of data through the use of space-time diagrams. Figure 6.2A, for example, depicts one of the principal information-gathering activities in fisheries science: the stratified random survey, which is used to estimate stock size.[7] The unit of information is the number of fish in a single haul of the net, which has a known duration (usually ten minutes). A single survey (H) of a large area (such as NAFO zones 2J and 3KL east of Newfoundland) might consist of 900 single hauls placed randomly in a larger area, the frame (F) of all possible hauls in 2J3KL. The area covered by the sample is ΣH (which takes about a month to survey). The number of fish in the entire area (the frame) is then inferred from the sample ($\Sigma H \to F$). This estimate at one point in time is then used to estimate stock size (s) for the year ($F \to S$). The length of the horizontal arrow ($\Sigma H \to F$) shows the burden placed on statistical methods when inferring from the sample ΣH to the frame F of all possible sample locations.

Here, knowledge gathered by way of the hauls is fed into a model (a model that includes estimates of mortality rates and other knowledge) that is combined, in computational form, to allow the stock size estimate for the frame F, at the space and time scale of year and a stock, to be generalized to stock dynamics.

Figure 6.2B contrasts the information-gathering activity in fishery science with the information gained through the experience of an individual fisher and a fishing community. The information gathered by fishers during the course of a single fishing trip occurs over a small area. Experience from each trip accumulates during the course of a career (and is passed down between generations), usually over a restricted area. The experience of the individuals in a community will cover a larger area.

Figure 6.2B depicts how fishers themselves "scale up" the information derived from their own experiences by accumulating and passing on knowledge through time and by communicating with others in their community. That is, they draw on (and add to) the accumulated knowledge represented by ΣC. As researchers, we have also sought to "scale up" this information. However, we have focused on particular pieces of information, have used a more formalized set of methods or proce-

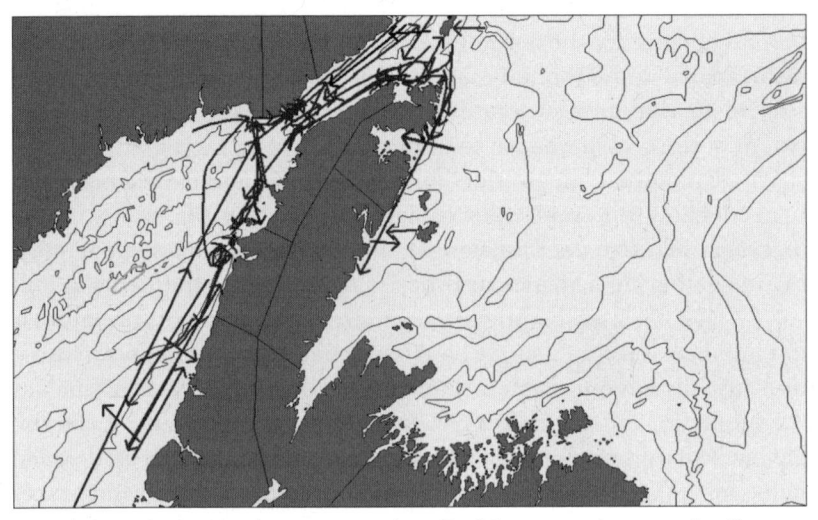

Figure 6.3 Cod migration patterns described by respondents on the Great Northern Peninsula and the Strait of Belle Isle. Each arrow represents an individual's description of cod movements and is associated with a particular behaviour and/or time of year.

dures for scaling them up, and have focused on regions that extend beyond the boundaries of traditional communities.

EXAMPLES

Following are three examples in which we describe the linkages among different sources of information. Each example approaches the challenge somewhat differently. We summarize across examples, paying particular attention to the sources of information utilized and how they are linked, as well as to how each example has enhanced our understanding of cross-scale and historical elements of the social-ecological systems in the study area.

Example 1: Local Stock Structure

One of the persistent concerns about LEK is its consistency and reliability, particularly when it contradicts scientific sampling. In this example information from LEK is used to interrogate and complement the knowledge system of science, and science is used to interrogate the validity of the assumptions in one LEK model. This example summarizes findings discussed in much more detail in Murray et al. (accepted).

RV survey data in Newfoundland are not available before the 1970s, are usually restricted to one season of the year, do not cover inshore habitat, and do not reveal much about the spatial structure of substocks, particularly in inshore areas. While acknowledging the existence of sub-stocks within larger populations (such as the "northern" or "Gulf" stocks), managers and fisheries scientists have operated on the idea that sub-stocks mix over large areas at the time of annual fall surveys. Likewise, the information from tagging studies is also socially and ecologically incomplete and "situated."

During the interviews, we therefore asked harvesters about the existence of resident, non-migratory, local, or "bay," stocks separate from the main, migratory body that tends to move into deeper water in the winter. Specifically, fishers were asked about the presence of cod in their areas during the winter or early spring, different morphological characteristics (see below), different behavioural patterns, and their opinions on the presence or absence of bay stocks. Fishers reported the existence of over-wintering stocks in several of the bays and sounds along the west coast of Newfoundland and the south coast of Labrador, including in Gilbert's Bay. The LEK establishes that not all sub-stocks move offshore and hence challenges the assumption that a fall survey timed to offshore movement will represent the aggregate abundance of all cod.

In addition to understanding stock structure, it is also critically important to understand how these groups (including the main body) of fish move, or migrate. Understanding the movements of fish is particularly important to interpreting RV data (usually collected over a relatively short term) and estimating the size of particular stocks. Figure 6.3 shows patterns of cod migrations in a GIS chart derived from interviews conducted in the area. Each arrow represents a migration pattern for cod as described by an individual fisher, and is associated with a particular "run" of cod, and is linked to the N6 database, where varying levels of detail are provided on the timing, direction, and nature of this movement. The complexity of movement here again suggests a correspondingly complex stock structure, and we have been able to verify that information in feedback meetings with both fishers and fisheries scientists and to use it to improve the general understanding of cod stock structure and movements in our broader study area.

Our work on local stocks also provides an example of how information from one knowledge system can be used to complement information from another. For example, fishers in Gilbert Bay largely distinguished local and migratory fish stocks by their colour, and in our interviews retired harvesters were asked (*inter alia*) to describe and locate their observations of brown or reddish cod on a nautical chart (Gosse et al. 2001; Gosse 2003; Gosse and Wroblewski 2004). These interview data were subsequently used as a starting point for more detailed work combining LEK and scientific research related to the relationship between diet and the colour of cod in Gilbert Bay.[8] A food experiment designed to examine the relationship between diet and fish body colouration showed that cod change colour within a relatively short period of time if their diet is changed (Gosse and Wroblewski 2004). At the same time, genetic testing confirmed that these "golden cod" were part of a genetically distinct sub-population of fish (see Wroblewski 2000). In this case scientific studies confirmed a possible relationship between LEK-based observations of different coloured cod and population structure but also called into question the assumption that colour differences, by themselves, were sufficient to distinguish between populations. Follow-up scientific research is required in other areas described in the interviews to verify the contemporary presence or absence of other local stocks. However, the interview results provide a very useful guide for selecting areas where there is probably a higher likelihood of finding such stocks.

Example 2: Understanding Processes of Intensification and Expansion in the Inshore

Example 2 represents a case where aggregating information across the study area is used to document and better understand the process of spatial, temporal, and ecological intensification and expansion in the inshore sector (Neis and Kean 2003). In this example, information from different knowledge systems is scrutinized and cross-checked to better understand the dynamics of these interactions.

Murray et al. (2008) used a multi-method, multi-scale approach to understanding historical patterns of intensification and expansion. They used landings data and archival information to demonstrate patterns of shifting aggregate effort across species (ecological expansion) (Neis and Kean 2003), emphasizing serial dependence on just one or two species at any one time and providing insight into aggregate effects on marine ecosystems such as declines in mean trophic levels.

Statistics such as these, however, cannot tell us much about the spatial or temporal dynamics of fishing processes such as variation in rates of catch and effort. Nor can these data inform us about possible interactions between the shifts described or about specific ecological processes involved (e.g., whether there were changes in the populations fished or the size of fish landed). Furthermore, statistics such as these tell us relatively little about the dynamic and complex processes of intensification of effort that underlie patterns of (temporarily) increasing landings, spatial expansion, and shifts across species.

Murray et al. (2008) found that an examination of LEK shows that the very process of aggregating information masks meso- (sectoral and regional) and micro-level heterogeneity in processes of intensification and expansion. Furthermore, while economic reasons (e.g., making boat payments) were often mentioned when fishers were asked why they changed their fishing operations, this was rarely the sole reason, nor even always the dominant explanation offered. Instead, these decisions were mediated by a variety of factors, including ecological conditions, regulations and other government actions, markets, access to capital, community, region, and the age of the fisher, local declines in abundance (which *sometimes* reflected larger-scale declines), management regulations (such as limited entry restrictions), the relative costs of entering new fisheries, the presence or absence of alternative species, and so on. The authors argue that findings such as these point to the need for actor-centred models (e.g., models based on fishers' actual behaviour) rather than simplified assumptions about causal mechanisms derived from analysis at a single scale.

Example 3: Individual-based Models of Harvester-Lobster Interactions in St John Bay:

Our experience in St John Bay highlights the fact that management concerns are sometimes specific to areas that are, relatively speaking, quite small. In this situation, the limits of a single, large-scale source of information are immediately apparent. NAFO landings statistics collected at a regional scale (in this case NAFO sub-division 4R) can tell us little about what is happening at a more local scale. Moreover, even if landings statistics were available for this smaller scale and effort information was incorporated, the data do not contain any insight about the causal mechanisms involved. On the other hand, micro-level LEK information can be aggregated to the level of a bay, making information about causal mechanisms that are most salient to management more accessible. LEK can also be combined with traditional fisheries science and used as the basis for developing individual-based models of harvester-fish interactions.

Whalen (2005) focused on the St John Bay lobster fishery, a valuable and productive fishery for many years. She interviewed over fifty lobster harvesters in this relatively small area (they amounted to a significant proportion of all license holders in the area) in an attempt to reconstruct changes in catch rates, fishing strategies, crew composition, management, fishing areas, and attitudes towards conservation in that fishery since the 1970s.

Whalen's LEK interviews showed that in the 1970s approximately 75 licensees landed somewhere between 250,000 and 600,000 lbs of lobster, and enjoyed catch rates that averaged around 15–20 lbs of lobster per trap per season. By 2003, 165 licensees were landing around 400,000 lbs of lobster, but catch rates had declined to 3–6 lbs. per trap per season. In addition, Whalen documented a shift in spatial effort into previously non- or under-exploited areas. Whalen traced this dramatic decline in catch rates, problems with over-crowding, and associated social turmoil to several causes. With the decline (and eventual collapse) of the northern Gulf inshore cod fishery, many fishers switched effort into the lobster fishery, often transferring lobster licenses into St John Bay from other areas, and the total number of licenses increased to over 200. Then DFO changed its policy and would not permit licenses to be transferred out of the area – again resulting in an overcrowded lobster fishery. Additional challenges for these harvesters include local license restrictions to the (potentially) lucrative crab and shrimp fisheries[9] and ongoing, small or nonexistent cod quotas. The situation has been only partially ameliorated by DFO license buy-back initiatives.

The computer-based model Whalen developed based on this LEK and on lobster biology allows her to try out "what if" scenarios (using information on fishing strategies, changes in number of boats, fishing areas, and lobster stocks) in order to assess the potential impact different management initiatives might have on lobster and lobster harvesters (2005). Using these models in combination with discussions with fishers, she has found that no one management initiative is likely to be

Historical Reconstruction 117

Table 6.1
Summary of Different Types of Information and Degree of Reliance (High, Medium, Low) in Each Sample

Example	Source of Information			Linkage
	LEK	Archival	Science	
Example 1	high	low	high	Micro-level LEK information used to complement R/V information and interrogate macro-level data
Example 2	high	high	low	Micro-level LEK information used to interrogate macro level data/analysis
Example 3	high	medium	low	Micro-level LEK information used to "scale up" and better understand management issues at a relevant scale

successful. Several potentially effective solutions would be particular to the somewhat unique conditions in St John Bay (such as targeted license buy-back programs to relieve overcrowding). The models we have developed are simplified starting points for further work, but we believe that they will be much stronger if they draw on these different knowledge systems.

CONCLUSION

In this chapter we have chosen several examples to highlight the importance of comparing and combining information from multiple sources and knowledge systems in understanding the complex interactions of fishers with marine resources over time. Linkages between these information sources have been made in several ways: by subject (broadly defined), by time, and by space. Different sources of information can also be used to make connections across multiple temporal and spatial scales. Thus, for example, the information derived from LEK interviews about individual fishing-related behavioural patterns can be used to better understand the complex suite of processes and factors at the micro-level that underlie and explain the macro-level shifts suggested by landings data. Table 6.1 summarizes the examples given above.

In most of the examples, trawl survey and archival sources were valuable for understanding macro-scale changes in fish populations. In a similar sense, our archival work has been invaluable in outlining the

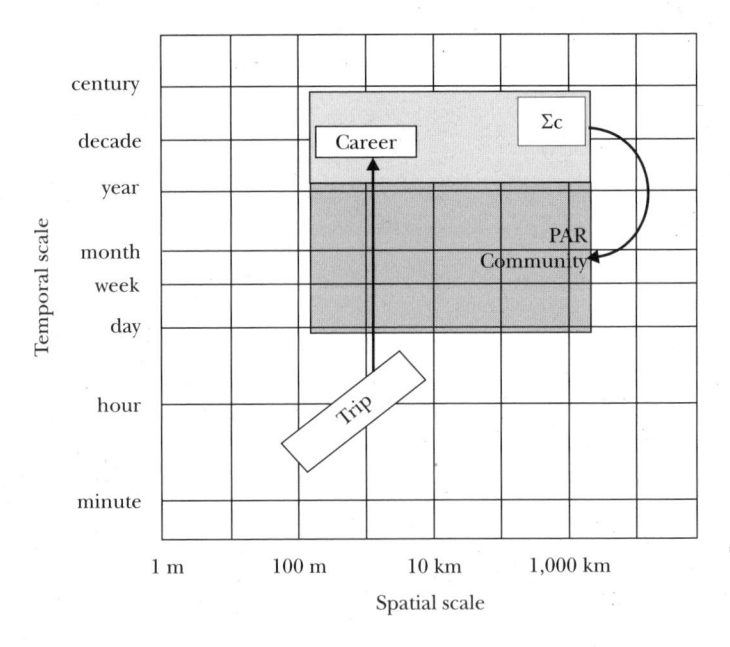

Figure 6.4 Knowledge assembly and flow through participatory action research, including the traditional or local ecological knowledge (TEK, LEK) of a community of people engaged in fishing. Adapted from figure 17.2 in Vodden, Ommer, and Schneider (2005, 294). With kind permission of Springer Science and Business Media.

shifting managerial regimes in our study area and how this macro-scale institutional framework has interacted with environmental change to shape fishing activity (see Murray et al. 2006; Murray et al. 2008). In most of these examples, however, we have focused on the importance of information derived from LEK interviews, particularly in linking these macro-scale changes in fish populations and/or institutional frameworks with the micro- and meso-scale activities of both the fish *and* the fishers.

As with any knowledge system, the picture LEK produces will be partial. However, we have found that LEK can be an invaluable addition to scientific and historical archival resources that are also partial. Harvesters are and were the central human actors in these social-ecological systems, and their observations and interpretations can contribute significantly to our efforts to understand the interactions in these systems. Furthermore, because it is built from the "bottom up," assembling knowledge through talking to fishers provides valuable insight into micro-scale processes, conditions, and variability. This better appreciation could help to shape management initiatives in a more targeted, nuanced, and effective way than prescriptions based on aggregate data or mechanical metaphors.

Figure 6.4 parallels figure 6.2 and provides a graphical representation of what knowledge assembly might look like in this sort of hybrid information system.[10] Here, the information is assembled and returned to the participants. The process is bottom-up, beginning at the resolution of a single trip, which harvesters assemble over time into knowledge at the time and space scales of their careers. Through informal exchange some of that knowledge becomes common to the entire community. Knowledge at this scale is expanded by interviews (which might be participatory) assembled in a way that can be taken back to participants. This participatory action research is iterative, as shown by the arrows in figure 6.4. A similar diagram could be constructed for scientific knowledge, which is situated within the experience of individuals, grows through exchange of knowledge (including the formal process of peer review), and is communicated through publication. The time and space scales of such a diagram (a modification of figure 6.2B) would resemble figure 6.4. This concordance in time and space scales (compare figures 6.2 and 6.4) suggests that knowledge systems develop at the scale of the social-ecosystem, despite the evident differences in the scale of knowledge of individuals (small scale over long time periods for harvesters, large scale with little or no direct observation over long periods by scientists). This correspondence in scale of knowledge systems opens the door to jointly developed information and insights and thus to come to cooperatively developed management plans. This is the ideal case in fisheries co-management.[11]

Our goal is find common ground that allows complementary use of both LEK and science (as well as archival information and the context provided by knowledge and methods in the social sciences) and movement towards a new information system that allows for a consistent, yet nuanced and informed, understanding of the complex environmental history in our study area. As our understanding of what to monitor grows, we can develop relevant time series, but we cannot work backward to reconstructing every relevant variable. If we are to do environmental history, we are therefore forced to piece together information fragments from multiple sources.

LEK seems poised to play a growing role in fisheries management, and we agree that there is a need for clarity and methodological rigour in this research, just as there is in any type of research. We should no more unquestioningly accept LEK as valid information than we should cease to hold traditional, peer-reviewed science to high standards. We believe that the methods outlined here, and a discussion of the associated challenges, are a step in the right direction.

7

Data Fouling in Newfoundland's Marine Fisheries

KAIJA I. METUZALS, C. MICHAEL WERNERHEIM,
RICHARD L. HAEDRICH, PARZIVAL COPES,
AND ANN MURRIN

INTRODUCTION

"If misreporting is ignored and catch data is worthless, what you have is an uncontrolled fishery" (*Halifax Herald* 2003). Sound fisheries management depends on the quality of catch data. Specifically, the estimation of stock abundance and the determination of quotas alike depend in large measure on accurate and precise[1] statistics on commercial landings. One of the most serious problems facing fisheries managers is how to improve estimates of the distortion resulting from "misreporting." Failure to obtain an accurate account from harvesters about activities at sea undermines the reliability of catch data, which can in turn introduce an (avoidable) element of uncertainty into the outcomes of fisheries policy: the greater the inaccuracy in the data, the wider the confidence intervals around the estimate of stock size. Data fouling causes the stock to appear healthier than it is, which, all else being the same, causes quotas to be set too high.

The problems associated with data fouling have attracted increasing attention in the literature and the popular media. There are several reasons for this. Recent resource crises in Canada and elsewhere have raised questions about the reliability of scientific stock abundance estimates, recruitment, and other key population characteristics. There is also growing recognition of the need for better enforcement, given the unrelenting pressure on stocks from both domestic and foreign fleets. Finally, it is well known that activities that distort fisheries statistics occur in virtually all fisheries and that they can cause entire fisheries to collapse (FAO 2002; Corveler 2002). But are some fisheries policy regimes "better" than others in terms of the quality of the data made available for management?

The fisheries economics literature on avoidance behavior and enforcement is rich in theoretical insight but provides very little in the way of empirical findings. Empirical work has been hampered by the lack of reliable data on activities at sea (legal or illegal) that are unobserved by the regulator. The empirical evidence is therefore scarce and often indirect or anecdotal. Apart from data on activities that violate the Fisheries Act there appear to have been few attempts to collect in a systematic and comprehensive manner information that can be used to estimate landings data inaccuracy in Canada. Our chapter seeks to address this gap by a) providing a descriptive analysis of the survey and anecdotal data collected from an interview study with Newfoundland fish harvesters on data fouling; and, b) by developing an analytical model of key elements that drive data fouling practices. By "data fouling" we mean legal and illegal fishing-related behaviors that distort or "foul" the statistics that form the basis for fisheries policy. Our larger intent is to design a framework that can be used with empirical data to estimate what we call the "data fouling factor." To this end we develop two models of high-grading and misreporting, respectively. The models and the analytical results, published in detail elsewhere (Metuzals et al. 2006; Wernerheim and Haedrich 2007) are summarized below. Our overall hypothesis is that data fouling is a much more important problem than fishers and fisheries management generally appear willing to recognize. Our survey of fishers in Newfoundland and our review of the international evidence (statistical and anecdotal)[2] support this hypothesis.

The personal interviews in our survey were structured so as to elicit first-hand information from current and former participants in the fishery about the nature, scope, and determinants of a range of legal activities that (perhaps entirely inadvertently) contribute to data fouling as we define it. The survey also shows an alarming lack of knowledge of conservation practices and protocols amongst respondents. Our modeling effort is informed by the findings from this empirical research.

THE CONCEPT OF DATA FOULING

Our definition of data fouling originates in the taxonomy of adverse side effects of quotas proposed by Copes (1986, 2000) and elaborated below (see also Alverson 1977; Alverson et al. 1994; Hall et al. 2000). Rather than treating data fouling as one such side effect, as does Copes, we define the term more broadly to refer to a wide range of fishing-related behaviors, legal and illegal, all of which have one aspect in common: they distort, or "foul," the statistics that form the basis for fisheries policy. These behaviors include overfishing, high-grading (selective dumping, usually by size), misreporting, discount- (or time preference-) driven overfishing, by-catch dumping (of incidental or nontargeted catch, because it is of illegal size of a regulated species or simply a low-value species), price dumping (of lower-valued specimens), quota busting, and the unrecorded dumping of bruised catch.[3] These activities occur in an essentially unobserved environment at sea and leave few traces in the statistics requested by and reported to the regulator. The expression "illegal, unreported, and unregulated fishing," or IUU fishing, has been used to describe a wide range of activities occurring on the high seas. The three main IUU categories are (1) illegal fishing on the high seas including poaching, (2) unregulated fishing whereby vessels operate outside management controls for whatever reason, and (3) unreported or misreported fishing (Bray 2000). The latter category has been subdivided by Pitcher et al. (2002) to capture categories not covered by the reporting system as follows: (3a) unreported (legal or illegal) discards; (3b) un-mandated catches, namely, catches that the fisheries agency is not mandated to record; and (3) illegal catch, i.e., catch contravening regulations in that it is unreported or deliberately misreported by species or size, usually to conceal quota violations. Treating these categories separately is difficult, since they intersect. The only difference between the extended definition of IUU given above and our concept of data fouling is that we do not distinguish between legal and illegal practices: any fishing behaviour that causes a discrepancy between the total mortality and the reported catch fouls the data and is categorized accordingly.

A number of methods have been used to examine "unreported fishing" for total catches (what happens at sea) versus landings (what is officially reported on land). For example, estimates of discarding can be obtained from observer data. Illegal landings are more difficult to quantify but may be estimated by comparison of reported landings with market sales or interviews with fish harvesters or by tracing techniques (Forrest et al. 2001). Estimates of by-catch and discarding for different fisheries have been obtained using biological models of the fishery (Allard and Chouinard 1997). Economic approaches have also been used to estimate incentives to discard (Arnason 1994). In 2003 the European Union, concerned about the widespread accuracy of official statistics,[4] confirmed that inaccurate reporting of catch statistics might have played an important role in the decline of the cod stocks in the North Sea.

Amongst the papers that seek to quantify aspects of data fouling, five stand out. The first is a theoretical analysis by Turner (1997). Second, Hutchings and Ferguson (2000) survey fishers in an attempt to generate upper and lower bounds on reported landings data in the Newfoundland cod fishery. Third, Pascoe et al. (2001) use Data Envelopment Analysis (DEA) to estimate misreporting in fisheries output data. Fourth, Angel et al. (1994) report that most regulations associated with quota management in the Scotia-Fundy region have not been enforceable, such as reporting by area and species, dumping, discarding, high-grading using correct gear, and so on. Finally, Pitcher and Watson (2000) also attempt to estimate the impact of illegal fishing practices in the North Atlantic.

In 2002, over eight thousand serious breaches of rules were recorded by all EU member states; these included falsifying and misreporting of the catch. Evans (2000) argues that fish stocks generally are probably over-estimated by 75 percent, and high-seas stocks by as much as 100 percent. Although the percentages for specific stocks are necessarily uncertain, it is widely held that not only does IUU fishing account for a large percentage of total catch, but IUU fishing is increasing worldwide as harvesters try to avoid the stricter fishing rules that follow declining catches. In response to this the Food and Agriculture Organization (FAO) has proposed an international plan of action for dealing with IUU fishing on the high seas (FAO 2002). Not all misreporting is under-reporting. Watson and Pauly (2001), for example, argue that *over*-reporting by China (catches beyond ecological limits) has masked decreases in global catches for more than a decade.

In Atlantic Canada there was widespread misreporting, concealment, dumping, and discarding long before the 1992 cod moratorium. Maintenance of two sets of logbooks and hidden holds for undersized, illegal catches were common occurrences (see, e.g., Anderson 1972; Harris 1998; Angel et al. 1994; Palmer and Sinclair 1997). Fishing pressure on cod was heavy in the 1980s, as certain fleet sectors exceeded their quotas twice over (Gough 2001). Misreporting seems to have declined from the early to mid-1990s but then increased again (Preikshot 2001) to the extent that it caught the attention of the federal auditor general, who reported in 1997 that information on fish stocks was considered inaccurate owing to misreporting and unsustainable fishing practices (AGC 1997). The cause was the blatant misreporting, under-the-table sales, and massive discarding of fish in Atlantic Canada (Mason 2002). The Fisheries Resource Conservation Council (FRCC) stated recently that briefs received from industry acknowledged that unsustainable fishing practices such as misreporting were indeed widespread and that anecdotal reports of cheating were increasing (FRCC 2003). Deep-sea trawler fishers were often described as "the biggest bunch of liars!" as under-reporting by skippers typically went uncontested by plant owners who had no incentive to verify skippers' reports (Anderson 1972). As Baum et al. (2003) aptly put it, missing values cannot be distinguished from true zeros in logbooks.

It has been estimated that in fisheries worldwide, fishers discarded about 25 percent of the catch during the 1980s and the early 1990s, or about 60 billion pounds each year (Alverson et al. 1994; Alverson 1998). Discarding and dumping are long-standing practices in all Newfoundland fleet sectors as well (Hache 1989; Harris 1990). By-catch was just "dumped over the side" (Martin 1990; Marshall 1990; Cashin 1993), sometimes in protest when there was no demand (Wiseman 1972). Large quantities of small cod were discarded at sea owing to the high costs of handling and storing small fish on trawlers (Task Group on Newfoundland Inshore Fisheries 1987). But by-catch was also dumped in ever-greater amounts during the 1980s (Atkinson 1984; Kulka 1982, 1984, 1986). Keats et al. (1986) estimate that discards of cod increased from 7 to 24 percent between 1981 and 1986, but decreased somewhat in 1987, owing to the use of larger mesh sizes and the introduction of the observer program.

Other major species such as redfish and flatfish were discarded at a rate that doubled in the early 1980s in NAFO division 2J3KL off the northeast coast of Newfoundland and southern Labrador. Hutchings and Myers (1995) estimate that the inshore fisheries discarded 5 percent by weight in the early 1980s and 28 percent in 1989. In more recent studies, Hutchings (1996) and Hutchings and Ferguson (2000) have estimated that discarded and unreported catches in the inshore fishery actually trebled in the same period. Unreported discards have been directly implicated in the erroneous estimates of fishing mortality on northern cod. Moreover, this high rate of discarding young fish contributed to the rapidity with which the cod stocks eventually collapsed (Hutchings 1996; Myers et al. 1997; Hilborn et al. 2003).[5] In 1993 the

Fisheries Resource Conservation Council (FRCC) agreed that dumping and misreporting have contributed to frequent underestimation of the mortality and hence to an overestimation of the Atlantic groundfish biomass (FRCC 1993, 9). In 1994 the FRCC reported testimony by fishers about selective dumping of catch in order to maintain quotas in mixed stock fisheries, a practice said to be tacitly acknowledged by fisheries managers (FRCC 1994, 2). This is borne out by a study of Scotia-Fundy fisheries in which twenty-three fishers interviewed admitted to dumping fish that did not match their quotas (Breeze 1998). It is important to note that although the Fisheries Act stipulates that no discards are allowed in groundfish fisheries,[6] it was only after the moratorium in 1992 that the regulations were enforced. Dwyer (2001) describes an instance where high amounts of deep-sea species were discarded as "garbage fish."

Observer programs covering the offshore fleet have existed in Canada since the early 1980s. Vessels operating within the 200-mile EEZ may be required by law to take an observer on board. Coverage levels for particular fleets vary between 1 and 100 percent.[7] The inshore and nearshore fleet we examined has low coverage, 1 to 2 percent. Interviews with fish harvesters are therefore a valuable source of information (Saila 1983; Neis, Schneider et al. 1999). However, fish harvesters' estimates of unreported catch will vary and have a bias toward underestimation (Saila 1983; Jensen and Vestergaard 2002).

THE SURVEY

We developed a survey questionnaire to elicit first-hand information about the nature and extent of data fouling fishing practices in the Coasts Under Stress (CUS) East Coast study area. We also carried out a search of Newfoundland court records on fisheries violations, along with an extensive search of print media for the purpose of collecting additional anecdotal information from a wider cross-section of fisheries participants than could be reached in our survey (Murrin 2003). The survey suggested a widespread lack of knowledge of conservation practices and of skills for participatory management. These findings were followed up in a separate pilot study of two communities in the CUS study area (Breen 2003).

Structured, face-to-face interviews of thirty minutes average duration were undertaken. One interview took three hours. Interviewees were selected using "snowball sampling," a method well suited for the study of sensitive issues and one that can increase the accuracy of the information collected (Lopes et al. 1996; Hutchings and Ferguson 2000). The interviews started from a list provided by the Fish, Food and Allied Workers Union, and subsequent interviewees were asked to identify other possible contacts. There were 8,675 licensed nearshore vessels in Newfoundland in 2002. A total of fifty fish harvesters were interviewed throughout Newfoundland from April to October 2003. Of these, forty-one were active harvesters and nine retired. Seventeen fish harvesters owned inshore vessels (< 35 feet), twenty-six owned vessels in the 35–65 foot nearshore sector, and three had vessels > 65 feet. Almost all respondents (96 percent) came from traditional fishing families; only two did not. All but one (a crew member) were full-time skippers. The respondents had on average of 30.6 (±1.56 SE) years of fishing experience, ranging from 11 to 73 years. Most were first- or second-generation fish harvesters (80 percent), but some were third- (4 percent), fourth- (10 percent), or fifth-generation (4 percent) fish harvesters. One respondent was a sixth-generation fisherman. Only two respondents had no direct fishing experience.

Results

Thirty-eight percent of interviewees said that misreporting occurs in their respective fisheries. This takes the form of dumping, discarding, and other potential data fouling activities that go on daily. Many (51 percent) appeared unaware that this might be in violation of the Code of Responsible Fishing, for the simple reason that what appears inconsequential on an individual basis is of no concern. In the crab fishery, 50 percent of harvesters admitted that misreporting occurs. Estimates range from 5 to 40+ percent by weight. Crab harvesters also report having witnessed the use of more than the allowed number of pots, as well as illegal sales of unreported crab. One person said that in the past this was done "quite a bit." Another informant claimed that now only "a handful of people are doing it, but it is not worth the risk for me." But the stakes are high. Two respondents alleged that bribes of twenty thousand dollars have been given to fisheries observers.

Regarding cod, it was claimed that in the past (pre-moratorium) "landings were never written down and misreporting happened all the time." Although some of the commercial cod fisheries in Newfoundland remain under moratorium, four respondents indicated that the misreporting of cod landings is still "extremely" high. Trucks are reported to off-load unobserved in some instances. In other cases monitoring is lax. One skipper claimed that he could smuggle a boatload past DFO without them seeing a thing. In the limited fisheries still open for northern cod, in particular the Sentinel and Index Fisheries, fish harvesters indicated that under-reporting of cod and redfish by weight is rampant. As much as 30 percent of cod landings were allegedly never reported according to some harvesters. Turbot landings were also said to be misreported. Adding to the confusion, two skippers said that some redfish landings have been recorded as cod landings. Two respondents noted that mackerel, herring, and capelin landings could have been misreported, since they were not monitored by boatloads. Interestingly, one skipper observed that the illegal activity centres on fishing in prohibited zones, concealing rather than misreporting illegal catch. The reasons for this are not hard to discern. Shellfish accounted for 83 percent (or $465.1 million) of landed value in the Newfoundland and Labrador fishery in 2003.[8] This exceeds the landed value of the cod fishery in its heyday in current dollar terms. While income in the cod fishery was relatively widely dispersed (at least in modern times), income in the crab and shrimp fisheries is concentrated in the hands of a comparatively small number of licence holders.

Misreporting: Discarding, Dumping, and By-catch

Discarding occurs when the crab is below legal size. This poses a problem if the discarded specimens die and the discards remain unreported. Most harvesters use a variety of mesh sizes in their pots. The regulated minimum mesh size is 5¼ inches, in order to allow escapement of adult males for reproduction (DFO 2003). A summary of the estimated discards from crab pots obtained from the respondents (Table 7.1) shows that, on average, a high amount of discarding takes place with 5½-inch mesh pots, whatever the season and fishing area. Very little discarding seems to occur with the 6-inch mesh. A number of skippers preferred the 6-inch mesh because it means "less picking to do." Only one harvester in our sample used an illegal 5-inch mesh.[9] The average discard estimates are 26.5 percent for the 5½-inch, 15 percent for 5¾-inch, and 10 percent for the 6-inch mesh. This is considerably lower than a recent DFO estimate according to which almost 50 percent of the crab landings are discarded (Wellman 2004).

Turning briefly to dumping, it appears that most of the pre-moratorium dumping of cod resulted from insufficient demand. Estimates

Table 7.1
Estimated Crab Discards by Weight and Mesh Size

Estimated Crab Discards (% by weight)[1]	Mesh Size of Crab Pot (inches)
10 (n=1)	5
10–20 (n=4), 50 (n=11), high (n=1)	5¼
10–20 (n=10), 20–30 (n=3), 75 (n=1), high (1), low (2)	5½
10–20 (n=5)	5¾
0 (n=1), 5 (n=2), 33 (n=1)	6

[1] Sample size in parentheses.

range from "medium" in the 1970s to "high" in the 1980s, when sometimes "the water was white with small fish" as "boatloads were thrown away since the plants did not take any more." Cod dumping from traps could vary from one to two loads per day or up to 50 percent by weight: "the harbour looked like it was covered with ice." The contrary view of others is summed up by a longliner skipper who stated, "No, I don't know anything about dumping ... we never dumped cod." Respondents indicated zero dumping since the beginning of the 1990s. In comparison, the Norwegian policy of banning dumping started in the 1980s, and it includes all major fisheries today (Geselius 2006). The principle is that all vessels are under a legal obligation to land all fish.

Cod by-catch is also an issue. In by-catch fisheries for cod the allowable proportion of cod is managed according to a set percentage of the overall catch. There is no quota monitoring, and extensive overfishing still goes on, according to one skipper. Another skipper estimated that 30 percent of these by-catch cod were never reported, since there was legally no quota. Two other skippers agreed that these catches are often known locally but go largely unreported. One respondent expressed dislike and contempt for the by-catch regulations, calling them "silly." One respondent claimed that the amount of cod sold illegally has increased since the moratorium.

Other Indications of Data Fouling

Canadian print media and regional court cases were also sources of information on data fouling. From 1970 to 1993 only forty-four cases were prosecuted in Prince Edward Island and Newfoundland (Table 7.2).

Violations ranged from illegal possession of undersized fish to failures to record catch. The most frequent offence was keeping undersized

Table 7.2
Summary of Fisheries Violations and Convictions, 1970–93

Violation and Conviction	Number of Cases
Overfishing – catching and retaining fish in excess of quota	4
Undersized catch	9
Fishing in closed season/waters	3
Fishing in a protected area	3
Misreporting	4
Fishing with an undersized net/mesh	3
Fishing without a license	5
Illegal possession of fish/lobster and/or equipment	2
Illegally entering Canadian waters	7
Destruction of fish habitat	2
Unlawfully transporting fish	1
Oversized catch	1
Total	44

SOURCE: *Newfoundland and Prince Edward Island Reports*, index.

catch. From 1994 to 2002, the print media were examined for reported instances of overfishing, misreporting, discarding, and other fisheries-related offences. Although a majority of articles referred to overfishing activities by foreign fleets, many discussed instances where domestic harvesters were said to have cheated on their catches, kept undersized fish, or high-graded their landings (Murrin 2003). Other irregularities, such as "bonuses" offered openly by the plants to secure delivery by the fish harvester to a specific plant, paint a complex and dark picture of the fishing industry. Some fish harvesters accused the plants of operating a cartel or a local "mafia" in order to control the supply and fix prices. Although the majority of crab harvesters in our survey say that they approve of management including the use of graders, monitors, offshore observers, and "black boxes" (vessel-monitoring systems and satellite monitors), they also say the fishery is fraught with illegal activity. More diligent enforcement makes cheating more difficult, but some respondents say they know that observers are paid off.

Analytical Results

In our analytical work (Wernerheim and Haedrich 2007), we formulate a theoretical model of two types of data fouling in a quota fishery: high-grading and under-reporting of catch. The model is solved analytically for the profit-maximizing effort level and the associated optimal number of high-grading operations. A second version of the model is solved for the optimal proportion of the harvest to under-report, given the perceived probability of detection and conviction, and the structure of fines for this offence. We demonstrate how the model can be applied to address some of the policy-related issues that surfaced in the survey research. Using available data on prices, costs, harvesting technology, and the biology of the resource obtained from independent sources, we parameterize the model and solve it numerically. Sensitivity analysis informed by the survey responses obtained can then be undertaken.

Consider high-grading first. We define high-grading as the sorting and selective discarding of the portion of the catch comprising small fish for the purpose of replacing it with higher-valued large fish. Assuming that each time a portion of the catch is replaced in this way the probability of catching large fish remains the same, the incentive to high-grade depends on the relative price of large fish, the cost of high-grading, and the cost of replacing the fish discarded by a new catch. Given that "large" fish fetch a premium relative to "small" fish, how many high-grading operations will maximize the profit on the quota in a given season? How sensitive is high-grading to the probability of finding large fish, to the price premium on large fish, and to fishing costs?

To address these questions, we assess quantitatively the sensitivity of the optimal (solution) values to changes in the key parameters of the model. This is useful for policy analysis, since some of these parameters are under the direct control of the regulator, while others can be influenced indirectly by other policy means. The calculations show that the optimal effort level is much more sensitive to the relative price of fish than to the number of discards. This result is consistent with the expected finding that the optimal number of discards is also highly sensitive to the relative price of fish. The most important result is a demonstration of how the model allows us to estimate the extent of error in the reported landings statistics as a result of high-grading. The "data fouling factor" measures the discarded (unreported) catch as a proportion of the total fishing mortality. That is, it captures the factor by which reported (observed) landings can be expected to differ from the unobserved actual kill at sea.

Turning briefly to misreporting catch, we suppose that incentives to misreport arise from balancing the benefits and costs of under-reporting. Failure to report all or part of the catch in a quota fishery (poaching) is illegal and if detected will lead to administrative penalties and prosecution in the case of serious and repeated offences. In the case of the Newfoundland snow crab fishery, administrative penalties are agreed upon by the DFO and representatives of harvesters in an attempt to limit prosecutions in cases where there may not be criminal intent. This amounts to a limited tolerance of errors in the harvester's measurement of the landed catch.[10] While misreporting all or part of the catch carries a risk of getting caught, prosecuted, and fined accordingly, misreporting can also increase profit, since the catch will not count against the quota if it can be landed unreported and undetected. The undetected (concealed) portion of the quota can thus be caught again. In general, the penalties are related to the extent of the offence: the higher the proportion of the quota overfished, the higher the penalty. The research questions addressed are as follows. By how much does the fine need to be increased above its base level (current practice) to bring the level of under-reporting down to some "margin of error" tolerated by the regulator? How sensitive is the optimal rate of concealment (under-reporting) to the unit price of fish for various probabilities of detection? What is the minimum viable price of fish at various rates of concealment?

Our modeling results are similar to those appearing in the enforcement literature. It is thus not surprising that in our model the effort level and the concealment rate are both sensitive to the price of fish. That is, as the price increases, the effort level and the concealment rate both increase, as intuition would suggest. What is more interesting is that the effort level turns out to be much more responsive than the concealment rate to a price increase. Moreover, the results suggest that if in a rising-price environment surveillance and enforcement are boosted, the concealment rate will be reduced more sharply than the effort level generally. This is as it should be, since if concealment drops off, less effort is required to land the legal catch only.

Management and the Canadian Code of Conduct

Most fish harvesters interviewed (84 percent) said that they like individual quotas (IQs) and that they like the way the crab fishery is managed today. But in direct reference to the data fouling problem, 10 percent of harvesters disapprove of IQ management, claiming that it destroys the fishery: "That's where the big guy gets the profit; the plants will get it all." The remaining 6 percent were retired fish harvesters. Some said that individual transferable quotas (ITQs) would be acceptable only if the plants/processors were exempted, as ITQs are believed to give control to processors. It is instructive that ITQs in particular are disliked primarily for reasons other than the strengthened incentives to highgrade and misreport that they give rise to.

The Canadian Code of Conduct for Responsible Fishing Operations is based on the FAO Code of Conduct established by the UN (FAO 1995). The code is provided by DFO with each license.[11] Yet, 51 percent of all fish harvesters (45 percent of active harvesters) interviewed said they were unaware of the code. Of those who were aware of it, 16 percent said they had not read it and were unfamiliar with it. The wife of one harvester said that he should be aware of the code since she had seen it in his mail.

Fish harvesters were also asked if they are aware of the Marine Stewardship Council (MSC), an independent, global, non-profit organization set up to solve the problem of overfishing. Established in 1997 by Unilever, the world's largest buyer of seafood, and the WWF, the international conservation organization, the MSC became fully independent of both organizations in 1999. Today the MSC is funded by a wide range of organizations, including charitable foundations and corporate entities around the world. It has developed an environmental standard for sustainable and well-managed fisheries following worldwide consultation with scientists, fisheries experts, environmental organizations, and other stakeholders with a strong interest in preserving fish stocks for the future.[12] Environmentally responsible practices are rewarded with a distinctive blue product label. There is currently no Canadian affiliation, and only two fish stocks in Canadian waters are undergoing certification. Only 23 percent of the thirty-four harvesters who responded to this question in the inshore, nearshore, and midshore fleets had heard of the MSC. But all agreed with the idea of eco-labelling, since it would appear to enhance the value of the product: "Must try to do something, if it is not too late already."

CONCLUSIONS AND POLICY IMPLICATIONS

The problem of data fouling is probably far greater and more urgent than commonly believed. One reason for this suggests itself immediately. Data fouling is intractable in that existing policy tools are ill-designed to curb most such behavior. In some cases, the policy instruments in use inadvertently encourage data fouling, or at least tacitly tolerate it. Only in some of the most egregious cases are regulatory effort and enforcement brought to bear in an attempt to limit the outright illegal forms of this behavior. Surveillance and enforcement are costly in financial as well as political terms. Financially it is difficult to argue for larger enforcement budgets when the benefits and costs are not supported convincingly by statistical evidence. Politically it is problematic because enforcement pits the interest of the present generation against that of future generations. But if our moral obligation to future generations includes a capacity to generate economic well-being from the fishery, it requires that decision makers face squarely the trade-off between poverty alleviation now and a sustainable fishery for the future.

The tensions in this trade-off are manifest in our survey. Many fishers are antagonistic to management for sustainability. Despite the FRCC's warnings, misreporting still appears to be common in Newfoundland. Approximately 40 percent of all fishers interviewed admitted to knowing that misreporting occurs, although they themselves would never do it. Nor would they report a buddy. This may be an underestimate, since many fishers who initially denied any misreporting did admit in the "verification" question that "some" cheating and poaching are going on. Fishers indicated that they knew that cod is being illegally poached and sold from door to door. A recent study comparing attitudes to poaching in fishing communities in Norway and Newfoundland (Gezelius 2003) found that in Newfoundland, in contrast to Norway, cod poaching for food is not considered morally wrong, whereas commercial poaching is, even though it has been going on for years. This supports earlier findings for Newfoundland's west coast (Palmer and Sinclair 1997).

We conclude from our small survey sample that fisheries management and fish harvesters in Newfoundland have not fully digested the lessons of the cod stock collapse and the socio-economic consequences of the subsequent cod moratoria. The fishery is still not prosecuted on a sustainable basis. Overfishing still occurs on an alarming scale. This not only jeopardizes individual species; it also undermines the benefits that could come from a diversified fishery. Despite the moratorium and increased surveillance and enforcement, reports of deliberate misreporting (of crab and cod landings) are still frequent. Findings from this small sample cannot be generalized to the whole population of harvesters, but they do indicate ongoing problems with discarding, high-grading, and other data fouling activities. As indicated by one harvester, "lots of things happen here in St John's that people in Ottawa are not informed about." In the words of another, "They don't have a clue." As Perry and Ommer (2003, 516) describe it, "Failing to comprehend and deal with scale issues like these creates a rich breeding ground for community rebellion against regulations, promoting various kinds of illicit practices that thwart the legitimate practices of fisheries management." We agree with this appraisal.

It follows that a better understanding is necessary of what drives these practices and how they distort the information on which management depends. The clearest general indication from this research is that a dedicated effort to improve education in matters of sustainability is urgent. As such, this study lends further support to a conclusion drawn in a number of previous studies in Canada and elsewhere. The role of education in changing the long-established habits and practices that undermine the scientific basis for fisheries management cannot be overemphasized. In the long term only education and proper enforcement can lead to acceptance of the idea that the very practices that are often perceived as privately rational are in fact socially irrational and destructive.

The implications for fisheries policy from this research can be summarized as follows:

1 In all but exceptional circumstances IQS and ITQS cannot be expected to resolve the problem of data fouling. IQ and, in particular, ITQ regimes strengthen incentives to high-grade and under-report in order to maximize the value of the quota. Since ITQS are unpopular with fishermen for yet other reasons, an opportunity may exist to build political capital by reconsidering the ITQ option (Copes 2000).

2 The Newfoundland groundfish community shows sustained shifts in overall size distribution and declines in average size of commercial species (Martínez Murillo 2001, 2003; Walsh 2001; Haedrich and Barnes 1997). The modeling effort we have undertaken in association with this research (Metuzals et al. 2006; Wernerheim and Haedrich 2007) indicates that while the economic incentive to high-grade is weakened as the probability of finding "small" fish declines, it does not go to zero until "large" fish are all but gone. This result is driven by the premium on large fish relative to unit harvesting costs. The higher this ratio, all else being the same, the more high-grading there will be. This is worrisome in light of the fact that harvesting costs trend downward with technological change, while the price premium for large fish in the market can be expected to trend

upward as the quality of the remaining resource is degraded. These factors thus combine to drive the price/cost ratio upward, which in turn fuels more high-grading. The damaging effects of this behavior need to be given much more attention by policy-makers. The Norwegian approach with a "no discard" policy warrants closer examination (see Geselius 2006).

3 Given the probability of being detected and subsequently convicted, a very sizeable increase in fines may be necessary in order to bring under-reporting within tolerable bounds. This may well be a more cost-effective means of controlling under-reporting, at least for low probabilities of detection. Even though we hypothesize that more effort is required to sell under-reported catch (as some avoidance may be necessary) than the reported catch (accepted directly by processing plants), the profitability of under-reporting makes it highly unlikely that moral suasion will curb such behavior measurably.

4 Few fisheries agencies can field the resources necessary to monitor and prevent illegal fishing. Local co-operation and control (where fishermen patrol themselves) is the appropriate approach (Hilborn et al. 2003). The rationale is that local fishermen know exactly who is doing what, when and where. Studies have shown that informal social control is more important than formal sanctions (Geselius 2002). Fishers need to be more involved in the process of management (Nielsen and Mathiesen 2000).

5 More research on the factors contributing to misreporting is necessary. We have strong indications of what motivates data fouling. We know much less about the most effective ways of dealing with it.

Acknowledgments

We are grateful to the many fishers for their participation in this study and for sharing their valuable experiences and insights. Thanks to Michael Ryan and Danny Ings, who provided helpful assistance, and to Martin Hall for many useful comments on the questionnaire. We also gratefully acknowledge the helpful editorial suggestions provided by Barbara Neis.

PART FOUR

Knowledge Flows, Policy Development, and Practice

8

Knowledge Flows around Youth: What Do They "Know" about Human and Community Health?

ANNE MARSHALL, LOIS JACKSON,
BLYTHE SHEPARD, SUSAN TIRONE,
AND CATHERINE DONOVAN

Within Western society, the biomedical discourse on health is the privileged form of knowledge about what constitutes health. Such privileging is evidenced in the allocation of resources to certain areas (curative medicine, for example, over health promotion) and the power and status of certain health care professionals over others (physicians, for example, over community health promoters). Alternative ways of understanding health and healthy practices and, by extension, health needs, exist within different cultures and communities. Although these alternative ways of knowing, or types of knowledge, may contribute as much, if not more, to health than has been hitherto acknowledged, they are infrequently sought and most often deemed less valuable than knowledge gleaned from the work of designated health professionals or experts (Bryant et al. 2004; Shucksmith and Hendry 1998). Indeed, the attempt to medicalize those that have traditionally relied on other ways of being healthy attests to the limited and potentially devastating impact of the biomedical model when it fails to attend to existing understandings of health and healthy practices.

Young people represent a group whose knowledge is not typically part of the biomedical discourse. In this chapter, we explore how youth understand, communicate, and make meaning of knowledge related to health and well-being within the context of social and economic restructuring in several Canadian coastal communities. We also consider the sources, processes, supports, and barriers related to what Landry et al. (2003) term "knowledge uptake." The specific research from which we have drawn data is focused on youth and their particular, situated understandings of health. Through individual and focus group interviews, as well as surveys, observations, workshops, photographs, and mapping exercises, we have explored the challenges and supports youth are experiencing as they approach and enter their adult years in communities that have undergone tremendous changes during the last decade. Our findings indicate that youth have distinct understandings or knowledge of health based on their social location as youth and their place in coastal communities undergoing significant changes.

CONCEPTUAL FRAMEWORK

Our research has been guided by social constructivist theories and approaches to learning and life-span development (Blustein 1997; Cochran 1997; Young et al. 1996; Hargreaves et al. 1996; Savickas 1995). Within these frameworks knowledge is socially constructed and is situated in time, space, and culture. Young people have a culture of their own, yet they are also situated within their larger family and community contexts. However, because of their dependence on adults for shelter and sustenance, as well as their relative lack of influence and life experience, youth can be considered a marginalized group in society, similar to other culturally marginalized groups such as the poor, or ethnic minorities (Cohen and Ainley 2000; Epstein 1998). Young people typically have little power on their own with respect to decision-making processes and outcomes in their communities.

Consistent with our conceptualization of knowledge as actively co-constructed in context, we use the terms "knowing," "learning," and "understanding" to label the processes in which these youth are engaged when making sense of their various social worlds and experiences. Our descriptions are necessarily tentative, since we are describing others' experiences, and we have used their own words to illustrate the interpretations and conclusions we have drawn from the data.

Any discussion about young people must take into account their developmental stage and the developmental tasks they are facing. Theorists and researchers agree that the teen years are focused on identity development and preparation for adulthood (Erikson 1968; Harter 1999; Super et al. 1996). Youth are learning about work and relationships and are making decisions about their future lives. They also depend on adults for both information and guidance. In adolescents' worlds, adults are the gatekeepers of information and access to services, education, and work. The major developmental task for youth has always been to separate from parental authority and dependence, and this time-honoured challenge is even more strained in situations of stress and uncertainty, such as that experienced in times of economic and socio-political restructuring. On the one hand, there is an emphasis on the importance of education, training, and future employment choices, and youth are experiencing pressure to make the right choices. On the other hand, parents, schools, and services that are struggling with the effects of restructuring have less money, time, and energy to support young people's exploration, and there are far fewer options available than in times of prosperity. In our study, we asked young people to tell us what it is like to be living in coastal communities that are undergoing this type of transition.

OUR RESEARCH

Our research methodology has blended focus group, narrative, and ethnographic elements. On both the West and East Coasts, individual and focus group interviews were our major means of data collection. Although there are slight differences in the ages of the youth participants on the two coasts, when we combine the data, we have spoken to a total of 101 youth between the ages of thirteen and twenty-six (in focus groups and one-on-one interviews). Also, forty adults have been interviewed formally in one-on-one interviews. In addition, we engaged in numerous informal discussions with adults and youth in the communities, spent time in the community participating in various community events, and held community feedback sessions to discuss research findings and our interpretations of the data collected.

On the West Coast, a number of the youth also participated in Possible Selves interviews (Markus and Nurius 1986; Shepard and Marshall 2000), life-space mapping (Shepard and Marshall 1999), and photo-assisted interviewing techniques, which provided visual and further descriptive detail relating to how these young people see themselves in present and future contexts. On the East Coast, we helped to organize a video production workshop for youth (led by the Newfoundland & Labrador Independent Film Co-operative [NIFCO]) and worked with youth (led by L. Clarke) to develop a video that allowed them to tell their stories about how changes in the community in the recent past have affected them and their future plans. For additional details of the methodology and results, readers are referred to (Ommer and team, 2007; Jackson et al. 2003, 2004; Marshall 2002; Marshall and Batten 2004). In this chapter, we focus on youth's knowledge of health, how they understand notions of health and well-being, and aspects of knowledge generation, as well as knowledge translation and transfer as experienced and described by our participants.

An important aspect of this research inquiry was continued attention to our own processes of knowledge creation and the transfer of knowledge both within the communities in question and within our respective academic settings. The lead authors and other members of the research team have been trained in varied disciplines and academic programs, including psychology, education, counselling, sociology, health promotion, leisure studies, and medicine. We are physically located in academic institutions on both coasts of Canada: the University of Victoria and University College of the Cariboo (British Columbia), Dalhousie University (Nova Scotia), and Memorial University (Newfoundland and Labrador). Over the course of the larger CUS research project, we have been able to combine our diverse skills and interests into two main integrated projects focusing on youth. Our collaborative process has included sharing and acknowledging our varied philosophies, backgrounds, experiences, theoretical orientations, writing styles, and institutional demands. We have developed a flexible and loosely structured format for this mutual process, involving email correspondence, telephone consultations, reading each other's work, team meetings, joint presentations at professional conferences, and serendipitous opportunities to meet afforded by participation in other professional projects. This ongoing relationship building and process of co-construction among academic researchers was mirrored in the relationship building and meaning-identification processes within our respective coastal-community research sites, which included multiple trips into the field and ongoing communication with youth and other key informants in the field. Bridging these two contexts, we worked together to shape the research design in an attempt to work collaboratively, while at the same time recognizing academic and community needs.

The participation of our community partners in the research was a critical aspect of our methodology. High schools, a community college, community agencies, First Nations bands, and government representatives, as well as other groups and individuals were instrumental throughout the process, from entry into the coastal communities, through data collection and data analysis, interpretation, and dissemination.

YOUTH VIEWS ABOUT HEALTH: WHAT DO THEY "KNOW?"

Canadian youth are among the healthiest in the world, according to population health data (Health Canada 2004; King et al. 1999; McCreary Society 2004). Consistent with this view, most of the youth in our research did not talk about disease, suggesting that they considered themselves to be physically healthy in a disease-free sense. However, their view of health was a holistic one; health risk or disease was only a part of that picture. The young people in our research described numerous instances of experiences and behaviors they associated with health in the broad sense – physical, mental, emotional, spiritual, and environmental health – suggesting that for them health goes far beyond a disease-centred model. They spoke of many activities related to overall well-being, such as family and social relationships, leisure pursuits, economic opportunities, and future career plans. This broad and complex view of health is consistent with recent research and scholarship related to adolescent health determinants and health behaviours (Puskar et al. 1999; Raphael 1996; 2003).

Although participants' understanding of health is suggestive of a broad definition, they were cognizant of health risks and lifestyle issues that are generally connected to poor health outcomes. In their day-to-day lives, youth described health risks that were usually related to accidents or injuries they might sustain in the course of sports or leisure activities. Many also commented on various lifestyle behaviours and specific practices that they considered unhealthy in the longer term, such as poor eating habits, smoking, excessive drinking, stress, and lack of physical activity.

Poor nutrition was one lifestyle issue discussed by a number of East Coast youth. One point they acknowledged was a local tradition of preparing food in a manner that is viewed as unhealthy. "I think it's just a way of cooking here. Like everything that everyone cooks ... you never cook without gravy or grease." There were some particular challenges described with regard to a healthy diet in more remote communities. Some youth commented that healthier eating was more expensive than "junk food" snacks. "There is a big issue here I know in this area of people who are overweight who are trying to loose weight and I find a lot of them when they do actually set themselves on a goal and go on their diets or whatever, they just find it too expensive to find foods that they need to keep themselves in that fit, because it is, it's very expensive to eat healthy." The following exchange was recorded in one focus group:

> I finds with eating healthy; it's hard to do, because you needs money.
> Yeah, that's true.
> I find healthy food is expensive to make, right?

A few youth commented on cigarette smoking as a health problem for youth, although some suggested that it might be less of a problem in recent years: "it [smoking] is less now." In contrast, the use of alcohol and drugs was identified as a current health problem for a least some youth. The variety of substances available in these coastal communities appears to be similar to what urban youth describe. One West Coast participant stated, "Well, there's lots of drinking, and pot and stuff ... yeah, it's a real problem in our town. Some say, like, there's nothing else to do." Another commented, "For instance drugs and alcohol are widespread and almost easier to access in a small community – one because most people know how or know someone who can access it."

The young people clearly know of the harms associated with tobacco and alcohol: "Smoking and drinking is not good for you. No, it's not. But, there's nothing else to do." However, there appears to be disagreement about whether the use of substances and alcohol has increased of late. One East Coast youth stated: "I think drugs are up too. Drugs are up. I don't think drinking is ... Drinking is the same as it's always been. And the difference in drugs too, like, a few years ago it would be like weed and oil and that kind of stuff, I'm saying, like five or 10 years ago. But now a lot of people are getting into acid and mushrooms and ecstasy."

It was generally acknowledged that some groups or individuals drink and others do not. Some youth mentioned peer support for non-use choices: "people respect who I am, and understand that she doesn't drink so don't ask her to, she's not going to smoke that joint with you so leave her alone you know, ... just things like that, it's ... it's good. I enjoy the feeling on my own that my friends and family understand about who I am and there not, none of my friends pressure me into doing things that I don't want to do." One young woman on the West Coast said that she has become a good example for others: "I guess I would consider myself a role model because ... I don't know, drug and alcohol free is a hard thing to do." One positive practice the British Columbia youth described was identifying a "designated" driver among a group of friends for a particular night. Also, some East Coast youth would choose not to drink at a gathering as a way of keeping others safe. "Yeah. If you're with a group of people that's drinking, then there's more than likely for every person that is drinking, there's probably someone there that's not to look after them anyway, right. That hasn't been happening in [name of place] a lot but out in the surrounding towns, there is a lot of it though."

East Coast participants commented extensively on the drinking among youth and were clearly concerned about the problems associated with heavy and continued drinking, especially among younger youth. For some, the drinking was a product of boredom and the fact that relatively few resources were allocated to youth-oriented activities.

> But what I am saying is that if we had a theatre, more people would do stuff like that, right? Like, I would.
> I would too.
> Like I wouldn't go out drinking every weekend, right? Yeah, instead of going drinking.

Social and leisure pursuits are very important aspects of young people's lives. Lack of or reduced leisure activities and opportunities for socializing with peers were identified by many youth as a problem. It was clear from their discussions that they considered it to affect their general well-being. A young woman observed: "Every weekend. That's all it is, a big scree every weekend. There's nothing else to do like for young people, it's just standing up by the shop. We'll all go to somebody's house or a party or cabin and drink." This statement also indicates that young people see the connection between availability of options and the likelihood of making healthy choices.

In contrast, a number of the youth commented positively on the wide range of outdoor activities available, and in some communities, the availability of sports. One young woman on the West Coast observed, "There is tons of outdoor recreation available: hiking in our provincial parks, boating/kayaking and fishing, biking, and skiing." This was echoed by several participants on the East Coast: "Yeah, there's lots to do ...

fishing, swimming, hiking, riding mountain bikes, dirt biking." The emphasis on sports activities was, however, seen as limiting for some youth. "If you're not into sports, it's hardly anything ... you know, it's just sports mostly."

Because of family stress and changes related to economic and social restructuring in their communities, mental health challenges were evident. Friends and social connections are a major focus in young peoples' lives. They have felt keenly the loss of friends whose families have had to leave these coastal communities in search of work elsewhere. The stress of continual out-migration was clearly evident, and there was even a feeling of hopelessness for some.

> INTERVIEWER: So what is that like for you when your friends move away?
> RESPONDENT: Well you feel almost like you are empty and like you lost a part and then you are sitting back like there was not hope for them [to make a life for themselves in the community] there's probably no hope for me.

One young man on the West Coast noted the overall effect on the community. "But the industries are shut down now, so it's kind of tough ... they tend to move out of the community and that just makes the community suffer more."

On the brighter side, some young people acknowledged that there are things they can do to cope with the on-going losses in their communities. One West Coast youth observed, "Hobbies are a big part of my life because the feeling of sitting around not doing anything also gets you down." A number of youth spoke in vivid terms of their attachment to their home community and the beauty of its setting. "I like the quietness. I like to be able to go down a dirt road and I find a little lake and to go fishing ... I love the sea, the mountains, the trees, and all that kind of stuff, it's ... it's my ... it's home."

Many of the research participants were thinking about job prospects and making plans for their future. Being able to work was acknowledged by many as an important factor related to healthy self-esteem and mental health, but it was often seen as out of their control. As one young woman put it, "If we are working it is not as bad because we are occupied and being productive, which I believe is most important in a healthy lifestyle."

Many of our participants spoke about the beauty of the physical setting and their attachment to their communities, or what Blustein (1997) has termed "place identity." The youth of today are particularly attuned to environmental issues, and the state of their physical surroundings was included in discussions of overall community health and well-being. An example on the East Coast of youth's concern about the physical environment is provided by the following exchange: "Yeah, it's ridiculous the stuff that people get away with when it comes to the environment. Yeah, it is. Well, for one thing, [name of community] has a garbage incinerator, right, and it's built above our hill. There's a salmon river down over the hill, right? This was done in the last 15 years, 10 years ... It's ridiculous. There's a brook there. How did they get away with doing that? Well that's stupid like. It's the dumbest thing I've ever seen."

Overall, the picture that emerged from the young people in our research indicates a view of health and well-being that is largely present-focused and closely tied to their social and emotional contexts. The impact of widespread educational efforts and attitude shifts regarding the health risks of smoking or drinking and driving is apparent. Youth appear to have accepted and internalized these messages, and provided many examples of decisions and practices that illustrated their beliefs that they are paying attention to healthy behaviours. Their perspectives, however, though influenced by bio-medical information, experts, and public health initiatives, are nevertheless firmly rooted in their social and identity-seeking developmental milieu. Youth views are consistent with a harm-reduction approach to health (Johnson 2004; McCambridge and Strang 2004)). Experimentation, limits testing, and a certain sense of invincibility are normal aspects of mid- to late adolescence. Also, young people are keenly aware of and affected by social and community aspects of health. Connecting with friends in leisure activities is a major part of their well-being.

ACCESSING KNOWLEDGE

How do young people access knowledge and resources regarding health? Where do they go and to whom? Youth have well-developed social networks that are major sources of knowledge, acceptance, and support. Hartup (1992) hypothesizes that social networks may be a requirement for positive psychosocial adjustment, because they provide opportunities for acquiring and practising social skills, provide sources of information about self and others and about the world, provide emotional support, and offer occasions for mutual regulation and management of personal relationships. A reading of our discussions with youth suggests that peers have similar "knowledge" or understanding of issues, so it is often one's friends to whom one turns for assistance, rather than adults.

> INTERVIEWER: Who would you turn to if you had a problem like that [being bothered by town gossip]?
> RESPONDENT: Go to your friends. Friends, yeah, definitely.
> RESPONDENT: I'd probably tell my friends before I'd even say anything to my parents.
> RESPONDENT: Your friends are ... like they knows kind of what you're going through because more than likely they've been there too. They knows, they went through it, so they know what's going on in your mind and stuff. They can relate.

Some of the youth suggested that school programs have had an impact on knowledge and behaviours related to health. For example, youth commented that smoking seemed to be one area where there had been improvement. "I would say it [smoking] is less [than a few years ago] because ... there's more education in school about smoking and stuff now." On the West Coast, the Career and Personal Planning (CAPP) curriculum in the schools includes learning objectives related to several health areas, such as smoking, nutrition, substance use, and personal safety. "We learned about nutrition and good eating and stuff in our CAPP class."

Use of media and the Internet was not directly addressed in our research questions. However, in the course of interviews and informal conversations, the youth participants acknowledged that they sought out information and were exposed to diverse opinions through reading magazines and surfing the Net. Today's young people have grown up with technology and computers; most can quickly access an astonishing variety of web-based information and sites related to any topic of interest. Indeed, adults and educators have expressed growing concern about young people's access to unedited and uncensored material of all kinds, including pornography, and a few youth noted access to such sites.

On the whole, the youth in our research generally saw adults as being the gatekeepers of resources and access to certain types of education and knowledge-building opportunities, either as a function of their specific roles as knowledge providers, especially within the formal educational system, or as wisdom accumulated over their lifetimes. They tended to view formalized knowledge as something "out there," something to be acquired in a designated learning environment such as a lesson or a school classroom. Beyond high school, pursuing knowledge or training often meant going away to a larger centre.

(DE)VALUING YOUTH KNOWLEDGE AND EXPERIENCE

Another key finding from our research relates to the value, or lack of, that is placed on youth knowledge. Some youth suggested that they believe their knowledge is often not taken seriously by adults, or that it is even rejected, because it does not fit with (some) adult understandings of issues or adult priorities. For example, a few youth on the East Coast argued that condoms in the high school would be useful for promoting positive sexual health, but they did not believe the school/adults would hear of it: "They're all too conservative. They just feel that'll promote it [sex]." Other participants observed that there appeared to be mixed messages about growing up and making your own choices on the one hand, but problems when those choices were not consistent with what significant adults wanted you to do. A West Coast youth commented, "Like, [an adult] can yell at you and call you stupid, but as soon as you try and defend yourself, you're sent to the office, and then you get sent home."

These adult gatekeeping and devaluing aspects of knowledge and knowing are clearly related to power dynamics. Youth participants described power over instances that they felt had hampered their progress or future options. Referring to an important opportunity related to his future, one youth commented, "maybe I didn't get the apprenticeship with them because, you know, I'm a kid and they don't listen to me much. Maybe it might have been easier to get [it] if a teacher would have talked to them."

Some youth expressed a desire for more hands-on experiential-learning situations within the context of the formal education system. Such desires point to the diversity in ways of learning and knowledge generation and to the need for an educational system that understands such diversity. In speaking about his high school experience, one young male on the East Coast observed, "It's absurd. We're not learning anything. We just get information, just memorize it and give it right back again." Another East Coast boy commented, "What should be in the schools is more classes where you can think and get some hands-on work doing different things, like shop classes and that kind of stuff." The need for information that is relevant to their everyday lives was also expressed by a few youth in terms of sex education classes.

> FACILITATOR: All right. Do you think that there is good education towards um sex you know in the ... school system or do you have access to knowledge?
> PARTICIPANTS: No ... We have one class where we have, well grade 9 I think, they had sex education and they just give us a book and we just go along, and they never give us like, all it was STDs and just little bits and pieces ... They didn't tell us all about safe sex and all that stuff.

Several of our participants talked about the "fishbowl" aspect of living in a small town and being "labelled" as good or bad. Once they were labelled, often in their early adolescence, that label tended to follow them. They related the labelling to not really being listened to or valued as having changed or matured. This type of "common knowledge" might be used against them, even though events connected to that label might have happened years earlier. Although labelling happens everywhere, it may be exacerbated in a small town, where you cannot really be anonymous no matter where you go.

A West Coast community story serves to illustrate youth knowledge uptake and persistence in the face of adult opposition and devaluing of you knowledge and experience. Several years ago, a number of youth in a coastal community came together to request a community skateboard park. They gathered knowledge about costs, park requirements, necessary materials, relevant by-laws, and procedural steps to make their dream a reality. On their own initiative they secured funds and in-kind donations from local businesses for a site, for concrete, materials, labour, and equipment. They prepared a proposal and brought their request to city council, arguing the positive outcomes (youth being out-of-doors but off the streets, engaging in skill-building activities, and co-operating in the use of limited facilities) and addressing potential objections (posting rules prohibiting the use of drugs or alcohol, promoting safety, and limiting access hours).

What followed over the ensuing years was a back-and-forth process of proposals and counter-proposals, site changes, and what the youth perceived as constant roadblocks and opposition. Each time the proposal was delayed, the youth regrouped, sought out additional information and advice, and returned. Some of the original group graduated or moved away, and others joined. Their persistence and commitment was finally rewarded in the fall of 2003 with the opening of the Kyle Scow Memorial Park. This story demonstrates what several youth called the "all-too-familiar" process of adult (negative) response to youth- driven initiatives. Even though they demonstrated creative energy, acquired knowledge and skills to support their project, and followed the rules, it took this dedicated group of youth and supportive adults several years to bring their community project to fruition. They felt that their knowledge, skills, and constructive input were not recognized or valued. Interestingly, on a recent visit to this community, we learned of a further outcome related to this story. One of the original youth advocating for the skateboard park is now on municipal council – using his knowledge of and experience with political processes in a community role.

WHAT WE HAVE LEARNED: IMPLICATIONS FOR RESEARCH, POLICY, AND PRACTICE

Our research indicates several areas for future investigation, policy development, and community-based interventions. First, a more inclusive definition of health and healthy practices is needed, one that goes beyond fact-based information and national averages. Young people inhabit multiple social worlds in which health and well-being are broadly defined and include physical, social, emotional, mental, sexual, relationship, family, community, and environmental aspects of health (Raphael 1996, 2003). Their view of health is different from the dominant biomedical discourse that is typically focused on health practices and environmental conditions that result in poor health outcomes, especially physical diseases. Our youth participants were vocal and articulate about the things that mattered most to them – friends, future prospects, leisure activities, and general well-being. They were also well aware of the multiple dimensions of health beyond the physical aspects. "If you are not happy, you are not healthy."

A second point is the importance of young people's context. The picture of youth knowledge and its applications that has emerged in our research is a blended one of formal learning in schools and institutions but also of much informal learning with peers and in social environments. More investigation is needed to better understand and tap the potential of these informal learning contexts. Knowledge process and products have been of particular interest to participatory action models and community-based researchers (Park 2001; Puskar et al. 1999; Small 1995) because of their emphasis on shared learning and mutual co-construction of meaning. Collaborative, ecological models of research not only meet the practical concerns of communities but also contribute to the academic goal of social-science advancement of knowledge. The youth participants in our research could clearly make the connection between social structural influences and healthy and unhealthy practices, such as when they spoke of the connection between lack of recreational/leisure opportunities and drinking.

Third, it is essential that parents, educators, health professionals, and policy-makers take into account the developmental context of youth and their identity projects. Normal developmental shifts make some level of stress and uncertainty a constant for youth. However, we found that this stress and uncertainty is heightened, as are the potential costs of mistakes – especially economic costs. With increasing pressure to make the right choices, coupled with fewer options, some youth resolve this dilemma with what developmental psychologist James Marcia (1994) and others (Harter 1999) have termed "foreclosing," or making a choice that severely limits remaining options. Among our participants, examples of such foreclosure situations that were related to physical, emotional, and mental health included quitting school, becoming pregnant, using substances, and depression. One participant on the West Coast expressed concern about the number of her friends who became mothers at a young age: "Um ... having children, there's a lot of young pregnancies, like a lot ... like at sixteen ... and I have about seven friends now that have graduated that have got children."

Although young people can temporarily decrease the anxiety associated with making choices about their futures by foreclosing, the problem is not actually resolved, and other negative consequences tend to accompany these foreclosure situations. Staying in their comfort zone of familiar but limited options instead of dealing with the stresses and uncertainty of leaving involves a big decision for young people in these coastal communities. Many stories surfaced, both of successes and failures. One strategy for dealing with this uncertainty is postponing a decision to move away for work or education. As one West Coast youth put it, "Well, if I don't leave, I don't have to come back a failure, do I?"

The devaluing of youth knowledge is another pattern that came out strongly in our interviews. Over and over again, we heard from the youth participants that their knowledge and needs were often discounted. From a social constructivist perspective, individuals, including youth, are the acknowledged experts about their own experience. Yet, like that of other marginalized groups, the wisdom of youth is seldom acknowledged. Although adolescents may take pains to define themselves differently, they still want their voices to be heard. And if adults want youth to act responsibly, it is important to involve them in meaningful discourse about health and other community issues. In spite of all that is generally accepted about the benefits of participatory decision making, young people are continually being left out of the policy process and decision making that affects their day-to-day lives. It is a universally accepted learning principle that those who are included in planning and decision-making processes are more engaged in implementing the outcomes. This principle is particularly relevant when considering youth, because they need to take on increasing responsibility for their life paths and outcomes.

A further key implication is the importance of adult support, role models, and meaningful dialogue with youth related to healthy choices and lifestyles. In small coastal communities, there are limited options and thus limited exposure to a range of live role models to facilitate exploration. Although information, Internet sites, and "virtual" opportunities are available, what may be missing, as Puskar et al. (1999) suggest, is a debriefing or grounding of the knowledge gained during youth's lived experiences in their particular (coastal) context, a debriefing that would make their experiences meaningful and connected. During our research, we observed concrete examples of intervention strategies and programs that facilitate knowledge transfer and uptake for youth. Many programs incorporate specific facilitated sessions to enhance sharing and the application of the young people's experiential learning. These included mentoring relationships with adults, field trips, and specialized community educational experiences.

How and when does knowledge become wisdom or "right judgment" (see Ommer et al., this volume, chap. 2)? Who considers young people to be wise, or does wisdom come only with age? If we take the time to listen and reflect on their views, young people can tell us a what they "know" about health, and by implication, about their health needs and priorities. In our research, we found that youth participants demonstrated particular perspectives and priorities in relation to the effects of restructuring in their communities. As is typical of adolescents, peer influences were often paramount. Other sources of influence included family and social groups. Familial closeness and attachment to community were seen to be key influencing factors.

If we are to support our youth in their quest for healthy and productive lives, it is important that we pay attention to how knowledge flows in their world. As one of our youth participants observed, "there is a lot of potential in these communities, and it's going to waste." It is in everyone's best interests that young people be encouraged to participate and take leadership roles with regard to knowledge uptake and application. It is their future that is at stake, and we cannot afford to squander it.

9

Promoting, Blocking, and Diverting the Flow of Knowledge: Four Case Studies from Newfoundland and Labrador

R. JOHN GIBSON, RICHARD L. HAEDRICH,
JOHN C. KENNEDY, KELLY M. VODDEN,
AND C. MICHAEL WERNERHEIM

Knowledge accumulates through experience and investigation and can be communicated through many different avenues, including scientific publications, university lectures, workshops, public media, policy documents, and oral tradition. Knowledge about natural resources includes data on the physico-chemical environment, population structure, behaviour, predator-prey relations, habitat, growth, migration, and related information about the impact of human activities on particular species and ecosystems. This information is necessary for the sustainable exploitation of natural resources for subsistence and sale and for recreation.

Knowledge about the local environment and the sustainability of the ecosystem is generated on a long-term basis by local communities (LK, local knowledge) and sustained by traditional knowledge (TK).[1] In aboriginal societies, for example, knowledge is gained and communicated through the practical activities necessary to make a living or engage in other customs and rituals and then passed on from generation to generation. This knowledge shares with conventional science the method of repeated observation and experimentation but adds the dimension of long-term lived experience and a holistic point of view that includes understandings and ethics based on cultural values (Sheehan 2001; Smith 1998).

Scientific knowledge originates from empirical data gathered through careful enumerations, measurements, and experimentation in laboratory and field situations. It generally involves the testing and/or generation of hypotheses and study over much smaller time scales than TK or LK. Investigative research may be motivated by intellectual curiosity, as is much research by universities and research institutions, or by policy requirements or practical problems that formerly motivated mainly government and industry but now, increasingly, local communities and academic institutions as well.

HOW KNOWLEDGE SHOULD MOVE

The standard view of science is that the scientific method ensures privileged access to objective reality. From this perspective, the first requirement for accepted scientific procedure is that it involves a careful, comprehensive, and objective study design directed at answering a clear and well-articulated research question using specified methods and that the results be presented in a form that would permit other investigators to replicate the study. This positivist approach, which equates science with objective, value-free knowledge production, has been challenged from many quarters. Critics argue that all knowledge is to some degree situated and socially constructed and thus, despite the scientific ideal, that facts and values cannot ever be fully separated. Nor can "the truth" ever really be found (Ommer et al., this volume, chap. 2). There is also increasing recognition of the potential contribution of different forms of knowledge (e.g., conventional science from multiple disciplines and approaches, along with local and traditional knowledge) to the pursuit of truth.

Nevertheless, scientists continue to aim for rationality, a measure of objectivity (by both recognizing and managing researcher influence and bias), and generalizable "truths." They stress the values of reliability, validity, accuracy, and representativeness as measures of quality research. Some researchers, such as Tobias (2000), have argued that these measures are important in the recording of TK as well. While the nature of scientific and other forms of knowledge, as well as the relationship between these knowledge systems, are in dispute, the aim of generating new knowledge remains highly relevant, particularly in fields such as ecology, resource management, and sustainable development, where not only lack of knowledge but also lack of quality knowledge (equivocality) are barriers to improved decision making (Wolfe 2000).

Other potential barriers to improved decision making can be found in the relationship between knowledge and policy. If scientific and local knowledge are to be utilized in addressing policy-relevant problems there needs to be a policy framework wherein the ideas generated from this knowledge can be applied in setting the policy agenda and captured in the resulting legislation. Additional requirements for knowledge to translate into the actual protection of natural resources and, in some cases, the recovery of degraded ones include effective monitoring and enforcement.

Of course this ideal model of how knowledge should move within the policy process does not always occur. It is a simplistic representation of reality that is open to criticism for being overly confident in our collective, technical problem-solving abilities and for its linear, rational nature (Homer-Dixon 2001). We suggest, however, that such an ideal is useful as a framework for the analysis and comparison of real-life situations and that it leads to an enhanced understanding of decidedly more complex situations. Policy analysts such as Pal (1992) and Doern and Phidd (1983) offer further justification for the ongoing utility of the rational-evaluation approach. The application (or lack) of such an ideal is indeed influenced by a host of ideological, social, political, and economic factors; economic considerations often dominate conservation concerns in policy outcomes, as both the literature and the case studies presented below suggest (Clapp 1998; Cashore et al. 2001; Hayter 2001).

In what follows (see table 9.1) we begin with a case study of a situation where knowledge flow has approximated the idealized model: knowledge has been generated and utilized to achieve a balanced approach to conservation and economic development at Indian Bay, in northeastern insular Newfoundland (figure 9.1). In co-operation with research scientists, the local community began to restore high-quality brook trout (*Salvelinus fontinalis*) stocks and, after a temporary hiatus, continue to be engaged in collaborative research efforts that are informing fisheries management in the immediate region, as well as in the province as a whole. As in the ideal model, legislative and policy measures have been accompanied by monitoring and enforcement activities.

Our second case study deals with the construction of a new road in Labrador (Red Bay to Cartwright, figure 9.1) and describes a situation where those responsible for monitoring culvert installations to protect anadromous salmon and trout populations ignored their legislative responsibilities, resulting in culvert installations that threatened these populations. The threat to these populations was invisible to the policy-makers and the general public until Coasts Under Stress researchers,

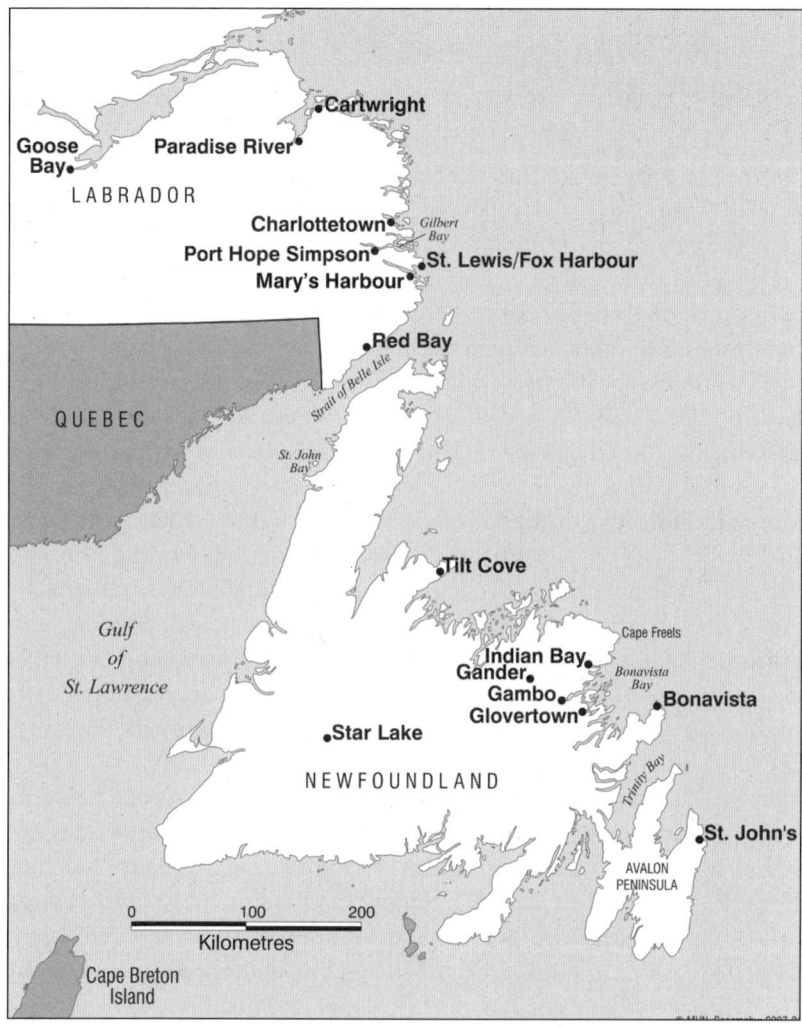

Figure 9.1 Locations of the case studies in Newfoundland and Labrador

working in collaboration with the Labrador Métis Nation (LMN), documented the problem, disseminated their findings, and generated enough political pressure to result in some rehabilitation of stream habitat.

The remainder of this chapter touches briefly on two additional case studies related to water systems and construction on the Island of Newfoundland (Star Lake and St John's, figure 9.1). The interests of industry in one case and those of developers in the other prevailed in the policy and decision-making process, blocking scientific knowledge

Table 9.1
Case Study Summary

	Knowledge Flow	*Comparison to Ideal Model*
Indian Bay	Scientific knowledge generation that includes local knowledge and actors contributes to policy generation and implementation	Close resemblance, but with diversions and feedback loops throughout the network of policy actors
Trans-Labrador Highway	Scientific knowledge and conservation mandate are ignored in practice (policy implementation failure), but the production of new knowledge and local mobilization results in commitments to reverse damage	Appears that process will ultimately resemble model but, again, with diversions linked to political, economic, and bureaucratic processes, lack of scientific knowledge and local input, lack of enforcement
Star Lake	A perversion of scientific knowledge through inadequate science and ignoring other knowledge sources, leading to uninformed and "unwise" decisions	Decisions are informed by limited knowledge
Urban Rivers	Economic interests and a change of political representation lead to scientific knowledge and conservation concerns being ignored	Decisions are not informed by scientific knowledge

about likely environmental consequences and resulting in environmental degradation.

Together these examples represent different points along a continuum related to knowledge flows, with the ideal model of the relationship between knowledge and policy at one end and situations where conservation concerns and scientific knowledge have been marginalized or blocked from influencing the policy process at the other (see table 9.1). The first and second case studies suggest that with some modifications to reflect real-life complexity and dynamism, the model can be closely replicated in some situations, although preservation of existing habitat is preferable to after-the-fact commitments to restoration. The other case studies remind us that in too many situations, local and scientific knowledge about the environmental risks of particular developments tend to be blocked or marginalized, rather than flowing among relevant stakeholders (e.g., users, scientists, policy-makers), owing to power differentials between different groups.

The cases of Indian Bay and Labrador, however, point to the potential offered by a learning-systems approach and offer insight into the circumstances under which learning can occur within a policy network. The concept of organizational learning has received significant attention in recent years (Easterby-Smith and Lyles 2003). Schön (1973), Hutchins (1970), and others have argued for three decades that "change" is a fundamental feature of modern life and that it is necessary to develop social systems that could learn and adapt through "reflection-in-action" (Schön 1983). Argyris and Schön (1974) emphasize the importance of learning strategies that involve not just corrective action in a specific situation but a reevaluation of governing goals, policies, values, and "mental maps." Fundamental to learning systems are networks of actors and "feedback loops" that operate throughout these networks (Smith 2001). The cases presented below reiterate and expand on theories of both learning systems and the policy process and their applications in Newfoundland and Labrador freshwater fisheries/habitat policy systems.

CASE STUDY ONE: THE INDIAN BAY ECOSYSTEM COMMITTEE

The Indian Bay case is one of a community system set up to be as democratic as possible that turned against "best practice" based on all the knowledge acquired, owing to conflicting objectives; misinformation; lack of communication between local, academic, and government partners; and inaction by those who should have intervened. These factors brought the research to an end temporarily, but the individual efforts of a few key people and commitment to the concept of local involvement in managing the watershed and its fishery have managed to get it back on track, demonstrating the durability of the community-based system (figure 9.2). Overall, this case study is an important example of community-university-government cooperation in knowledge generation and improved management practices. It demonstrates that policy systems can approximate the ideal process, while also illustrating that, unlike the model presented above, real-life problem solving in social-ecological systems is highly complex and vulnerable and reliant on ongoing learning and adaptation.

Indian Bay is a fishing and logging community on Northwest Arm at the head of Bonavista Bay, Newfoundland. Logging was the major industry in this area until 1966, when Bowater Pulp and Paper Com-

Promoting, Blocking, and Diverting Knowledge 161

```
                        Indian Bay
                History of the brook trout fishery

Trophy brook trout fishery                    Restoration
         ↘                                    (following 1994)
         Deterioration  →  Overfished    ↗
         from about 1979    1985-1990         ↑
                                              |
                 Movement of knowledge        |
    Local knowledge                     Local stewardship
    (anglers and cabin owners)          (Indian Bay Ecosystem
         ↗  ↙  ↘                        Committee, IBEC)
     MUN              DFO            ↗
    (Research)  →  (Formulation of special
                    regulations in 1994)
```

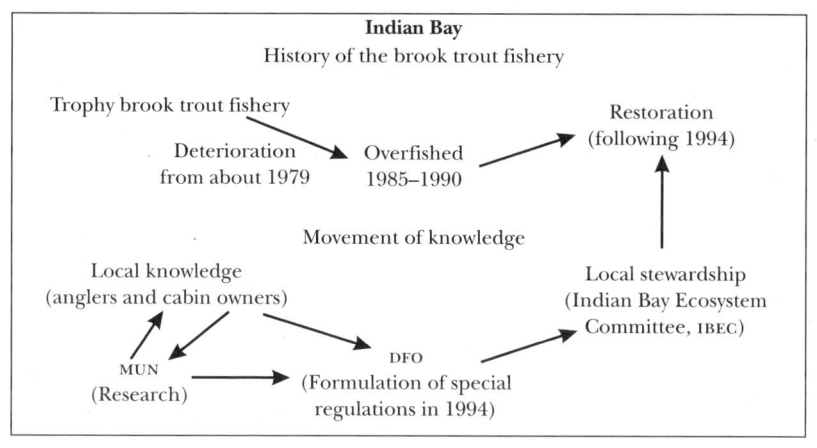

Figure 9.2 The loss and remediation of the trophy trout fishery at Indian Bay, illustrating the movement of knowledge during this process. MUN = Memorial University of Newfoundland; DFO = Department of Fisheries and Oceans

pany closed up shop after a major forest fire. The Indian Bay River and associated lakes were renowned nationally for their exceptional angling, and especially for trophy brook trout of "five- or six-pounders" (Power 1997). Access and angling was controlled by Bowater until they ceased operations in 1966. With the construction of the Trans-Canada Highway around 1957 and an access road to Indian Bay in 1959, better access was available to anglers (locally and from further away). Snow machines appeared in the mid-1970s, along with more float planes and more vehicular traffic as forest access roads were improved. All these changes led to increased exploitation.

The bag limit in the 1970s was twenty-four fish or ten lbs. plus one fish per day, with a possession limit of twice the daily limit. These regulations were not enforced, and fish were also taken by nets and other illegal methods, leading to overexploitation and loss of the large trout. When fishing declined to its lowest level between about 1985 and 1990, local people realized that something had to be done "if the resource was not to go the same way as the cod." Restoration of the ecosystem was initiated entirely by the local communities. The Cape Freels and Gambo–Indian Bay Development Associations formed the Indian Bay/Cape Freels Ecosystem Committee in 1988. Their first initiative was to remove the large amount of garbage that had accumulated in the watershed area. In 1990 over five thousand bags of garbage were collected, along with about fifty tons of heavy items such as discarded stoves, refrigerators, oil tanks, beds, and car wrecks. Since the clean-up and as a result of sign installations and an awareness campaign, there has been no serious littering. In 1992 the Indian Bay Ecosystem Committee (IBEC) was formed. Habitat improvements were made on thirteen tributaries, with removal of obstructions caused by debris and pulpwood jams, logging dams, and old beaver dams and culverts. Four collapsed bridges were reconstructed, and cribbing was installed for river-bank erosion control. The committee conducted a public awareness campaign and surveyed people using the area for sport fishing. The results showed that there was concern about the declining trout stocks.

It was IBEC's original intention to build a permanent hatchery for a long-term restocking program with brook trout. Luckily this program was not implemented, as a result of scientific advice that introducing hatchery stock leads to deterioration in genetic diversity and declines in numbers and in the size of wild fish. Scientific advice was given by Dr R.L. Haedrich and the Salmonid Research Group at Memorial University. Together they showed that the water quality of the system was good and that growth rates of trout in Indian Bay remained the same as before: greater than those for stocks on the Avalon Peninsula in southeast Newfoundland. They also developed models to show that the stocks would recover if special regulations were implemented for the area. Experiments with these regulations and the closure of two lakes to fishing coincided with the demonstrated return of large trout. A four-year trout assessment project was launched with funding from federal and provincial sources (van Zyll de Jong et al. 2002). IBEC recommended to the federal Department of Fisheries and Oceans (DFO) that special regulations be implemented. DFO agreed and these regulations are now enforced by IBEC. Seasons have been shortened, and a bag limit of six fish or two lbs. plus one fish was applied in 1994. Since that time, angling has improved and the fishery is presently operating near full capacity. Because the present regulations are not effective when effort is high and size-based regulations are needed to accommodate increased effort and sustain high-quality fishing, IBEC is discussing additional regulatory changes with government and community actors.

IBEC's long-term objective is to use the system's superb recreational angling as the basis for enhancing economic opportunities within the ecosystem area, while also maintaining local opportunities for socially and culturally important recreational activities such as angling, hunting, and cabin ownership. There is close cooperation with several universities, and a number of graduate theses have been written on research questions related to brook trout, anadromous and resident Atlantic salmon (*Salmo salar*), and some other species. IBEC has a main office at Indian Bay and a field station upriver. There are plans under way to build more laboratory facilities, accommodation, and an interpretation centre, in order to create a nationally important field research centre (the Indian Bay Centre for Cooperative Ecological Studies, or ICCES). With these developments has come a broader focus on the ecosystem as a whole, with studies relating not just to fisheries but also to forestry practices, invertebrates, plants, anthropology, and rural development.

As a result of these successes, neighbouring communities have sought IBEC's assistance in conserving their fisheries resources. In a watershed east of Indian River, the Southwest Pond watershed, the Atlantic salmon display an unusual life history tactic in that they behave similarly to sea trout. In fact the locals refer to the species as "sea trout." In the spring, "smolts" and larger stages migrate to feed in the estuary and adjacent marine area. However, unlike the usual anadromous strain they do not overwinter at sea but after a couple of months return upriver, where the mature fish spawn in the late fall. The fish grow to 2 to 6 lbs. and provide excellent sport.

Because these salmon congregate in the estuary in the early spring and feed avidly, they are easily angled. Until recently, existing regulations, which were the same as those for trout, led to overexploitation. A graduate student at Memorial University of Newfoundland (MUN), Steve Sutton, undertook angler surveys and interviews and presented the information to the local community (Sutton 1997, 2000). With help from some members of IBEC, DFO was asked to implement regulations reducing the season length and bag limit in order to restore the fishery, which has now recovered. This is a nice example of local knowledge interfacing with scientific knowledge, and the appropriate authority implementing the legislation.

Although considerable progress has been made, the Indian Bay program is vulnerable. In 2001, at the annual spring meeting of IBEC there was a "coup d'état," in which a new board of directors was elected that had no agenda other than that it was anti-science and wanted no more studies in the system. The board did want government funding to continue, but it wanted that funding to go towards trail construction and a hatchery. The coup appears to have been triggered by local resentment among some members of the community of those who had supported the initial program. Those responsible for the coup were also concerned that fishing procedures might be contributing to fishing mortality (fyke netting).

Community concerns grew to exaggerated proportions. Distant graduate supervisors were unaware of the extent of the fish mortalities and of the level of community discomfort, and local staff and graduate students also failed to recognize the extent of the problem. Geographical, physical, and ideological gaps between the community and outside scientific advisors contributed to downplaying the issue of research-related fish mortality. This lack of communication led to misinformation, exaggerations, and false rumours, which were presented at the annual meeting. Scientists were not present to refute the arguments, defend the research, or gather constructive feedback that might have been used to improve research procedures. Government representatives who were at the meeting and who could have dealt with some of the misinformation chose not to intervene – possibly in reaction to the "tiresome, juvenile turf war" between federal and provincial officials (Schindler 2001).

The efforts of a few key people and the failure of government to provide funding for the hatchery and trail construction have helped restore the original program. Those from the "opposing party" have become more informed about the benefits of research and have had an opportunity to express their concerns. Similarly, further investigation of the matter through CUS research has informed scientists about some problems associated with the research methods that were being employed in Indian Bay when people became concerned. This shows effective and sustained knowledge transfer from scientists, researchers, and communities into policy requires ongoing and effective communication at all levels. The Indian Bay example also shows that one requirement for a good scientific program is for it to have a solid research framework and for it to be run by a consortium of university members and federal and provincial governments who are committed at a very senior level, but also involving local people and effective leaders. In the case of Indian Bay, a local non-profit institution and a skilled and committed local manager have been critically important.

The decline of the trout resource and its recovery in Indian Bay is an excellent example of how management failure and the lack of scientific data led to the collapse of a resource, but also of how local initiative and a "bottom-up" approach, coupled with assistance from outside scientists and policy-makers, has helped to restore the system. The trout resource is regarded as more important than the salmon angling, and it is of social and cultural importance to the local community, who were responsible for the restoration of the aesthetic appeal and the angling in the watershed. They may have succeeded because they are an old and established community with pride in the resource and with members who are determined to conserve it for future generations. The approach of the Indian Bay group is different from that of some other groups, in that their primary objective is scientific management and conservation of the ecosystem, incorporating, rather than being driven by, economic sustainability, whereas some other watershed management groups appear to be primarily interested in make-work projects for their community, and acquiring funds for this purpose.

This case study illustrates how a natural resource can be restored and conserved based on a foundation of knowledge that is used to inform the development of an alternative policy framework. The residents themselves brought about the change, asked for scientific input, and had financial assistance from government sources. However, it was key individuals, particularly IBEC personnel with support from a local board of directors, who appreciated the value of the system, who had the wisdom to apply the knowledge and the incentives and initiative to attract volunteers and sources of funding that made it happen. The interaction of local and outside knowledge holders and decision makers, facilitated through the IBEC organization, has resulted in changes not only in government policy-making but also in the policies and behaviour of individual and corporate users of the watershed and of the IBEC organization itself. Despite the apparent resilience of the Indian Bay model, however, reliance on key individuals introduces an element of vulnerability, as does the need for ongoing yet fragile public, government, and academic support.

CASE STUDY TWO: FISH PASSAGE AND THE TRANS-LABRADOR HIGHWAY (TLH)

The history of roads in the Labrador portion of the Canadian province of Newfoundland and Labrador dates to the 1960s. Initial road construction was enabled by funding from the federal government, mainly from the Department of Regional Economic Expansion (DREE). The first all-weather gravel roads connected the single-industry communities of western and central Labrador. The second round of road construction was from L'Anse au Clair to Red Bay in the Strait of Belle Isle.

In 1997 the province reached an agreement with the federal government to fund the construction of the so-called Trans-Labrador Highway (TLH) from Red Bay north along the coast to Cartwright and inland to Happy Valley-Goose Bay. The TLH was to be funded by amortizing long-term savings achieved by phasing out federal subsidies to the region's coastal boat services. Roads would replace boats for the movement of people and goods.

Most of the people living in communities from Lodge Bay to Cartwright favoured construction of the TLH (Kennedy 1995, 243; Fiander-Good Associates 1993, 9–2–9–3), considering it of fundamental importance to the future of their region. Concerns about potentially negative environmental impact associated with road construction were drowned out by hopes for the future, which the TLH appeared to symbolize. Local people also assumed that the government knew how to protect the area's rivers and that it would monitor road construction to ensure that they would be protected. While aboriginal groups expressed some concerns regarding increased fishing pressure on their territories (the Innu Nation) and potential negative impacts on fish habitat (the Labrador Métis Nation (LMN) (Fiander-Good Associates 1993, 8–6–8–9), most people in the region, many of whom belonged to the LMN, felt the concerns of the Innu and Métis Nations were extreme and continued to press for the road.

Phase II of the TLH, from Red Bay to Cartwright, was constructed in 2001 and 2002, connecting communities from Mary's Harbour to Port Hope Simpson, Paradise River, and Cartwright, with access roads to St Lewis/Fox Harbour and Charlottetown (figure 9.1). This road crosses 20 different watersheds and 166 watercourses (Jacques Whitford Environment Limited 1998). The provincial government's Department of Transportation and Works (T&W) has thirty years of experience dealing with stream crossings. In the early days there were no environmental restrictions on the structures installed, but over the past fifteen years, regulation has increased in response to concern about the need to provide adequate fish passage. In the past five or six years concern has extended beyond fish passage to include a more general need to protect fish habitat (T. McCarthy, T&W, personal communication).

Three basic structural designs for stream crossings are in use: round pipe, bottomless corrugated iron pipe, and bridges. The key factor in the choice of design by T&W is the flow rate, which is important for two reasons: (1) the structure must withstand a "fifty-year flood" requirement and the lesser floods that occur more frequently; and (2) the structure must permit fish passage.

In late June and early July 2002, CUS conducted a survey of a 210 km section of the newly constructed road, in co-operation with the LMN (Gibson et al. 2005). The team evaluated crossings of permanent streams using the DFO's guidelines for stream crossings (Gosse et al. 1998). These guidelines stipulate that in order to conserve a waterway's integrity, streams under road crossings should simulate natural conditions and that a bridge length or culvert width should be selected to "clear span" the active channel. In relation to fish habitat, bridges and open-bottom/bottomless arch culverts are preferred. Where cylindrical culverts are installed, they should simulate open-bottom or pipe arch culverts and should thus be countersunk 30 cm below the stream bed elevation, or for culverts with a diameter exceeding 200 cm, 15 percent of their diameter should be below the stream bed. Water depth above the substrate should be similar to or greater than that found in the natural channel. Water velocities can be up to $0.3-0.6$ m.s^{-1} if a coarse substrate is present to allow slower flows near the bottom, in order to facilitate migration of small fish (young salmonids will migrate many kilometers up small streams above spawning areas) (Erkinaro and Gibson 1997; Erkinaro et al. 1998).

The team found that 53 percent of the crossings on permanent streams presented barriers to fish migration, and only two out of forty-seven culverts examined were of open-bottom types. None of the pipe culverts were embedded, as is required to conserve productive capacity of fish habitat (most stream invertebrates, which provide the major food of small salmonids, require stony stream substrate). The result was loss of benthic stream habitat and of riparian habitats at crossings, as well as loss of some wetland habitat with filling and constriction at crossings by filling materials. From the 210 km sample of highway surveyed it appears that more than 50 percent of stream crossings are barriers to fish migration and will result in loss of spawning and rearing habitats. Fish species negatively affected are brook trout, Atlantic salmon, Arctic char (*Salvelinus alpinus*), and rainbow smelt (*Osmerus mordax*). These species are the basis for important recreational fisheries, they are also an important part of the LMN diet and have a very high cultural value to the LMN.

Publication of the results from this relatively inexpensive study resulted in a high-level meeting with DFO (17 October 2002) that included the regional director for the Science, Oceans, and Environment Branch, the division manager of Marine Environment and Habitat Management, and the president of the LMN. The Regional Director emphasized that DFO was keen to cooperate with the LMN, provincial authorities, and researchers in conserving fish habitat and in remedying any problems. Culverts were to be checked by DFO, so that remediation work would be done. Also LMN fishery guardians were to be trained to ensure proper stream-crossing techniques would be implemented for Phase III of the TLH. These discussions resulted in a comprehensive and exhaustive study of all stream crossings associated with Phase II of the TLH, a study carried out in co-operation with the LMN, the province, and DFO. Prior to this study, DFO had required T&W to undertake stream remediation (i.e., to undertake an initial effort to protect habitat and to do *ex post* work on the original structure to restore habitat) on the Island but not in Labrador. However, in response to the CUS report, five culverts on the Labrador road were identified as in need of remediation in 2003. The problems on these sites have since been rectified.

On streams where DFO identifies a fisheries concern, culverts are to be countersunk to protect the minimum flow levels required to ensure fish passage. T&W insists that where fish passage is a concern, culverts are countersunk, and other measures suggested by DFO are implemented as requested to protect habitat. In crossings of temporary streams or where there is an upstream barrier close to the road, there is no countersinking. T&W notes that remediation can be very costly, as it involves blasting bedrock from stream beds. If the pipe is insufficiently countersunk, leakage under the pipe can reduce the flow rate inside the pipe below the minimum required by DFO to protect fish passage. DFO is sensitive to the cost of remediation and does not often require it. T&W takes the view that given a limited budget, the most prudent approach is to spend scarce "remediation dollars" on the streams where the return to remediation is the greatest, with the result that small streams tend to be ignored.

Why were so many TLH culverts not installed according to DFO guidelines? The failure to properly install some culverts is probably related to the very large number of potential sites along the road and to the fact that, in each instance, T&W's decision making involved a trade-off between cost considerations and environmental priority. Given the significant costs involved in appropriate construction, it is perhaps not surprising that all crossings did not receive the attention warranted by due consideration of fish habitat. Other contributing factors may have been a lack of awareness by the construction companies responsible for installation of the importance of small streams for the spawning and rearing of salmonids and a lack of adequate government enforcement in the field.

Round pipe is stronger than any other pipe and the most cost-effective. Round pipe can also easily be adapted with fish baffles. Arched pipe with a flat bottom can be an alternative to round pipe if the ground is level. Because arched pipe is cheaper than round but not as strong, rock will normally have to be placed inside the structure to guard against collapse. Furthermore, arched pipe needs a bedrock stream and concrete footings. Installation is very costly, since it requires blasting, adding at least Can$100,000 to the cost of arched pipe if it is to be installed correctly. Round 800–900 mm pipe costs about Can$200 per meter (about Can$4,000 for the average stream crossing). In contrast, 20-meter single-span arch structures cost about Can$800,000 each. The 30-meter span at South Feeder cost Can$1.2 million, as did the 35-meter span on Gilbert River. The bridges at St Lewis, Alexis River, and Mary's Harbour cost Can$8 million, Can$5 million, and Can$1.2 million respectively. Since the road was funded entirely by the provincial government and funds are limited, cost alone means that bottomless structures are used only at DFO's insistence (T. McCarthy, T&W, personal communciation).

All construction work is outsourced, as the T&W is set up to do maintenance and not construction. In contracting for and managing this work, T&W strives for cost-effectiveness, subject to the guidelines issued by DFO. Before any construction at a stream crossing begins, a permit or clearance from the DFO is required. This takes the form of a "letter of advice" in which protective requirements regarding fish habitat are specified. In addition, T&W has biologists on staff who provide advice in situations where DFO does not express specific concerns. In practice, T&W staff generally carry out an initial assessment and, based on experience, identifies situations where fisheries issues can be expected to attract DFO's attention. It is DFO that ultimately decides whether habitat or fish passage is an issue at a given stream crossing, and it is DFO's responsibility to identify such situations, to suggest appropriate remedies, and to monitor and enforce compliance. However, it appears that DFO's enforcement is inconsistent and generally dependent on the DFO officer in the area.

Ignoring small streams because of an insufficient road construction budget is one thing. Ignoring small streams because they are dry part of

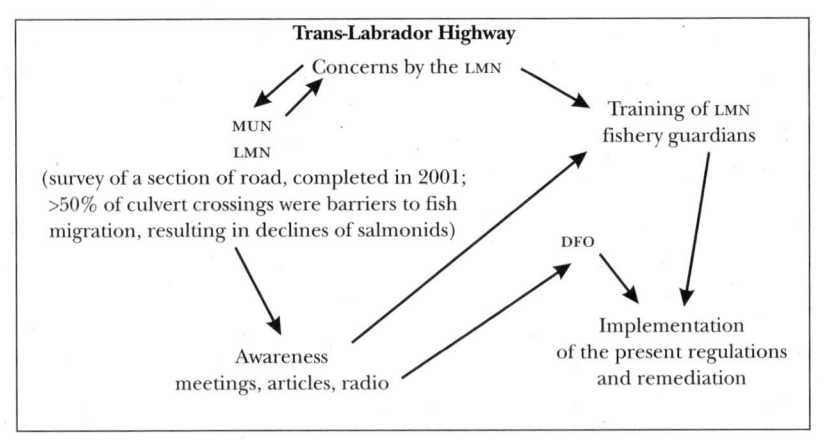

```
                    Trans-Labrador Highway
                      Concerns by the LMN
            MUN                              Training of LMN
            LMN                              fishery guardians
(survey of a section of road, completed in 2001;
>50% of culvert crossings were barriers to fish
migration, resulting in declines of salmonids)
                                      DFO
                                             Implementation
              Awareness                      of the present regulations
       meetings, articles, radio             and remediation
```

Figure 9.3 An example showing the importance of interactions between local ecological knowledge and scientific knowledge, and co-operation between the various authorities. MUN = Memorial University of Newfoundland; DFO = Department of Fisheries and Oceans; LMN = Labrador Métis Nation

the year or encompass less habitat overlooks the fundamental contribution to the food web and the general ecosystem that such streams make. The policy problem appears to be two-fold, but it has a common source: an apparent barrier to the flow of knowledge. The role of small streams in fluvial ecosystems along the TLH is probably not sufficiently well understood by decision makers. That is, expenditure to protect parts of the ecosystem functions in some areas may be wasted if remedial action is not taken in other areas. In addition, when knowledge about the role of small streams is lacking, it is hard to make a persuasive case to senior decision makers about the need for a road construction budget that pays the same attention to fish habitat-friendly stream crossings as it does to road gradients. As a result, although the loss of stream habitat owing to improperly constructed stream crossings is serious and illegal and although it can be as damaging to fisheries as overfishing, the problem is very common (reviewed in Gibson et al. 2005). The CUS study generated scientific knowledge in a collaborative and effective way, however, and this knowledge empowered the LMN and the scientists to promote the flow of knowledge to decision makers and to exert pressure on government to implement its own policy (figure 9.3). The follow-up studies have emphasized the value of small streams to policy-makers, and increased effort is to be put into small stream conservation in the future.

This case study also suggests that concern and awareness must exist at multiple levels within government, including the local level, if legislation is to be at all effective. It suggests that effective enforcement is critical and that it takes more than good academic science to raise awareness, particularly in the face of strong economic incentives to ignore that science. It was the combination of the political influence of the LMN, now involved in monitoring and enforcement, and the scientific information about road impacts that led to remediation measures being put in place by DFO. It is to be hoped that some learning has occurred throughout the system and that Phase III of the TLH will result in better protection of fish habitat and passage in both large and small streams.

Both with the Indian River basin and with the Labrador stream crossings it was basically a love of nature and respect for their natural environment by the local communities that resulted in the decision to take action in order to conserve their resource.

Political and economic pressures surround the conservation of any natural resource, and where there are sufficient political pressures from developers, limited scientific information, and blockages in the knowledge flows, the authorities may cheat. In the last part of this paper, we briefly discuss two situations from Newfoundland where interest groups blocked the flow of scientific knowledge in order to enhance their benefits to the detriment of an ecosystem and society as a whole.

CASE STUDY THREE: THE STAR LAKE DEVELOPMENT

Star Lake was once a large (15.7 km^2) lake in west central Newfoundland (figure 9.1). Two species of fish were present, a race of brook trout that matured late, was relatively long-lived, and grew to a large size, and a very small arctic char that was a major prey for the brook trout. In 1997 the lake was transformed into a fluctuating (8 m over winter) reservoir for hydroelectric (15 MW) generation. The impoundment was projected to cover 25 km^2, but by mistake an extra 2.2 km^2 was flooded. Spawning and rearing areas, at the lake outlet for the large trout and in littoral areas for the arctic char, were lost. "Mitigation" was to take place using a hatchery for brook trout designed for stocking up to one hundred thousand fingerlings annually. Since hatcheries have failed elsewhere to conserve unique genetic stocks (Vøllestad and Hesthagan 2001) and frequently result in reduction or loss of wild stocks (Myers et al. 2004), such management measures are unsuitable in Newfoundland and

Labrador, where it is likely that numerous, but so far unquantified distinct population segments or stocks remain (Adams and Hutchings 2003; van Zyll De Jong et al. 2004).

The Environmental Impact Statement (EIS) for the Star Lake development predicted that effects on fish would be minor, that they could be mitigated, and that they could, and in fact, be positive. The international scientific literature illustrating the consequences of water level regulation – the oligotrophication process, the loss of littoral invertebrates, and the indirect loss of benthic and large salmonid fish – is monumental (e.g., Stockner et al. 2000), but this literature was not acknowledged, and these risks dismissed. Based on the projected increase in the flooded area and a projected "trophic upsurge" from increased dissolved nutrients, a theoretical net gain of productive habitats was emphasized. But this projected gain ignored the fact that studies have shown that after the original "trophic upsurge" the productivity of reservoirs declines to below the original productivity of the lake. The littoral areas of a lake are the most productive for plant, algal, littoral plankton, and benthic invertebrates and have the highest biodiversity of the lake. These food items are impoverished and in some cases eliminated by fluctuating water regimes (e.g., Smith et al. 1987).

While it has been shown that with new reservoirs over acidic rocks, as in Precambrian areas, mercury is released and accumulated up the food chain where it can reach unhealthy levels in piscivorous fish, and that these elevated levels can last for more than twenty years (Anderson et al. 1995), the EIS stated that the "mercury content in sport fish will remain unchanged." Contrary to this claim and as predicted by the existing science, since 2000 both the brook trout and the arctic char in Star Lake have acquired high levels of mercury, resulting in restrictions on human consumption of these fish (annual advisories by Health Canada; the actual mercury levels are not publicly available).

New roads associated with the dam have increased access and angling pressure, so that decreased seasons and bag limits are now in place. Sticklebacks (*Gasterosteus aculeatus*) have appeared in the lake and have become abundant. They were probably introduced in nets used for an annual monitoring program "to determine the suitability and success of the brook trout breeding program, the long term survival of the fingerlings, and the assessment of the status of brook and arctic char in Star Lake." (Jacques Whitford 2006). This is being carried out by the proponent on behalf of DFO, but the reports are internal and not publicly available.

Recent assessments submitted to DFO have shown that the Arctic char population has collapsed and few large brook trout remain (Jacques Whitford 2006). The report documents that angling effort declined in the previous two years (2004 and 2005) and that success rates have fallen off considerably. The catch per unit effort (fish/h) from standardised deeply set gill net sets for brook trout declined from 2.50 to 0.00 and for Arctic char from 3.50 to 0.00. Insufficient broodstocks were collected in 2004 and 2005, in spite of greatly increased levels of effort in time spent and gear deployed in both years. In 2005 only 14,560 trout eggs were collected (collection target 100,000 eggs). The mean length at age of the trout increased from 1999, but subsequently there has been a decrease in mean lengths. For the three-year- and four-year-old trout in 2003 mean (fork) lengths were 217 mm for the 3+ and 285 mm for the 4+ fish. There was a decrease after this time, and in 2005 the fork lengths averaged 172 mm for 3+ and 219 mm for 4+ trout. In addition, the annual mean condition factor of both species (the ratio of weight to length cubed) has declined significantly, indicating that oligotrophication has now followed any trophic upsurge. The condition factor for brook trout declined from 1.09 in 1999 to 0.88 in 2005. That for Arctic char declined from 1.09 in 1999 to 0.68 in 2004. Thus, the lack of adequate forage is quite clear. Over half the brookdstock now collected come from the artificial rearing program. From these new data it appears that the unique Star Lake salmonids are headed for extinction in their natural habitat. The striking degradation of a formerly pristine area and virtual elimination of the valuable trophy trout fishery are seen as sad losses by members of local communities (Byrne 2002).

Star Lake is a classic example of the changes science indicates should be expected when a lake is converted into a fluctuating reservoir. During the environmental impact assessment, several scientists, including one who had done research in the lake, and many local people expressed concern about the negative changes that would probably occur. However, federal and provincial authorities accepted an inadequate study, despite considerable criticism from these groups (Gibson et al. 1999). An EIS is conducted and financed by the proponent. As a result, the science it contains is often poor and biased in favour of the project proceeding. It is not uncommon for such studies to conclude that things will improve (Campbell and Parnrong 2000). The Star Lake development provides an example of scientific and local ecological knowledge being perverted owing to political and corporate pressures and weaknesses in the EIA process that combine to limit scientific and other forms of input to sources and interpretations that favour the corporate proponents.

As shown by other studies, weaknesses in the EIA process include assumptions that the future can be predicted, the marginalization of local and traditional knowledge, and a tendency to favour the implementation of monitoring programs that do not adequately address post-development impacts (Berkes 1988). Berkes suggests that post-EIA monitoring has primarily been done "to fulfill legal obligations rather than aiming to mitigate real impacts and trying to improve understanding of environmental systems so that similar mistakes can be avoided in the future."

CASE STUDY FOUR: URBAN RIVERS IN ST JOHN'S

The urban rivers and lakes of St John's are unusual for a city in that they are in general healthy ecosystems, and although enriched with nutrients from farm and urban sources, they are not polluted. Scientific studies have shown that salmonid production is exceptionally high in these systems (Gibson and Haedrich 1988). These studies and popular appreciation of these river and lake resources have put pressure on authorities to cease the unplanned degradation of the rivers (through channelization, input of sewage, and so on). Streams have been enhanced to restore habitat diversity, and sources of sewage have been diverted to sewage systems. When these initiatives were undertaken, the St John's City Council consisted of members who were co-operative with conservation groups. It adopted a resolution (in October 1982) "that priority be given to good conservation practices in any development affecting waterways undertaken or approved by the city," and it assisted with enhancement of streams and with education related to stream ecology. Unfortunately, today the council and staff appear to have little interest in conserving the city's rivers and have a confrontational attitude towards conservation groups.

An example of present planning that is hostile to the conservation of these rivers is a proposed development, the Southwest Expansion Area, in which the remaining headwaters of the Rennies River, a major river in the city, will be developed. At a public hearing a number of presentations from scientists, conservation groups, and concerned citizens pointed out that in the absence of changes to this proposal, the loss of wetlands and forest cover would cause radical changes in the hydrology, so that flooding would increase. They argued that increased erosion and resulting "flashiness" of the river and related deterioration in water quality would have deleterious effects on the biological resource. They also suggested that eco-hydrological management be implemented in the form of water retention devices to control water discharge and to treat runoff by wetland construction and by means of phytoremediation techniques, which are well known and sustainable (Gibson 2003). It was suggested that council take advantage of the significant expertise in watershed management and stream ecology that is available in the city, and professional scientists volunteered to help. The council rejected suggestions for water control; some councillors commented that the suggestions were "scandalous," and the mayor thought it insulting for scientists to try to advise city staff (*Telegram* 2003a). Instead, downstream flood defence measures such as flood walls have been built, bridges and the river outlet have been widened, and environmental science has been ignored. The Southwest Expansion Area is being paved and developed with apparently few constraints.

The effects of increased runoff on discharge and stream biota are well known. Conceptually, the effects of development are not difficult to understand and have been demonstrated in some parts of the system. This suggests that pressure from wealthy developers is behind the Council's rejection of the scientists' advice and offer for support. By way of comparison, a second river, the Waterford River, flows into the western part of St John's. The headwaters of this system are under the jurisdiction of a second city, Mount Pearl. The Mount Pearl council collaborates with conservation groups to conserve this beautiful river system. The city staff participate in meetings with (NAACAP) Northern Avalon Atlantic Coastal Action Program and has supported the correct construction of bridges and culverts, conservation of wetlands and buffer strips, construction of settling ponds, and so on.

CONCLUSION

In Indian Bay, members of the local community were concerned about the collapse of their freshwater fishery and were appalled at the deterioration of the watershed. The fishery management plans in place were inappropriate and were not enforced. A combination of local knowledge and scientific research helped set the stage for restoration of the resource and for the ecosystem as a whole, with benefits to the community. A hiatus occurred briefly because of incomplete transfer of knowledge but in general, the Indian Bay case provides an ideal model for moving knowledge and harnessing it in support of conservation that could be applied elsewhere.

In the case of the TLH, everything appeared to be in place to ensure that the road did not threaten fish habitat or passage: a sound objective study (ecology and habitats), an appropriate policy framework (no "net loss" of productive fish habitat), targeted legislation (the Fisheries Act), and effective enforcement (DFO agents on the ground). However, very serious habitat destruction and fragmentation of streams occurred. This is a common problem and may occur because construction companies can get away with careless construction at road crossings, and so have little incentive to take more care, and because governments concerned about costs tend to trade off habitat and passage concerns for cost concerns unless they are subject to scrutiny and to challenge. Authorities that should be enforcing habitat conservation like to be seen as cooperative with developers, and not interfering with "progress," and field personnel may not always be fully cognizant of the regulations and the risks associated with poor culvert installation. Whatever the reason, it took the local communities, the LMN leadership, and the availability of appropriate scientific expertise and funding from a university research project to generate the research and political pressure required to reverse significant environmental damage. The University interface provided the scientific knowledge (published) and the quantitative data needed to have regulations enforced (Gibson et al. 2005).

In the ideal model, knowledge production and knowledge flows should maximize ecosystem health and community health, incorporating LK, TK, and scientific knowledge, and linking these to existing research and to existing policy frameworks, in order to influence policy development, implementation, enforcement, and local actions. The Indian Bay case fits this model, despite a minor hiatus and ongoing vulnerability related to access to leadership and other resources. In this case, success has been based on the willingness of all parties to pursue this ideal. The Labrador stream crossings study appears to have harnessed LK and science to achieve some restoration, but the full extent of the improvements that will be achieved is not yet known. Knowledge can of course exist but nevertheless be ignored, as in the case of the rivers of St John's, or perverted, as in the case of Star Lake. In the case of Indian Bay and the TLH work, a love of nature and respect for their natural environment within the local communities, linked to the social and cultural importance associated with this environment and its fisheries resources, provided the impetus needed for knowledge to channel the political process in the direction of conservation.

Political and economic pressures surround the conservation of any natural resource, and where there is sufficient political pressure from developers, the authorities will not always enforce existing policies and laws and, in the process, will fail to put into effect ecosystem conservation measures. The flow of knowledge from design to implementation of regulations for the benefit of ecosystem and community health may be perverted or blocked, despite the presence of an appropriate policy framework. Sufficient political pressure must be applied so that legislation is enforced, and the network of policy actors must be willing and able to learn and adapt their approaches and policies. The cases of Star Lake and the urban rivers in St John's illustrate situations where poor science and economic power, in the case of Star Lake, and arrogance and probable political influence on the part of developers, in the case of St John's, have blocked or perverted the influence of science on policy.

In the first two cases, local and Métis residents considered ecologically responsible policy development and implementation to be in their social, cultural, political, and economic best interests. In the latter cases, powerful corporate interests were able to marginalize the issues and concerns of other groups concerned with environmental impacts, and scientists and their allies lacked the political power of the Métis or the grassroots conflict-resolution structure of the Indian Bay case. These findings are consistent with theories of political economy that suggest capitalist accumulation often prevails as a policy objective, portraying the policy process as dynamic, conflict-ridden, and socially and politically driven with an economic bias (Hessing and Howlett 1997). Knowledge becomes only one of a host of factors that determine policy outcomes in an environment where powerful economic actors exert substantial influence over government policy-makers.

10

Knowledge Flows, Conservation Values, and Municipal Wetlands Stewardship

BRIAN MCLAREN, TIM HOLLIS,
CATHERINE ROACH, KATHLEEN BLANCHARD,
ERIC CHAURETTE, AND DEAN BAVINGTON

The official program goals of Municipal Wetland Stewardship (MWS) in the town of Gander, a small inland centre in Newfoundland with an economy dependent today on air traffic control of international flights over the North Atlantic, read this way: "To restore, enhance, and protect important wetlands in Gander; to promote a greater appreciation of wetlands and wetland values; to have wetland values included in the municipal plan." These goals approximate the goals of eleven other rural Newfoundland and Labrador communities that have signed on to the Eastern Habitat Joint Ventures (EHJV) program, and they reflect the community-level dissemination of the goals of a government-initiated program employing voluntary stewardship agreements to protect, maintain, and enhance the abundance and quality of wetlands. The goals are consistently interrelated, in that knowledge and values are not separate but intertwine. The goals are both cognitive, seeking knowledge gain, and affective, seeking attitudinal or value changes.

This chapter discusses knowledge and its role in determining and predicting conservation values as they relate to Newfoundland's MWS program. Our study was motivated by the Coasts Under Stress goal to examine the interaction between scientific and local knowledge in developing resource management policy, specifically the contributions of each to decision making and to education. The chapter considers the concepts of "knowledge" and "values," and their often-blurred boundaries when employed in environmental education and conservation programs, especially in relation to the broader issue of policy-making. We examine whether an increased willingness to protect wetland resources, which are normally subordinate to "upland" resources in a Canadian society with agrarian roots, occurs as a result of increased knowledge or as an exercise in the instruction of values, as witnessed in some rural Newfoundland communities.

More specifically, we discuss how knowledge, or a particular construct of knowledge, is used by the program managers of the "official" MWS in Newfoundland and Labrador and how this knowledge is received by people in rural municipalities. We find that because of its value bias, residents of some communities may discover a re-interpretation of natural surroundings, new knowledge, or enhanced attitudes and values that promote a conservation ethic among people in the community, while residents of other communities will find that the program challenges the traditional ecological knowledge that sustained early settlers in rural Newfoundland and that may still be drawn upon to sustain local resources in modern times. We start with these ironies. We then explore uncertainty, deterministic and stochastic thinking, and we describe a special dissonance that appears as a lack of agreement among community members, or even as a dissonance in the mind of the same community member, on how to approach wetlands in a modernized society. We close with an ambitious advocacy for stewardship as a way to address new environmental challenges in an uncertain world.

Stewardship has succeeded in entering popular consciousness through numerous public policy applications. It is recognized in both Canada and the United States through initiatives such as the government of Canada Habitat Stewardship Program for Species at Risk, the Stewardship Action Plan for Canada, the Marine Stewardship Council (a global NGO that certifies commercial fisheries as sustainably managed), and the Pesticide Environmental Stewardship Program (developed by the US Environmental Protection Agency as a voluntary public/private partnership to reduce pesticide risk). Stewardship, however, is a much-used term with no commonly accepted definition (Meidinger 1998), being employed to describe activities as diverse as those of "NIMBY" activists (Lerner 1993) and of government land acquisitions aimed at preserving endangered species. We limit the term to those environmental philosophies, policies, and actions that incorporate a notion of people caring for or being responsible for a local area or resource. People involved in stewardship may be a neighbourhood group opposing the development of a nearby treasured area or residents taking responsibility for management decisions about a local resource. In the sense adopted here, stewardship properly refers to the wide range of actions that people take to care for their local environment. The key component of a stewardship definition is that the actions of environmental protection that people undertake must be *voluntary* – they are not a response to the threat of punitive measures.

The knowledge flow in the functioning of the MWS program can be described thus: the EHJV transfers knowledge to the community members that their local wetlands provide critical habitat for waterfowl – something they may not have known – and knowledge of how local wetlands can best be preserved and enhanced. Stenmark (2002) describes these stages as "the what is" (wetlands are critical to waterfowl), "the what can be" (they can be preserved and enhanced), and "the means to attain it" (the expertise of the EHJV scientists) of environmental decision making, which is informed by knowledge. However, communities have to "learn" to want to protect the wetlands in order for any of this knowledge to be of practical consequence. It may appear that the educational role that MWS performs itself has effected change among community members, but the missing link between knowledge and actions remains to be filled by a value statement prioritizing the role of wetlands in waterfowl survival over competing philosophies and demands on the wetlands resource. If such a void in local understanding exists, it surely follows that the value statements directing the MWS program must be adopted by the community for this knowledge to create stewards of its members. There are instances where it is reasonable to suggest that the value statements have been adopted as a result of an instruction in values, not in knowledge.

If considered as a model for sharing knowledge alone, MWS creates new and explicit links between the local decision maker, scientific knowledge, and the knowledge of the consumptive user (figure 10.1). In traditional resource conservation programs in Canada, hunter-based goals are transparent at any scale, as are the knowledge dissemination goals of MWS. Traditionally, hunters provide information about their resource consumption and behaviour, which allows provincial decision-making bodies to complement it with largely scientific survey information, in order to set quotas or to open and close areas to hunting (figure 10.1A). Without a stewardship model, appreciative (non-consumptive) nature activities are carried out with local support and knowledge only, but local decision making is rarely integrated with matters of conservation, except perhaps in steering the urgency for

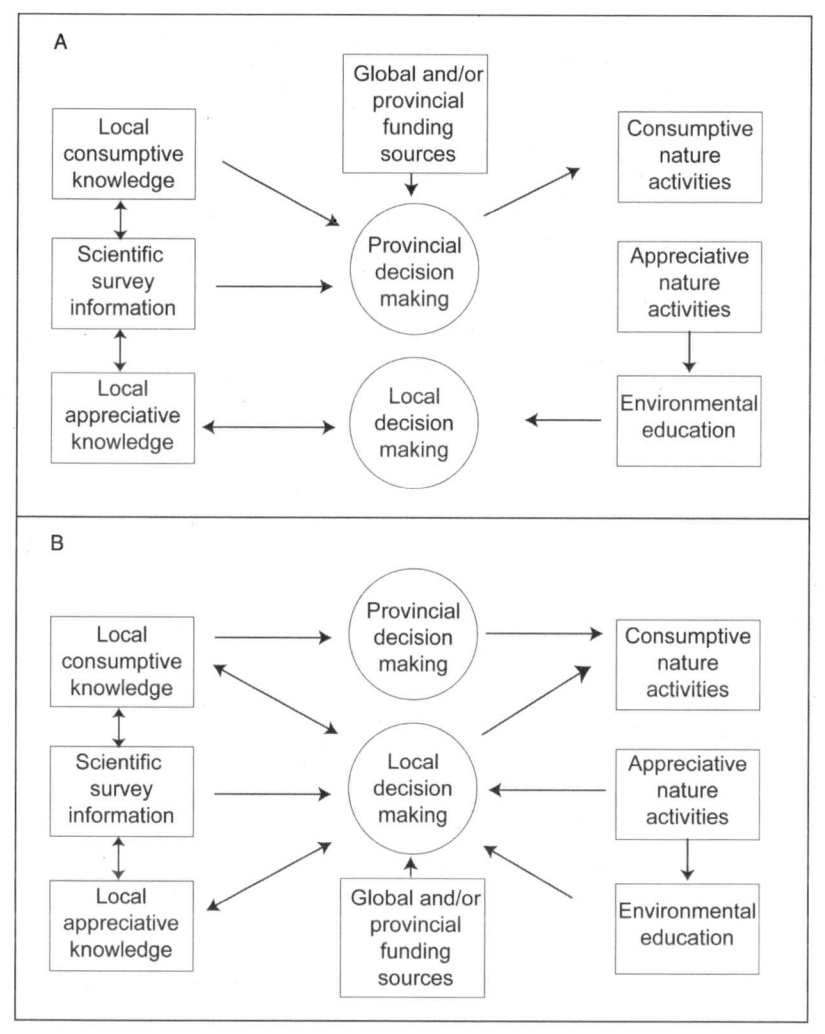

Figure 10.1 Knowledge flow in (A) traditional resource conservation programs in Canada and (B) Municipal Wetlands Stewardship (MWS) programs in Canada. MWS programs provide more opportunities for input based on local decision making.

scientific surveys or in garnering support for the creation of reserves. MWS results in a higher level of inclusiveness of individual views. As one advocate and community leader put it, "It has opened a lot of eyes. Overall, stewardship has made everybody more aware of what they've got." Also, stewardship appears to involve local decision making in preference to elite, centralized, and scientific-based decisions (figure

10.1b). Appreciative users share in the decision-making process that affects hunting policies, for example, at least as we saw in most MWS communities. One of our informants said, "It seems that people are more aware, not of the word 'stewardship,' but of the waterfowl around here. Talk to anyone and they will say the bird population has increased." No measurement substantiates this claim of an increase in bird populations. In fact, at least one hunter, who exhibited an impressive knowledge of local birds and wetlands, had formed a different opinion, without however discounting the value of the stewardship program's conservation role: "There aren't more birds now, people just think there are more birds because they've been made aware of them."

Admittedly, consumptive users are less privileged at higher levels of authority in stewardship relative to provincial hunter-based programs. Moreover, MWS does not allow for budgets to count birds, as might be expected in a science-based survey of stewardship efforts. Yet, hunters can possibly be more empowered locally in MWS. In the words of one life-time hunter: "Stewardship for me is protecting the ecosystem and keeping habitat in natural shape, and spreading information to the community as a whole so that they follow the lead of the environmental groups."

The MWS program seeks to move people from a non-environmental to a pro-environmental perspective and to make unnecessary the threat of legislated sanctions or expensive land acquisition. Laws are passed because citizens and political leaders feel that they represent the will of the majority and that in a democracy, the roots of legislation may be found in the wishes, requirements, and values of the public that the lawmakers represent. True authority, natural authority, is not frozen in hierarchy but is continuously recycled back through the society from which it emanates (M'Gonigle 1986). While the goal of all citizens taking responsibility for the environment seems to belong to an ideal world, stewardship and legislation are perhaps not as far apart as they appear at first sight, since a wish to protect the environment is required of the majority of citizens for such laws to exist in a democracy. Consequently, in order for legislated conservation policies to work, people at all levels of society must understand that it is in their own interest to work for conservation (Myers 1990), an understanding that is also required for successful stewardship.

Thus, the key theoretical difference between legislation related to stewardship and command-and-control legislation may be stated in terms of the knowledge and values of the steward, which flow directly into the decision-making process, rather than being filtered through centralized policy-makers (Holling 2003). This point is part of the depiction in our schematic of MWS (figure 10.1). Stewardship is succinctly summarized as empowering community members to act directly on their local knowledge, values, and motivations to protect the natural environment. At all levels, when stewardship is in place, knowledge quality improves over legislated sanctions, and knowledge flow is increased over both legislation and land acquisition.

The use of "formalized" stewardship agreements is seen as a way to accomplish wetlands protection goals at a community level "through indirect programs of policy change and public education related to wetland values" (EHJV, n.d.). Although the MWS program may produce direct changes that foster habitat-related objectives, such as a town plan that bans wetland development, the changes in perception of residents of the community that indirectly contribute to these objectives are arguably more important. In addition to drawing on observations from Gander and other MWS communities visited by our research team, we will now draw extensively from research results from three rural Newfoundland communities: Stephenville Crossing, one of the first signatories to the EHJV; Parsons Pond, a more isolated and economically depressed Northern Peninsula community; and Glovertown, a more prosperous community with a varied economy, one that is also home to many employees of an adjacent national park. Neither Parsons Pond nor Glovertown are part of the MWS program, but they served for us to provide good comparisons for understanding local ethics.

Major achievements in Stephenville Crossing include no-hunting designations for The Sanctuary within the municipality, rejuvenation of the Prairie, a small fen in the centre of town, and an increase in community participation in bird watching. Attributing all these changes to the program is misleading; for example, the town plan had already designated the protected area as a no-development zone. In Parsons Pond, recreational use of wetlands, other than as a part of subsistence hunting and berry-picking, is nearly unknown, and interest in developing trail infrastructure for community use is very low. Glovertown, in contrast, hosts a system of over four kilometers of trails and boardwalks around a fen and bog system near the community. The privately developed recreational area is prized by many community members and offers viewing opportunity that leads to a protective attitude toward these wetlands specifically. The area used by the trail system, Ken Diamond

Memorial Park, was not chosen for its significance as waterfowl habitat, and protective attitudes have arisen for recreational rather than ecological stewardship reasons.

In 1986, Canada and the United States signed the North American Waterfowl Management Plan and committed themselves to a long-term program of joint ventures aimed at assuring the survival and increase of waterfowl populations and the preservation of the habitats on which their survival depends. These ventures, including the EHJV, combined the resources of federal and provincial governments with those of non-government conservation organizations to protect and manage important wetland habitat in particular regions. Regions were chosen both for their biological significance and by application from communities containing significant waterfowl populations within their municipal boundaries. Thus, MWS may be considered as a form of co-management involving a partnership between the EHJV and a community. While co-management arrangements can involve no more than a token participation of the community, the MWS arrangement appears to constitute a level of community empowerment and participation tending toward "citizen control" (Arnstein 1969). At the same time, it is important to recognize the *real* goals for the EHJV. Their primary objective is to preserve wetlands considered important for the survival and increase of waterfowl populations.

Of the 75 percent of the program's funding that comes from the United States, one-half is contributed by the US Fish and Wildlife Service and the other half by Ducks Unlimited, a group pursuing the interests of sport hunters. The remainder comes from Wildlife Habitat Canada, whose funding derives from hunting licenses and conservation stamps. An anthropocentric basis, then, motivates the EHJV and, consequently, the MWS. Furthermore, managers do not measure, as examples, a wetland's role in water purification, in reduction of soil erosion, or as a source of food for moose. These choices are value-based directives, originating from the anthropocentric motivation to protect waterfowl. The most serious limitation imposed by the EHJV, by virtue of its underlying motivation, is in the selection of qualifying "stewardship communities" (Hollis 2004). Thus, while the program functions in such a way as to appear to have delegated power to local communities, the extent to which it reflects "citizen control" is ultimately limited by the fact that the EHJV chooses the values that underlie the participatory management arrangement.

A first irony, then, is that the utility of the program varies according to the scale at which it is viewed. Why do local people choose to voluntarily protect and enhance their local natural environments and resources? Ultimately, any conservation effort is motivated by some perceived benefit: the natural environment is valued when it is perceived to possess utility, be it economic, recreational, or purely psychological utility, a use tied to a particular goal of an individual or a community (Burningham and O'Brien 1994), which can motivate that individual or community to act to protect it. We heard it this way in one community, and similar words were expressed in many other communities: "I don't know of any use of the wetland, so why would I want to preserve it?"

Generally, the globally embedded goals of the EHJV are unknown to local communities participating in MWS. The program theoretically empowers local knowledge (of wetlands and waterfowl habitat) to protect local wetlands, but actually functions by creating a *new value* that belongs neither to EHJV nor to traditional rural ethics: local wetlands formerly perceived as "useless bogs" become "beautiful." In this discussion, Glovertown's Ken Diamond Memorial Park is the best example. As one resident of the community stated, "It's a beautiful area in the way it has been developed. It was perceived as a bog, as useless land. Now you can see the fragile ecosystem." Ken Diamond Memorial Park conveys no more superior ecological benefits than it did as a "useless bog," but because it now conveys benefits to a new community by way of the development of boardwalks and trails that allow those with no prior reason to come in contact with the wetland to "see its beauty," it is valued accordingly (Hollis 2004). This perception is more a change in values than a change in knowledge.

Since Confederation, Newfoundland has undergone considerable economic and physical modernization, such as the switch from a merchant to an open market, a cash economy, and pursuit of the material goods of its mainland North American neighbours (Philbrook 1968; Omohundro 1994). While not independent of these, a further change that is less visible includes new cultural standards, such as the way Newfoundlanders perceive and relate to their natural environment. We heard frequent references to how community members have, since the inception of the MWS program, learned about the role of wetlands and about different ways of valuing nature and relating to it. This new knowledge frequently conflicted with that expressed by hunters (Hollis

2004), creating the appearance of knowledge tensions that are, in reality, value differences.

Value conflicts arise when one particular set of values is promoted or privileged, since by necessity it is privileged at the expense of another (Stenmark 2002). The new way of knowing nature, which seems to supplant traditional values, is what may be referred to as "intellectual modernization" (Hollis 2004). Some respondents reflected, even acknowledged, such a change or tension within themselves, one that arises acutely as a result of the value dissemination of the MWS program: in reference to the changes at The Sanctuary in Stephenville Crossing, "I've been hunting since I was a child and I love the land, but the world is moving on."

Knowledge changes as needs change, brought about by modernization. As the local environs become less important to everyday survival, people form a new relationship with the land. More accurately, the value of the local environs alters itself in the hierarchy of community needs and decision making. MWS can be portrayed as part of this modernization, arguably by necessity, as traditional ecological knowledge diminishes; it represents a "new knowledge" of the value of local wetlands. In summary, there are positive and negative effects of facilitating wetland access through the development of passive recreational facilities ("nature trails") in natural areas. Such development fosters attachment and protective attitudes, and particularly affords the opportunity for people who would not normally do so to come into contact with nature (Hollis 2004). Hunters in our surveys were more ambivalent toward MWS, since they were, to paraphrase one respondent, left to wonder why anyone would wish to walk around a wetland, having spent a day of work in one. Hunters learned through years of using wetlands of their importance for subsistence, even survival, purposes, but this traditional stewardship ethic appears to be marginalized by the EHJV (Hollis 2004). A second, rather acute irony arises here. From the point of view of environmental ethics, a conservation program funded by sport hunters and dependent upon the continuation of sport hunting, which also tends at a local scale to marginalize subsistence hunting, is problematic.

The adaptation of communities to a new way of understanding wetlands when exposed to MWS (part of what we term "modernization") relative to the ironic inertia identified in the sport hunters' motivations for the EHJV program (they are slower to change) is precisely an example of the interplay between scales referred to by Ommer et al.

(this volume, chap. 2). Moreover, marginalizing local community members who prioritize consumptive use values is not merely ironic; it is also unjust (Hollis 2004). If it were to be taken to the extreme, privileging preservation values would leave human society precisely nowhere to live and survive in the natural environment (Cronon 1995). Also in a practical sense parks or waterfowl sanctuaries cannot be created out of every locally accessible piece of the natural environment in order to fulfill the protective goals of sport hunters or environmentalists elsewhere.

Thus, the knowledge and value changes brought about by the stewardship program are complex, and they highlight issues of cognitive dissonance, irony, and gentrification. "New" knowledge creates an altered perception of traditional practices and their value in the modern world. Significantly, this change is the opposite of the creation of "wisdom" as Ommer et al. present it (this volume, chap. 2), from the perspective of Eastern philosophy, where to live knowledge is to have wisdom. Thus, "new" knowledge in MWS is both humbling and enabling in a startling way. Consider this quote from an advocate of the program: "I think people are becoming more cognizant of the damage done by prior generations and they want to protect this for future generations. I think that in rural communities people are more aware now. You have some activists around, too. Newfoundlanders have been demonized as ignorant and evil during Greenpeace seal campaigns. Many were turned off the term 'environmentalist,' although that is in effect what they are."

A third irony, expressed in the above quote, involves the appearance of new social norms in embedded communities that marginalize hunting activities that were once part of rural life. An important part of this process is the way that MWS provides a new context for the evaluation of local wetlands. The "new" knowledge of the role of wetlands as habitat for waterfowl is actually, not new to those who continue to hunt for subsistence purposes, and the key is not the knowledge but the promotion and subsequent adoption of environmentalist values. New ways of knowing nature – increasingly, developing aesthetic appreciation at the expense of valuing its role as a subsistence resource – will inevitably become more important as traditional stewardship practices become less relevant to everyday rural Newfoundland life.

Traditional ecological knowledge has diminished because reliance on, and thus everyday contact with, local nature has diminished. It is becoming less important to know about nature, and thus nature itself is becoming less important. A final irony or complexity here is the recurrent and problematic assumption by local residents when they first hear about stewardship that it is associated with an alienation of their traditional rights. They fear that managers of a stewardship program might dismiss traditional rights and values by fostering new, appreciative uses and dictate unwanted community changes by assuming that residents are embarking on stewardship for the first time. In fact, stewardship as a way of life in using and protecting resources – although other words were used to describe it – must have existed for centuries among residents of Newfoundland and Labrador. As defined by Roach (2000), stewardship means that the caretakers and the beneficiaries are the same. Historically, this form of autonomy and self-legislation existed in rural Newfoundland through a hunter-gatherer relationship between community members and the land (Nemec 1993). The relatively pristine natural environs on the doorsteps of communities that were, by and large, treated as common property (Okihiro 1997) have for centuries been a key source of subsistence activities such as hunting, trapping, wood cutting, berry picking, and small-scale farming (Overton 1980; Omohundro 1994). These concepts of stewardship may be lost by delivering the message that only looking at resources, rather than using them for subsistence, will allow people to appreciate and protect them. Thus, managers of the MWS program who work with the local interest in consumptive activities repeat frequently that "stewardship is not about taking away hunting areas." These managers may be taking a preferred, though unspoken, route toward motivating people in conservation. That is, if traditional knowledge and uses are not respected, an older wisdom may be lost, and the environment may suffer.

Moving to our next section, we distinguish between knowledge movement and value instruction by providing examples. One can learn about the role of wetlands as habitat for waterfowl and as an integral part of a functioning ecosystem, but that knowledge alone does not dictate either a protective or a harmful decision or act. Empirical research that finds little correlation between increased environmental knowledge and pro-environmental behaviour or concern (there are several examples: Tracy and Oskamp 1983; Vining and Ebreo 1990; Krause 1993; Grob 1995; Furman 1998) brings into question the role that knowledge plays in the functioning of the MWS program. That the bog was previously "useless" most likely suggests that it was merely useless to the individual. It may be of more "use" since it serves the purpose of waterfowl habitat (about which the individual has now been educated), but it may become significantly useful only when the individual has learned an appreciation of waterfowl. None of this is to say that the knowledge imparted by MWS is entirely redundant. As stated by one community leader of the MWS program, "What we've been doing is slowly educating ourselves." And by another, "[The program] has certainly increased awareness of birds. No one knew we had so many birds before." We heard many statements of this kind: "I know that the wetland gives me a nice place to walk so I would like to see it preserved."

Some of the knowledge exchange becomes formalized as environmental education, especially for children and visitors to the community. One recurrent example is the construction of interpretive centres. Attitudes change as a result of this kind of activity initiated by MWS. The pattern was described by one community leader in this way: "Kids are educated now and they then educate their parents. At first, people misunderstood wetlands protection. They thought it would mean their rights being taken away, land expropriated." So what is being taught and learned? People begin to learn specifics about the visitation by ducks and other waterfowl and gain an appreciation for diversity of waterfowl. They learn about the role of wetlands as habitat for waterfowl and as an integral part of a healthy ecosystem. They learn different ways of valuing nature and of relating to it.

In some ways, then, the mechanism by which stewardship arises from new knowledge is fairly straightforward: as knowledge increases in one individual or community, an interest in sharing this knowledge grows. In general, people involved in co-management will talk about a change in their own awareness, attitudes, and values (Blanchard, unpublished data). Because the MWS agreements are knowledge-based (people speak of "new awareness"), a unique form of empowerment acts in favour of the stewardship efforts. For example, consider this statement from a resident of an MWS community: "I know that I have a greater appreciation for wetlands and from talking to others I believe they have learned quite a bit and feel that just walking around the park is, in itself, a learning experience." The result of knowledge sharing is expressed by the same respondent in an enthusiastic fashion, revealing even a desire to return information to government in a progressive rather than punitive, fashion: "There's a growth in our own awareness and what our residents and other people come to know about us. People here say, 'It's no longer just about [our community]. We're helping birds outside, all up and down the coast.' Governments and politicians need to be made aware of our efforts."

Yet, values provide the lens through which one interprets knowledge. In demonstrating how science alone cannot be employed to formulate environmental decisions, Stenmark (2002) notes how all environmental policies are based on attitudes and judgments, more often implicitly than explicitly stated, about what is valuable, what should be encouraged, and whose interests should be satisfied. As Ommer et al. (this volume, chap. 2) note, since all theoretical knowledge falls short of reaching full truth, uncertainty is inherently involved in policy decisions. It is further impossible to formulate any decision unless our knowledge is supplemented with certain value judgments. We may *know*, for example, the maximum sustainable yield of a waterfowl population, we may possess the knowledge of how to realize it, and, additionally, we may know that to do so would destroy a neighbouring endangered species. We may indeed be certain about all of these things. However, what *ought* to be done is not something we "know" in any scientific sense (Stenmark 2002), since a value statement, prioritizing either productive values or values of preserving the endangered species, is required to make a decision pertaining to a wetland. Knowledge itself may be capable of being distinct from opinion, but the decisions on which that knowledge is based are always a matter of value-laden opinion.

The stewardship arrangement, in which the community is both the caretaker and the benefactor of its decisions, tends to eliminate externalities, the situation in which the full costs or benefits of a decision are not borne by the decision maker. Employing local knowledge tends to reduce or eliminate such externalities, not only because decisions informed by such knowledge are more likely to be made with an awareness of the damaging or depleting consequences of those decisions but moreover because they are more likely to be made with consideration for the needs, aspirations, and values of *local* people.

Among random interviews, there are unsurprisingly many comments that suggest that local knowledge is simply more accurate. Such comments may be motivated by local value judgments and a distrust of centralized power. It can be difficult to differentiate between those who assume they know more and consider managers' knowledge inferior and those who, for many reasons, just resent government. Furthermore, a wish to be involved in the management of a wetland, based on a judgment of its value, is probably as likely to produce such a response. The most frequent responses illustrating a view that local knowledge and decision making are superior to government initiatives came from residents of Parsons Pond. These ranged from the well-elaborated ("I'd like to see more protection, but I don't want to see a bureaucrat who has never stepped on a marsh telling us what to do. It has to be very carefully thought out. [For example,] I'm concerned with the ban of lead shot. You've got to employ local knowledge. That study [on which the ban on lead shot was based] was made in the US and it doesn't apply in Canada. We don't have the problems they did. Now we are injuring more birds [with steel shot] than killing them") to the more succinct ("People here know more about the area than anyone else. Government should listen to the people who know") to the more provocative ("It's not really necessary [to educate the community about the wetland]; everybody is aware of what it is and its benefits. I don't think the government should have any say at all [in managing the wetlands]; it should be someone who grew up around these areas").

Respect for traditional "rights" to the commons is separate from respect for traditional knowledge and must be applied cautiously against modern transportation tools that provide greater access, such as all-terrain vehicles, speedboats, and snowmobiles. The alienation felt by many new-generation residents from a natural wisdom that came from living off of the land must also caution managers. Local people cannot claim in-depth knowledge about local ecosystems or profess any commitment to stewardship simply by virtue of membership in families of long-standing residency in a community. However, it is also a misassumption that environmental education will, at worst, have no effect (De Young 1993), and the danger exists that this new knowledge will prevail at the expense of a traditional knowledge that encompasses exactly the environmental ethic that the program seeks to foster.

Stewardship can act as a safeguard against the notion that knowledge and science are infallible. MWS can avoid the problem inherent in the "control" style of managerial ecology of failing to recognize that nature is much more variable than ecologists and biologists generally know it to be from their observations of only a small time period (Pimm 1991; Bavington 2002). While wildlife managers dominating decision making in other programs may seek to produce the desired number of ducks by working with habitat conservation and hunting regulations, evaluations of the success of MWS tend not to rely on such simple assessments of duck numbers. Hence, the program is also not frustrated by unexpected variability in natural populations. Managers perceive that part of the program's success results from its recognition of natural change; they give up on the idea of fully controlling population numbers or of creating and managing a stable ecosystem where nature is "in balance." This change of perspective from deterministic modelling of nature to a recognition of the role of stochastic variables fundamentally alters human thinking that nature can be managed. It moves us from a hierarchical "dominion model," in which we see ourselves as exerting rightful mastery and control over nature, to a more ecologically sound "stewardship" model, which seeks to flatten the hierarchy and to emphasize, instead, care, restraint, and sustainability. Such a change is part, as well, of a conceptual shift in philosophy of resource management. Biologists today are increasingly advised to recognize control as an impossible task. This change does not diminish the importance of habitat conservation, but it does invoke a new challenge to work with human communities, in addition to the protected areas themselves, in order to offer species the greatest chance of recovery.

Knowledge must be treated with caution when it is employed by managers as an unchallengeable basis for decision making, not only because it is not infallible but equally because values, not knowledge, ultimately dictate decision making. The traditional relationship, whereby science has spoken and therefore there is nothing left to discuss, is no longer acceptable (Leiss 2001). As Gibbons (1999, 83–4) states, "The old image of science working autonomously will no longer suffice. Rather, a reciprocity [*sic*] is required in which not only does the public understand how science works but, equally, science understands how its public works." The problem of how knowledge affects very different outcomes, depending on the values upon which it is engaged, needs to be clear at the outset. When knowledge, whether scientifically or locally generated, is merely employed to disseminate a particular value or ideal, then we feel this motive must be made explicit. When it is not, knowledge can become a tool of power, and stewardship will operate merely under the illusion that local values are not filtered through centralized policy makers, as happens with legislation and land acquisition strategies when the role of values in shaping environment decisions are often peripheral in technical debates that accord greater weight to expert knowledge (Leiss 2001). In a successful conservation strategy, the values are honest and open.

Despite very thorough discussions of indigenous environmental ethics, Berkes (1999, 181) argues that the conservation practices of traditional peoples depend more on the fact that they will bear both the costs and benefits of their decisions rather than an inherent ethic toward conservation. This engages the question of whether hunters value local wetlands and other environs only because of their subsistence resource value and thus whether this "traditional" form of stewardship is motivated primarily, or only, by needs to protect and conserve, dictated by a restricted economy and the need to survive. This is an important question, since this anthropocentric stance dictates that, should the local natural environment no longer directly benefit the community, it would cease to be of value (cease to be the beneficiary of stewardship). That is, if uses could be made of local wetlands that better benefited the community, including destructive uses, they would be chosen: in a restricted economy, wetlands would be sold out for jobs. However, this is not what Hollis (2004) found.

We argue that communities with "traditional" stewardship values have learned lessons that can be used to address modern resource problems but that these lessons are being marginalized by modernization. In rural Newfoundland, there is a unique way of knowing the local natural environment, because people are participants in the landscape. Hollis (2004) found that this was particularly true for residents of Parsons Pond. As Rolston (1995, 377) argues, "Science understands how landscapes come to be and how they now function as communities of life. But people, too, form their own communities of life." This is what is unique about stewardship in rural Newfoundland. Today, local wetlands are valued by community members in rural Newfoundland for reasons as diverse as providing venues for moose hunting or rabbit snaring, places for the peace and tranquility of a walk, tourist attractions, waterfowl habitat, filtering systems for the water supply, or just because they have been there for thousands of years (Hollis 2004).

In many cases, it is important to community members that these values will continue to benefit future generations, and the values that the local wetlands hold for them bear significantly on their approach to decision that are made about them. The way that arguments are constructed that result in decisions pertaining to the local wetlands' environment suggest that ethical orientations influence individuals' positions on environmental issues. "Unfettered access to the great outdoors" (Felt and Sinclair 1995, 22) continues to be one of the most important values to residents of parts of Newfoundland. Traditional hunting and gathering activities continue to be perceived as a right of rural life (Okihiro 1997), a "regional mark of distinction," an "expression of self-esteem" (Omohundro 1994), and a revered part of community life, if not an imperative for survival during harsh economic climates (Cadigan 2002). So would these rights be sold out for new, strictly economically motivated initiatives? We will use the words of one of our respondents to answer this question: "It's a deep question. I feel that if we do that then we have nothing. I feel very strongly about that. I don't like that people can't stay [to find work], but we can't destroy it. I'm for finding a job somewhere else when you can always come back."

Relevant models for stewardship must be about using new knowledge and accepting new values only insofar as they prepare community members for new challenges in environmental management, like climate change, introduced species, and shifting social interest in outdoor activities. The mere fact that an individual knows that a decision or act is harmful or beneficial to the natural environment does not necessarily imply that he or she will or will not undertake it; thus stewardship, an explicit values exercise, has a unique role. Environmental crises are as much crises of technology as of (value-dictated) maladaptive behaviour (Weigel and Weigel 1978). In the sense that MWS explicitly articulates the goal of *changing* values, it recognizes the importance of changing behaviours in an uncertain world.

Alienation from nature is not what we hope "intellectual modernization" creates. Encouraging the appreciative enjoyment of the natural environment has benefits, but it does not always connect humans with nature (Cronon 1995). We close with a quote from one former town employee in Stephenville Crossing, who identified and articulated the actual time when he saw stewardship engaged in a new way. "[After the oil spill into the estuary in 1997], I was asked about the cleanup; I was asked numerous times 'how are the birds doing?' I knew for sure that the [wetland's] birds were important to the community."

PART FIVE

Moving Knowledge across Disciplines and between University and Community

11

Knowledge Movement in Response to Coastal British Columbia Oil and Gas Development: Past, Present, and Future

CHRISTOPHER R. BARNES, ROBERT H. DENNIS,
LORNE F. HAMMOND, MARJORIE J. JOHNS,
AND GREGORY S. KEALEY

INTRODUCTION

The principal challenge for humankind in the twenty-first century will be to achieve a truly sustainable relationship with the environment while developing socio-economic and cultural systems that ensure human rights, comfort, and dignity. This goal will require an improved understanding of the earth system and of its ability to respond to different scales of anthropogenic forcing (Zobeck 2001), as well as a better understanding of the dynamics of knowledge production and the interaction between scientific knowledge, government policy, and community values. Increasingly, there will be demands for new forms of social behaviour, strategic planning, and research funding and collaboration.

In this chapter, we use oil and gas exploration in British Columbia as the starting point for a discussion of the success and efficiency (or not) of knowledge transfer to date and the implications for both science and public policy, and we suggest ongoing transformations that are required to address the growing urgency of environmental and social restructuring.

We start by laying out a generalizable model of knowledge transfer that treats knowledge as inseparable from values. In a current example, the focus is on issues surrounding potential development of oil and gas reserves off the West Coast of British Columbia, Canada, issues that are politically charged and divisive and that have large socio-economic and environmental implications. Over the past decade, hydrocarbon development has occurred in the offshore Atlantic coast, and currently there is a debate whether to lift the moratorium on hydrocarbon development on the offshore Pacific coast. We briefly compare the British Columbia situation with the development of oil and gas resources in Newfoundland and Labrador, where the issue has not been contentious and has proceeded comparatively expeditiously.

The past, present, and possible future development of hydrocarbons reveals how knowledge is discovered, interpreted, archived, forgotten, and selectively considered within the political and decision-making processes in public policy formulation. This chapter discusses knowledge movement from different aspects of coastal British Columbia oil and gas development as it has occurred in the past and as it is being considered today and for the future. The complexity of the knowledge structure and movement is considered within a new model. We examine two components in detail: the relationship between knowledge transfer and values among the public and elected officials and the relationship between knowledge transfer and values within the community of science, particularly the earth sciences.

MODEL OF KNOWLEDGE MOVEMENT

The components of our model of knowledge movement include all or some of (1) stakeholders (government, communities, individuals, industry, academia); (2) locations (places, regions, environments); (3) individual and group biases (based on adopted values and accepted practices); (4) communication pathways (verbal, written, symbolic); (5) outcomes (policy, health, culture, technology, education/learning); (6) scale and types (ideas, questions, data, information, knowledge); and (7) time (past, present, future).

At the core of our model (figure 11.1) is an event (e.g., a proposal for offshore British Columbia oil and gas development) that directly affects a location, environments, communities, industries, and inhabitants. The event triggers identification of issues, questions, ideas, actions, and information that starts a process of knowledge movement. Distinctive to the example of proposed offshore oil and gas development (symbolized by the rig) is that such an event interfaces with all of Earth's physical systems: earth/land, ocean, and air/atmosphere. The sensitivity of the interfaces and their greater extent and visibility play

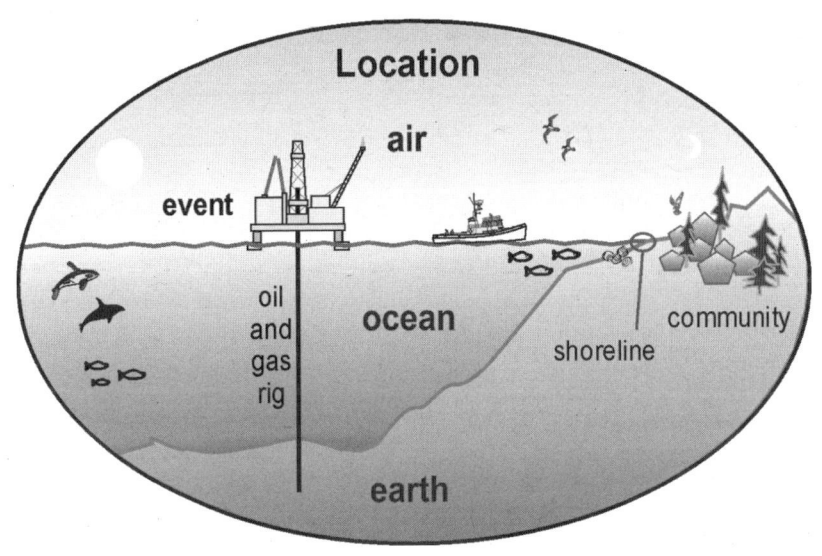

Figure 11.1 Dispersed impact of knowledge movement. An event that produces knowledge flow directly influences a region (e.g., a proposal for oil and gas development in coastal BC) and its communities, industries, and natural environments, including interfaces with the earth, ocean, and atmosphere.

important roles in the scale and development of issues. In our coastal British Columbia example, all three interfaces can move surfaces towards the shoreline, for example, through winds, ocean currents, and plate tectonics, which indicates a particularly vital and sensitive ecosystem. This sensitivity may pose additional challenges for West Coast oil and gas industries to prevent environmental damage, and it therefore makes this a particularly real and valuable example to model.

People as individuals and as members of groups (figure 11.2) identify issues and set forth to resolve them. People may be influenced by individual filtering systems, values, beliefs, and biases that they adopt through learning and lived experiences and that result in various forms of knowledge. People with similar value systems may naturally associate, collaborate, or work together in communities of knowledge, but sometimes people with different value systems also collaborate. This collaboration may promote a broader learning environment, but issues may also take longer to resolve because of greater available data, information, experiences, and potentially conflicting values. People may be involved in groups in different categories: community, academic, government, and industry groups (figure 11.2). We argue that the keys to

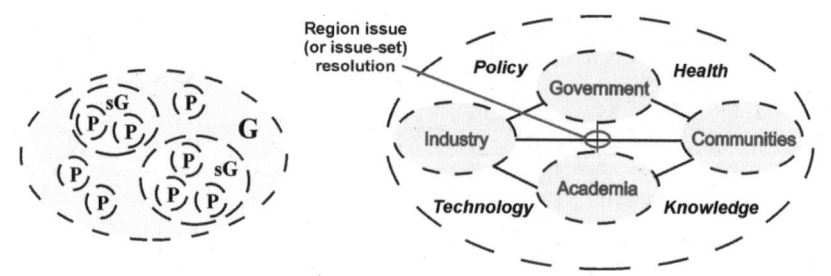

Figure 11.2 Participants and patterns of knowledge flow. Individuals (P), subgroups (sG), and groups (G) interact in categories such as a community, academia, government, and industry. Participants may be influenced by values adopted through experience and knowledge. Value systems and resolution of issues are critical for arriving at beneficial outcomes.

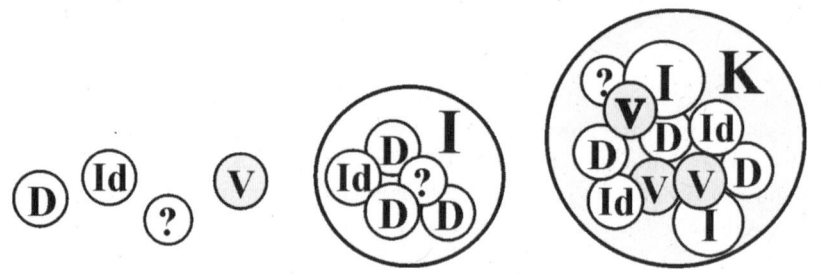

Figure 1.3 Components of Learning and Knowledge Bundels. Components of learning involve ideas (Id), questions (?), data collection (D), and values (V) and movement of "knowledge bundles" of information (I), and knowledge (K). A greater number of interactions may result in more complex knowledge bundles and outcomes.

issue resolution are communication, collaboration, knowledge transformation, and recognition and understanding of different value systems, so that negotiation may proceed. The positive outcomes that might result include new policies, regulations, technologies, and learning, accompanied by improved individual, community and ecosystem health.

Learning takes place at different levels and initially may start with questions, ideas, values, and data. When these are organized, movement to "knowledge bundles" occurs with the development of information and knowledge (figure 11.3). Knowledge movement (figure 11.4) initiated by an issue or issue-set may start in a historical archive of ideas, values, data, and knowledge bundles, which may be written, verbal, symbolic, or in some other form of record. New questions and ideas are formed and data and information is sought from locations, environ-

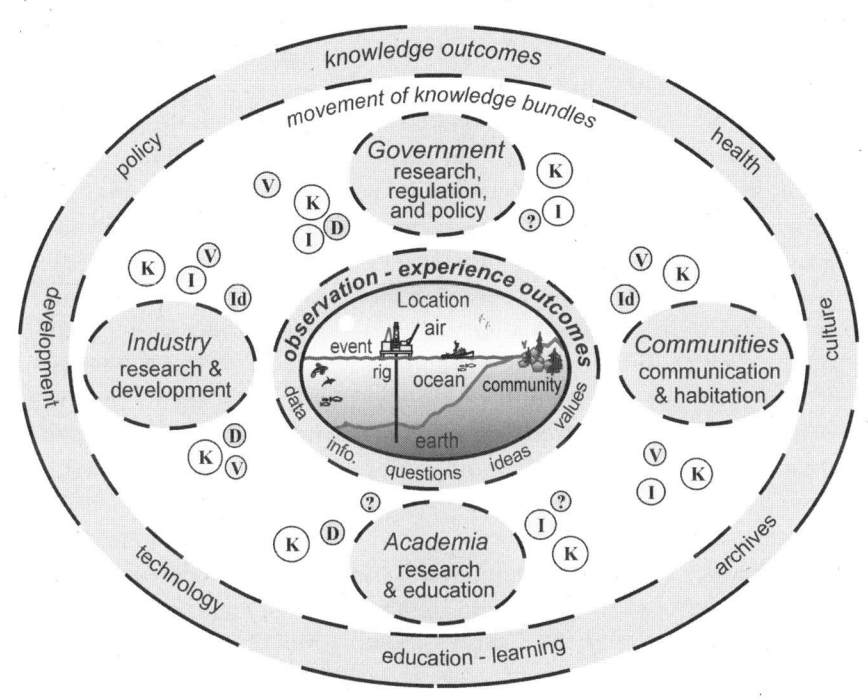

Figure 11.4 Time slice of knowledge flow. Knowledge bundles are born at a location and grow when new ideas and questions are formed. New data are collected and transformed to information in the process of conflict and resolution. Knowledge bundles develop and transfer from interacting individuals or groups. Knowledge flow is filtered (dashed lines) by values adopted by individuals and groups and by their experiences and knowledge. Components of learning involve ideas (Id), questions (?), data collection (D), values (V) and movement of "knowledge bundles" of information (I) and knowledge (K).

ments, and peoples. A complex set of issues, such as those triggered by potential offshore British Columbia oil and gas exploration, which interacts with all of Earth's interfaces (figure 11.1), may be best resolved with multiple participants, preferably from the four categories of academia, community, government, and industry (figure 11.2). If each group, with their own values and filter systems communicated, collaborated, and exchanged information and knowledge, a broader understanding of the issues, approaches to resolution by the groups, and the potential development of beneficial outcomes might result. Once resolution has occurred (even if it has been deferred), some knowledge bundles will descend to historical archives for future reflection, ideas generation, adaptation, and use.

In the rest of this chapter we look at two aspects of this model in detail, the relationship between values, knowledge, and policy in the interplay between government and the public (communities) and the role of disciplinary values (another type of community value) in the creation and application of scientific knowledge around oil and gas development. Examples from the early coastal British Columbia oil and gas economy show that this small-scale industry was accepted by the coastal communities, that it was integrated with and essential to them. Important were communications and links between the peoples and their activities within a mainly community resource-based economy. Changes to these communities occurred as the resource economy declined, oil spills occurred that were outside their control but affected their coastlines, and new economies developed (e.g., tourism). With these changes came new individual, group, and community values, growth, and knowledge.

Knowledge follows certain pathways and practices accepted by individuals and groups. Issues related to the Canadian Newfoundland and Labrador Accord and the British Columbia Moratoria illustrate how people with a variety of knowledge and value systems have produced different environmental, political, and economic outcomes. The knowledge pathways involve the opposition between economic benefits and environmental preservation. This conflict demonstrates the power of political and public will when in British Columbia events such as nearby oil spills are and locked in the minds of members of the West Coast public who favour environmental protection and when in Newfoundland disasters and loss of life (e.g., involving fishing boats or the *Ocean Ranger* oil rig collapse), which are not new to the culture, although obviously tragic, are accepted and oil and gas development is allowed to proceed.

APPLYING THE MODEL I: UNDERSTANDING ACCORDS, MORATORIA, AND GOVERNMENT POLICY ON THE BRITISH COLUMBIA AND NEWFOUNDLAND AND LABRADOR COASTS

Within the broader issues surrounding the history of Canada's East Coast development and West Coast non-development of offshore oil and gas, two defining features have come to characterize government policy: accords and moratoria. In Newfoundland and Labrador, a logical coastal context to juxtapose with British Columbia, the language of accord is appropriate because it signals both popular sentiments and inter-governmental co-operation on establishing a regulatory framework for development to proceed, despite the landmark sinking of the *Ocean Ranger* drilling rig in 1982, with the loss of eighty-four lives. An array of factors – including generally amiable environmental conditions, the location of the resource, and the need for industrial and economic development – led both the polity and the policy-makers alike to pursue development vigorously.

By contrast, a strong environmental movement, substantial economic diversification, and political opposition hindered the potential for development in British Columbia. While the polity remains divided over the desirability of development, federal and provincial policies have remained highly consistent in their opposition to offshore development, making "moratoria" the *mot de jour* since the early 1970s.

In this section we look at the role that epitomizing events, historical patterns, and economic self-interest played in shaping the values that explain the difference between the West Coast pattern and that on the East Coast. In Newfoundland and Labrador, science and human tragedy were "read" against a profound desire for economic and social development and thus proceeded; in British Columbia, conversely, even talk of development ceased in the wake of environmental disaster. The interaction of these considerations influenced public policy: by unpacking the epistemological underpinnings of "accord" and "moratoria," one sees how they have been historically and socially constructed and entrenched culturally on the East and West Coasts of Canada.

Newfoundland and Labrador

Oil and gas development became a policy issue on Canada's East Coast when the Hibernia oil field was found in 1979.[1] Little scientific opposition arose to counter the prospect of offshore development in Newfoundland and Labrador, where government allowed development to proceed even though jurisdictional and regulatory issues were not immediately resolved between the provincial and federal governments. The strong forces in support of development in Newfoundland and Labrador were its provincial identity and sense of distinctiveness within Confederation, and thus an entitlement to the resources of the offshore. Premier Brian Peckford took the issue to Supreme Court, and it ruled that the federal government had both ownership of and jurisdiction over the offshore areas and its resources. With the rise to power of the Progressive Conservative Party in 1984, Prime Minister Brian Mulroney and Newfoundland cabinet minister John Crosbie affirmed a commitment from the federal government that regardless of the court decision that the offshore would be treated as though it belonged to the province. When federal energy minister Pat Carney came to Newfoundland later that year, she stated, "Why don't we just leave the issue of jurisdiction. Why don't we just treat it 'as if you owned the resource' ... Why don't we run the offshore 'as if you owned it like Alberta'" (Nameth 1997, 116–17). This spirit of co-operation led to formally entrenching these principles in the Atlantic Accord in 1985 and in the Canada Newfoundland Atlantic Accord Implementation Act (creating the Canada–Newfoundland Offshore Petroleum Board) in 1987.

Along with the Atlantic Accord came a set of expectations, understandably, from both the government and the people of Newfoundland and Labrador that have not been fully realized. Among the agreement's purposes, it aimed "to recognize the right of Newfoundland and Labrador to be the principal beneficiary of the oil and gas resources off its shores" and "to recognize the equality of both governments in the management of the resource, and ensure that the pace and manner of development optimize the social and economic benefits of Canada as a whole and Newfoundland and Labrador in particular" (Canada 1985: section 2a and 2b). With scientific data and public opinion both favourable to development, it has proceeded. The blockage to moving knowledge, in this circumstance, can be found between the promises of the Atlantic Accord and its implementation act and other legislation involving fiscal redistribution, like equalization, all within the bureaucracy of the federal government. The people of Newfoundland and Labrador waited until 2005 for policy-makers to remedy this structural gap, so that they would be accorded the near-term social and economic benefits that the province promised. In 2005, a renegotiated Atlantic Accord promised a greater share of the oil and gas royalties to the Atlantic provinces.

Forgotten Flows of Knowledge: Coastal British Columbia's Early Oil Economy

The early history of the oil economy on British Columbia's north coast is worth remembering. About 1910 the first marine engines become available to small fishing boats. The oil-based economy had begun somewhat earlier on a very small scale. Fuel came from California to storage tanks and small refineries in Vancouver. In 1904, Union Oil barges began to supply Vancouver's BC Sugar Refinery. In 1911, Standard Oil delivered fuel to Powell River's pulp and paper plant and to mills at Port Alice and Ocean Falls. That same year, CPR began converting steamships from coal to fuel oil (Clapp 1985). The 1912-13 Nanaimo coal strike led other coastal steam operators to look at alternative fuels.

World War I encouraged Imperial Oil to build the IOCO refinery on Burrard Inlet. By 1923 the last steam tug had left British Columbia's shipyards as the marine industry converted to fuel oil, diesel or gasoline. The new fuels offered fast turnaround on refuelling, quick departures, compact storage, and reduced engine room crew size. Cheap marine transportation costs for moving oil made imports from east of the Rockies uncompetitive until completion of a pipeline in 1953. By then, Peruvian and Californian oil had changed life on Canada's north Pacific coast.

Typical of the 1930s was the north-coast fuel ship *B.C. Standard*. With a small, 150-horsepower engine, it carried 65,000 gallons of fuel. Its young, motivated crew drummed up accounts from fishing camps, float camps, and small logging operations, while salesmen went after the Vancouver head offices of large companies (McNeill 1980). The *Standard*'s owners commissioned a survey of the new energy market on the north coast (Mackenzie 1936) that revealed the extent of the oil industry in the area's economy.

In 1935, about 75 percent of the 5,000 boats in British Columbia's gill-net fishing fleet operated north of the Gulf of Georgia. Their small seven horsepower motors consumed 750,000 gallons of gasoline annually. The fleet of almost 300 diesel purse-seiners began their hundred-day season on the Nass and fished their way down to the Gulf of Georgia, following the salmon and burning 1.5 million gallons of diesel fuel. The troller fleet, one-quarter owned by First Nations, burned 2 million gallons of gasoline and 200,000 gallons of diesel fuel. Another 1 million gallons of fuel oil went to pilchard and fish reduction plants (Mackenzie 1936).

The *Standard*'s survey looked at coastal logging operations, such as Green Point Logging. The latter burned 5,000 barrels of fuel to operate nine miles of logging railway and used 15,000 gallons of diesel to produce 40 million foot board measure (FBM) of logs. By 1935 they were already abandoning steam donkey engines for caterpillar engines. At that time, the logging fuel market on the north coast was estimated at $270,000, and fossil fuels were used to cut and move 600 million FBM of logs a year (Mackenzie 1936).

By 1935, without even counting the fuel bought by major pulp mills or Prince Rupert's Grand Trunk Pacific Railway, the isolated wild north Pacific coast consumed large amounts of sea-delivered petroleum products. Even the subsistence family economy, whether based on logging or fishing, depended on oil produced by offshore wells along the coast of California, or fields in distant Talara, Peru, or Mexico.

World War II increased refinery capacity, demand, and the size of coastal tankers. Typically, postwar period is Chevron Canada's *Standard Service*, a small diesel-electric vessel that carried 12,000 barrels of oil to small railway-based logging operations. They rapidly switched over to logging trucks and the cargo of the *Standard Service* changed to diesel. Yet the customer base remained much the same: fish-rendering plants, logging operations, canneries, and small communities.

The localized scale of the operation meant that the fuel ship captains had intimate knowledge of the coast, weather conditions, and the small operations with whom they dealt. It was not unusual for the captain to be asked to tow a float camp to a new location or to have to search the bays for a missing customer who had moved on since the last delivery. Stories of blank cheques with fuel orders left in jars on empty docks are part of the community of trust remembered by crew members (McNeill 1980).

This fuel industry history is now forgotten knowledge. In that history, the fuel industry was not seen as a threat, because it was integrated into the small-scale industrial and social activity along the coast. Unlike today's supertanker, the fuel ship had a human face, and operators shared an awareness of the dangers and the complexity of the local marine environment. Fuel spills did occur, but their ecological footprint was small and dispersed as the float camps moved frequently. People's livelihoods depended directly on the delivery of oil and gas to them, and they shared the benefits as well as the risks that the transport of oil and gas involved. That is not to say that the fuel ships had little impact. They powered railroad and truck logging, industrial fishing fleets, fish canneries, and rendering plants. They accelerated the transformation and destruction of the ecology of the north coast. Yet their history seems unanchored in the memory of communities, despite almost a century of existence.

Conversely the captains behind modern tanker spills, such as the *Exxon Valdez* and the *Arrow* spills, seem unconnected to the commu-

Figure 11.5 Shell Canada Ltd, Sedco 135F semi-submersible drilling rig under construction in Victoria, 1966–67. Royal BC Museum, I-31974

nity's sense of moral responsibility within the marine environment. They serve machines whose scale dwarfs the vessels that are part of the community's daily lives, foreshadowing the massive scale of potential ecological disaster. The smaller fuel boat had a human dimension that made it, not invisible, but an accepted part of the seascape. Further, whereas the local tanker supplied coastal populations directly and contributed to their livelihood, the new tankers bypassed their communities. Far from seeing any direct benefit, coastal British Columbians saw these leviathans as a threat to their way of life.

Perception, Filters and Flows of Knowledge

The modern industry became visible slowly. Exploration for oil in 1949 on the Queen Charlottes, in Richfield Oil's 1958 series of test wells on Graham Island, and in the seismic surveys out at sea were barely noticed. However, from 1967 to 1969 Shell Oil drilled fourteen test wells off Vancouver Island, Queen Charlotte Sound, and Hecate Strait. This activity was visible. The large drilling rig was built in Victoria (figure 11.5) and survived a hundred-foot wave in Hecate Strait. The actual impact of test drilling activity on local peoples and the environment seemed minimal, but it had a major impact on First Nations leaders as they considered the implications of oil and gas development.

Two oil spills outside British Columbia did much to make the industry visible to communities. Information flowed through the media and in activist and science reports concerning Europe's *Torrey Canyon* spill (1970), which covered 270 square miles of ocean and 73 miles of coastline, and concerning the 1969 blowout at Union Oil's *Platform Alpha* near Santa Barbara, California (Clarke and Hemphill 2002). Santa Barbara was a cognitive anchor, a defining proof and rallying point for environmental fears and debates over marine-spill regulation along the Pacific coast. From a public perspective, the combination of spills discredited the idea that tankers and platforms were "safe."

For Canada's federal government, the pivotal cognitive anchor was neither of those events, however. Instead it was the wreck of the tanker *Arrow* in Chedabucto Bay, Nova Scotia, in 1980. The report of the royal commission investigating this disaster, the Hart report revealed the weakness of the mechanisms of response and the vulnerability of the regulatory framework. Yet that regional experience is almost invisible to most British Columbia communities, although it contributed to the federal government's imposition of a moratorium on oil and gas exploration in 1972 (discussed in more detail below).

Anti-American sentiment also filters British Columbia's concerns over oil spills. The Amchitka nuclear tests above the province's north coast created the Stop the Wave campaign and Greenpeace. Quite unlike the experience of Labrador and Newfoundland, this 1960s environmental antiwar legacy gave the tanker traffic debates of the 1970s a deeper level of political meaning, one shaped by the arrival of draft refugees and by the Vietnam War. From the West Coast perspective, the critique of America is a major regional subtext.

A sense of geographic threat to national borders is more pronounced in British Columbia in the debates over oil. The province is threatened by spills along its coast but also from the south and the north, a threat that hits a sensitive nationalist nerve. British Columbia became caught between two halves of US national energy policy when a tanker route was proposed from Alaska, down the coast to Puget Sound, in Washington State (Freeman 1972). And there were negotiations about a tanker port on the north coast of British Columbia at Kitimat, to connect to the pipeline network for the American Midwest.

Subsequent cross-border incidents hardened British Columbia's environmental resistance. In 1989, oil from the barge *Nestucca* came north from Oregon to wash ashore at Long Beach on western Vancouver Island (Webster 1999). A few months later the spill of the *Exxon Valdez* happened to the north, in Alaska, a spill that was predicted years earlier in a popular West Coast novel (Becker and Coburn 1974). From the West Coast perspective, the dual-border tanker traffic routes have been a major concern, and may flair up again as demand increases for items such as isolated liquefied natural gas (LNG) tanker ports.

In response to these events and community fears came two major studies. The West Coast Oil Ports Inquiry (Thompson 1978) drew attention to a weak capacity to respond to even minor spills and presented the concerns of the fishing community and First Nations. It suggested studies on the environmental impact of port and tanker traffic and of the socio-economic impact on communities. The *Report and Recommendations of the West Coast Offshore Exploration Environmental Assessment Panel* (1986) looked at ecological issues, emergency response and compensation, and job training. It concluded that First Nations' title to the seabed was not extinguished by any treaty and that spills threatened seafood resources critical to cultural survival.

The hearings led the federal and provincial governments to draft the *Pacific Accord*, a regulatory mechanism comparable to the ones agreed to in the East. Talks between the governments broke down, however, and, following the Exxon Valdez disaster, the government of British Columbia asserted a provincial moratorium in 1989.

The nature of the federal and provincial moratoria is largely misunderstood. Federally, in 1972 Prime Minister Pierre Elliot Trudeau, at the request of David Anderson, a long-time environmental activist and later minister of the environment in both Jean Chrétien's and Paul Martin's governments, issued an order-in-council (OIC) to ban development. The order itself has been lost, but Anderson argues it retains its effect until the government decides otherwise: "I'm not even sure anyone can find the original piece of paper ... I've never seen it. But technically, in a sense, it's sort of like, you know, common law. At this stage it doesn't really matter very much where it is. It's a technical issue of whether or not you can find a piece of paper. But nobody can rant that we haven't had it all these years. Yes, we have. It has been firmly planted in peoples minds; it has been acted as though it's in existence, so it has been created by custom".[2] Public perception, in this instance, has become as important as government policy in maintaining a ban on offshore development.

Provincially, several orders-in-council have been passed regarding potential offshore reserves, but the most important include OIC 35/82, approved on 7 January 1982, which includeed note 2 to schedule 2 of the Petroleum and Natural Gas Act, stating that "no drilling licenses will be issued within the Provincial Inland Marine Zone defined in BC regulation 237/81."This became B.C. Reg. 10/92 when filed on 11 January 1982. Following the Exxon Valdez disaster, this note was maintained when the Government of British Columbia announced the moratorium would remain in effect for another five years, even though tanker traffic was a distinct issue from exploration. It remained in effect until the legislation was amended by the government of Premier Mike Harcourt with OIC 231/94. Note 2 to schedule 2 was dropped, and with it, the province's legal basis for its moratorium. The next day, 25 February 1994, OIC 231/94 became B.C. Reg. 55/94. To speak of "lifting the moratorium," then, as if it had been a long and arduous process, is largely a misnomer: the legal basis of the moratorium is a matter of government policy and can be changed by announcing a policy shift or a willingness to consider new applications for exploration.

Although much of the current interest around oil and gas exploration focuses on the Queen Charlotte Basin, it is only one of the four offshore basins that probably contain oil and gas, and the development of each would have different cost-benefit structures for nearby communities. Offshore hydrocarbon exploration and development in the Tofino Basin will have rather different implications for the nearby coastal communities than for the Queen Charlotte and Georgia Basins. The Winona Basin, which lies to the northwest of the Tofino Basin, has the least potential and would probably be the most difficult to develop.

The Tofino Basin lies offshore but close to the west coast of Vancouver Island, and large segments of that coast are now developed as parks (the federal Pacific Rim National Park and the provincial Juan de Fuca Park). The communities along this coast have depended on logging and fishing for their existence and as both of these industries have declined, the communities have focused more recently on tourism. Thus, there could be substantial opposition to offshore hydrocarbon exploration and development if there was a perception that such activities could deter tourism. An opposing view may be that more diversified economic activities would support healthier coastal communities (e.g., through supply industries, accommodation, and shore facilities), which could be seen as attractive to some communities (e.g., Gold River, Port Alberni, and possibly Ucluelet).

There are other locations in the world where offshore hydrocarbon exploration and development are occurring close to major coastal parks and tourism centres, most notably off the southwest corner of the North Island of New Zealand (near Palmerston). In British Columbia the different communities have not fully explored their options and can be expected to take different stances, depending on the balance of their anticipated future economic options for development, especially with tourism. This observation emphasizes the need for open and transparent knowledge transfer to ensure full public participation in decision making and public-policy formulation.

With recent reports like the 2004 report from the Royal Society of Canada commissioned by the federal government, which identifies no discernable scientific rationale for non-development, with a widely stated desire for development on behalf of Premier Gordon Campbell's provincial government (elected 2001), and with public opinion in constant flux, the battle for offshore development in British Columbia will continue.[3]

Knowledge, Values and a Tale of Two Coasts

"Accord" and "moratoria," therefore, provide apt characterizations of development and non-development and of the products of the interplay between government policy, public perception, and scientific research. Here the transfer of knowledge creates diffuse boundaries between the three, each influencing and shaping the others and forcing the interaction of the micro- and macro-structures of society to produce accords and moratoria in each coastal context.

The role of history and values that shape local culture and legal frameworks are highlighted by the comparison of East and West Coast oil development. In addition to the different history of environmental activism and wealth distributions, in the past twenty years, the issue of unextinguished aboriginal title has loomed large on the West Coast. Courts have accorded Aboriginal people offshore rights, as well as unextinguished title to most of British Columbia where no treaties were signed.

Potential treaties to settle Aboriginal title issues, fear of environmental damage, regulation, the scale of development, nationalism, and cultural and regional barriers to knowledge are all factors that provide part of the explanation of the differences between Newfoundland and Labrador and British Columbia. However, the forgotten knowledge discussed in this chapter suggests that part of the answer may lie with finding the appropriate human scale for development and knowledge exchange and communicating local ecological knowledge in a way that makes the ecological sense of risk more visible to industry, and it may also lie in creating an industry that is part of, not apart from, community.

APPLYING THE MODEL II : FROM GEOSCIENCE TO EARTH SYSTEMS SCIENCE

The future challenges are profound, and they affect most disciplines and cultures. In this section we discuss specifically the evolution of the earth sciences and how they must change in order to contribute to developing better solutions for a sustainable future.

Movement of Knowledge Bundles: Examples from Pacific Coast Geoscience

At the core of our model (figure 11.4), geoscience history and knowledge is archived by humankind (e.g., in research papers, reports) and recorded within the geological and fossil record. A review of more than one hundred of Canada's West Coast and offshore geophysical, geological, and paleontological publications reveals that geoscience has moved through data collection, information analysis, and knowledge development (figure 11.3).

Early Canadian Pacific coast geoscience involved exploring frontier areas in the onshore and offshore. Locating resources (e.g., coal, oil, gas, gold, silver, copper, and other resources) was a key onshore exploration activity. The science involved observation, description, dating, correlating, and mapping rock units (e.g., Clapp 1912; McLearn 1929; Usher 1952) and interpreting geology and assessing resources (e.g., Sutherland-Brown 1968; Muller et al. 1981). Early studies were strongly data- and information-based (figure 11.3), and they were positioned near the core of the knowledge model (figure 11.4). Later, results were organized (bundled) and communicated (moving out from the model core) to serve the purpose of resource assessment for growing societal needs. However, broader questions involving past depositional environments, tectonic displacements, and the impact of resource extraction on both communities and the environment were not well understood initially. As issues surfaced (e.g., scarcer resources, declining community health, unemployment) broader questions were asked. Collaborative science, partnerships, and training became important for stimulating scientific discoveries and technological development, improving communications, and maximizing knowledge movement (figures 11.2, 11.4).

Scientific work in the offshore frontier required research vessels, technologies, and instruments that were commonly supported by industry. Magnetic, gravity, seismic (geophysical), and other instruments and surveys were used to locate oil and gas. Science-industry collaborations and research in the deep oceans led to the discovery of magnetic anomaly patterns locked in magmas/basalts that had been deposited, cooled, and moved away from oceanic ridges. These observations resulted in a major shift in earth science thinking with the development of the theory of plate tectonics (e.g., Raff and Mason 1961; Vine and Wilson 1965). Improved funding and research followed (e.g., Deep-Sea Drilling and Ocean Drilling Programs). In the British Columbia offshore, early data collection and coastal geophysical surveys and seismic (e.g., earthquake) monitoring were followed by oil and gas exploration (e.g., Shouldice 1971). Data were quickly bundled into information (figure 11.3) as magnetic, gravity, seismic, and other anomalies were observed and as new questions were asked; and research resulted in the interpretation of basin structures, tectonic processes, volcanism, and mountain building (e.g., Gabrielse and Yorath 1992).

Obstacles to the Movement of Knowledge

Early geoscience publications commonly had one author, reflecting the independent thinking and research style of frontier scientists. The rationale behind this model might include immediate recognition, power, and control of a project, and apparent reduced risks of losing scientific ideas and results. Checks on research quality were commonly operated through the traditional science publication peer review process. Seminars and other presentations probably were the platform for research discussion and debate. Collaborations may have expanded between professor (mentor) and student, but roles and a working hierarchy were clearly defined. A benefit of this style of research was that results could be rapidly disseminated, but at the cost of forgoing the broad thinking that could be achieved through collaboration.

Competition is a significant factor in science, and it may create obstacles to knowledge movement. It may be more visible during periods of funding shortfalls and scientific controversies when research results do not agree. Competition can be distracting to scientists, or it can be invigorating when new ideas are explored. An example of a small-scale conflict involving two scientists is provided by the different interpretations of ancient depositional environments of the Nootka Sound area presented by Jeletzky (1973) and Cameron (1980). In this case, additional science at the location was delayed for many years until new offshore data allowed alternative interpretations of the complex geology and tectonic environment. Research results from a larger unresolved controversy, the "Baja BC" controversy (e.g., Irving et al. 1996; Cowan et al. 1997), indicate varied results and interpretations for the timing, mechanisms, and displacements of British Columbia rocks over thousands of kilometers.

What appear to be obstacles have the potential for fostering scientific discovery, the movement of ideas, and creative thinking and creative solution. When controversies are brought to the forefront, public awareness is raised. Science funding and acknowledgement of scientific research may be achieved. A four-quadrant model by Kort and Reilly (2002) illustrates the phases of learning and how confidence, fascination, enthusiasm, excitement, enlightenment, and being proud provide a positive "affect" for constructive learning and knowledge movement, whereas frustration, insecurity, embarrassment, and anxiety lead to non-learning and a negative affect (e.g., in which scientists insult each other, lack funding, and experience employment downsizing). Positive affects are elevated with acceptance in the science community and through communications and awards for science excellence. This creates a positive learning environment where discovery, ideas, and productivity can flourish.

The period from the 1960s to the 1980s, when research moved beyond the earlier forms of data collection and information analysis, was a productive time for geoscience. Larger integrated projects involved the development of knowledge structures. Science management partitioned roles, developed work ethics, provided funding and mechanisms for acknowledgement and recognition, developed collaborative science visions and directions, and planned and defined project and product outcomes. Large projects initiated by the Geological Survey of Canada (e.g., International Boundary Studies, the Frontier Geoscience Program, Lithoprobe – the latter with NSERC), the British Columbia Ministry of Energy and Mines, universities, and the Ocean Drilling Program encouraged multiple science collaborations. In part, they provided significant funding for extensive data collection, dissemination of information, and development of knowledge bases.

The successes of these projects are demonstrated by the discoveries that resulted. Some coastal British Columbia examples include discoveries of new faults and earthquakes at spreading ridges; the subducting (plunging) Juan de Fuca plate and the associated accretion of island terranes, uplifted sea floor, and volcanism (e.g., Mounts Baker, Rainier, and St Helens); the movement of triple-plate junctions; a deformation front of crumpled strata at the junction of the Juan de Fuca and North American plates; fluid expulsion and gas hydrates inboard of the deformation front; movement of strata sometimes over great distances along faults (e.g., the San Andreas, West Coast, and Queen Charlotte faults); a locked non-subducting part of the Juan de Fuca plate and a high potential for a future mega-earthquake; and offshore hydrothermal vents rich in heated fluids, mineral deposits, and novel life forms. Publication of these and other results provided larger-scale geological and Earth process interpretations (e.g., Monger et al. 1972; Hyndman et al. 1990; Gabrielse and Yorath 1992; Yorath et al. 1999), delivered information on resource potentials (e.g., of hydrocarbons, minerals, aggregates, water) (e.g., Woodsworth 1991; Hannigan et al. 2001) and assessed onshore and offshore geohazards (e.g., of volcanic eruptions, earthquakes, tsunamis, landslides, mineral/soil toxicity, ground stability, erosion, and flooding). This latter knowledge is used to improve building codes; to develop regulations, safety guidelines, and emergency plans; and it is to be hoped to prevent or reduce the use of high-risk areas.

The shift from resource-driven, data-information geoscience to "earth system science" – environmental/human-impact studies linking earth, ocean, and atmospheric sciences (Barnes, Bornhold, et al. 1996) – produced a vision for a larger-scale research, technological, education, and collaboration platform. To achieve broader thinking, improved earth science might integrate human value systems and communication pathways. The outcome could involve a re-bundling of the components of the knowledge framework and alternative directions for knowledge flow.

Current Challenges for Knowledge Transfer in the Earth Sciences

Many earth sciences institutions and academic departments and programs are partitioned in to the subcomponents of the earth system. Thus, traditionally geology, geophysics, oceanography, and atmospheric sciences have been taught as separate programs within separate departments at universities. Over the last two decades, it has become increasingly apparent that the earth system is a complex of interacting coupled systems and that there is both a scientific and a societal need to study the earth system in its totality, not just its separate component systems. A number of major publications have emerged that have defined and advocated the concept of earth system science (ESS) (e.g., NASA 1988; NRC 1992, 1993; Malone 1994). This ESS concept has provided the basis for some new visions for the future of the discipline in Canada (e.g., Barnes 1993; Barnes et al. 1996), but there are significant barriers to the diffusion and acceptance of this concept (knowledge bundle) within science and government.

Institutionally, university and government departments have been slow to adapt: academic units currently have aging faculty and limited opportunities to hire in new directions; governments units are commonly mandated by government legislation based on issues/needs of the past. The conservative nature of the recommended programs in geosciences of the Canadian Council of Professional Geoscientists of the Association of Professional Engineers and Geoscientists is a strong impediment to moving Earth Sciences education in Canada toward a more comprehensive and socially relevant curriculum. This academic reform is urgently needed to train the next generation of earth scientists in ways that prepares them for the range of issues noted above.

The Canadian federal government departments are organized to reflect the past and present emphasis on revenues from the resource sectors: e.g., the departments of Agriculture, Fisheries and Oceans, and Natural Resources. All of these have been downsized by Program Review in the last decade, so that they are typically one-half to two-thirds their earlier size. The lack of hiring opportunities for young scientists has sent a sobering message about future opportunities to graduating classes, while at the same time deferring radical renewal and reform of the government and academic units based on a strong focus on ESS.

The last decade has seen available operating and research budgets stagnate or decline at a time when major increases are required to solve the societal problems noted above. This is apparent for the federal science departments and the national granting councils, and it is apparent in the dramatic reductions in the R&D budgets of, for example, the CANDU Nuclear Operators Group (CANDU Nuclear Operators Group 2000). However, in the last few years, new optimism has emerged in the academic community in response to new federal government programs that have introduced two thousand new research chairs over ten years. Furthermore, the Canadian Foundation for Innovation (www.innovation.ca) will distribute directly and leverage indirectly over $10 billion to improve the research infrastructure (e.g., with new equipment and facilities).

The main driving force behind many of these new funds from the federal government has been the philosophy that to be economically competitive, Canada must invest in innovation (in industry and universities) (Environment Canada 2000; PAGSE 2000). Canada ranks seventh among the G8 nations, barely above Italy, in the percentage of the gross domestic product it invests in R&D. A new Innovation Strategy has been published further promoting excellence and investment in advanced education and training (Industry Canada 2002a, 2002b; www.innovationstrategy.gc.ca).

Novel Technologies to Improve Knowledge Generation and Transfer

An example of the application of the earth systems science approach is provided by the novel techniques and multidisciplinary research just being started and proposed for the northeast Pacific region in both coastal and deep-sea areas. The main objectives are to better understand the interacting components of the earth system and the marine environment. The benefits will include improved understanding of the severe seismic/tsunami hazard, gas hydrates (as an energy resource and an environmental threat), ocean/climate dynamics as applied to the fisheries, and the nature of the deep-sea ecology and biodiversity. Two related and sequential research projects (Project VENUS and Project NEPTUNE) have been formulated, which together represent a major mega-project in the earth sciences that will last several decades. The principle behind both is the same: to use recent advances in powered underwater cables and in high-bandwidth telecommunications using fibre-optic cables to establish "smart/intelligent" underwater observatories that will not only record observations but will allow data and information transfer and interactive experiments.

VENUS (Victoria Experimental Network under the Sea; www.venus.uvic.ca) will operate as two cable arrays from 4 km and 40 km in length in relatively shallow coastal waters around Victoria, British Columbia. Funding of $10.3 million was received in late 2002 from the Canadian Foundation for Innovation, the BC Knowledge Development Fund, and other partners (with Dr Verena Tunnicliffe, University of Victoria, as principal investigator).

NEPTUNE is an innovative facility that will transform marine science (www.ooi.washington.edu: program director, John Delaney, University of Washington; NEPTUNE Canada, www.neptunecanada.ca: project director, Christopher Barnes, University of Victoria). As a network of more many subsea observatories covering much of the 200,000 km^2 Juan de Fuca tectonic plate in the northeast Pacific, it will draw power from shore and exchange data with scientists on shore through more than 2,000 km of submarine fibre-optic cables (Delaney et al. 2000). Each observatory will host and power many scientific instruments on the surrounding seafloor, in boreholes in the seafloor, and buoyed up into the water column. Remotely operated and autonomous vehicles will reside at depth, recharge at observatories, and respond to distant labs. Continuous near-real-time multidisciplinary measurement series will extend over twenty-five years. Free from the limitations of battery life, ship schedules, shipboard accommodations, bad weather, and delayed access to data, scientists anywhere in the world will monitor their deep-sea experiments in real time on the Internet and routinely command their instruments to respond to storms, plankton blooms, earthquakes, eruptions, slope slides, and other events.

This revolutionary approach, with its significant scale and reliable technology, will lead to fundamental advances that would be impossible using periodic ship voyages. Scientists will be able to pose an entirely new set of questions and perform experiments to understand complex, interacting earth system processes. The NEPTUNE regional cabled observatory will be operated by a Canada/US partnership that will design, test, build, and operate the network, as two cable arrays, on behalf of a wide international community of scientists. The total cost of the project is estimated at about Can$250 million from concept to operation. About Can$30 million has already been funded for design and development. NEPTUNE Canada will receive over Can$80 million over the years 2003–9 to install the northern part of the facility. About Can$20 million per annum will be required to operate the full network. The 800 km Canadian Portion will become fully operational in 2009, while the US portion will likely be completed in 2015.

Resource extraction is moving into the deep sea, climate change is affecting fisheries, and populations are expanding in earthquake-prone coastal regions. NEPTUNE, which will be among the first of many such cabled ocean observatories, will attract worldwide attention. There is much to be gained from being among the scientific and industrial pioneers. Industry can develop new products and expertise and gain exposure in new markets, worldwide. New scientific understanding will help with real key problems ranging from seismic-hazard assessment to fish stock management in a changing climate. The

Oil and Gas Development   219

multidisciplinary data archive will be an amazing, lasting resource for scientists and students. The public will share in the research discoveries of one of the last unexplored places on earth through educational and entertainment/tourist programming of the real-time, scientific data and video imagery.

This example illustrates how developments in other sectors (e.g., telecommunications, computation and data management, engineering, and robotics) can be employed to transform the methods of investigating the earth system. Instead of using just research vessels, which have serious imitations when it comes to making time-series observation and being present for rare or extreme events, the new technology of powered, optical-fibre cables will revolutionize ocean science. New applications are envisaged in climate science and climate predictions, fisheries management, "smart" deep-sea oil field development, national security, and educational programming.

This transformation of the ocean sciences by cabled ocean observatories such as NEPTUNE is fundamentally related to the transformation of how knowledge moves. Data and imagery will be transmitted at gigabits per second; they will flow in real time to scientists, to schools and the public, and to policy-makers. Teams of scientists can work on multidisciplinary experiments, irrespective of their physical location. The data sets will evolve into a huge archive that will itself become an invaluable interactive research tool. Virtually all the data and imagery will be publicly available, thus becoming a liberating and democratizing factor, removing impediments for the rapid and widespread movement of information and knowledge while ensuring lack of proprietary control by vested interest groups.

SUMMARY

In this chapter we have proposed a general model and explored past, present, and potential future knowledge movement in response to coastal British Columbia oil and gas development. Knowledge movement can start with an event that affects places (e.g., earth, ocean, and air interfaces) and its inhabitants. In the context of coastal and offshore oil and gas issues, recognizing the scale of the event, identifying participants and issues, understanding interactions of the earth systems, and locating and estimating potential resources are important first steps. The bundling of information and knowledge by community, industry, academic, and government participants could allow economic and environmental planning to proceed and potential beneficial outcomes to be recognized.

Obstacles to knowledge movement involve the continuously large and growing quantity of data and information and the selection and filtering processes that are required to determine what is relevant. Relevancy may change with different people and with local issues and events, and it may also change as knowledge grows or value systems evolve. Examples from the early oil and gas economy of coastal British Columbia showed that the industry was small in scale and accepted by, integrated into, and also essential to the coastal communities. Important were the communications and links between the peoples and their activities within a mainly community resource-based economy. Changes to these communities occurred as the resource economy declined, oil spills occurred outside their control but impacted their coastlines, and new economies developed (e.g., tourism). With these changes came new individual and group and/or community values, growth, and knowledge.

Knowledge follows certain pathways and practices accepted by individuals and groups. Issues of the Canadian east coast Accord and the west coast Moratoria, illustrate how people with a variety of knowledge and value systems have produced different environmental, political, and economic outcomes. The alternative pathways involve economic benefits as opposed to environmental preservation. This demonstrates the power of political and public will when events such as nearby oil spills are held and locked in the minds of the West Coast public, that favour environmental protection, and on the East Coast, where disasters and loss of life (e.g., involving fishing boats, the *Ocean Ranger* oil rig collapse) are not new to the culture, are tragic, are accepted, and oil and gas development proceeded.

Values are an important part of knowledge bundles when it comes to public perception and government responses, but they also play a role in disciplinary cultures and knowledge bundles within academic and government scientific communities. In the example of Canadian West Coast geoscience, data collection and information analysis originally mainly served resource economies. Geoscience knowledge moved and matured with increased collaborations to serve broader social needs (e.g., knowledge of the earth's processes; environmental and hazards assessments). Outcomes included important West Coast geoscience discoveries, technological advances, and knowledge to support development of policies and regulations.

At the perimeter of our model are the outcomes of research and collaborations. A vision for the future is presented in the context of environmental problems and human socio-economic-cultural systems. In order to develop solutions to critical issues that go beyond the immediate question of oil and gas exploration, such as ozone holes, global warming, depleted resources, environmental degradation, and biodiversity loss, research and political strategies must be developed that are applicable locally, regionally, and globally. Given the urgency involved and the huge costs of inaction, it is essential to develop new levels of inter-sectoral collaboration on a scale and efficiency not yet attained.

One partial solution involves a major reorganization of the education curricula and research programs in earth system sciences so that they interface more effectively with social sciences and humanities. This could be further improved with movement of knowledge between researchers and policy-makers and into public education and through the development of new technologies for environmental monitoring. We have emphasized the importance of a multiple-collaboration model and the impact of anthropological activities on all of the earth's systems, and we have argued that the natural and physical sciences of the future would benefit from a better understanding of human value systems and how their application may change scientific thinking and outcomes. Enhanced knowledge and effective knowledge transfer are critical and can be generated in new and novel ways, especially with the growing capacity to wire the planet electronically (by means of satellites, cabled observatories). The NEPTUNE regional cabled observatory will be the first in the world, and it will transform not only the ocean sciences by the way that knowledge, information, and imagery is moved, transforming the speed, volume, and diversity, and the distribution, and improving free access. The problems of the safe exploration and exploitation of hydrocarbons and the sustainability of coastal communities on the West Coast of Canada have created issues in which effective knowledge transfer is critical for sound public-policy formulation and public acceptance. The earth sciences will be a core discipline in seeking and defining science and technical solutions. Science, social, political, cultural, and industrial participants and various aspects of society will determine the types of outcomes and their timely implementation.

12

The Process of Large-Scale Interdisciplinary Science: A Reflexive Study

PETER TRNKA

INTRODUCTION

In the last couple of decades we have witnessed a transformation in the paradigm of natural scientific research, a paradigm shift from disciplinarily specific individual or small-team research to multidisciplinary large-team work (see, for example, Rabinow 1999 and Knorr Cetina 1999). By "a paradigm shift" I mean what Thomas Kuhn (1970) refers to as a substantial change in the beliefs, methodologies, experimental procedures, and culture of scientific work. I do not mean to suggest that all work in natural science is now multidisciplinary and big, but only that this model of research is more and more prevalent and is beginning to define the field, though not without opposition. This essay tracks a similar shift as it pertains to the rise of large-scale team research combining various disciplines across the natural, social, and human sciences.

The reasons for such shifts in the organizational structure of the sciences (and I shall use the word "science" in this broad form throughout as including the natural, social, and human sciences) are many and diverse. In the natural sciences the move to so-called *big science* is the result of a number of factors: completion or exhaustion of highly specialized disciplinary research; the discovery or creation of big problems that require many researchers and many disciplines to solve (in part because of, for example, systematization in genomics and technological requirements in physics, and also because of new global-scale environmental problems);[1] and the provision of large research budgets by national granting councils. The corresponding tendency toward big projects in the social and human sciences may share some of these causes and is in part the result of the rise of large-scale natural science (work in genomics and ecology, for example, has included, by necessity, questions falling within social and humanist enquiry, such as questions about the organization of work, the nature of technology, ethics, and law).

There may be ideological reasons for such changes in science as well. Whether or not the provision of large research budgets for scientific work is merited (by the significance of the problems to be addressed and our likelihood of solving them in this or that manner), the processes by which societies and their institutions and citizenry decide upon the allocation of public funds include a broad range of concerns. To believe that one of the reasons for big science and big research budgets is promotion of science and scientists within society at large does not require undue cynicism or skepticism concerning science; rather, such a view extends theories and findings concerning class and interest from the social sciences to the domain of science itself.[2] Such a view does, however, allow for a critical inquiry concerning the validity and justification for big science.

To put the question bluntly, Do trends (and corresponding budgetary allocations) toward large-scale interdisciplinary science make sense in terms of improving science (and/or its application) or are they mainly exercises in the self-promotion and the self-aggrandizement of researchers? Putting the question this way serves to set out the extreme options (which, even so, may not be mutually exclusive). Between the extremes lie more likely alternatives, such as changes to the hierarchies between sciences; the character of scientific work and accountability; and the links between research institutions such as universities and their funding agencies, governments, corporations, and communities. In short, the trend toward big science encapsulates a diversity of factors in need of analysis if we are to improve our decisions as to whether or not to continue to promote and to participate in such work. This question is especially pressing given reasons to believe that the university and its professional staff play a more and more important role in mediating class formation in society.[3]

Recent developments in the philosophy and sociology of science have made it possible to pose questions such as the ones above and to begin to answer them. The study of science has itself shifted from a preoccupation with the justification of scientific claims to inquiries into the social and economic structure of science. While there has been substantial research on natural science in this context, little has been done on the social and human sciences or their interrelation with natural science. This study, intended as a first attempt at some redress of this problem, took as its occasion a unique Canadian case. The large-scale multidisciplinary project Coasts Under Stress offered researchers a unique opportunity in 1999: to participate in the largest research grant awarded to date by two Canadian federal granting agencies (NSERC and SSHRC) in tandem.[4] Approximately seventy academic faculty, primarily at Memorial University of Newfoundland and the University of Victoria, took up the opportunity in the name of scientific research into the relation between ecological and human health.[5] The goal of this reflexive study was to collect information on and analyse the process of work that was being called into existence by the awarding and taking up of the grant. How would knowledge be made and moved in this large, multidisciplinary and multi-agency research framework?

THEORY AND METHODOLOGY: REFLEXIVITY IN INFINITE REGRESS

The theory and the method chosen for this reflexive study are modelled on the work of Pierre Bourdieu (1984b, 1996), a leading sociologist of the twentieth century and pioneer of studies of academics and academic institutions. His reflexive methodology (Bourdieu and Wacquant 1992) is premised on the belief that the more we know about the people that produce knowledge, the more we are likely to know about the objects of knowledge: making investigators the objects of knowledge improves the likelihood of objectivity in knowledge. Reflexive knowledge is generated by way of questionnaires, interviews, demographic data, observation, and analysis. Objective knowledge of a knower's conditions of knowing is generated neither by quantitative measurement and statistics alone nor by theory alone but by way of an empirically and theoretically sophisticated analysis of the position of the knower in a field of forces. Field analysis, adapted from contemporary physics, considers a subject to be constituted by its position relative to an entire field of similar forces, at different positions, and travelling in different vectors (Bourdieu 1996; for a general study of field concepts across disciplines, see Hayles 1984). Such an approach rejects the view of knowledge as a given object or entity in favor of the view that knowledge is something that is made, torn apart, and remade as it moves from one conglomeration of attributes in a field to another.

A premise of field analysis applied to society is that individuals are partially constituted by – and so their aims will be determined by and in accordance with – the social trajectories that they come to expect and to seek. Bourdieu insists that an adequate social explanation of actions, including actions of knowledge acquisition, does not take away from – rather, it bolsters – claims to freedom (understood as the amplification of consciousness based on knowledge of one's environment). Bourdieu's notion of *habitus* – an agent's set of dispositions to act – encompasses habits of which a subject might be unaware, as well as explicit decisions.

Originally, my reflexive study had three empirical prongs: questionnaires, interviews, and ethnographic participant observation.[6] Difficulties in securing ethical consent for the latter, together with administrative discomfort with such investigation and changes in my research team, lead to limiting the study to two empirical prongs, plus my own experience.[7] I hoped to be able to analyse quantitative and qualitative data from the questionnaires together with interview material, research documents, and my own observations and experiences. I proposed to handle my own involvement as both a participant and an observer of CUS by way of an extension of the reflexive method to my own study. The first stage of this reflexive extension was the last question on my questionnaire: "What do you think of this questionnaire?" The answers to this question form the start of a dialogue with CUS researchers that will continue the critical evaluation of this study and CUS as a whole.[8] My own position as a member of the research team added, I believe, to my ability to understand and analyse the research process.[9] While my own self-interest (or other conscious or unconscious motives) could and probably did prejudice research judgments, I have sought to put my decisions and instruments to various tests (of which the reader's evaluation of this essay is one).

The questionnaire, at first targeted toward all CUS members,[10] was designed to document attitudes and measure expressed valuations concerning science and discipline, and to allow for the matching or correspondence of these attitudes with background information concerning the position of subjects in the academic and economic fields. A great value lies in the subject speaking for herself, and so various quotations, at times lengthy, follow.[11]

The initial aim was to represent the views of all members of CUS, from faculty investigators and research associates to students and community partners. Eventually the set was narrowed down to include only faculty co-investigators and research associates.[12] Eliminating the views of students and community partners from this reflexive study meant a significant narrowing of scope relevant to an important aspect of the research structure of CUS. I have in no way tried nor been able to remedy this resultant neglect, except to feature the sayings of my research subjects on such matters. I regret the absence of these views and can only speculate as to how they would have changed the final outcome.

The second phase of this research (not discussed here) relied on interviews planned as face-to-face open-ended discussions, guided by a short set of general questions, with six individuals on each coast of the study.[13]

SOME FINDINGS CONCERNING RESEARCHERS' VIEWS ON SCIENCE, DISCIPLINARITY, AND THE ORGANIZATION OF RESEARCH

My sample is formed by 27 questionnaires, representing 35 percent of the set of 60 co-investigators and 70 research associates. I sorted the respondents along the following axes: type of science (natural, social, human); discipline; East/West Coast; junior-senior; male-female.[14] Much of the detailed work, in part statistical, analyzing the subgroups within this population remains to be done in the form of correspondence analysis.[15] It remains to be seen whether any valid generalizations may be made concerning differences in attitude between, e.g., East and West Coast participants or researchers employed in departments in the natural as opposed to the social sciences. The questionnaires that form the sample indicate a balance of respondents along various axes, together with some significant areas of unknowns (as set out below – respondents were informed of their right to answer only the questions they wanted to and were warned of the possibility that answering all questions would provide potentially identifying information).

Overall, the respondents represent a diversity of university departments, faculties, and academic disciplines, including from both the East and West Coasts of Canada and across a range of career stages. Specifically, 8 hold highest degrees (preponderantly PhDs) in natural science disciplines, 7 in social science, 4 in the humanities, 2 in education, and 1 in health, with 5 unidentified. Nine respondents either did not specify a department of affiliation or said the question was not applicable; the remainder is distributed in anthropology, education, earth and ocean sciences, economics, environmental studies, geology, health, history, nursing, and political science.[16] Nine respondents are employed by Memorial University and 6 by the University of Victoria; 2 others are from other East Coast universities and 1 from another West Coast university, while 8 respondents did not specify their place of work. The significant portion of non-answers to such questions (approximately a third of respondents in some cases) suggests a reluctance to provide either identifying information or information useful for disciplinary and coastal comparisons.

The respondents range in age from their thirties to their late sixties and older, with the largest group (13) falling in their fifties. Sixteen are male and 11 female; of those who provided their birthplace (20) approximately half are Canadian-born and half foreign-born (primarily from either the United States or the United Kingdom); the majority of respondents are married. Only one respondent earns under $40,000 p/a, with the largest group of respondents (12) receiving over $80,000 p/a; respondents better represent senior than junior levels of academic life.[17]

I have structured my analysis of the themes in the questionnaires in three categories: views on major classifications in science and knowledge, views on disciplines and disciplinarity, and views on scale.

Sciences Natural, Social, and Human: On Meaning and Definition.

How do scientists define science?[18] This is perhaps an obvious question, but one hard to put to scientists. First of all, one has to decide who they are. Then they must be willing to answer. Some may claim that doing science and defining it are two very different things. Some hold that natural science and natural science alone is science, others include social science into the sciences, and still others (notably French speakers) have no problem of speaking of the human sciences. Would different positions on the definition and meaning of science within a multidisciplinary research project be a problem or an asset? Would these positions change through the course of our work together? How? These and related questions were what I sought from the first series of questions.

The very term "science" (or "scientific" as in, e.g., "your views on scientific research" in the title of the questionnaire) confused several respondents. Some wondered whether when I mentioned science I meant natural science.[19] Other difficulties lay with more specific terms that were uncommon to some, e.g., "human science" and "transdisciplinary." Such problems concerning terminology are only to be expected in a broadly multidisciplinary population, where different disciplines will feature different terms, meanings, and usages. Nevertheless, such terminological differences may reveal much concerning the culture and history of disciplines and their relations between each other. The use of "science" to refer exclusively to natural science, for example, implies a relatively narrow geographic, cultural, and historical perspective on the term (confirmed, e.g., by responses that find contrary terms like "human science" incomprehensible or oxymoronic).

Often it was my impression that "science" functioned mostly as an honorific term for the respondents, designating something akin to "those like me who perform research well." When asked to specify the nature of scientific research more explicitly, respondents tended to offer disciplinarily specific answers. Furthermore, distinctions between sectors of knowledge production are not commonly well understood or agreed upon, respondents showing uncertainty whether it is methodology or the nature of the object that distinguishes the three main branches of knowledge, social science, natural science, and the humanities (whether this should be taken as a criticism of the knowledge of respondents or of the confusion of the state of the academy and methodology is another question).[20]

The questionnaire contains seven long answer questions concerning the meaning of science and scientific knowledge, as well as a series of ranking questions (these shall be given little attention in what follows).[21] As was expected, notwithstanding the respondents' participation in a self-styled interdisciplinary research project, many of the answers to these questions were little more than advocacy for one's particular or general affiliation. For example, all distinguished between "scientific knowledge" and "local knowledge,"[22] with nine expressing a clear preference for the former,[23] only three siding somewhat with the latter, and the remainder crafting some balance. As with many of the responses in the questionnaire, the longer and more complicated ones raise more food for thought and question the categories implicit in the question, often suggesting much more needs to be said: "Both share common elements and goals – to better understand and communicate knowledge about the world. 'Scientific knowledge' to me (Western scientific knowledge) arises from a European tradition and relies on testing hypotheses through experimental method – knowledge conveyed through presentation and publication in specialized journals; purports to be value-free; local knowledge methods are less formal – also seek to predict; communication often oral; may include (strongly) a specific world view – a *lot* more on this."

This response also recognizes that many terms of classification are made to have a certain image and that it is important to be able to distinguish the image from the real thing; responses could be sorted, accordingly, by way of whether or not classifications are (a) accepted as given or (b) contested as made. Noting that classifications of science are themselves constructed (made) and historically and geographically shifting (on the move) does require some acknowledgement of social construction (the social construction of human classificatory structures), without entailing any stronger thesis concerning the social construction of reality or science.

Most respondents associated "expert knowledge" with both "scientific" and "local" knowledge, but where an exclusory choice was made, it was, with one exception, in favor of the "scientific".[24] Most did not expand on their choices, here, though when they did it seemed to be assumed that "expert" was something good and positive, with one exception:

> It is about granting or claiming a position of power in the sense that [Michel] Foucault discussed (see, e.g., Foucault 1997 and 2000). I do not wish to be an expert but sometimes have this role forced upon me by audience expectations. I am uncomfortable with the term and feel its exclusion of other knowledge outweighs the good associated with it. That said many people wish to have an "expert" as an ally. One can use the expectations positively to support them, but I prefer to be known as one with "experience" in an area. To be "trusted" to give advice is better than being an "expert."

The challenge to both the scientific-expert and the local-expert views articulated here shows how academic fighting over valued terms may miss the point; we should be wary of the packaging of knowledge and aware of the powers conferred upon and expressed by those in positions to make knowledge.

On the distinctions between major branches or types of knowledge, be they all called science or not,[25] the answers become less obviously polemical and more informative (this may also be a function of progressing through the survey and the form of the questions). On the distinction between natural and social science, responses drew the distinction in terms of (sometimes singly, sometimes in combination)

- object of study
- method
- language
- community
- indeterminacy

- rhetoric
- cause
- truth
- power
- ethics

The variety of types of distinction here surprised me, even though the majority fell under the first two, expected categories (and quite often singly and simply).[26] Some reflected the kind of work that we had been discussing as an interdisciplinary team: "Methodologies in doing science. Natural science: minimal community; human contact up front; obtain results and knowledge and then go to the community to share knowledge. Social science: learn; observe, attain information at the community level and share knowledge with the community. Involve the community. Thought."

This response uses community, control, and focus as distinguishing variables; it also includes both knowledge making and knowledge moving, in diverse forms. Surprising variables, for me,[27] included the simplicity or complexity of language: "The natural sciences tend toward explanation, often terse, of the behaviour of inanimate objects, organisms that cannot speak, or people if we ignore language. The social sciences tend toward explanations that incorporate the complexity of language." The answer is difficult to interpret conclusively, since no obvious preference attaches to terseness or complexity. The writer speaks, it should be noted, of tendencies, of movements rather than fixed states.

Distinguishing between natural science and the humanities elicited a similar range of classifications,[28] with object of study and method also being common, but other terms featuring as well: life, reason, imagination, history, and politics, most notably. The answers themselves are not as interesting in my judgment as those to the previous question (this could in part be a function of exhaustion), but one stands out, and, I would add, gets it right: "See above [previous question on natural and social science], since I have no idea what the difference is between 'social sciences' and 'humanities' other than the vague hopes of the 1930s instrumentalist school of structuralists (The New School NYC,

Rockefeller's funding of social science at Chicago, LSE, etc.), and the whims of university administrators."

Disciplines: Single, Multiple, Between, Across

Whatever scientific specialization – in the sense of a specialized investigation in the natural, social, or human sciences – a respondent may have, they will also (and to some extent as a function of the former) have a *habitus* in relation to disciplinarity, multidisciplinarity, interdisciplinarity, and transdisciplinarity.[29] Discipline and scientific orientation are related and in some cases coextensive; in other cases they are contraries, in the sense that scientific orientation (what I want to study and how) may point outside a narrow specialization, outside a discipline. Comfort with distinctions within one's discipline is usually greater than the comfort with distinctions across disciplines or with distinctions concerning interdisciplinary methodology. Extra-disciplinary science may be multidisciplinary, interdisciplinary, or transdisciplinary.[30] Multidisciplinary work combines separately achieved knowledges. Interdisciplinary work lies between disciplines, both in terms of the aggregation of several methods and bodies of knowledge and in terms of the cross-fertilization of methods and inquiries. Multidisciplinary work is considered less "innovative," while interdisciplinary work exhibits methodological "innovation." "Transdisciplinary" is a term used most often by those suspicious of the methodological laxity of multidisciplinary and interdisciplinary approaches to extra-disciplinary work. From this perspective, revolutionary, if not normal, science, in Kuhn's terms, is transdisciplinary even in its narrow, disciplinarily specialized modes (usually because it initiates a reconstruction of a conceptual field by importation of an alien structural configuration) and explicitly in its large-scale, multidisciplinary research projects.

Something like the latter claim, the seeming oxymoron that good disciplinarity is transdisciplinarity, might be the point one respondent makes by refusing to distinguish: "Fundamentally, no [distinction]; specifically, methodology is already established within a discipline." All the other responses did find distinctions, of fundamental and other sorts. The three primary categories of answers are the problem, the scale, and the community. How a problem is presented for research and the scale and complexity of a problem were cited numerous times in distinguishing interdisciplinary and disciplinary research. The following expresses many similar responses well: "Disciplinary research adopts a particular subject and methodological approach (and a particular technical terminology) and develops very specialized knowledge of a problem. Interdisciplinary research brings together the methods, technical languages, and insights of several disciplines in the attempt to analyse a complex and multi-faceted problem."

The contrasts between analysis and synthesis, simplicity and complexity, specialization and generalism are invoked elsewhere in the questionnaire responses commonly. This answer betrays no beliefs concerning incompatibility of the approaches, thus suggesting compatibility; the answer also does not state an explicit preference for the value of solving one type of problem over another. Another, similar response puts the contrast in another common way: "Disciplinary research focuses on a major theme or type of knowledge; interdisciplinary research seeks to integrate the common elements from different themes in achieving a better understanding of a question or a problem." The language of integration was central to the administrative rhetoric concerning methodology (see, e.g., the grant proposal); the interdisciplinary approach appears to be preferred here precisely because of the operation of a synthesis of a plurality of themes or disciplines.

Perhaps the most interesting answer of the set is the following: "Disciplinary research works within a known, usually well understood community. Interdisciplinary research works within an imagined community. It is to the credit of the granting councils in the industrialized countries that they fund this." The reference is to Benedict Anderson's *Imagined Communities*, a highly regarded critical work of history.[31] This response links to the ways in which science was discussed in relation to community earlier; it also invokes themes of reality and unreality in doing so and moves us on to a discussion of questions of scale and Coasts Under Stress specifically. Before moving on, one final response comparing disciplinarity to interdisciplinarity bears quoting, if only for its being the most condemnatory of the whole project and because it challenges the form of some of the previous distinctions:

> Depends on the discipline. Archeology is extremely interdisciplinary in every context. Archeologists look at the trend to interdisciplinary research as a confusion between ends and means. Interdisciplinary research often confuses these two. The CUS program for example has all along been about the means and it has

never been about the ends. You would struggle to find a more aimless project than CUS – it is ID [interdisciplinarity] for the sake of ID and has never had a clear research goal. So disciplinary research tends to be more focused, and where it needs to be interdisciplinary, it is. The research question must be given pride of place.

Small, Medium, Large: Scale and Management

The scale of scientific research includes the scale of its theories, methods, instruments, objects, subjects, and financial awards.[32] More often than not, financial scale determines administrative scale which determines who does what kind of research how. What happens to knowledge makers – and to the institutions in which they work, the students they teach, etc. – when they invest their time in projects where disciplinarily-specific value is not optimized? For some, this is the movement from knowledge maker to knowledge mover, from researcher to publicist (a move that is perceived by some in the Canadian granting councils' affinity for interdisciplinarity and applied or targeted research). The large-scale character of the interdisciplinary research project necessitates, for example, that the project director becomes first and foremost a knowledge manager.

The promises as well as the problems of the CUS project were made acute by the duration of the study, the span of time across which commitment to collective work was secured by a budget, and, to a lesser extent, the projected span (based on promise and trust in a new application) for a continuation of the project, perhaps for another five years.[33] The time commitment required for participation was high, and so concerns regarding the value of the project were acute. If participation was highly valuable to a participant in terms of estimated potential gain in academic and financial capital (more likely for junior and student participants than mid-level or senior faculty, though more likely for faculty occupying very high places in the administrative structure than for those in the nebulous middle strata), then continuation of involvement in the current project was important, and hopes of participation in its projected continuation were likely. The situation was reversed for those who believed their academic capital might be idling or depreciating as a function of involvement.

Responses to the ranking questions having to do with personal experience in Coasts Under Stress reveal nothing overly surprising.[34] The questions were of two sorts: (a) questions concerning how a respondent's ideas about science, research, disciplinarity, community activism, and politics had changed over the course of the project and (b) questions concerning how well organized the project was.[35] Regarding the first set, a handful of responses to each question claimed participating in the project had had no effect at all, while an even smaller handful, half a handful or so, claimed their ideas had changed entirely. The majority of responses fell in the "changed a little" and "changed moderately" categories. The strongest indication in the "very much" category concerned interdisciplinary research, as might be expected.

In the second set of questions, questions concerning the organization of the project, each statement affirms a positive experience of integration in the project (e.g., "The project as a whole is well-organized") and the respondent is asked to agree or disagree (or agree or disagree strongly). The majority of responses to each question/statement – with one notable exception – lie in the "agree" category.[36] This is a positive assessment by a majority of respondents of the organizational structure.[37]

Respondents were then asked to comment on whether they thought "the overall organization of CUS could be improved" and if so, how. A number of responses mentioned overly large size and lack of integration:[38] "The organization and administrative structure of CUS is fine. However, the program overall is too big. Half the number of researchers would have been better. There should have been more integration of the projects from the original proposed stage." A number of criticisms deal with this issue of better planning and initial definition of issues and goals;[39] another one gives the following advice: "[I]f we could start again, I would (i) plan the project and then recruit the participants as necessary and (ii) reduce the size and (iii) budget more face-to-face meetings."[40] Another, similar response also notes that now that things are set in motion, the question is redundant or in the wrong tense: "Let me answer this by rephrasing the question to read 'could have been improved.' It would have been better to put together teams of researchers to address defined issues as drawn up to frame the overall project. As it was, it became necessary to create form out of the proposals that happened to come in."[41]

This response raises numerous issues. First, there are issues concerning time and how large-scale and relatively long-duration projects use time and capital (including symbolic capital) compared to more traditional, shorter-term disciplinarily aligned work. Large projects usually take more time, in part because of the organization involved and in part perhaps because of the complexity of the object of study. Investment in such projects thus ties up or fixes research capital in a certain way. Different durations and structures of research work create their own problems and promises. What may be deficiencies for a certain mode of scientific work may be necessary hurdles or potential values for another mode of work. There might be some truth to the idea of throwing the dice and working with the results, though this is not the usual image of science that scientists like to portray.[42]

Some of the responses to this question were quite personal and went into detail concerning a respondent's particular experiences. The CUS project adopted the seastar as a metaphor for its organizational structure: the team was organized into five arms (they were eventually reorganized or merged), each of which had sub-studies (or suckers) that might also be cut or merged. The following response features a much-discussed and contentious topic for the team, namely, a cut of part of the fourth research arm (having to do with seismic and geological assessment) that was requested in the granting councils' mid-term site review report.[43] The response points to the need for reflexivity in the project and practical guidelines flowing from such reflection:

> I was incredibly disappointed when part of Arm 4 was cut. I had learned a considerable amount, put a lot of time (some extra) into the project, and felt I had much more to learn about collaboration with social scientists. I found the 'cut' insulting and it leaves me wondering about the knowledge of the funding advisors. As a natural scientist, I had to get my study completed before considering going into the communities but I definitely wanted collaboration with social scientists on how and when to enter communities and what the communities may want. I am at the community stage, [about] to enter [the] phase, but with the 'cuts' I wonder if this will ever be achieved in CUS for my project. I have had some initial good feedback from CUS [from] social scientists. But time and cuts may not allow community entry. Also no future CUS meetings I feel is a large mistake which will reduce collaboration, one of the main goals of the project. I hope CUS will come up with some recommendations to funders as to new ways of thinking about science funding and flexibility.

This is one of the longest responses to any question in the questionnaire. It raises issues concerning loyalty to other members of a research arm, the need for guidance and collaboration (especially at the stage of moving knowledge), and, centrally, the nature of the community in which the researcher is taking part and the support from that community upon embarkation on an activity apparently new to this natural scientist: entering the community outside the universities to discuss their research.

It is with regret that I have said little concerning the relation between university researchers and administrators, on the one side, and the variety of communities and partner organizations either implicitly or explicitly involved in the research. In part this has been a question for me of focus and scope, but not one that I am much satisfied with. The connection between university, that is, academic, expert, or scientific, knowledge and local and community knowledge is, after all, one of the main themes of the project as a whole and a strong concern of many of the researchers.[44] The response above articulates the respondent's frustration with the loss of what was above described as a tying up or fixing of research capital (which includes resource and collaborative personnel). The response lays blame outside the research team and, in this case, with the funders' direct intervention. The strength of the attachment to the research community is marked, as is the desire to maintain cross-disciplinary collaboration (repeated frustration is expressed regarding the threat to the interdisciplinary research community, which threatens, in turn, this particular researcher's confidence in approaching the community outside the academy). Withdrawal from the community is by implication a great loss, against which the respondent again turns to the research community for aid, by way of an appeal for reflexivity with practical recommendations.

The final response I will quote from this section emphasizes the above-mentioned desire for stronger links between the university and the outside community. The issue is here put again in terms of moving knowledge from one community to another but holds implications as well for the impact this may have on what knowledge is made and how:

> I think if we all went to a community for six weeks we'd get further. We do almost no team reporting to communities. We lack a professional dissemination and media approach. That includes a newsletter circulating within the group, not just outside. What we

do away from meetings is only seen as power point slides. We are overly reliant on "books = knowledge." Books are commodities with limited shelf-life usually, and that shelf-life decreases exponentially the wider the focus. No one even indexes knowledge in team proceedings. Communities cannot penetrate the language cultures. Nor do academics produce knowledge fast enough for policy makers, who should have been integrated into the team from the start, think tank style. Why are we running after trains? How does that serve the advancement of knowledge or improve the lives of people in coastal communities? I still do not know how we are improving those lives. Is that our goal?[45]

In addition to providing a neat principle by which to estimate the value of books, this one included, this response gives various positive suggestions for improving the community channels by which knowledge moves and through which knowledge is made. Language, the language of specialization and science, is here cited as a primary block to knowledge flows. The language of the newsletter and the media is offered as a way of stimulating knowledge circulation. This answer, like an earlier one quoted, makes direct reference to policy recommendations and for an antidote draws on the culture or community of the think-tank, which is alien to and in some ways a competitor of the university in the field of knowledge making. Whatever one may think of this assessment of the goals and value of the project, the frustration and intelligent grappling with ways to reduce it is manifest.

The penultimate question on the questionnaire asked respondents what they thought was the project's "primary goal." A variety of answers followed. Some gave what is close to the officially stated goals of the project, such as the following exemplar: "To understand the impacts of environmental and economic restructuring (especially as caused by humans) on the health and well-being of coastal communities, individuals, and environment."[46] There are a number of other kinds of answers. Some feature advocacy and political change, rather than research problems. Others emphasize the interdisciplinary or research community experiment (with some respondents praising this and others bemoaning it): "Networking"; "Discipline-Bridging"; "Consilience of interdisciplinary science and social studies."[47] Some are more pointed: "Demonstrate effectiveness of large-scale interdisciplinary research and influence public policy."[48]

PROBLEMS AND PROMISES OF REFLEXIVITY

Bourdieu applied his reflexive methodology to the study of French academics (1984b), hypothesizing relationships between academic and class position and receiving substantial resistance to his questionnaires from knowledge producers who did not think that they should be subjected to research. In a more recent work (1996), he studies the field of academic institutions in France in order to assess how class is mediated by institutions of higher learning. In both cases, in his reflexive study of members of the academy and in his field analysis of the power of institutions of higher learning, Bourdieu's work has shown in precise and quantifiable ways (see, e.g., his correspondence analysis in both 1984b and 1996) the power relations in which academics work and the effects of such power relations on attitudes and practices.

This reflexive study, like the body of knowledge which it is tracking, has transformed through time, as a result of chance, decisions, interests, politics, and so on, to a point where some of its original aims have been abandoned (ethnographic participant observation) and others remain to be completed (interviews, correspondence analysis, archival analysis, conclusions).

The location (geographic, administrative, institutional, and financial) of this reflexive study within the larger body that it took as its object raised both promises and problems in terms of fulfilling the reflexive mandate. On the one hand, my involvement as primary investigator on the reflexive study, within the group as a whole likely lessened the distrust, suspicion, and animosity that an academic researcher might feel at the prospect of becoming an object of study. Mutual involvement in a shared enterprise ordinarily lessens distrust and increases openness. The extent of such an effect is hard to measure, though, and familiarity has countervailing tendencies, such as the breeding of mistrust and contempt. My participation in the larger body was also seen as an issue for the methodological validity of the study.[49] Often such objections took it for granted that inclusion of a subjective point of view in a study immediately negates any claim to scientific status.

The participation rate in the reflexive study was not high.[50] The response rate was affected by a variety of variables, including dislike or disapproval of the study, concerns about confidentiality, the time required (approximately one hour, estimated in the pretest), and forgetfulness. Misunderstanding of the study contributed also. There were continual confusions between the study and management personnel or management function. Some of these confusions resulted, I believe, form the location of the reflexive study in the centre of the sea-star.[51] Other confusions were attributable to what I believe were questionable decisions concerning the presentation, discussion, and criticism of my study and lack of attention to the explanation of the study distributed in written form with each questionnaire and discussed in numerous oral presentations.[52]

Judgments concerning the value of the project, as well as corollary decisions about involvement in it, were brought to a point of intensity in the reflexive study, in that the mandate of the reflexive study was to assess the very thing that participants themselves were attempting to figure out (i.e., the value of the project and their engagement in it). How would participation in the reflexive study increase or decrease the value of the project as a whole (which might be estimated to be high or low, depending on the particular subject) and so, perhaps, require revisiting one's commitment to it? A participant would have to estimate the value of the reflexive study itself to be able to answer the previous question, which, expressed differently, means that trust in the reflexive study was yet again a prerequisite for participation (trust here corresponding to an explicit or implicit evaluation of the reflexive study as somehow "worth my while").

The value of the reflexive study could be defined in various ways, as determined, e.g., by how much the reflexive study would corroborate the general experiment, or, on the other hand, by how much light the reflexive study would shed on the nature and value of large-scale interdisciplinary science and so be of use in determining, at least to some extent, the future direction of large funding initiatives (by promoting, transforming, or negating them) and the organization and methodology of interdisciplinary and transdisciplinary work.[53]

It is easy to see how my reflexive research could be confused with something like an administrative performance review. I tried to remedy such confusion by emphasizing the research character of the study and distinguishing it from the anthropological study out of which it had initially grown. Such remedies only went so far, however, and I would speculate that suspicions about the administrative uses of my research explain some of the refusals to participate, especially the low rate of student participation (where fears of the consequences of such an administrative review would be felt most strongly). The elimination of the students from the study – their self-elimination and then the consequent elimination called forth by me in the name of scientific method – cuts out one of the most fruitful areas for commentary, for three primary reasons: the major power relation amongst researchers in Coasts Under Stress was between research assistants (often students at the master's or doctoral level) and faculty (professors of various ranks, with or without doctorates); the granting councils emphasized student training, including by way of stipulations concerning levels of funding; and, consequently, Coasts Under Stress emphasized student training. My apologies to the few students who did take the time to fill in the questionnaire, though I assure you that I have read it and I have listened to what every individual involved with Coasts Under Stress has told me.

The trust that was required for participation in the reflexive study was not based on any guarantee of ethical or dignified treatment of data and identifying information but in the promise of something like fair treatment. The writing up of my analysis of the study, especially given my reserve in commenting on what I was finding out, has been the first opportunity for the subjects made objects in the reflexive study to witness the results of that objectification.

My subjective "take on things" is inescapable, no matter how the methodology (of the quantifiable, qualitative, and theoretical aspects) of the study is conceived. I would argue that this fact does not impede, but rather strengthens, my ability to understand the situation. I would argue further that no science escapes this subjective situation (though this need not weaken science thereby). Involvement in discussion of study results and the collective writing up of the results of the project as a whole necessitated various decisions concerning how the reflexive study was itself to take up the requirements of the whole (some of which might jeopardize its independence).

The attempt at interdisciplinary, collective work in the writing of this book has shaped my writing of this essay in various ways. First, it should be noted that the contributors to this volume include the project director, Rosemary Ommer, another member of the Executive committee, Harold Coward (one of the few humanists), and Barbara Neis, once a member of the East Coast steering committee, who first engaged me in the project. The writing of this piece, like all the others in this volume, went through a collective critical regimen. All the pieces, perhaps only excepting this one, were written by two or more individuals. This essay itself builds on the work of a number of individuals in a team and outside the team over several years. Such work includes collaborative writing (e.g., of abstracts and proposals), as well as intellectual challenge and development through conversation, criticism, and formal presentation of ideas.

It is difficult to quantify the intellectual or scientific progress that comes from the encounter of minds in various settings. Part of the allure of interdisciplinary work is the opportunity to be taken out of one's familiar zone into a novel area of work and thought. I have certainly learned a lot through the course of various meetings (often tedious and longer than they should have been) and met people that I like to exchange ideas with. I have not, however, felt that my ability or my project has been well understood. I could have done much more, I believe, in contributing to the project in the spirit of its mandate and method.

Trained as a philosopher and having worked in interdisciplinary contexts over a long time, I attempted to introduce the elements of my scholarly training at the opportune times – in discussions of ethics, the ethics of research, definitions, definitions of health, the relation between ecological and human health – but with what I believe was little success. I remember being rebuffed, for example, during a plenary discussion of definitions of health for suggesting that we should broaden our bibliography to include significant French and German contributions to the debate (e.g., Canguilhem 1978; Luhmann 1989). In general I found the theoretical and methodological point of view of the social science researchers to be constrained by a preference for local and national authorities. Theoretical discussion concerning, e.g., the interaction between natural and social systems and theories of health and illness, was markedly low in references to theoretical or international texts.

While I discussed what I was doing with various individuals in CUS throughout my involvement, it was not until a meeting in Victoria in 2004 for the preparation of publications that I presented my work. Each essay in the volume had a lead author and two critical readers, each of whom presented a report. Round-table critical discussion followed. I was critical of various essays, and various individuals were critical of mine, including a collaborator on the project, John Kennedy, and Rosemary Ommer. I had expected some grief because my essay was not yet finished (not unlike others and in part because I hesitated to reveal some of my findings and interpretations, a hesitation due to my distrust about getting a fair hearing) and because of what I indicated about the project. The discussion was animated but polite. At one point

I said that in writing a preliminary analysis of a study and presenting it to my research subjects, I wanted to outline to them some of the more negative potential findings. The complication of critical participatory writing is shown in such a situation. I was surprised to receive the support that I did for the essay, especially since it urged me to do what I had wanted from the start, namely, to make my own voice clear in the writing and not to hide behind my instruments.

The critical comments on this essay by the authors of this book have transformed it by showing me that I can be kinder and by pushing me to say what I think I ought to say.

CONCLUDING REMARKS

"Theory" may mean something like the "foregone conclusion" the mistrustful scientist projects onto the work in progress of the humanist.[54] It may also mean the considerations, aims, and means by which a methodology is assembled and against which it is tested. That theory and method may be seen at one and the same time, if not by the same individual, as oppositional *and* intrinsically related reveals the confusion and variety of attitudes toward scientific research today. Dividing theory and method assumes an oppositional stance between them, as if one could win out without the other. The reason for doing so is no more than a preference for one or another discipline or group of disciplines,[55] a preference that separates inseparables and dichotomizes and stratifies intellectual work, disciplines, and whole groups of disciplines.

The question of soundness is often confused with the issue of origins. Attempting to define a good approach, we search back for a safe harbor, a launching point of impeccable qualifications that will somehow guarantee the voyage. What Kuhn has called "normal" natural and social scientific research is overly concerned with method, while everyday humanities research is overly concerned with reading and writing (absent, in appearance or reality, method).[56] We should be aware of the distinct (and perhaps incompatible or incommensurable) attitudes toward method and scientific research that exist among academic researchers, attitudes that encompass disciplinarily specific points of view concerning exact definitions and statistical approaches, as well as theoretical and political points of view on the relative merits (and meanings and interconnections) of research, data, statistics, analysis, thought, practice, and politics.

If the apparently untenable and ideological opposition of theory and method is rejected,[57] the question remains as to how much of which goes into making a science.[58] How do theories and methods change during the course of research? Are these changes good or bad? How are research results to be evaluated (results such as the corroboration of the methodological design; conclusions concerning behavior of the object studied drawn within the parameters of the research design and hence limited by the specific states measured at specific locations and times; conclusions concerning trends and tendencies that may be extrapolated from measured coordinates; conclusions concerning the inadequacy of the research design or the limitations of research knowledge concerning a phenomenon owing to the nature of that phenomenon – e.g., in the case of human populations, their capacities to understand and change)?

Minimal attention was given at the start of the large project to issues of theory and method concerning the whole (for example, to the interdisciplinary research that was to be the working together of a large number of diverse scientists from across the academic spectrum). Interdisciplinarity was talked about in only general terms as a process of integration of specific bodies of knowledge; the process of integration was described in terms of an administrative hierarchy (using the metaphor of the seastar, with a centre and five arms, initially).[59] Questions concerning theory and method were bound to come up in an explicitly interdisciplinary and large-scale research project. The working hypothesis, made explicit at times, was something like the following: no prior resolution of methodological or theoretical differences is likely; they will be worked out in practice. Coasts Under Stress thus positioned itself as an experiment, without wanting to give up some of the value and status of established, accepted science.

The case appears to have preceded theories and methods. This may be an anomaly of interdisciplinary research or a truism of good science. That this is an open question opens another possible question, namely, whether in this case, the theory and method of this large-scale interdisciplinary research group had more to do with facts of administration (that individuals had agreed to participate and were being funded to do so in a particular administrative structure by two federal granting councils)[60] than with requirements of science. Administrative requirements, which is to say financial and political requirements, created an opportunity in which science would, so to speak, have to work itself out in terms of its theory and methodology.[61] Science might, presumably, either advance or not, depending on the outcome (so that the theory and methodology of the whole, in this case, come out close to last). Whichever the case, the ambivalent role of theory and method in such a process of scientific research should be studied.

13
Circularizing Knowledge Flows: Institutional Structures, Policies, and Practices for Community-University Collaborations

KELLY VODDEN AND KELLY BANNISTER

INTRODUCTION

The once-contested idea of integrating local, traditional, and scientific knowledge for policy decisions has now become an accepted notion by decision makers from local to international levels. While not long ago the experiential knowledge of local fishermen and aboriginal elders alike was dismissed as unreliable, M'Gonigle (1999, 131–2) notes that "as part of the broader historical movement that is now challenging the larger political economy of science, these [local and traditional] forms of knowledge are increasingly being recognized for the sophisticated understandings built into them and for the benefits to sustainability that would attend the operationalization of these understandings." One indicator of this recognition is the increasing number of funding opportunities for university research collaboration with community-based organizations and First Nations that encourage research outcomes of social relevance in both practical and policy realms.

Canada's research granting agencies have launched a host of new collaborative research programs over the past few years. Some examples include:

- the Community-University Research Alliance (CURA) Program of the Social Sciences and Humanities Research Council (SSHRC),

- the Community Alliances for Health Research (CAHR) Program of the Canadian Institutes of Health Research (CIHR),
- the Major Collaborative Research Initiative (MCRI) Program of SSHRC and the Natural Sciences and Engineering Reasearch Council (NSERC),
- the Northern Research Development Program of SSHRC,
- the Aboriginal Research Program of SSHRC, and
- the Centres for Research in Youth, Science Teaching, and Learning (CRYSTAL) Pilot Program of NSERC.

The Coasts Under Stress (CUS) Project, supported by the SSHRC's MCRI program, with matching funds from NSERC, reflects a willingness to fund research that is interdisciplinary and that involves government and civil-society partners to varying degrees.

Some authors applaud efforts to forge a stronger link between university research and contemporary social, economic, and ecological problems, while others argue that university research within Canada is falling victim to corporatization, barely concealed under the guise of greater relevance (Newson 1998; Lieberwitz 2000; Gould 2003). What all sides agree on is that the university is changing in a fundamental way and that research is increasingly driven by more applied, practical questions. Markey et al. (2004) suggest three reasons for this shift. First, in an era of budget restraint and demand for increased accountability, government policy-makers and funding agencies are seeking to demonstrate more clearly the value returned for public dollars invested in research. Second, many researchers themselves are adopting a more critical approach, increasingly acknowledging the situatedness and limitations of "expert" (i.e., academic, scientific, or technical) knowledge and expressing a desire not only to better understand but also to have a positive impact on communities and society in general (Raffensperger et al. 1999). Moreover, Canadian practices have been influenced by international recognition of the potential contributions of local and traditional knowledge to scientific research and sustainable development (IUCN et al. 1991; WCED 1987).

Third, many communities and individuals are feeling "researched to death," and thus are reluctant to participate in new projects governed by outsiders unless the research aims to transform their contributions into results that are meaningful at a local level. The term "research" is often equated with exploitation, particularly in an aboriginal context (CIHR-IAPH 2002; Smith 1999; Weinstein 1998; Pepall 1998). An "enough is enough" sentiment is evident. In some cases, such as the James Bay Cree Nation, a moratorium on outside research has been imposed (Batten 2002). In many other cases, communities and local/ First Nations governments are establishing research protocols, legislation requiring research licenses, and contractual agreements for information and benefit sharing.[1] Generally, there is a trend toward communities insisting on more involvement in and control over the research process.

While barriers to forging common meanings remain, at least in *principle*, it appears that the conceptual challenge of bringing together different contextual and situated ways of knowing, in order to address current issues, is beginning to be addressed. Our chapter explores the interrelated challenges of *practice* in such work. In particular, we examine how knowledge does or does not move between universities and communities and why. We argue that while the collective *will* to attempt to merge knowledge systems is growing, the *way* is still lacking. Thus, a "discussion of how the bringing together of local knowledge with scientific knowledge results in wisdom" (Ommer et al., this volume, chapter 2) would be remiss without critical reflection on systemic barriers to knowledge flow and consideration of how institutional policies and practices support or impede this process. Such reflection suggests that the motivation behind the will to do this, and the level of commitment (individual and institutional) to integrate knowledge forms, can have considerable influence on the long-term outcomes of collaborative partnerships.

University research involving communities does not occur in a void; individuals and community groups often have developed their own capacities, styles, and expectations around the research endeavour, be it through informal networks, local institutions, or customary practices. Similarly, community-university collaboration must operate within the context of the institutional policies and procedures of the university, such as the protection of academic freedom, rights to intellectual property, ethics policies for research involving humans, and constraints on allocation of funds. As the following case studies demonstrate, these policies may lead to conflict between university and community expectations. For example, community partners may expect university researchers to exert political influence through dissemination and application of research results, while university researchers may consider exerting this influence to be outside their role, or even unethical. University researchers may feel constrained by project budgets, while community members may see them as "rich," with research funds much larger than most community projects. Differences in power, values, traditions, and resources all influence the community-university relationship, as do past experiences, including feelings of mistrust or suspicion that may be inherited by current researchers, whether they are based in the community or the university.

Genuinely collaborative community-university partnerships involve broadening and democratizing the research process (Schroeder 1997; Freire 1970/1992). As Ansley and Gaventa (1997, 53) note, "Questions about these matters involve recognizing that there are competing rights and values in a democracy – hard issues from which researchers and their institutions should not be immune. Rather than being ignored, or routinized through deadening procedures, these challenges should be injected into debates about research in administrative halls, faculty offices and classrooms." Such debates must consider both the advantages of incorporating new sources and types of knowledge (e.g., local and traditional knowledge into the academic research process, and academic science into community processes), as well as the potential costs and challenges.

The risks of the community-based research approach include becoming "too close" to communities (or to one subset of a community) and thus losing the illusion of autonomy and objectivity that lends academic research greater credibility than, for example, studies commissioned by industry or other interest groups. It is this air of neutrality, however questionable, given our understanding of socially constructed knowledge, that allows the university to uphold the role of "honest broker." Communities and others in civil society often use the neutral, critical thinker and her work to challenge the status quo and/or advance claims for social benefit. Thus, it is in everyone's interest to protect a degree of separation, while at the same time seeking to build partnerships. This is but one example of the risks, challenges, and complexities that both parties must consider in the design and implementation of university-community collaboration.

Various institutional models for university engagement with "community" exist,[2] ranging from extension services and continuing studies departments, to US land grant universities and their cooperative research and extension services, to community-based research centres and European science shops.[3] Such models are the basis or inspiration for university-community partnerships by Canadian researchers and their institutions, but none can be considered standard within the country. Some models are mostly research-focused, while others promote education and outreach, but all are predicated on sharing of information and facilitating new understandings. In this chapter we look at some specific examples and explore "how" and "how well." That is, how are ideas and information transmitted from universities to communities and vice versa? How well does knowledge move and how do understandings flow? What are the essential components of reciprocal interchanges and what are the main barriers to such exchanges?

We seek preliminary answers to these questions from a retrospective analysis of three case studies of community-university partnerships from different geographic areas on the west and east coasts of Canada, including the Northern Barkley and Clayoquot Sound region of western Vancouver Island (British Columbia), northern Vancouver Island (British Columbia), and the Indian Bay watershed (Newfoundland). Additional insight has been gained through associated field research in the Bras d'Or Lakes watershed of Cape Breton. The following section provides contextual background on each of these areas, a description of the university-community partnership model employed, and an analysis of its respective advantages, disadvantages, opportunities, and challenges. Structures, policies, and practices that facilitate or impede reciprocal knowledge exchange are examined within the case study regions. Case study information was gathered through a combination of a literature survey, interviews, and participant observation, including direct participation in institutional operation and/or development by the authors. Our participation in and our analysis of the case studies were supported in part by the CUS project.

CASE STUDIES

Northern Barkley and Clayoquot Sound: The Clayoquot Alliance for Research, Education and Training

The Clayoquot Alliance for Research, Education and Training (CLARET) is a formal partnership between the Centre for Public Sector Studies at the University of Victoria (UVic) and the Clayoquot Biosphere Trust (CBT). The CBT is a non-profit organization formed in 2000, following designation of Clayoquot Sound (west coast of Vancouver Island) as a UNESCO Biosphere Reserve. It received a $12 million federal grant to establish an endowment fund, the income from which is intended to foster conservation and sustainable development and support local research, education, and training initiatives in the Biosphere Reserve region. As the community partner in CLARET, the CBT is meant to be a conduit for First Nations and non-aboriginal communities of the Biosphere Reserve region who live in Northern Barkley and Clayoquot Sound. Likewise, as the university partner, Public Sector Studies is envisioned as a link to other academic units at UVic, as well as to other university campuses.[4]

The idea for the CLARET partnership grew out of a shared desire to understand fundamental social transformations occurring due to economic structural readjustment and evolving understandings of human relationships with uncertain and complex natural ecosystems (Bannister et al. 2003). A large part of the labour force in the region has relied on forestry and fisheries industries that have been seriously affected by declining fish stocks, environmental concerns, and corporate decisions (Dobell and Bunton 2001). First Nations communities, logging interests, environmental groups, and local communities hold a wide diversity of local views on land use and resource management. Although the region has experienced a "volatile history" of "confrontation and conflict," Dobell and Bunton (2001, 11) note that the consensus-building process leading to the UNESCO designation of Clayoquot Sound as a Biosphere Reserve is evidence of efforts "to build mutual respect and trust, and to tackle problems in a more participatory manner."

The CLARET partnership received three years of funding from the CURA program of SSHRC.[5] Partnership goals included

- linking community needs and interests with academic concerns and making the education and training resources of the university more accessible in the region;
- creating better understanding of how research and knowledge can support policy formation, decision making and action (in communities and governments); and
- establishing a long-term resource centre, or "science shop," for ongoing community-university connections designed to foster collaborative research, education, and training initiatives (Bannister et al. 2003).

The region includes the two villages of Ucluelet and Tofino and five Nuu-chah-nulth First Nations living in several small villages.[6] About half the region's population of approximately four thousand, is of First Nations descent.[7] The communities are located in coastal temperate rainforest amid a diversity of ecosystems, including unlogged watersheds, old-growth forests, streams and rivers, mudflats, and marine environments that are rich in biodiversity. The region's natural wonders attract almost one million visitors a year, and with further increases in tourism are expected (Dobell and Bunton 2001).

The "research culture" within the area is intense, largely owing to the vast opportunities provided to outside researchers by the natural environment. Significant research capacity exists within the region, as well; there are skilled individuals with research experience and academic qualifications and individuals such as First Nations elders who are highly respected for their cultural and experiential knowledge. Many research-oriented local organizations and institutional innovations have developed around governance and natural resource management.[8] As well, many university researchers from Canada and elsewhere have established collaborations with organizations and First Nations in the region.

Some residents and members of local First Nations expressed high levels of frustration at feeling "researched to death" and "meeting'ed to death." At the same time, most local people who are interested and involved in research indicated they did not know how to access the large body of collective information and knowledge that presumably has resulted from all this research. Among other things, CLARET was seen as an opportunity to understand the local socio-political and cultural contexts in which research occurs and to contribute to building a more organized network of collaborators to facilitate longer-term, sustainable research relationships and higher degrees of local involvement.

Within CLARET, activities have been undertaken by co-op students, graduate students, community research associates, and university researchers, many of whom were "borrowed" from other projects to make an in kind contribution. Community members also "borrowed" from their jobs in the public or non-profit sector. A significant challenge initially for researchers and community members alike was how to engage with each other, given a high degree of community distrust of outside researchers, the feelings of being over-researched and over-burdened by contributing to research as volunteers, and the sense of being uninformed about the end results in the region.

The academic researchers initially set aside their enthusiasms and preconceptions regarding the research vision and initial research priorities in the face of competing visions within the community. Rather than initiating work from the outset on topics for which good academic models and resources already existed, they redirected their plans as community interests were made clear. Initial projects were developed in direct response to specific, community concerns. For example, to better understand how collaborative research ought to be conducted across the various "cultures" involved (academic, non-aboriginal community, and First Nations), an overarching initial project was undertaken to co-define research protocols, resulting in an agreed standard of research conduct for the region.[9] The process was critical for the CLARET partnership but lengthy in terms of academic research timelines (i.e., two years of meetings and workshops) and thus costly. The resulting *Standard of Conduct for Research in the Northern Barkley and Clayoquot Sound Communities* is instructive, but challenges remain concerning how to get it out to the university research community (CLARET 2005). One solution currently being explored is for university research and ethics policies to formally acknowledge local research protocols and require affiliated researchers undertaking activities in the communities to comply.

To address local concerns about the lack of access to an accumulated body of knowledge about the region existing as "grey literature" (e.g., industry, government, and NGO reports; discussion papers; and other non-peer reviewed sources), a systematic inventory of social and environmental research was undertaken by a community consultant, in order to create a local research archive and electronic database. The database is meant to serve as a reference point for future research in the region, to eliminate redundancies, and to build on the knowledge base that already exists. The work was subsequently extended into a community mapping project and regional information system undertaken in partnership with the West Coast Vancouver Island Aquatic Management Board. Significantly more time and funds will be required to develop an appropriately sophisticated cataloguing and database system to enable culturally sensitive information (e.g., some local First Nations' traditional knowledge) to be included and password-protected. A remaining challenge relates to how to make this kind of information accessible to university researchers without the communities giving up too much control.[10]

Communication between communities and universities is challenging, but communication across cultural differences is even more challenging. As a fundamental part of building cross-cultural relationships and with the recognition that First Nations understandings about the natural world are embedded in language, CLARET supported a local Nuu-chah-nulth language revitalization project. A new non-profit society called the Nuu-chah-nulth Central Region Language Group was created. The group recently released a multimedia CD-ROM, produced in partnership with Parks Canada, documenting Nuu-chah-nulth names and cultural knowledge of flora, fauna, and the local environment.[11] Other research priorities identified more recently from the communities include understanding and contributing to community health,[12] and understanding the effects of the growth of tourism on local economies, the environment, and social health (CLARET 2004). However, the three-year SSHRC/CURA grant ended in 2004, and an application for a two-year extension was unsuccessful, so the capacity of CLARET to undertake projects on these themes is uncertain.

Since three years is much too short a time frame to build a collaborative partnership and complete a research program, an ongoing commitment from both community and university ends will be required to continue the partnership. An application for a further round of CURA funding for 2005–10 was also unsuccessful, despite strong support in principle expressed by the president of SSHRC at the time. The community partner (CBT) has indicated its support to carry the administrative and financial burden of the partnership to the extent that is possible, but the university partner (UVic) lacks any resources to support infrastructure and costs. However, a new Office of Community-Based Research has been created through the Office of the Vice President Research at Uvic. This new office is a core-supported structure that aims, as its name implies, facilitate community-based research, and it may help maintain community-university partnerships during periods between project funding.[13] The university side of the partnership, at least in the interim, will depend on committed individual researchers who can continue to borrow their own time from other funded projects or participate as volunteers, and in that way offset, to some degree, the problem of inadequate core funding.

This tension between the need for ongoing commitment in community-based research and the need for continuing accountability associated with competitive processes for research funding is a central element in the institutional misalignments that inevitably attend such cross-cultural research initiatives. The underlying question is, once a partnership such as CLARET has proven itself to be viable with limited-term project money, can an ongoing commitment by the university be institutionalized (e.g., by establishing a science shop-like entity or some other facilitative entity)? If not, researchers are left to continually re-invent the wheel in building partnerships anew with each new round of grant funding, thereby losing valuable potential to move collaborative research to more sophisticated levels that build upon previous work. It is the more sophisticated and longer-term collaborative research relationships that will lead to the integration of knowledge systems and the co-production of knowledge that projects such as CLARET and CUS seek to achieve.

Northern Vancouver Island, British Columbia: The Inner Coast Natural Resource Centre

The "North Island" region encompasses the top third of Vancouver Island (north of Campbell River), the adjacent mainland area, and islands in between. The region generally corresponds with the boundaries of Mount Waddington Regional District and the territories of the Kwakwaka'wakw peoples. Like Clayoquot Sound, ecologically the region is rich and diverse. It is also large and sparsely populated, with approximately 11,650 residents[14] (less than 0.7 people per square km) (Statistics Canada 2006). There are six municipalities in the region, ranging in size from 400 to almost 5,300 residents, as well as several smaller, unincorporated communities and twelve First Nations, whose villages and traditional territories lie within the regional district boundaries.[15] An increasing proportion of the population is made up of people of First Nations descent, with 17 percent reported in 2002 (BC 2002). Logging and forestry make up the region's largest employer, followed by manufacturing, retail trade, accommodation, food and beverages, and education. Both the logging and the fishing industries have been hard hit by economic restructuring and resource decline or degradation over the past decade (Vodden 1999).

North Islanders have long realized that information and knowledge are key requirements for increasing local control over resource management and economic development. Studies of the region had often been done by outside agencies that came in, conducted research and, as in Clayoquot Sound, took their results with them. In 1995, a group of Alert Bay residents launched an initiative to resolve this problem. A steering committee was formed through the Alert Bay Economic Development Commission to work towards forming what was to become the Inner Coast Natural Resource Centre (ICNRC), a locally driven research and education centre. In 1996, a successful application was made to the provincial Crown corporation Forest Renewal BC for funds to complete a viability analysis and a business plan. A number of local and external organizations offered their support, signing partnership agreements indicating how they would be involved. The ICNRC developed such agreements with more than twenty-five organizations, including local First Nations, municipal and regional governments, industry, non-government and labour organizations, government agencies, and post-secondary institutions (both universities and colleges).

Located in a formerly abandoned school, the ICNRC officially opened its doors in June 1997. Since then more than twenty-five initiatives have been undertaken, including research projects, workshops, and conferences. Projects have addressed a broad range of topics, such as linking science and local knowledge; community development planning; value-added seafood processing; non-timber forests products research and development; selective fisheries; sea lice research; Geographic Information Systems; coastal planning; resource mapping; the habitat productivity of a highly valued estuary; and development of a resource library, website, research registry, and draft research protocol.[16] The protocol is modelled in part on and is compatible with the 'Namgis First Nation research protocol,'[17] which also must be adhered to when research is conducted within 'Namgis traditional territory.

Projects are developed in one of two ways. Over the years various exercises have been undertaken by the ICNRC to identify research priorities for the region, beginning with an extensive consultation in 1996 and periodic priority reviews since then with local representatives that form the ICNRC Board of Directors. Projects are either initiated from this prioritized project "wish list" or introduced by outside agencies. When a university wishes to conduct a project in the region, staff and board members will review it and, if it is deemed appropriate and beneficial to the region, offer their support and involvement.

Significant capacity exists in the region in the form of skilled individuals with research experience and qualifications. This capacity has been strengthened by the role of the ICNRC and its partners in providing research training and experience, along with a local research institution that can be mobilized when resources are available. The ICNRC has established credibility as a neutral forum for dialogue and information sharing and has completed a number of worthwhile projects. Conferences have brought hundreds of visitors to the region. Further, the academic community has benefited from the experience of working and learning in a remote coastal community, integrating academic with local and traditional knowledge. However, for various reasons, ultimately the ICNRC has not lived up to its vision or full potential and remains limited in capacity.

Lack of core funding support is the primary barrier to the ICNRC's success, since it has limited the organization's ability to foster new relationships, maintain existing ones, or initiate new projects. Initial seed funding was received in 1997 from the Regional District and the Vancouver Foundation. Since then the organization has operated with in-kind support and project funding, including a project administration charge that has financed costs such as rent, telephone services, and part-time administrative staff but that has not enabled the ICNRC to hire an executive director. Such a position has always been considered critical to the organization's success. Volunteers who have attempted to fill the coordination void have experienced burnout.

While university-initiated projects have brought important achievements in addressing local research needs and facilitating public education and dialogue, there is limited scope for channelling funds to local research partners under programs sponsored by agencies such as SSHRC. Key university partners such as Simon Fraser University (SFU) Continuing Studies in Science have been innovative in finding ways to direct project administration dollars and funding to the organization for collaborative initiatives. At the same time ICNRC staff and volunteers have contributed significant amounts of time and energy to these initiatives of mutual interest. The strong ivolvement of SFU Continuing Studies, along with the affiliated Centre for Coastal Studies is facilitated by both departments' mandates for community service and outreach. Most recently partnership initiatives have been supported through a SSHRC- and DFO- funded Ocean Management Research Network and the Linking Science and Local Knowledge node of that network, based at the Centre for Coastal Studies and inclusive of community partners such as the ICNRC, along with government agencies and academic researchers from coast to coast. That said, the ability of the network to financially support the activities of partner/member organizations is limited.

A second major barrier has been created by local politics and difficulties in sustaining genuine local support. Despite the agreement of local governments and organizations to be active partners in the ICNRC, only a limited number have lived up to this commitment, in part owing to tensions between communities. Alert Bay is seen as "anti-aquaculture," for example, and therefore in opposition to towns and organizations that consider themselves "pro-industry." ICNRC is located in Alert Bay and is thus associated with the anti-aquaculture stance, despite declarations of neutrality. It remains committed to a regional mandate, yet a perception persists that the ICNRC is focused on Alert Bay rather than on the region as a whole. To address this issue, meetings and events are rotated among communities and regional projects are pursued. Some residents believe that all regional services should be based in the larger centers of Port McNeill or Port Hardy. Alert Bay–based organizations such as 'Namgis First Nation, U'mista Cultural Centre, and Alert Bay Marine Research Society have been among the most active local partners. Without strong support from all communities in the region, however, the ICNRC does not have the credibility it needs to succeed.

On several occasions, outside research institutions have approached a local "partner" organization and not being referred to the ICNRC. For example, Community Futures Development Corporation (the key development agency in the region) agreed to sign a memorandum of understanding (MOU) with the ICNRC stating that all research activities would be undertaken by or in partnership with the ICNRC. However, the MOU was never signed and Community Futures Development Corporation has since acted as lead partner in research partnerships with both Royal Roads University and University of British Columbia. North Island College, another ICNRC partner organization, entered into a partnership with SFU's Centre for Distance Education to deliver a $1.3 million research and capacity-building project called "Bridging the Divides" without any initial ICNRC involvement. Lack of coordination and communication was a problem at both the local and the university levels in the establishment of the project. Despite a close affiliation, Distance Education had not communicated with Continuing Studies at SFU, which had fostered strong working relationships in the region through the ICNRC. Staff and resources allocated to the local area for this project are directed to the college, which is also suffering from budget cutbacks. The failure of local partners to refer projects to and fully support the ICNRC is in part responsible for resource shortages. The lack of ICNRC organizational capacity is, in turn, used as a justification. Clearly, competition for scarce outside funding, as well as issues of power, control, and recognition among north island organizations and communities represents a significant barrier to collaborative efforts to generate and share knowledge within the region and with external agencies.

Indian Bay Watershed, Newfoundland and Labrador: The Indian Bay Ecosystem Corporation

The Indian Bay Ecosystem Corporation (IBEC) began when community members became concerned about pollution, habitat degradation, and the depletion of socially, culturally, and economically valuable fisheries, particularly trophy-sized brook trout populations, in the Indian Bay watershed (see Gibson et al., this volume chap. 9, for a related discussion of IBEC). The Indian Bay watershed is an extensive freshwater system made up of more than seventeen lakes feeding into Indian Bay River and then into the Atlantic Ocean in northern Bonavista Bay. It is highly productive in terms both of fish diversity and of fish growth. The watershed is also home to many other species, including furbearers and moose that have traditionally been hunted and trapped by community members. Despite a fire that swept the entire area in the 1960s, virtually destroying the primary industry at the time (forestry), pockets of old-growth timber remain throughout the watershed. Some have been set aside for protection as pristine study areas under agreement with the logging companies, others as part of the Indian Bay water supply area.

In socio-economic and cultural terms the Indian Bay watershed region is extended to the whole of "Bonavista North" or "the Kittiwake shore." The communities of the shore (population approximately 10,000) extend well beyond the biophysical watershed boundaries but are connected to it through historic and continual use. The freshwater system empties into northern Bonavista Bay at the town Indian Bay (population 196: Statistics Canada 2006). Outdoor recreational activities, of which fishing is among the most common, are very important to local residents. These activities largely account for the area's reported high quality of life. A seasonal pattern of subsistence and recreation includes moose hunting in the fall, snowmobiling and ice fishing in the winter, and salmon and trout fishing in the spring and summer. The Indian Bay watershed, a popular cabin location, is used for each of these activities.

IBEC has accomplished a great deal since its formation in 1988, including debris cleanup, habitat restoration, stock monitoring, and harvesting agreements with logging companies to establish buffer zones and no-harvest areas and with the DFO to implement special fisheries management regulations and a local enforcement program. A land use plan was developed to consider cabin development and other uses, along with conservation and research needs. Results have been achieved in both habitat and stock recovery. In partnership with government and universities, particularly Memorial University (MUN), considerable information about the system has also been gathered. The group now has input into inland fisheries management not only in the watershed but province-wide (see Gibson et al., this volume, chap. 9). IBEC has been recognized for these efforts provincially, nationally, and even internationally.

To date IBEC has hosted undergraduate and graduate students conducting field research in the watershed on topics as diverse as ecological modelling, resident attitude surveys salmonid population genetics, threatened and endangered species, frogs, vegetation, forestry, and governance. Partnering universities have included MUN, SFU, Dalhousie University, University of New Brunswick, Middlebury College Vermont, Trent University, and the Universities of Hamburg, Hull, and Toronto, among others.

Looking to build on these successes, generate local employment, and create revenues for the non-profit corporation, IBEC has proposed to establish a Centre for Cooperative Ecosystem Studies. Funding was acquired from federal and provincial agencies for a feasibility analysis. A steering committee, including university and government partners, has been established, a business plan has been completed, and construction under way. The centre will build on existing research facilities within the watershed. A diverse range of services is envisioned, including an undergraduate program, field courses, research projects, training programs, kid's camps, school programs, educational adventure tourism, and consulting (Vodden 2004a).

Research capacity has been built over time in the Indian Bay area. Local students have been trained (undergraduates, MAs, and PhDs) and have gone on to work in their respective fields, primarily in Newfoundland resource management and development agencies (a provincial capacity building benefit). Executive Director Winston Norris, credited for much of IBEC's success, has gained significant experience in research and project management but lacks "recognized" scientific qualifications and, therefore, has required a research partner if results are to be peer reviewed and accepted in the scientific community. IBEC staff members have gained considerable experience in data collection, but analysis has been done primarily by outside researchers. With the development of the centre, however, internal capacity has increased. A former provincial freshwater fisheries biologist and a recent PhD graduate from the area were hired to work with the new centre.[18]

Once again lack of core funding threatens the long-term ability of IBEC, as a local institution, to enter into research partnerships. Despite skill at fundraising and remarkable success over the past twenty years, reliance on government money directed to short-term projects makes the organization vulnerable to policy change. Atlantic Canada Opportunities Agency (ACOA) is a major funder, confident that the resource can be rebuilt and managed by IBEC to a point where the recreational fishery can be expanded as a tourism activity and, more recently, that research can also make a significant economic contribution to the region and the province. However, the experience of the ICNRC shows that finding core funding or operating on project administration fees for research and education programs is a difficult road. The ACOA should be recognized for its long-term view and ongoing commitment to the initiative. Ultimately the core priorities of IBEC and the ACOA differ, however. While the ACOA's mandate is regional economic development, IBEC's mandate also includes the protection of social, recreational knowledge creation and conservation values. Unless IBEC can attain financial self-sufficiency and/or generate significant economic benefits, future support will be jeopardized.

Institutional barriers are also faced at the university level. In establishing the new centre IBEC is seeking to establish partnership agreements with MUN as a core local university partner, along with several other post-secondary institutions and government agencies. A former MUN biology chair served on the centre's steering committee and arranged meetings with the university president that have resulted in formal, written expressions of support for the initiative. The challenge, as laid out by MUN's steering committee member, is that intellectual freedom within the university means that the university cannot force individual researchers to conduct research on any particular topic or in a given region. Thus, while high-level institutional support may help to establish credibility for such a local centre, working relationships with individual professors and graduate students with a compatible research interest are needed to operationalize the partnership.

Opportunities have been explored for providing a space on campus for a centre staff member/representative (perhaps an adjunct professor) to liaise with faculty and staff to build these relationships. However, space is limited and the centre as of yet does not have a "home department" or university-based centre to be located within. The CUS project allowed IBEC (a CUS community partner) to use a desk at the CUS research office but could do so for only a limited time because of space constraints and priority given to students and researchers. Just what form of institutional support MUN will be willing to provide, therefore, remains unclear. A model may exist in the new Leslie Harris Centre of Regional Policy and Development in 2004 to create university-community partnerships and to keep track of which MUN researchers conduct research related to regional policy and development in the province. The centre helps fill a gap in university community service left by the elimination of Memorial's Extension Services in the early 1990s.

LESSONS FROM THE CASE STUDIES

A number of important similarities and differences can be seen through comparative analyses of the three cases, which are summarized briefly in table 13.1. Each case demonstrates a desire on behalf of local communities for increased involvement in research activities, including defining priorities, establishing a research agenda for their regions, and ensuring results are returned to the region; education and training opportunities are essential features. This desire has manifested itself in various forms of action, such as

- the establishment of local institutions capable of entering into research and education partnerships;
- local research training and capacity building;
- the development of research protocols that outline both principles and practices that external partners should follow when conducting research in the region; and
- the creation of research libraries, archives, bibliographies and databases.

Ecological baseline studies have provided an important starting point for using information and knowledge to generate sustainable local-development solutions. While ecological studies are often central to the local research agenda, particularly in the initial stages, the local institutions examined also address social and economic elements. CLARET, the ICNRC, and IBEC all share an integrated focus on social, cultural, economic, and environmental values, demonstrating local awareness of complex interconnections within social-ecological systems.

In all the cases, traditional and local knowledge or insights have been incorporated into (or in some cases have guided) community-based

Table 13.1
Characteristics of Community-University Partnership Models

	Indian Bay Ecosystem Corporation	Clayoquot Alliance for Research, Education, and Training	Inner Coast Natural Resource Centre
Year initiated	1988	2001	1996
Initiator	Community	University/Community, responding to the SSHRC/CURA stimulus	Community
Organizational structure	Non-profit corporation	Unincorporated partnership of non-profit charitable organisations	Non-profit charitable organisation
Board of directors	Community representatives elected by area at open public meeting	2 directors (1 UVic, 1 CBT) plus 11 appointed steering committee members (3 UVic, 3 CBT, 3 external, plus 2 ex-officio CBT)	Representatives appointed by each local partner (municipal, regional, and First Nations governments, NGOs) plus one external partner (university)
Partners	Universities (8+), governments, forest industry	1 university and 1 community NGO as conduits for collaboration between numerous universities, NGOs, and First Nations	Universities and colleges (5+), governments, NGOs, tourist industry association, fisheries union
Role of senior governments (provincial and federal)	Funding, receive policy input, advisors, members on field school steering committee	Some project-specific funding	Occasional project funding, or use as venue to gather and disseminate information
Dominant partner	Community/federal government	Formerly university (UVic); currently community (CBT)	Community/university (SFU)
Primary funding sources	Federal (core funds negotiated annually) with some provincial project funds; NSERC/SSHRC	Formerly SSHRC/CURA; currently community endowment fund (CBT); significant in-kind local and university volunteer support	Community in-kind (no core funds); project-specific funders (foundations, university, government); significant in-kind local and university volunteer support

Table 13.1 continued

	Indian Bay Ecosystem Corporation	Clayoquot Alliance for Research, Education, and Training	Inner Coast Natural Resource Centre
Year initiated	1988	2001	1996
Activities and their applications (prioritized)	Research; local and provincial management and policy input; annual workshops; website	Research; education; training; website; protocols development; workshops; symposia; field courses; database and archives; policy input	Workshops and conferences; research; resource mapping; input into policy and planning; library; website; database
Key project topics	Fisheries; logging impacts, community culture/desires re fisheries; botanical and amphibian research	Natural resource management; aboriginal language; broadband access; property rights; tourism; community health	Community development, fisheries, non-timber forest products, coastal planning, aquaculture, oil and gas
Local research protocols in place?	No	Yes	Partial/in development ICNRC; 'Namgis yes
Role of First Nations	Low	Significant	Significant
Perceived institutional commitment[1]	U: medium (formal) C: medium F: medium/high P: medium	U: low (increasing) C: medium (increasing) F: low P: low	U: low/medium C: medium F: low P: low
Individual commitment[2]	U: medium/high C: high F: high P: medium	U: high C: high F: low P: low	U: high C: high F: low P: low
Priority capacity issues	Project funding, infrastructure, university partnerships, citizen education	Project funding, cumulative data management, infrastructure (especially at university), aboriginal participation	Project funding, communication and partnership support, local leadership, commitment and volunteer capacity

NOTE: The characteristics indicated in the table reflect the interpretation of the authors based on available data and refer to the individual partners within the context of the partnership only.
1 U = university; C = community; F = federal government; P = provincial government.
2 I.e., personal commitment of individuals involved (for key see note 1).

projects through direct involvement of local people in activities. Their involvement has been instrumental to project outcomes, whether it be through providing knowledge of the formerly undocumented distribution of an endangered fish species (IBEC) or of methods for engaging remote local communities in coastal planning (ICNRC), to give just two examples. In each of these examples, external partners such as universities and government agencies also played crucial roles in gathering and disseminating information and then attempting to apply this knowledge in policy and practice. Thus, two-way collaboration was required not just to enhance the dissemination and impact of results but to ensure the quality of the research itself.

The establishment of agreed-upon procedures and protocols has helped facilitate community participation, as have other measures taken to facilitate cross-cultural sharing and accurate interpretation of results. In two of the three cases examined, First Nations played a significant role in establishing new local research or educational institutions, as well as university-community collaborations. The Nuu-chah-nulth language revitalization project (CLARET) is one example that led to creation of a new aboriginal NGO.[19] The establishment of the Elders Committee, University College of Cape Breton Integrative Science Program, and Scientist/Elder Talking Circles are examples from Bras d'Or Lakes, while 'Namgis First Nation has been instrumental in the achievements of the ICNRC (Vodden 2003, 2004b).

An understanding of local governance and organizational structures is important for determining appropriate links with local governments, organizations, and sub-groups. Complexities in local governance and community dynamics take time to understand, but without this awareness, research collaborations may not be considered legitimate, and they risk becoming highly political, biased, and unstable. It is important for university researchers to gain a situated awareness of the sociopolitical and cultural contexts of their work, in order to understand the authority vested (or not) in local organizations and individuals, local decision-making processes, and local capacity. Community-based research institutions can provide a "portal" to the community that will facilitate community partnerships, outreach, and understanding for external researchers. However, these community institutions must be effective (in themselves or through partners) at communications and networking both within and outside their regions, informing and engaging their local constituents, as well as external government and scientific partners and funders.

In all three cases, nearby universities (i.e., within the given province) are the most significant academic partners for local institutions. At the same time local institutions engage or seek to engage university partners from across the country, seeking assistance in both research and education. Difficulties were encountered in securing long-term funding for specific projects and particularly for basic infrastructure and operations. There has been heavy reliance on committed individuals from both community and university, individuals who are often volunteers or are able to donate some of their paid time in-kind (the latter often through "creative" arrangements with their employer).

University researchers involved in the case studies have faced common challenges, including lack of recognition within the academic system for much of the time, financial costs, and non-academic outcomes associated with community-university partnerships (Miller et al. 1999). The two-year development of research protocols for CLARET, for example, resulted in an agreed standard of conduct that was deemed essential to any collaborative research within the partnership, but the results (although of academic interest) were not appropriate for publication in a peer-reviewed journal, because participants agreed that the work was explicitly a development project rather than a research project.

Another challenge evident at the university end was a lack of coordination of individual researchers working within the same communities; much community-based research appears to be led by individual faculty members and conducted project by project (based on competitive external grants), with no overarching coordination or support by the sponsoring institutions. This feature contributes to some of the problems mentioned previously, namely, the drain on community members' time and energy if they are participating in multiple projects led by different researchers (often on related topics) that, at least in some cases, could be coordinated so as to use everyone's time most efficiently. In addition, when project funds end, so too do the collaborations, unless more project funds can be raised. Given the significant time and cost required for relationship-building and formation of partnerships with communities, there may be justification on economic as well ethical grounds not only for regional research centers but for a campus-based coordinating or facilitating entity, such as the Extension Services model, the Leslie Harris Centre at MUN, or the office of Community Based Research established at UVic.

Some notable differences also exist between the three cases. Differences in the size of the regions in question and in their populations, socio-political, cultural, and ecological contexts, and differences in economic circumstances all significantly influence research priorities and programs. Perhaps the most prominent difference is the role of government in the research partnership. For IBEC and the Unama'ki Institute of Natural Resources (UINR) in the Bras d'Or Lakes, senior government representatives (from both policy and science sections) play a strong role in the research partnership, providing funding, input into research agenda, and technical expertise/involvement. In these cases, knowledge flows most readily from research into the policy realm (e.g., to produce changes in fisheries management).

The role of the university also differs in each case. For the ICNRC, university researchers have played a key role in initiating community-university partnerships and setting the research agenda. This is also the case for CLARET, although to a lesser degree, since all the initial activities were redesigned in response to community perspectives and priorities. By contrast, in IBEC and the UINR, university involvement has been an "on request" support function. In these cases, which also have strong government involvement, university researchers have provided additional influence to local institutions in their negotiations with senior governments, as well as in management and policy decisions.

Funding is a challenge common to all the cases, but that challenge has been addressed in various ways. The ICNRC has attempted to supplement project income by providing contract research and outreach functions. An initial SSHRC/CURA grant was decisive in the formation and early years of CLARET, but SSHRC funds have not provided support in the other cases. CLARET benefits from the unique case of continuing support (however constrained) from the community partner (CBT), an institution with independent core funding from an endowment. This is certainly an effective interim measure and makes possible some leveraging of significant funding from other partners; however, without comparable support from UVic and renewal by SSHRC for a further round of funding that is prerequisite to placing the CLARET partnership on a self-sufficient basis, an ongoing partnership is unlikely. In the cases of the UINR and IBEC ongoing federal funding (albeit project or program-based) has been critical and has been linked to the involvement of government as a third research partner with communities and universities.

SYNTHESIS OF LESSONS: TOWARDS CIRCULAR KNOWLEDGE FLOWS

Community-university research collaborations are an important tool for addressing many types of research questions, but they often fall short of their potential, partly owing to a tendency toward linear, extractive flows of knowledge. That is, knowledge and information gained by university researchers working in or with communities are necessarily channelled into a centralized system of production that transforms data, observations, insights, and ideas from their social and ecological contexts into currencies for academe (such as peer-reviewed publications, conference papers, and course materials) as the first priority. As long as these professional and institutional debts are paid, the university researcher is free to attend to other (read lesser) priorities, such as lay articles, workshops, and meetings for sharing research results and their meanings at a local level, or reports, recommendations, and policy briefs for promoting policy changes at various government levels that would positively affect the people and places that were the original sources of research data.

We suggested at the onset that the collective *will* appears to be developing but not a clear *way* to foster socially relevant research through community-university partnerships. Given a finite amount of time, energy, and funds, neither the proverbial "carrot" nor the proverbial "stick" has been institutionalized in ways that would enable the university researcher to meet the expressed needs of most community collaborators without impinging on the demands of the academic system. A new framework is needed that conceptualizes collaborative research as a circular, rather than a linear, exercise that begins and ends in the same place – i.e., in the community.

Reciprocity – an exchange of mutual benefit – is fundamental to any circular system for pragmatic as well as ethical reasons. In other words, if source communities are depleted or degraded by the research process, they will not be available for future research opportunities. A system for production of knowledge that is based on extraction is destined to be the architect of its own demise; eventually university researchers will run out of people and places to research. Our suggestion to "circularize" flows of knowledge should be seen as a means of both addressing practical problems in research and democratizing the research process. While space constraints have prevented a more detailed review of a larger number of case studies, even the preliminary review of a small number of cases provided here suggests several lessons that can inform a discussion about flows of knowledge.

First, communication is central to effective partnerships, channels for communication must be built rather than assumed, and the barriers of physical distance should not be discounted. Difficulties in creating virtual communities of interest bonding university researchers with distant communities of place are real. Communication begins with engaging in a process of trying to understand one another (at the individual and institutional levels) – it begins with time and effort spent in relationship building, developing mutual understandings, fostering trust and respect, overcoming cultural barriers, and working out institutional procedures. These are both prerequisites and co-requisites to research; certain elements need to be in place before the research begins, but others will likely be figured out only during (and as a result of) the research process. Thus flexibility and reflectivity are important. This relationship building *ought* to be conceptualized as an integral part of the research process. Clearly, the timeline required extends beyond that of a graduate thesis. It requires the longer-term commitment of individuals at the faculty level, as well as graduate students, to participatory, community-based research approaches (Reason 1994; Green et al. 1997). Long-term individual commitment, in turn, requires institutional support, which can come in multiple forms (e.g., through professional recognition, funding, staff support, and new organizational structures of various forms, as outlined in table 13.1) and is ideally present at multiple levels (e.g., at the level of the community, the university, and government).

Second, partnerships work well when communities' as well as university researchers' needs are met in the process – when there is mutual benefit. Community benefits should be locally defined. The kinds of benefits commonly specified in community research protocols include local training, education, mentoring, income generation (when possible), and answers to locally important questions. Providing those answers depends on returning results to communities in useful forms: results published in theses or academic journals that are not readily available to communities or in forms that are not readily understood by the layperson are not likely to be useful (Elias 2002). An extra effort is often required by the university researcher to "translate" scientific data into clear, concise, and appropriate forms, whether written, verbal, or otherwise.

While these kinds of lay publications tend to be seen as a service to communities rather than part of scholarly works, because they do have significant value within the academic system as a vehicle for communicating scholarly works to benefactors and the wider public (to whom publicly funded institutions are accountable), their value to universities in public relations and communications should not be understated.[20] The various added "costs" of collaborative partnerships are reduced for individuals when they are given professional credit for their individual efforts. Added "costs" to universities are reduced when there is a local organization to work with that shares a similar mandate and already has some capacity. Similarly, the time and effort required by community groups to develop research relationships with appropriate university researchers is reduced when there is a designated point of contact to facilitate communication at the university. In effect, community-university collaborations require institutional support and coordination at both the community and the university end. A prerequisite to effective and mutually beneficial partnerships is making a good match between the partners.

Third, given that the advancement of knowledge is the central goal of academic research and that scholarship is predicated on diligent review of existing literature, our increasing awareness of large bodies of knowledge that are *not* widely accessible merits careful consideration. Here we refer to the elusive "grey" literature – such as government and industry contract reports, newsletters, working papers, bulletins, fact sheets, and the like that are not peer reviewed and not controlled by commercial publishing interests. Our case studies (especially of CLARET and the ICNRC) indicate that grey literature is a valuable source of information to communities and university researchers alike, but it is often excluded from the cataloguing systems created and used as the basis of academic literature. There are several consequences of this practice, such as gaps in contextual information (cultural, social, ecological) and repetition of research. Inventorying, cataloguing, and archiving such information is an enormous task (i.e., it is time-consuming, expensive, and specialized), but it is one that would serve all partners in community-university collaborations. Universities typically have far greater capacity to undertake or facilitate such tasks, but it is the communities that tend to make the effort, however inadequate the resources they are able to direct to the task. Similar observations can be made in relation to databases of local and traditional knowledge, although the latter has the added layer of complexity related to aboriginal rights involving access to and use of cultural knowledge (not discussed here). As the examples above suggest, inclusion of these existing, diverse, and underutilized information sources can significantly improve the outcome of knowledge generation and dissemination endeavors. Their exclusion is often at the cost of research quality.

We conclude that how knowledge flows between universities and communities is directly related to the ability of research collaborations to address the priorities of the partners in mutually beneficial ways. Knowledge flow, like reciprocity in research, depends on capacities of the collaborators, as well as the investment of time and resources to develop mutual understandings and establish collaborative processes for decision making and sharing control. Contextual understandings, such as existing governance structures and the appropriate process or protocol for entering into a legitimate partnership, are essential to effective and mutually beneficial research partnerships. Personal, informal relationships built over time underpin most community-university research collaborations, but sustaining these collaborations beyond merely a "project-based" timeline also requires an ongoing commitment at the institutional level to operationalize the necessary incentives and support the individuals involved and their successors over timelines that are meaningful and useful to communities as well as universities.

Acknowledgements
We are grateful to Dr Rod Dobell (UVic/CLARET), Dr Patricia Gallaugher (SFU), Winston Norris (IBEC), and Michael Berry (ICNRC) for helpful comments on an earlier draft of this chapter.

14

Conclusion

BARBARA NEIS AND JOHN SUTTON LUTZ

In a world increasingly supplied with information, how do we know what is "knowledge" and how can we act wisely? This book is among the first in Canada to directly engage these vital issues. Here we have explored how knowledge is created and transferred and used, and perhaps most importantly, how it is blocked and how it atrophies. We have sought to present in a critical and reflexive fashion some of the results of our Coasts Under Stress (CUS) research that inform larger issues related to producing and moving knowledge and fostering wise choices.

Two essential concepts emerge across the essays in this book, and they often seem to be at odds with each other. First is the importance of community. Communities are where life is lived, where we feel comfortable and understood. We all want healthy communities in the broadest sense of that term: safe, clean, prosperous, caring communities where we feel understood and valued. There are other kinds of communities, for example, communities where research is done. Universities, government, and industrial research teams and scientific associations all constitute communities of learning where people come together, within particular disciplinary cultures, develop specialized terminology and tools and try to solve problems. Community and university are not opposed; they are just different types of "communities," and research does not start with the one and operate on the other. The two should be interwoven like an Escher painting so that it is hard to tell where one starts and the other ends.

The second lesson is that while we need our bounded communities, the paradox is that we must also learn to operate beyond them. We live and work in communities that by definition are bounded but all the big problems transcend the boundaries of particular communities (academic or otherwise). We are inevitably part of a larger community that includes plants and animals and the aquatic, terrestrial, or celestial environments in which we and they live. To thrive we must understand how our community is linked to all the others. In the academy this requires a transdisciplinary approach that has only rarely been embraced. In research it means learning how to make mutually comprehensible and link traditional knowledge in indigenous and settler communities with the "academic" knowledge of the university.

CUS was an experimental Major Collaborative Research Initiative. Central to our research was an exploration of the ways in which industrial, political, and social restructuring have interacted with the restructuring of biophysical environments and food webs to affect the health of people, communities, and environments. In our view, disciplinary boundaries (between social, natural, humanist, and health researchers) have tended to mask interactions between these realms, resulting in partial knowledge, impoverished policy frameworks, related unanticipated and frequently negative outcomes for the health of people, communities, and their environments, and missed opportunities for recovery. Thus, a key point of departure for CUS research (and for many of the contributions to this book) is the assumption that exploring these interactions requires cutting across traditional disciplinary boundaries between the natural and social sciences and humanities and boundaries between academic science and applied science, departmental boundaries within government, and boundaries between these knowledge forms and various forms of vernacular knowledge.

To accomplish these goals, we have had to develop new conceptual frameworks, models, and methodologies. We have also experimented with novel applications of existing ones and developed tools for comparing the knowledge and perspectives that derive from different approaches. We have found that working on the boundaries between disciplines and between social groups is a challenging but fertile place to work. If we think of science as linked to discovery, these neglected boundary areas provide a rich space for discovery because they interface and are hence transitional areas.

This collection and the project on which it is based would not have been undertaken without a leap of faith from two national research councils: the Social Sciences and Humanities Research Council and the Natural Science and Engineering Research Council. Their joint funding of the project is too rare and exceptional. CUS is an example of the new "big science," in that it was a large-budget, multi-year project involving a huge team of researchers from multiple disciplines. It was somewhat unique within this tradition, in that the social scientists played a central role relative to the natural scientists in the definition of the problem and design of the work. Books on "knowledge" and "power" are unusual outputs from contemporary big science.

Trnka (this volume, chap. 12) has addressed some of the challenges and issues associated with big science, challenges that are not only "scientific" but also administrative and cultural. CUS consisted of multiple administratively and thematically linked projects that in their design reflected the personal histories, knowledge, and interests of members of the research team and the diverse points of entry into multiple, social-ecological systems entailed by their research trajectories. The researchers within CUS shared a research focus on interactive effects. This shared focus took time to develop, as did the basis for stronger collaborations. When measured against an idealized model for big science as deductive, hypothesis-driven, experimental research carried out by a tightly knit research team with shared concepts, goals, and methods, CUS may seem to fall short. However, if one starts from the assumption that all forms of knowledge production involve multiple social, cultural, and ecological processes engaging multiple audiences and diversity in practice and point of view, the CUS approach can be seen as a real strength of the project. It can be seen as a model for transdisciplinary "science in action," (Latour 1987).

One challenge Trnka does not mention is the ambiguity within granting councils regarding what they and others expect from interdisciplinary and transdisciplinary projects (Tress et al. 2005). As indicated by McNeill (1993, 13), embarking on interdisciplinary work entails serious challenges for researchers in the world of academic science as we know it:

> To undertake interdisciplinary research is not easy. Some of the problems are intellectual, others are of a practical/organizational nature, either for the individual or the institution concerned. For the individual, a central question is the reference group – both for undertaking research and for getting it published. And these are linked. The individual who works with other researchers from other disciplines must resolve certain problems: How will they communicate? Whose language will they speak, and whose values will they adopt? Whose knowledge will count? For the researcher who chooses to cross disciplinary boundaries, a break is made with

an established community. The need is to find, or even if necessary to create, another: no easy task.

McNeill's points about interdisciplinarity also apply to the challenges of connecting the "ways of knowing" practised in the academy with the different knowledge bases that exist in communities in the form of lay or vernacular knowledge and traditional ecological knowledge in its varied forms in different ethnic, religious, and socio-economic groups. The same applies to crossing the divide between research and policy. All these types of interdisciplinarity or transdisciplinarity require new ways of "learning to learn" and new commitments to listening across our differences. The CUS project has experimented with these ways of learning, tested and developed new methods and pointed to other possibilities. This volume is an attempt to model learning across boundaries.

We often talk about information as something that is mobile, portable, transferable, or exchangeable, and in today's world it can be moved in more ways than ever before. But knowledge requires a social context that includes people who have a will to know. Knowledge is still transmitted across a campfire or as a part of a ceremonial meal, but more often it moves from person to person in age-stratified institutions like schools that are largely isolated from wider communities; in places of worship or prayer; in books and periodicals; through the courts, and political and lobby groups; and, increasingly digitally by way of television and the Internet. The essays in this book have looked at a range of key sites, or nodes, where knowledge is generated, transmitted, or blocked: big science (Trnka; Barnes et al.), schools (Turner et al.; Harris and Umpleby; Marshall and Jackson); communities (Turner et al.; McLaren et al.; Gibson et al.; Metuzals et al.; Vodden and Bannister); research communities (Barnes et al.; Trnka, Schneider et al.; Murray et al.; Metuzals et al.), media (Barnes et al.), and policy contexts (Schneider et al.; Metuzals et al.; Gibson et al.; Murray et al.). Barnes et al. model the movement of knowledge bundles in their chapter, while others (especially Ommer et al.) explore some of the institutional and other processes that shape knowledge production, flows, and the outcomes of knowledge application.

Some contributions have explored the spatial and temporal scales inherent in knowledge production (Schneider et al.; Murray et al.) and their significance for the ways knowledge can highlight certain interactive processes and their effects, while masking others. Latour captures the scaling problem when he notes, "The weather forecasts over a whole region entail continuous clashes with local people who want predictions about local weather" (1987, 213). The organizational scale of our work can either tell the "local" story or the "regional" story, but seldom both. For example, if the organizational scale of our work is a community of fish or a fishery community, we may miss internal differences in the dynamics and effects of restructuring between social groups within that community and among fish species, or between older fish of a particular species and younger fish, female and male fish. A focus confined to these particular human or fish communities will miss their relationship to more global relationships, such as the effect of fish decline in the food chain on other species or the effect of a loss of the main livelihood in the human community, which may increase exploitation of other ecosystems. If the town that loses its fish plant turns to pulp and paper and if unemployed fishers turn to logging, they start another round of impacts on water flow and water tables, on carbon absorption, and on wildlife, and the effects spread out. These differential effects may be relevant not only to our understanding of interactive restructuring and its effects within these groups but also for larger-scale processes and outcomes.

Our focus on interactive restructuring has reminded us forcefully of the problem of complexity and the challenges it poses not only for knowledge production but also for its application to real-world problems and for the related, larger problem of governance. In relation to coastal areas, new approaches to governance are being advocated and tried that require a different approach to knowledge production and new mechanisms for moving knowledge. Co governance, some have argued, is "well equipped to deal with diverse, complex, and dynamic situations," such as those found in coastal areas, but other forms of governance are also essential (Kooiman and Bavinck 2005, 22; Vodden and Bannister, this volume, chap. 13). The knowledge production and transfer requirements of these alternative governance forms are substantially different from those associated with twentieth-century Western resource science and management (Finlayson 1994) – variants of which, in certain contexts, led to natural and human disaster (Scott 1998).

Trans-disciplinarity can help us grapple with problems that cross-cut spatial and temporal scales, as well as multiple social and ecological units. Historians and literary scholars may study individuals; sociologists and anthropologists, communities; sociologists may study nations;

and scientists, populations and data sets that stretch to numbers towards infinity. Conclusions valid at one end of a scale have less and perhaps no validity as you move up or down. One of the vast gulfs in our ability to understand knowledge flows is how to connect the micro studies to the macro (Murray et al., this volume, chap. 6). Failure to understand the ways social-ecological dynamics influence the information from which we build our knowledge can seriously undermine our capacity to see what is happening in the world around us and why (Metuzals et al., this volume, chap. 7).

Will Wright (1991) and others have argued that much of science as we know it is based on the incorrect and indeed incoherent claim that through science we can gain access to "pure," "objective" nature. The claim is incoherent because we can never observe "pure" nature and because all forms of science are inevitably social-ecological products linked to social legitimation. The claim is also dangerous because it leads us to attribute environmental disaster or scientific failures exclusively to social and political processes, drawing our attention away from problems within normal science itself. What sorts of problems? In the 1990s, one of us was asked to speak to a group of American fisheries stock assessment scientists about the social and economic impacts of the collapse of the northern cod stocks. You could have heard a pin drop as Neis explained that more than twenty-thousand people had been laid off in Newfoundland and Labrador and that there would be significant and enduring (intergenerational) impacts not only on the incomes and employment of the fish harvesters and processing workers but also potentially on their health and that of their families and communities – impacts that are still unfolding today, more than a decade later. Like their counterparts in Canada, for these stock assessment scientists, normal science did not include considering what could happen to people and communities if they make a mistake. The collapse of the northern cod stocks was, of course, a result of more than flawed stock assessments, but they played an important role (Finlayson 1994). Imagine that these and other stock assessment scientists were surgeons operating on a human being or engineers building a bridge. Would we not find it problematic if, in carrying out their objectives, they ignored potential risks to the health of people and society? As with other environmental disasters, the collapse of the northern cod stocks called into question the naïve assumption that science can be fully separated from management and policy, with the latter, social elements taking responsibility for socio-economic and health impacts.

Knowledge can be applied to any purpose, constructive or destructive. Wright has argued that "a coherent and ecological form of knowledge must incorporate social *and* natural criteria for validity, criteria that evaluate knowledge claims in terms of the interactions between social practices and natural processes ... this means it must be made *reflexive*, where the criteria for the validity of explanations include a critical evaluation of the social-natural effects of those explanations, as legitimated social actions (1991, 10). This is the approach we adopt when discussing medical knowledge, and it leads us to reject certain medical claims on the grounds that they may endanger health. Wright is arguing that this approach needs to be extended to all science as an essential first step in the journey from information to knowledge and ultimately to wisdom.

Wisdom, according to the *Oxford English Dictionary*, is the capacity of judging rightly in matters relating to life and conduct. What is right, of course, is also culturally and temporally bounded, and so what is "wise" will vary between observers. Yet almost every observer would agree that it was not wise to fish our commercially vital northern cod or pacific coho salmon stocks to the edge of extinction. The institutions we have created in these cases, but in so many others too, are not structured to promote wisdom. As Metuzals et al. (this volume, chap. 7) show, some of our institutional arrangements are practically guaranteed to generate unwise solutions.

James C. Scott's *Seeing Like a State: How Certain Schemes to Improve the Human Condition Have Failed* focuses on land-based examples of such "great human tragedies of the twentieth century" (1998, 3) as Soviet and Tanzanian forced "villagization." He argues that a key element in these tragedies was the introduction of social and natural simplifications through modern statecraft, i.e., through efforts on the part of states to make the social and natural world "more legible – and hence manipulable from above and from the centre" (2). These simplifications and the associated social legibility provided the capacity for large-scale social engineering. Where this social engineering was associated with "high-modernest ideology," or hyper-confidence in scientific and technical progress, an authoritarian state, and "an incapacitated civil society" the social and environmental outcomes were frequently tragic (5). To counter these weaknesses in bureaucratic and capitalist planning and high-modernest ideology, Scott argues for the importance and relevance of local knowledge, informal institutions, and improvisation in the face of uncertainty.

If we can create institutions that stifle wisdom, surely we can build others that foster it: institutions that ensure that knowledge flows from communities to policy-makers, that it gets refined and tested, and circles back to communities. We can build institutions that promote awareness of uncertainty and complexity without promoting paralysis and that connect knowledge and governance. Many of the chapters in this volume (Ommer et al.; McLaren et al.; Gibson et al.; Turner et al.; Harris and Umbleby; Marshall and Jackson; Vodden and Bannister), suggest institutional arrangements that do foster the movement from knowledge to wisdom, and these arrangements are urgently needed. If we are thoughtful, we can create infrastructure that resolves the paradox of the need to work at a community level and to work across communities.

Wisdom, from our point of departure, means taking decisions, action, and giving advice based on the careful accumulation and selection of knowledge that has been both thoughtfully/theoretically and practically/experientially verified (Ommer et al., this volume, chap. 2). Wisdom involves the critical assessment of innovation based on the principle of the inherent uncertainty of knowledge, but it is not the same as conservatism, since wisdom involves the critical assessment of tradition and "received wisdom." Unafraid to try new things when opportunities or exigencies arise, wisdom means acting from a position beyond the interests of a single community and a single species, with the precautionary principle, taking the long term health (multiple generations) of the society-environment nexus as its measuring stick. The essays in this book suggest that as a society we can choose to make laws, develop methods, and create institutions that can turn knowledge into wisdom and degradation into recovery. Paraphrasing Robert Frost, they also tell us that we have "miles to go before we sleep."

Notes

CHAPTER TWO

1 Rosemary E. Ommer is a geographer and historian, Harold Coward a specialist in religious studies, and Christopher Parrish a marine chemist.
2 They move to recipients such as communities and bureaucrats, by whom they may then be used in policy decisions.
3 This type of methodology can be difficult for scientists who are often left wondering about the randomness of subject selection and the proportion of subjects who actually made a given quotation.
4 The paradigmatic text here is Kuhn (1970).
5 See, for example, Pauly (1994).
6 Although the debate appears to have been resolved, there is some chance that the big bang may turn out to be a big splat instead. However, that would require a parallel universe, and Stephen Hawking has just announced, with regret, that the "parallel universes" theory cannot be sustained (see Seife 2003).
7 Lower-case omega is used in fatty-acid nomenclature.
8 See, in particular, chapter 10, "Techno-Hubris" (247–77). The book, for all its unsatisfactory way of skimming over vast quantities of highly complex material and offering random examples to make its points, is a useful, popularly written warning to a world that is so far not paying attention.
9 We note in passing that Coasts Under Stress has been organized as a complex adaptive system which we thought of, metaphorically, as a seastar, with each arm having the independence to innovate. We then fostered the spread of successful innovation to other arms.
10 That is, there is a danger of thinking that human systems behaviour can be reductively equated with that of natural systems.

11 We are grateful to Dr Schneider for these comments on complexity. See also Berkes et al. (2003).
12 http://www.resalliance.org
13 This is a major reason for the current appeal of fundamentalism.
14 "Multiple renewable-resource use" is a better term than "exploitation" for this kind of resource use, because the environment was used as needed rather than exploited for profit.
15 We distinguish here between the faith-based and dogma-directed wisdom of the medieval church and the broader knowledge of the academy, whose domain was secular.
16 That is not to say that wisdom resides only there but to say that we found it there.
17 Although they may do consulting from time to time, but the activity is differentiated from their formal academic role as producers of new knowledge.

CHAPTER FOUR

1 Most social-equity funding, now called "CommunityLink funding," was provided for schools through the Ministry of Children and Family Development. This funding, now reduced, is allocated today to all districts according to statistical records of unemployment and welfare demands, and regardless of existent programs.
2 To provide partial anonymity, pseudonyms have been used for the elementary school and the students and staff of the secondary school.
3 Ms. Noonan described some opposition to these machines, but said that "resistance was totally overwhelmed by the people who want it there, for it raises funds ... five thousand dollars this year for the PE department."
4 Haughey (2002), in pointing to the value of Foucault's insights for an understanding of educational administration, names parent councils among a growing number of "technologies of self-management" (9).

CHAPTER SIX

1 Social-ecological systems include political, economic, social, and cultural institutions and processes, as well as the biological and physical environments within which these institutions and processes are embedded. Social-ecological systems are nested, historical products that operate at varying spatial, temporal, and organizational scales ranging from the level of individual people and organisms up to global systems. Such systems are interactive and these inter-

active processes are associated with complex, non-linear processes and outcomes (Dolan et al. 2005).

2 While FEK might be considered a more specific term than LEK, we use the two interchangeably here, as our focus has been on fishing.

3 For example, they can say little about how a shift to shrimp trawling might affect recruitment in other fisheries like Atlantic halibut (*Hippoglossus hippoglossus*), given by-catch issues or possible negative impacts on benthic habitat.

4 For example, knowledge about the conditions that predict when a stock will arrive in an area where it can be harvested is subject to more ground truthing than is knowledge about where that stock goes once it has left the area and can no longer be harvested.

5 Note that by using the term "expert," we do not mean to distinguish our respondents from "inexpert" others. By definition, every fisher has some expertise. We use the term "expert" to refer to this expertise.

6 Tapes were transcribed by a person from the study area, in the hopes of both returning some work to that area and improving the overall quality of the transcript (based on an assumption of greater familiarity with local expressions and place names).

7 Figure 6.2A and accompanying text adapted from Vodden, et al. (2005, 293–5 and fig. 17.1): "A Comparative Analysis of Three Models of Collaborative Learning in Fisheries Governance: Hierarchy, Networks and Community," in T.S. Gray, ed. *Participation in Fisheries Governance* (Dordrecht, Netherlands: Springer/Kluwer Academic Publishers). With kind permission of Springer Science and Business Media.

8 Note that in this particular study Whalen was working with a known local cod stock.

9 Access is limited to these fisheries owing to a combination of a limited licensing policy and the economic costs associated with entering these distant, deep-water fisheries.

10 Figure 6.4 is adapted from figure 17.2 in Vodden et al. (2005, 294): A Comparative Analysis of Three Models of Collaborative Learning in Fisheries Governance: Hierarchy, Networks and Community," in T.S. Gray, ed. *Participation in Fisheries Governance* (Dordrecht, Netherlands: Springer/Kluwer Academic Publishers). With kind permission of Springer Science and Business Media.

11 It should be noted that in suggesting such a model, we acknowledge that building bottom-up information sources that would attend to management concerns in each of the myriad locations and fisheries is a daunting task and would require the re-thinking of research priorities.

CHAPTER SEVEN

1 Precision is a measure of the variability of data around its mean value, whereas accuracy is a measure of the closeness of a measured or computed value to its true value (NRC 2000).
2 The anecdotal evidence from Canadian print media and the findings from court records of convictions on fisheries violations cannot be reported fully here for reasons of space (see Murrin 2003).
3 Other terms for dumping used in Atlantic Canada are "shacking," "pitching," "biffing," "culling," and "capacity dumping" (Breeze 1998). In Newfoundland discarding is sometimes known as "tripping the cod end."
4 http//:www.Europe.int.
5 See also Finlayson (1994), M. Harris, (1998), and others for analyses of the collapse of the Atlantic ground fishery.
6 Notwithstanding section 33 of the Fishery (General) Regulations, no person who catches groundfish of any species with fishing gear other than a cod trap shall return the groundfish to the water unless the person is authorised by a condition of a licence to return groundfish of that species to the water.
7 D. Kulka, DFO, St John's, personal communication.
8 Economics and Statistics Branch of Newfoundland, http://www.economics.gov.nl.ca/bulletins/fish.asp.
9 The harvester claimed not to know the mesh size of his crab pots. Our measurement showed 5 inches. The harvester explained that he had bought them second-hand in an outport 300 km away. The previous day his wife had been contacted by DFO regarding the mesh sizes of the crab pots. When the wife, who fishes with her husband, said that she did not know, the caller responded, "Well, I guess it's 5¼ inch mesh, isn't it?" Investigation concluded.
10 Most often, misreporting amounts to understating the catch. It is worth noting that in some cases harvesters may have an incentive to *overstate* the catch or misrepresent the catch location. For example, this has been said to occur in the lucrative snow crab fishery off the east coast of Newfoundland. When commercial catches are low (well below quota levels) or consist mostly of immature crab, harvests in certain locations may be overstated to the regulator so that quotas are less likely to be lowered for the next season. The source is an anonymous informant. (personal communication, 9 December 2003).
11 See http://www.dfo-mpo.gc.ca/communic/fish_man/resp98/index_e.htm.
12 See http://eng.msc.org

CHAPTER NINE

1 "TK" is an extension of the more common term "TEK". While "TEK" refers to traditional "ecological" knowledge, "TK" is intended to recognize the broad, holistic nature of this knowledge – including ecological, but also economic, political, cultural, and social aspects. TK is distinguished from LK because of its unique multi-generational nature, particularly in the case of TK held by First Nations peoples about their territories.

CHAPTER ELEVEN

1 Hal Stanley, chairman and chief executive officer of the Canada-Newfoundland Offshore Petroleum Board, personal interview, Tuesday, 23 March 2004.
2 David Anderson, Minister of the Environment, Government of Canada, personal interview, Thursday, 30 January 2004.
3 Two important conclusions regarding the moratorium and oil and gas activities include the following: (1) provided that an adequate regulatory regime is put in place, there are no science gaps that need to be filled before lifting the moratoria on oil and gas development; and (2) the present restriction on tanker traffic in transit along the West Coast of North America from entering the coastal zone should be maintained for the time being (Royal Society of Canada 2004, xix).

CHAPTER TWELVE

1 Michel Serres refers to these global-scale problems as *objets du monde*, or world-objects (1995a), and much of his writing on knowledge and science concerns how transdisciplinarity is necessary to address such problems (1995b, 1997).
2 This line of thought has been developed most forcefully by the Strong Programme in the sociology of knowledge, namely in the work of Barry Barnes and David Bloor (Barnes et al. 1996) and that of Stephen Shapin (1998).
3 Bourdieu (1996) makes the argument that this is indeed the case in contemporary France and while the disanalogies between the French case and the Canadian, American, or British scenes (to consider a few examples) are numerous, the similarities should not be quickly dismissed.
4 SSHRC was the lead agency and set the evaluation context.

5 See the section "Some Findings concerning Researchers' Views," below, for a fuller discussion of the constitution of the research team, the fluctuating nature of that population, and the sample population for this study; the approximate number given here conforms to that used in CUS promotional literature.
6 More history of this reflexive study may be found later in this chapter in the section "Problems and Promises of Reflexivity."
7 Evidence of animosity towards the reflexive study is found, first, in the fact that I was told at least twice that my original study proposal (entitled "Researchers Under Stress," I recall) was disliked (or hated) by the executive committee. I was also told that Coasts Under Stress already had an anthropologist on the West Coast who was already going to be studying and videotaping the group. Although I learned later that the East and West Coasts were supposed to partner together in sub-studies, this opportunity was not suggested to me. After I dropped that proposal (and entered an end-of-term ethics study instead, from which I was eventually displaced) the anthropological proposal was debated lengthily and strenuously (including by me) at the first East and West Coast CUS team meeting in Victoria. Ethical approval of such a study was one major point of contention. I and others then joined the anthropological project to revise and develop it. This study is the result of that initiative, though the original anthropologist resigned from the project not long after. Finally, during the course of this study there were various disagreements and conflicts between me or a member of my team and the executive. More of the history of the reflexive study can be found below in the section "Problems and Promises of Reflexivity."
8 Person-to-person interviews will also add to this and the broader autocritique. In the process of this reflexive study, various components have been shed or deferred, in part owing to overly ambitious initial objectives: ethnographic participant observation, document and archive analysis, some statistical analysis of the questionnaire data, and all of the correspondence analysis of the questionnaires. I still hope to complete face-to-face interviews with individuals from both the East and the West Coast in the near future.
9 Knorr Cetina (1999) and Rabinow (1999) illustrate some of the difficulties and promises of being present during the study of science in process.
10 At first I sought as large and representative a sample of the population forming Coasts Under Stress as possible, including individuals in partner organizations and community contacts. This naive expectation may be partly explained by my naïveté concerning how large the project was and how it could be surveyed. A current count by one of the CUS staff is as follows: 61 co-investigators (including the project director), 16 research associates, 12

collaborators, 69 masters and doctoral students, 208 research assistants, and 12 post-doctoral fellows; however, the staff member notes that "[t]he numbers are not straightforward. There are cases where individuals have started with us as graduate students and then worked later as research assistants. There are people who worked as Conservation Corps Interns and later as masters students. In these cases I count both positions." Dissemination of the questionnaires was by hand at meetings and electronically through e-mail project lists.

11 The ranking questions dealt primarily with assignation of value in some vague sense – a feature of the scale that various respondents noted critically – and form one of the areas of the study whose results will be analysed with the help of statistics.

12 The team meetings at which my reflexive study was introduced and explained were attended primarily by researchers and consultants. The familiarity and trust that was required to participate in this reflexive study was difficult for me to establish with all members of CUS, and even those who I did work with occasionally and attend team meetings with were often somewhat curious or suspicious of what I was doing. Very few students answered the questionnaire, so few that I removed them from the study, fearing the sample was too small to draw on.

13 I learned quickly that the original plan to videotape the interviews would not fly, partly because I did not have my purchase of a digital video camera approved (griping by me, for sure, but also not irrelevant) and primarily because I recognized that consent to the interviews would likely be difficult, especially if they were to be videotaped. I now plan to audiotape them.

14 Some of these axes, e.g., male-female, are straightforward, since they correspond directly to a single question on the questionnaire; others, such as discipline, are more difficult, depending on what information a respondent chose to give and the detail provided (so in some cases, e.g., department and faculty of affiliation, and department of the PhD are given, while in others only one of the above is given). In the more complicated cases of classification I have on occasion made a judgment based on the implication of partial data; however, a significant portion of respondents left all such questions blank, thus making any attempts at cross-comparison between sub-groups rather difficult and obviating the need for classification of all respondents along all axes.

15 In brief, correlating views as represented in answers to thematic questions on the questionnaire with the biographical and demographic data collected on the first page of the questionnaire; see Bourdieu (1984a) and (1996).

16 I did not include myself in the study by way of answering my own questionnaire (if I had, the lone entry for philosophy would appear above), although I

was tempted to do so – the desired inclusion of my own attitudes in the study will be in the form of this analysis and my involvement in discussion in the interviews, as well as my replies to objections from others in the project.

17 How seniority and status are to be determined is somewhat complex, given the need to weigh together earnings, professorial status, administrative status, research track record, etc., only some of which information was collected in the questionnaire.

18 It should be clear that I am here not trying to find the right meanings of the terms "natural, social, and human", nor to judge responses based on my beliefs about this, but that I am analyzing what the responses show about the clarity or confusion concerning these meanings.

19 This type of response, anticipating a certain point of view in terms of what the questionnaire was looking for, was interesting to me, in that often the guesses were quite wrong or cancelled each other out; often respondents would ask, for example, in response to the questions calling for valuations of significance, what I meant by significance, or whether significance was a fact or a norm, ignoring the possibility that I was interested in their reaction to what – I was aware – was an ambiguous term. One response captured fairly well the investigator's assumption: "These are all positional power statements. I can't answer them simply. My position distorts my answer. This all depends on who is judging. Nevertheless I will give you a shallow response if it will help." He went on to answer all the questions with "substantially significant." This response recognizes the complexity of the notion of significance, its shallow objective and deep subjective meaning, and its contentious hold on reality and unreality (the subject makes something significant, thereby complicating naïve assumptions concerning subjective unreality and objective reality).

20 I am here attempting to suspend my own views concerning the meaning of these contested terms, though it is clear that my own assumptions and prejudices inform both the construction of my questions and the interpretation of those results.

21 What follows is a partial analysis of only the most salient points in the responses – some questions are analysed rather fully, others left almost untouched.

22 With one anomaly – one respondent claimed no difference but then implied one by stating that the two must "resonate" together.

23 Science is often identified with natural science implicitly, as in the following, typical remark: "I consider most scientific knowledge to be valid because it has been subjected to statistical analysis; local knowledge that has proven the test of time is my guidepost; otherwise I am skeptical." Does the former show prejudice toward science? There is balance in the answer, but while science is

associated with validity, local knowledge is associated with skepticism. Another pro-science answer: "Scientific knowledge is published in peer reviewed journals and is validated by reproducibility under controlled conditions. Local knowledge is often not published, but may be published in non-scientific literature. Local knowledge is often the opinion of lay persons, not tested for validity." Apart from the reassertion here of a form of hard natural scientific value from within a multidisciplinary project, what this response allows, in relation to the others, is a mapping of the diverse and often incompatible ways in which pro-science or other attitudes are expressed (with natural science, e.g., being identified in the shorter and simpler answers with method, truth, validity, duplication, statistics, peer review, and scientific publication).

24 Interestingly enough, the exception was made by a natural scientist.
25 In part this is a question of language and tradition (the study's location on the East and West Coasts, and not in Quebec, should be noted here). In the French tradition, e.g., we speak of human sciences, whereas in contemporary English Canada, this is still seen by some as an odd term. How much are disputes concerning the meaning of methodological descriptions in fact disputes or misunderstandings concerning traditions, cultures, and institutions?
26 For example, natural and social science were distinguished by reference to subject matter – the physical world and social relationships. A variety of different goals were given.
27 This analysis needs to be deepened through a correspondence or matching, as far as possible, of the types of distinction given and the discipline of the one making the distinction.
28 This generalisation is also true of the question on social science and the humanities, where another respondent noted the institutional reasons for such distinctions.
29 That respondents to the questionnaire in the reflexive study often expressed confusion at the latter term, and sometimes also at the previous, shows the lack of understanding of the meaning of basic terms related to interdisciplinary research.
30 This discussion is informed by the analysis of disciplinarity, interdisciplinarity, and transdisciplinarity in Serres (1995b, 1997), Stengers (1997), and Guattari (1996).
31 Note the style of answers: from something like a true and false test to essays with references; the embodiment of disciplinary and institutional habits.
32 In moving to this as the third theme in the responses to the questionnaire, I am following the structure of the questionnaire but skipping a set of questions on coastal life and health, which I have not turned to yet.

33 At the time of this writing, namely, the fifth and final year of the project, which is also the time of the collective writing up of "results" and so the "pressure cooker" stage of the long process, the projected continuation of the CUS project under the SSHRC/NSERC MCRI funding rubric, referred to as CUS II, was dealt a blow by SSHRC's rejection, at the first stage of adjudication, of the project's Letter of Intent. How does such an event alter the commitment and involvement of participants at the final year of the project?

34 Again, a fine-tuned consideration of the responses, linking them to the disciplines and academic careers of their subjects by using the biographical details of the first page of the questionnaire, may lead to more interesting conclusions.

35 The questionnaires were collected over a period of approximately six months during the third year of the project. It is very possible that estimations of the integration of fields of research in the project went up and down substantially, given the advance of that research, especially as research plans came to completion and the project moved into the stage of synthesizing results (which is as close to the stage at which I and others are now in terms of writing up results and writing together). Like other partialities the one of time has correctives, and the idea for objections and replies to this study is warranted in part as an update on ideas and attitudes (as are the interviews and further analysis to come – thus approximating something like the reflexivity to the nth or infinite degree advocated by Bourdieu).

36 Almost no-one (at most 2 and usually 0 or 1) agrees strongly or disagrees strongly. Almost no-one is undecided, except on the organization of the project as a whole (4). The one exception to the majority support of the organization of the project (from between 14 to 22 responses) was articulated in the case of the integration of the arms of research with each other. A majority of respondents approve of the integration of work within a single arm of research and especially of the interchange of research information within an arm (22 agreed); a majority approved of the organization of the project as a whole and that the "goals of the project as a whole are becoming more clearly defined over time"; a majority (18) agreed that "team meetings and plenary session [were] generally productive."

37 Thanks to John Lutz for suggesting I highlight this point, as well as to him and Barb Neis together for their criticisms of this essay. I would also like to thank all of those who criticized my work, especially Barb Neis, from whom I continue to learn a lot, John Kennedy, Stuart Lee, Rosemary Ommer, Dave Schneider, and many others. I would also like to thank members of the staff, especially Cathy King and Janet Oliver, for their help throughout.

38 Voiced in 9 of the responses to the question of whether Coasts Under Stress could be better organized.

39 Other criticisms of the organization focused on a perceived centralization and hierarchization of power in the project, as evidenced by comments such as "too much left to one person" and "a little less top-down driven decision-making." How the values and perspectives implicated in such statements could be made to align with the desires documented earlier concerning more planning and structure is open to speculation.
40 The answer continues, "and (iv) reduce," followed by an illegible word.
41 Here, as in many cases, matching this statement with the respondent's declaration or lack thereof concerning their position in CUS would shed further light on the response, but this work still needs doing.
42 Here and elsewhere the differences should be noted between "big science" within one or several cognate disciplines and "big science" that, like CUS, crossed over macro-divisions between disciplines; the experimental character of big science methodology likely applies much more to the latter than to the former.
43 The review cited the lack of fit between this particular research activity and the overall purpose of CUS: "the committee was at a loss to determine how some research activities (the most obvious is the work on seismic and geological assessment of oil and gas reserves) could contribute to the overall goal ... [T]he underlying assumption that restructuring and health are inter-related must be made explicit rather than implicit throughout the research program. There needs to be a higher level of integration of this theme with projects within and between arms. For example, the committee wonders how the seismic and geochemical studies off the West Coast in case study 2 of Arm 4 fit into this overarching theoretical framework. The committee does not doubt the scientific value of this work but seriously questions its relevance to CUS. The committee feels it would be appropriate for this work to be funded separately by industry, NSERC or other sources but not by CUS."
44 On the same question another respondent writes: "I'm sure it [CUS] could [be better organized] but [this] would be difficult and expensive. I'd like to see local communities more involved and integrated in a real way. I don't feel that their voices are central to our work and they should be, in my view."
45 One of the main ways in which this reflexive study is biased (and in this way it is also collaboratively and collectively written) is by way of the responses I have chosen to quote. In the case of this respondent, occupying in some ways a marginal relation to the population, I have chosen to quote their responses at least a couple of times, in part because the respondent took the time to write what I consider thoughtful and intelligent responses. Whether or not I agree with the responses is another issue, though I would not be so naive as to insist that the two have nothing to do with each other.

46 Another 9 responses say much the same. How does one count or analyse answers like the following: "As stated in the proposal"?

47 These are some of the more critical: "I honestly can't say [what is the primary goal]! I know the buzzwords but ... I suppose it would have to be to research the environmental and social issues surrounding community life between the two coasts and somehow learn something. The stated aim is so vague it is hard to see how it can fail to meet it"; "To fund people's research (just kidding) – although this is clearly a significant part of it."

48 It may be seen from such comments why this reflexive study received a fair bit of attention.

49 Various comments of this sort were made on the questionnaires and also orally to me in between various meetings.

50 The feelings, opinions, experiences, and judgments of the student participants is especially interesting for the reflexive study, since this marginal population is vulnerable and at times, it appeared to me, largely incredulous and alienated from the faculty researchers. Rumblings of dissent, disquiet, and complaint were voiced to me most frequently and most vociferously by students, yet, for similar reasons, students were least likely to wish to participate and to be identified (for fear of reprisals from management).

51 This locational error, though natural for an administrative decision concerning study organization, reveals either misunderstanding or perplexity about the nature of the study. The metamorphoses of the study: from an improvised partnership at the first joint East-West Coast team meeting, to the retirement of the anthropologist, the addition and then quick subtraction of a graduate student anthropologist, whose participant observation arm of the reflexive study was also subject to scrutiny, to the final, single investigator form, with assistance from John Kennedy, Memorial University, anthropology, and graduate students Dwayne Avery, Dan Ferguson, and Yusuf Baydal.

52 These factors were evidenced in numerous oral communications and responses to the questionnaire that voiced surprise at the fact that identifying information was requested on the first page of the questionnaire – a questionnaire that respondents were instructed they were to answer according to their discretion, without having to answer any questions they did not want to – respondents who, as academics, would have readier access to information concerning questionnaires and confidentiality issues, albeit more so in the social than in the natural or human sciences.

53 I was told the funding councils took interest in the stressful course of the reflexive study.

54 Theory, in the pejorative sense of a foregone conclusion, will be associated with the humanities to a great degree, less so with social science, and hardly

or not at all with (good) natural science, with method receiving the opposite associations and valuation.

55 That this study posed questions in terms of "natural science," "social science," and the "humanities" reveals how groupings of disciplines are accepted and to some degree partially ratified (or trust in these designations is continued). Whether or not these groupings – and affiliated ones such as "pure" and "applied" – have a scientific, administrative, and/or broader social sense is a good question. The adoption of these large-scale groupings by Canadian federal granting councils (as evidenced, e.g., in their names, NSERC and SSHRC) gives credit to these classifications at one and the same time that the "integration" of these large groupings in CUS constitutes a type of "experiment" as to their worth.

56 Drawing such a generalization risks foreclosing upon the object of this study and in doing so, raises, on a small scale, the very problem of the relation between theory and methodology here being discussed, as well as related issues of the disciplinary awareness and valuation of different methods and theoretical orientations.

57 Such a split between theory and method may be denied by basic facts about scientific process (a method fits with a hypothesis, which is a theory of some sort) or by attention to quality research and reflection on the processes of science (see, e.g., Bourdieu 1996).

58 Consider that these remarks on theory and method are being written after I have begun processing my data on scientists' attitudes towards large-scale, interdisciplinary research.

59 In retrospect, I would say that the paucity of explicit and detailed discussion of the theory and methods of interdisciplinary research was filled by an administrative solution.

60 The confusion – real or illusory – between scientific and administrative requirements, in science in general and in this large-scale, interdisciplinary project is one of my themes.

61 I do not mean to suggest that there was no concept behind the project but that the absence of a well-worked-out method and theory make it easy to ask whether the concept was driving the machine or the administrative apparatus.

CHAPTER THIRTEEN

1 Examples of protocols and research licences other than those discussed below include Inuit research principles and guidelines, Dene Cultural Institute guidelines, Akwesasne Nation Protocol for Review of Environmental and Scientific Research Proposals, Tangentyere Research Policy, Mi'kmaq

Research Principles and Protocols, Nunavut Research Institute research principles. Hill (1997) and Voumard (2000) discuss contractual agreements.
2 The term "community" can be defined in many ways, for example, by a geographic area ("communities of place") the boundaries of which may be identified by political jurisdictions; biophysical characteristics; historical patterns of settlement; land use, or affiliation among residents. Communities can also be defined as "communities of interest," people with something in common other than their place of residence, such as gender, kinship, ethnic background, or political beliefs (Bryant 1999; Vodden 1999). While both definitions are relevant here (e.g., the community of academia or citizens within a geographic community interested in research), we use the term to mean the collection of people living within a community of place.
3 Science shops are considered a model of community-based research. They originated in the Netherlands and were created as mediators between citizen groups and research institutions. The International Science Shop Network (http://www.scienceshops.org/) defines a science shop as providing "independent, participatory research support in response to concerns experienced by civil society."
4 See http://www.clayoquotalliance.uvic.ca/structure.html for a schematic of the structure of CLARET.
5 http://www.sshrc.ca/web/apply/program_descriptions/cura_e.asp.
6 The First Nations communities are Maaqtusiis, or Ahousaht (Ahousaht First Nation); Hot Springs Cove (Hesquiaht First Nation); Esowista (Tla-o-qui-aht First Nation); Opitsaht (Tla-o-qui-aht First Nation); Ittatsoo (Ucluelet First Nation); and Macoah (Toquaht First Nation).
7 Information from www.clayoquotbiosphere.org.
8 For example, the former Long Beach Model Forest Society, Clayoquot Sound Central Region Board, West Coast Vancouver Island Aquatic Management Board, as well as several non-government organizations and businesses such as the Tofino Botanical Gardens and Clayoquot Field Station (for an overview see Dobell and Bunton 2001).
9 The protocols development was facilitated by one of the authors (Bannister) as part of both CLARET and the CUS project.
10 See http://www.clayoquotalliance.uvic.ca/Database/index.html.
11 See http://www.clayoquotalliance.uvic.ca/Language/index.html.
12 "Community health" is locally defined as "involving social, economic, and environmental factors that need to be integrated with individual health needs" (CLARET 2004).
13 See documents posted at http://www.research.uvic.ca/CBRF/.

14 Utilizing Mount Waddington Regional District as the regional boundary (Statistics Canada 2006).
15 First Nations in the region include the Da'naxda'xw/Awaetlala, Gwa'sala-'Nakwaxda'xw, Kwakiutl, Kwicksutaineuk-ah-kwa-mish, Mamaleleqala-Qwe-Qwa Sot-Enox, Mumtagila, 'Namgis, Tlatlasikwala, Tlowitsis, Tsawataineuk, Quatsino and Kwa-wa-aineuk Nations.
16 See www.icnrc.org.
17 'Namgis First Nation Guidelines for Visiting Researchers/Access to Information. Available at http://www.namgis.org/governence/Programs/index.asp.
18 The recent PHD, now a postdoctoral candidate, receives a stipend for his contribution to the centre.
19 The Central Region Nuu-chah-nulth Language Group.
20 A Canadian survey, reported in *University Affairs*, indicates that "non-traditional research activities" such as efforts to communicate research results to end-users or to translate knowledge are still undervalued in university promotion decisions, despite recent emphasis on such activities by SSHRC and CIHR (Charbonneau 2004).

Bibliography

Adams, B.K., and J.A. Hutchings. 2003. "Microgeographical Population Structure of Brook Charr: A Comparison of Microsatellite and Mark-Recapture Data." *Journal of Fish Biology* 62:517–33.

AGC (Auditor General of Canada). 1997. *Fisheries and Oceans Canada, Sustainable Fisheries Framework: Atlantic Groundfish*, chap. 14. http://www.oag-bvg.gc.ca.

Agrawal, A. 1995. "Dismantling the Divide between Indigenous and Scientific Knowledge." *Development and Change* 26:413–39.

Alcock, E., D. Ings, and D.C. Schneider. 2003. "From Local Knowledge to Science and Back: Evolving Use of Local Ecological Knowledge in Fisheries Science." In *Ecosystem Models of Newfoundland and Southeastern Labrador: Additional Information and Analyses for "Back to the Future,"* ed. J.J. Heymans. Fisheries Centre Research Reports 11(5):20–39. http://www.fisheries.ubc.ca/publications/reports/report11_5.php.

Allard, J., and G. Chouinard. 1997. "A Strategy to Detect Fish Discarding by Combining Onboard and Onshore Sampling." *Canadian Journal of Fisheries and Aquatic Sciences* 54:2955–63.

Alverson, D.L. 1998. *Discarding Practices and Unobserved Fishing Mortalities in Marine Fisheries: An Update*. Washington Sea Grant Program, 98-06. Seattle, WA.

– 1977. *Report of the Advisory Committee and Marine Resources Research Working Party on Marine Mammals.* FAO Fisheries Report no. 194. Rome: FAO

Alverson, D.L., M.H. Freeberg, S.A. Murawski, and J.G. Pope. 1994. *A Global Assessment of Fisheries Bycatch and Discards.* FAO Technical Paper no. 339. Rome: FAO.

Anderson, G.L., and F. Jones. (2000). "Knowledge Generation in Educational Administration from the Inside Out: The Promise and Perils of Site-Based

Administrator Reasearch." *Educational Administration quarterly* 36(3): 428–64.

Anderson, L.G., and D.R. Lee. 1986. "Optimal Governing Instruments in Natural Resource Regulation: The Case of the Fishery." *American Journal of Agricultural Economics* 68 (4): 679–90.

Anderson, M.R., D.R. Scruton, U.P. Williams, and J.F. Payne. 1995. "Mercury in Fish in the Smallwood Reservoir, Labrador, Twenty-One Years After Impoundment." *Water, Air and Soil Pollution* 80:920–30.

Anderson, R. 1972. "Hunt and Deceive: Information Management in Newfoundland Deep-Sea Trawler Fishing North Atlantic Fishermen." In *Anthropological Essays on Modern Fishing*, ed. R. Anderson and C. Wadel. Newfoundland Social and Economic Papers no. 5, Memorial University, NL.

Angel, J.R., D.L. Burke, R. O'Boyle, F.G. Peacock, M. Sinclair, and K. Zwanenburg, eds. 1994. *Report of the Workshop on Scotia-Fundy Groundfish Management from 1977 to 1993*. Canadian Technical Report of Fisheries and Aquatic Sciences 1979.

Anonymous. 2001 *Queen Charlotte Islands Herring*. DFO Science Stock Status Report B6–03.

– 2000. *Pacific Region 2000/2001 Management Plan – Food and Bait Herring*. DFO Management Plan.

– 1999a. *Fisheries Management Plan. Newfoundland and Labrador Snow Crab Fishery, 1999–2001*. DFO Integrated Fisheries Management Plan.

– 1999b. *Fisheries Management Plan. Scotia-Fundy Fisheries Integrated Herring Management Plan, 1999–2001*. DFO. Integrated Fisheries Management Plan.

– 1997. *Fisheries Management Plan. Area 12, 25–26 Snow Crab 1997–2002*. DFO Integrated Fisheries Management Plan.

– 1996. *Fisheries Management Plan. Area 19 Snow Crab, 1996 to 2001*. DFO Integrated Fisheries Management Plan.

– 1984. "Future Management of the Herring Fisheries of the Newfoundland and Labrador Region – A Discussion Paper." 1984. DFO.

– 1981. "The Management and Utilization of Atlantic Herring and Mackerel in the 1980s – A Discussion Paper." DFO.

Ansley, F., and J. Gaventa. 1997. "Researching for Democracy and Democratizing Research." *Change* 29:46–53.

Argyris, M., and D.A. Schön. 1974. *Theory in Practice: Increasing Professional Effectiveness*. San Francisco: Jossey-Bass.

Armstrong, Karen. 2000. *Buddha*. London: Phoenix Press.

Arnason, R. 1994. "On Catch Discarding in Fisheries. *Maritime Research Economics* 9(3): 189–207.

Arnstein, S. 1969. "A Ladder of Citizen Participation." *Journal of the American Institute of Planners* 35:216–24.

Atkinson, B. 1984. "Discarding of Small Redfish in the Shrimp Fishery off Port au Choix, Newfoundland, 1976–80." *Journal of Northwest Atlantic Fishery Science* 5 (1): 99–102.

Bak P., C. Tang, K. Wiesenfeld. 1988. "Self-organized Criticality." *Physics Review* A 38:364–74.

Bakhtin, Mikhail. 1996. *The Dialogic Imagination: Four Essays by M.M. Bakhtin.* Ed. Michael Holquist, trans. Caryl Emerson and Michael Holquist. Austin: University of Texas.

Bannister, K., T. Behr, S. Boychuk, N. Crookes, R. Dobell, S. Harron, S. LeRoy, A. Morgan, G. Schreiber, and J. Yakimishyn. 2003. *Clayoquot Alliance for Research, Education and Training: Exploring Borderlands, Bridging Boundaries.* Poster presented at the Community-University Expo Conference, Saskatoon, May.

Bannister, K., and P. Hardison. 2006. *Mobilizing Traditional Knowledge and Expertise for Decision Making on Biodiversity* Report prepared for the consultative process towards an International Mechanism of Scientific Expertise on Biodiversity (IMOSEB). German Federal Agency for Nature Conservation. Online at http://www.polisproject.org/PDFs/Bannisterhardison%202006.pdf.

Barnes, B., D. Bloor, and J. Henry. 1996. *Scientific Knowledge: A Sociological Analysis.* Chicago: University of Chicago Press.

Barnes, C.R., ed. 1993. "Future Research Trends in the Earth Sciences." *Geoscience Canada* 20:1–148.

Barnes, C.R., B.D. Bornhold, L.L. Mayer, I.A. McIlreath, B.J. Skinner, D. VanDine, and R. Wallis. 1996. "Future Challenges and Trends in the Geosciences in Canada." *Geoscience Canada* 22(1–2):1–99.

Batten, S. 2002. "Some Ethical Considerations for Research with First Nations." Coasts Under Stress Working Paper – Arm 5, Case Study no. 2, University of Victoria, Victoria, BC.

Baum, J., R. Myers, D. Kehler, B. Worm, S. Harley, and P. Doherr. 2003. "Collapse and Conservation of Shark Populations in the Northwest Atlantic." *Science* 299: 389–92.

Bavington, D.Y.I. 2002. "Managerial Ecology and Its Discontents: Exploring the Complexities of Control, Careful Use and Coping in Resource and Environmental Management." *Environments* 30:3–21.

BC (Government of British Columbia). 2002. *North Island Straits Coastal Plan.* Government of British Columbia: Victoria, BC.

- 1989. *Petroleum and Natural Gas Act*. Victoria, BC: Government of British Columbia. http://www.qp.gov.bc.ca/statreg/stat/P/96361_01.htm.
Becker, M.K., and P. Coburn. 1974. *Superspill: An Account of the 1978 Grounding at Bird Rocks*. Seattle, WA: Madrona Press.
Berkes, F. 1999. *Sacred Ecology: Traditional Ecological Knowledge and Resource Management*. Philadelphia, PA: Taylor and Francis.
- 1993. "Traditional Ecological Knowledge in Perspective." In *Traditional Ecological Knowledge: Concepts and Cases*, ed. J. Inglis. Ottawa: Canadian Museum of Nature, International Program on Traditional Ecological Knowledge.
- 1988. "The Intrinsic Difficulty of Predicting Impacts: Lessons from the James Bay Hydro Project." *Environmental Impact Assessment Review* 8:201–20.
- Berkes, F., J. Colding, and C. Folke, eds. 2003. *Navigating Social-Ecological Systems: Building Resilience for Complexity and Change*. Cambridge, England: Cambridge University Press.
Biron, M., R. Campbell, and M. Moriyasu. 2000a. "Historical Review (1994–1998) and Assessment of the 1999 Exploratory Snow Crab (*Chionoecetes opilio*) Fishery off Southwestern Nova Scotia (NAFO Division 4X). DFO CSAS Res. Doc. 2000/018.
Biron, M., E. Wade, M. Moriyasu, P. DeGrâce, R. Campbell, and M. Hébert. 2000b. "Assessment of the 1999 Snow Crab (*Chionoecetes opilio*) Fishery off Eastern Nova Scotia (Areas 20 to 24)." DFO CSAS Res. Doc. 2000/017.
Blustein, D.L. 1997. "A Context-Rich Perspective of Career Exploration across Life Roles." *Career Development Quarterly* 45:260–74.
Bourdieu, Pierre. 1996. *The State Nobility: Elite Schools in the Field of Power*. With the collaboration of Monique de Saint Martin. Trans. Lauretta C. Clough. Oxford. Polity, and Stanford: Standford University Press.
- 1984a. *Distinction: A Social Critique of the Judgement of Taste*. Trans. Richard Nice. Cambridge, MA: Harvard University Press.
- 1984b. *Homo Academicus*. Trans. Peter Collier. Les Editions de Minuit. Stanford: Stanford University Press.
Bourdieu, Pierre, and Loic. J.D. Wacquant. 1992. *An Invitation to Reflexive Sociology*. Chicago: University of Chicago Press.
Bray, K. 2000. *A Global Review of Illegal, Unreported and Unregulated (IUU) Fishing: Expert Consultation on Illegal, Unreported and Unregulated Fishing*. FAO: IUU/2000/6.
Breen, E. 2003. "Community Confidence in Fisheries Management and the Potential Use of Fisheries Indicators: A Study of Two Newfoundland Communities." Master's thesis, Memorial University of Newfoundland, St John's.

Breeze, H. 1998. *Conservation Lost at Sea: Discarding and Highgrading in the Scotia-Fundy Region Ground Fishery in 1998*. Ecology Action Centre and the Conservation Council of New Brunswick.

Bromley, Hank, and Michael W. Apple. 1998. *Education, Technology, Power: Educational Computing as a Social Practice*, SUNY Series, Frontiers in Education. Albany, NY: State University of New York Press.

Brown, John Seely, and Paul Duguid. 2000. *The Social Life of Information*. Boston: Harvard Business School press.

Brundtland, G.H., ed. 1987. *Our Common Future: The World Commission on Environment and Development*. Oxford, England: United Nations Commission on Environment and Development and Oxford University Press.

Bryant, C. 1999. "Community Change in Context." In *Communities, Development, and Sustainability across Canada*, ed. John Pierce and Anne Dale. Vancouver: UBC Press.

Bryant, T., I. Brown, T. Cogan, C. Dallaire, S. Laforest, P. McGowan, D. Raphael, L. Richard, L. Thompson, and J. Young. 2004. "What Do Canadian Seniors Say Supports Their Quality of Life? *Canadian Journal of Public Health* 95(4): 299–303.

Burningham, K., and M. O'Brien. 1994. "Global environmental Values and Local Contexts of Action." *Sociology* 28:913–32.

Butler, G.R. 1983. "Culture, Cognition, and Communication: Fishermen's Location-Finding in L'anse-a-Canards, Newfoundland." *Canadian Folklore Canadiene* 5 (1–2): 7–21.

Byrne, M. 2002. "Star Lake Remembered – Then and Now." *Spawner* 2002: 66–7.

Cadigan, S. 2002. "The Role of Agriculture in Outport Self Sufficiency." In *The Resilient Outport: Ecology, Economy, and Society in Rural Newfoundland*, ed., R.E. Ommer, 241–62. St John's, NL: ISER Books.

Calcutt, R., and R. Boddy. 1983. *Statistics for Analytical Chemists*. London: Chapman and Hall.

Cameron, B.E.B. 1980. *Biostratigraphy and Depositional Environment of the Escalante and Hesquiat Formations (Early Tertiary) of the Nootka Sound Area, Vancouver Island, British Columbia*. Geological Survey of Canada Paper 78–9.

Campbell, I.C., and S. Parnrong. 2000. "Limnology in Thailand: Present Status and Future Needs." *Theoretical and Applied Limnology* 27: 2135–41.

Canada. 1985. *The Atlantic Accord: Memorandum of Agreement between the Government of Canada and the Government of Newfoundland and Labrador on Offshore Oil and Gas Resource Management and Revenue Sharing*. Ottawa: Government of Canada.

CANDU Nuclear Operators Group. 2000. *CANDU Research and Development: Capability Review*. CANDU Owners Group Report: COG–00–059.
Canguilhem, Georges. 1978. *On the Normal and the Pathological*. Trans. C.R. Fawcett. Boston: D. Reidel.
Cashin, R. 1993. *Charting a New Course: Towards the Fishery of the Future*. Report of the Task Force on Income and Adjustment in the Atlantic Fishery. Ottawa: Communication Directorate, DFO.
Cashore, Benjamin William, George Hoberg, Michael Howlett, Jeremy Rayner, and Jeremy Wilson. 2001. *In Search of Sustainability: British Columbia Forest Policy in the 1990s*. Vancouver: UBC Press.
Cassirer, E. 1965. *The Philosophy of Symbolic Forms*. Vols. 1 – 3. New Haven, CT: Yale University Press.
Charbonneau, L. 2004. "Publish or Perish Still Holds Sway." *University News*, October. www.universityaffairs.ca.
Chiasson, Y.M., M. Hebert, and M. Moriyasu. 1992. "A Retrospective Look at the Development and Expansion of the Southwestern Gulf of St Lawrence Snow Crab, *Chionoecetes opilio*, Fishery. *Canadian Technical Report of Fisheries and Aquatic Sciences*, no. 1847.
CIHR-IAPH, (Canadian Institute of Health Research – Institute of Aboriginal Peoples' Health). 2002. *Five-Year Strategic Plan: 2002 to 2007*. Ottawa: CIHR-Institute of Aboriginal Peoples' Health.
Clapp, C.H. 1912. *Southern Vancouver Island*. Canada Department of Mines, Geological Survey, Memoir 13.
Clapp, F. 1985. "Coastal Tankers of British Columbia." *Steamboat Bill* 42 (4, winter):232 –45.
Clapp, R.A. 1998. "The Resource Cycle in Forestry and Fishing." *Canadian Geographer* 42 (2): 129–44.
Clark, K.J., D. Rogers, H. Boyd, and R.L. Stephenson. 1999. "Questionnaire Survey of the Coastal Nova Scotia Herring Fishery." DFO CSAS Res. Doc. 99/137.
Clarke, K.C., and J.J. Hemphill. 2002. "The Santa Barbara Oil Spill: A Retrospective." http://www.geog.ucsb.edu/~kclarke/Papers/SBOilSpill1969.pdf
CLARET, (Clayoquot Alliance for Research, Education and Training). 2005. "Standard of Conduct for Research in the Barkley and Clayoquot Sound Communities," version 1.1. Document prepared for the Protocols Project of the Clayoquot Alliance for Research, Education and Training. University of Victoria. online, http://www/clayoquotbiosphere.org/science/resources/php.

- 2004. *Clayoquot Symposium 2003: Health Across the Water. Proceedings.* Victoria, BC: CLARET. http://www.clayoquotalliance.uvic.ca/Symposium2003/index.html.
Cochran, L. 1997. *Career Counseling: A Narrative Approach.* Thousand Oaks, CA: Sage.
Cohen, P., and P. Ainley. 2000. "In the Country of the Blind? Youth Studies and Cultural Studies in Britain." *Journal of Youth Studies* 3(1): 79–95.
Cooke, R.M. 1991. *Experts in Uncertainty.* Oxford: Oxford University Press.
Copes, P. 2000. "Adverse Impacts of Individual Quota Systems on Conservation and Fish Harvest Productivity." Discussion Paper 00-2 Institute of Fisheries Analysis, Simon Fraser University, June.
- 1986. "A Critical Review of the Individual Quota as a Device in Fisheries Management." *Land Economics* 62:278–91.
Corbett, Michael. 2007. *Learning to Leave: The Irony of Schooling in a Coastal Community.* Halifax: Fernwood Books.
Corsiglia, J., and G. Snively. 1995. "Global Lessons from the Traditional Science of Long-Resident Peoples." In *Thinking Globally about Mathematics and Science Education,* ed. Gloria Snively and Allan MacKinnon, 25–51. Research and Development in Global Studies. Vancouver: Centre for the Study of Curriculum and Instruction, University of British Columbia.
Corveler, T. 2002. *Illegal, Unreported, and Unregulated Fishing: Taking Action for Sustainable Fisheries.* Wellington: WWF New Zealand.
Cowan, D.S., M.T. Brandon, and J.I. Garver. 1997. "Geologic Tests of Hypotheses for Large Coastwise Displacements: A Critique Illustrated by the Baja British Columbia Controversy." *American Journal of Science* 297:117–37.
Cronon, W. 1995. "The Trouble with Wilderness: Or, Getting Back to the Wrong Nature." In *Uncommon Ground: Toward Reinventing Nature,* ed. W. Cronon, 69–90. New York: W.W. Norton and Company.
Davis, A., and J.R. Wagner. 2003. "Who Knows? On the Importance of Identifying 'Experts' When Researching Local Ecological Knowledge (LEK)." *Human Ecology* 31(3): 463–9.
Davis, W. 2001. *Light at the Edge of the World: A Journey through the Realm of Vanishing Cultures.* Vancouver, BC: Douglas & McIntyre, and Washington, DC: National Geographic Society.
Dawe, E.G., D.W. Kulka, H.J. Drew, P.C. Beck, and P.J. Veitch. 1999. "Status of the Newfoundland and Labrador Snow Crab Resource in 1998." DFO CSAS Res. Doc. 99/136.

De Young, R. 1993. "Changing Behaviour and Making It Stick: The Conceptualisation and Management of Conservation Behaviour." *Environment and Behaviour* 25(4):485–505.

DeGrâce, P., M. Hébert, E. Wade, A. Hébert, D. Giard, T. Surette, M. Biron, and M. Moriyasu. 2000. "Assessment of the 1999 Snow Crab (*Chionoecetes opilio*) Fisheries off Western Cape Breton (Areas 18 and 19)." DFO CSAS Res. Doc. 2000/015.

Delaney, J.R., G.R. Heath, B. Howe, A.D. Chave, and H. Kirkham. 2000. "NEPTUNE: Real-time Ocean and Earth Sciences at the Scale of a Tectonic Plate." *Oceanography* 13(2):71–9.

DFO (Department of Fisheries and Oceans). 2003. "Newfoundland and Labrador Snow Crab Stock Status Report 2003/021." Canadian Science Advisory Secretariat. http://www.dfo-mpo.gc.ca.

Diamond, Jared. 2005. *Collapse: How Societies Choose to Fail or Succeed*. New York: Viking.

– 1997. *Guns, Germs and Steel: The Fates of Human Societies*. New York: Norton.

Dobell, R., and M. Bunton. 2001. *Sound Governance: The Recent Emergence of New Networks and Collaborative Institutions in the Clayoquot Sound Region*. A draft monograph commissioned by the National Roundtable on Environment and Economy for the Policy Research Secretariat, for a series of workshops on Adaptive and Community-Based Management. Victoria, BC: CLARET. http://www.clayoquotalliance.uvic.ca/PDFs/Sound_Gov_2.

Doern, G.B., and R. Phidd. 1983. *Canadian Public Policy: Ideas, Structure and Process*. Methuen Publications.

Dolan, H., M. Taylor, B. Neis, J. Eyles, R. Ommer, D. Schneider, and W. Montevecchi. 2005. "Restructuring and Health in Canada's Coastal Communities: A Social-ecological Model of Restructuring and Health." *EcoHealth* 2: 1–14.

Dwyer, M. 2001. *Sea of Heartbreak*. Toronto: Key Porter Books.

Easterby-Smith, M.P.V., and M. Lyles. 2003. "Introduction: Watersheds of Organizational Learning and Knowledge Management." In *The Blackwell Handbook of Organizational Learning and Knowledge Management*, ed. M.P.V. Easterby-Smith and M. Lyles. Oxford: Blackwell.

EHJV (Eastern Habitat Joint Venture). n.d. *A Prospectus for the Eastern Habitat Joint Venture*.

Elias, B. 2002. *The Shape of Things to Come: The Second National Gathering of Graduate Students on Building Capacity in Aboriginal Health Research*. Report on the Second Annual National Gathering of Graduate Students, 28 March. Ottawa: Canadian Institutes of Health Research – Institute of Aboriginal Peoples' Health (CIHR-IAPH).

Bibliography

Eliot, T.S. 1963. *Collected Poems 1909–1962*. London: Faber.
Environment Canada. 2000. *Technology, Competitiveness and Canada's Environmental Industry: An Outlook into the Future Development of the Canadian Industry*, Ottawa: Environment Canada.
Epstein, J.S., ed. 1998. *Youth culture. Identity in a Post-Modern World*. Malden, MA: Blackwell Publishers.
Erikson, E.H. 1968. *Identity: Youth and Crisis*. New York: Norton.
Erkinaro, J., and R.J. Gibson. 1997. "Interhabitat Migration of Juvenile Atlantic Salmon in a Newfoundland River System, Canada." *Journal of Fish Biology* 51:373–88.
Erkinaro, J., M. Julkunen, and E. Niemelä. 1998. "Migration of Juvenile Atlantic Salmon *Salmo salar* in Small Tributaries of the Subarctic River Teno, Northern Finland." *Aquaculture* 168:105–19.
Evans, D. 2000. *The Consequences of Illegal, Unreported and Unregulated Fishing for Fishery Data and Management. Expert Consultation on Illegal, Unreported and Unregulated Fishing*. IUU/2000/12. Rome: FAO.
FAO (Food and Agriculture Organization of the UN). 2002. Stopping Illegal, Unreported and Unregulated Fishing. Rome: FAO.
– 1995. The Code of Conduct for Responsible Fisheries. Rome: FAO. http://www.fao.org/fi/agreem/codecond/ficonde.asp.
Felt, L.F., and P.R. Sinclair. 1995. Introduction to *Living on the Edge: The Great Northern Peninsula of Newfoundland*, ed. L.F. Felt and P.R. Sinclair, 1–25. St John's: ISER.
Fiander-Good Associates. 1993. *Trans Labrador Highway: Social and Economic Project Feasibility Analysis Condensed Final Report*. Fredericton, NB.
Finlayson, A.C. 1994. *Fishing for Truth: A Sociological Analysis of Northern Cod Stock Assessments from 1977 to 1990*. St John's, NL: ISER Books.
Fischer, J. 2000. "Participatory Research in Ecological Fieldwork: A Nicaraguan Study." In *Finding Our Sea Legs: Linking Fishery People and Their Knowledge with Science and Management*, ed. B. Neis and L. Felt. St John's, NL: ISER Books.
Fischer, J., and R.L. Haedrich. 2002. "Thermodynamics for Marxists." In *The Resilient Outport: Ecology, Economy, and Society in Rural Newfoundland*, ed. R.E. Ommer. St John's, NL: ISER Books
Ford, J., and D.R. Martinez, ed. 2000. *Ecological Applications* 10 (5). Special Issue on Traditional Ecological Knowledge, Ecosystem Science, and Environmental Management.
Forrest, R., T. Pitcher, R. Watson, H. Valtysson, and S. Guenette. 2001. "Estimating Illegal and Unreported Catches from Marine Ecosystems: Two Case Studies." In *Fisheries Impacts on North Atlantic Ecosystems: Evaluations and*

Policy Exploration, ed. T. Pitcher and D. Pauly. UBC Fisheries Centre Research Report 9(5): 81–93.

Foucault, Michel. 2000. *Power: Essential Works of Foucault, 1954–1984* Vol. 3. Ed. James D. Faubion, trans. Robert Hurley and others. London: Penguin.

– 1997. *Ethics: Essential Works of Foucault 1954–1984*, Vol. 1. Ed. Paul Rabinow, trans. Robert Hurley and others. London: Penguin.

– 1980. *Power/Knowledge: Selected Interviews and Other Writings, 1972–1977*. Brighton, England: Harvester Press.

Fowler, H.W., and F.G. Fowler, ed. 1964. *Oxford Concise Dictionary*. Oxford: The Clarendon Press.

FRCC (Fisheries Resource Conservation Council). 2003. *2003/2004 Conservation Requirements for 2J3KL Cod Stocks*. Ottawa: FRCC.

– 1994. *Conservation Stay the Course – 1995 Conservation Requirements for Atlantic Groundfish*. Report to the Minister of Fisheries and Oceans, Fisheries Resource Conservation Council. (FRCC.94.R.4) Ottawa: FRCC http://www.frcc.ca/scanned%20reports/ FRCC94R4.pdf.

– 1993. *We Must Stop Chasing Quotas Down to the Last Fish: 1993 Conservation Requirements for Atlantic Groundfish*. Report to the Minister of Fisheries and Oceans. (FRCC.93.R.1) Ottawa: FRCC http://www.frcc.ca/scanned%20reports/FRCC93R1.pdf.

Freeman, M.M.R. 1992. "The Nature and Utility of Traditonal Ecological Knowledge." *Northern Perspectives* (Canadian Arctic Resources Committee) 20 (1). http://www.carc.org/pubs/v20no1/utility.htm .

Freeman, M.M.R., and L.N. Carbyn, ed. 1988. *Traditional Knowledge and Renewable Resources Management in Northern Regions*. Occasional Paper No. 23. Edmonton, AB: Canadian Circumpolar Institute (formerly the Boreal Institute for Northern Studies).

Freeman, S.D. 1972. "New Policies for Energy and the Environment." In *Energy and the Environment: A Series of Public Lectures*, ed. I. Efford and B. Smith, 32–44. University of British Columbia, Institute of Resource Ecology, Vancouver.

Freire, P. 1970/1992. *Pedagogy of the Oppressed*. New York: The Continuum Publishing Company.

Furman, A. 1998. "A Note on Environmental Concern in a Developing Country: Results from an Istanbul Survey." *Environment and Behaviour* 30:520–34.

Gabrielse, H., and C.J. Yorath, ed. 1992. *Geology of the Cordilleran Orogen in Canada*. Geological Survey of Canada, *Geology of Canada*, no. 4, and

Geological Society of America's Geology of North America, v. G-2, Decade of North American Geology Project.
Galbraith, John Kenneth. 1992. *The Culture of Contentment*. Boston: Houghton Mifflin.
– 1977. *The Age of Uncertainty*. Boston: GK Hall.
Gaventa, John, and Andrea Cornwall. 2001. *Power and Knowledge*. In *Handbook of Action Research: Participative Inquiry and Practice*, eds. Peter Reason and Hilary Bradbury, 70–9. London: Sage Publications.
Gezelius, S.S. 2006. "Monitoring Fishing Mortality: Compliance in Norwegian Offshore Fisheries." *Marine Policy* 30: 462–9.
– 2003. "The Morality of Compliance in Coastal Fisheries: Cases from Norway and Newfoundland." Paper presented at the IASCP Northern Polar Regional Meeting, Anchorage, Alaska, 17–21 August 2003.
– 2002. "Do Norms Count? State Regulation and Compliance in a Norwegian Fishing Community." *Acta Sociologica* 45:305–14.
Gibbons, M. 1999. "Science's New Social Contract with Society." *Nature* 402:81–4.
Gibson, R.J. 2003. "Potential Threats and Recent Surveys of St John's City Rivers." *The Osprey* 34(2): 11–16.
Gibson, R.J., and R.L. Haedrich. 1988. "The Exceptional Growth of Juvenile Atlantic Salmon (*Salmo salar*) in the City Waters of St John's, Newfoundland, Canada." *Polskie Archiwum Hydrobiolii* 35: 385–407.
Gibson, R.J., R.L. Haedrich, and C.M. Wernerheim. 2005. "Loss of Fish Habitat as a Consequence of Inappropriately Constructed Stream Crossings." *Fisheries* 30(1): 10–17.
Gibson, R.J., J. Hammar, and G. Mitchell. 1999. "The Star Lake Hydroelectric Project. An Example of the Failure of the Canadian Environmental Assessment Act." In *Assessments and Impacts of Megaprojects*, ed. P.M. Ryan, 147–76. Proceedings of the Thirty-eighth Annual Meeting of the Canadian Society of Environmental Biologists, in collaboration with the Newfoundland and Labrador Environment Network, St John's, NL, Canada, 1–3 October 1998. Toronto: Canadian Society of Environmental Biologists.
Gitga'at Nation and Coasts Under Stress. 2003. *Gitga'ata Spring Harvest – Traditional Knowledge of Kiel*. Gitga'at Nation, Hartley Bay; Coasts Under Stress, University of Victoria; and Sierra Club of British Columbia, Victoria. Directed by Robin June Hood, filmed by Ben Fox. Distributed by McNabb Connolly, Mississauga, Ontario.
Glantz, S.A. 1997. *Primer of Biostatistics*. New York: McGraw Hill.

Gomes, Manuel do Carmo. 1994. *Predictions under Uncertainty: Fish Assemblage and Food Webs on the Grand Banks of Newfoundland*. St John's, NL: ISER Books.

Gosse, K.R. 2003. Brown Cod and Bay Stocks: Science and Fish Harvester's Knowledge of Colouration in Populations of Atlantic Cod (Gadus morhua) in Newfoundland and Labrador. Master's thesis, Memorial University of Newfoundland.

Gosse, K.R., and J.S. Wroblewski. 2004. "Variant Colourations of Atlantic Cod (*Gadus morhua*) in Newfoundland and Labrador Nearshore Waters." *ICES Journal of Marine Science* 61:752–9.

Gosse, K.R., J.S. Wroblewski, and B. Neis. 2001. "Utilization of Local Ecological Knowledge (LEK) in a Scientific Study of Coastal Cod in Newfoundland and Labrador." Conference proceedings, Putting Fishers' Knowledge to Work, an international conference investigating the role of local and traditional ecological knowledge in fisheries management. University of British Columbia. Vancouver, British Columbia, August 2001.

Gosse, M.M., A.S. Power, D.E. Hyslop, and S.L. Pierce. 1998. *Guidelines for Protection of Freshwater Fish Habitat in Newfoundland and Labrador*. St John's, NL: Fisheries and Oceans.

Gough, J. 2001. Key Issues in Atlantic Fishery Management. Web address for Museum of Civilisation, Ottawa. http://www.civilization.ca/hist/lifelines/gough2e.html.

Gould, E. 2003. *The University in a Corporate Culture*. New Haven, CT: Yale University Press.

Gray, T. 2002. "Fisheries Science and Fishers' Knowledge." ENSUS 2002 – Marine Science and Technology for Environmental Sustainability Conference, University of Newcastle upon Tyne, December. http://www.efep.org/TSGENSUS.pdf.

Green, L., M. George, M. Daniel, C. Frankish, C. Herbert, W. Bowie, and M. O'Neil. 1997. "Background on Participatory Research." In *Doing Community-Based Research: A Reader*, ed. Danny Murphy, Madeline Scammell, and Richard Sclove, 53–66. Washington, DC: The Loka Institute.

Grob, A. 1995. "A Structural Model of Environmental Attitudes and Behaviour." *Journal of Environmental Psychology* 15:209–20.

Guattari, Pierre-Felix. 1996. *The Guattari Reader*, ed. G. Genosko. Oxford. Basil Blackwell.

Gunderson, L., and C.S. Holling. 2002. *Panarchy: Understanding Transformations in Human and Natural Systems*. Washington, DC: Island Press.

Hache, J.E. 1989. *Report of the Scotia-Fundy Groundfish Task Force*. Halifax, NS: Department of Fisheries and Oceans.

Haedrich, R.L., and S.M. Barnes 1997. "Changes Over Time of the Size Structure in an Exploited Shelf Fish Community. *Fisheries Research* 31: 229–39.

Halifax Herald, 20 January2003. Halifax, NS.

Hall, M., D. Alverson, and K.I. Metuzals. 2000. "Bycatch: Problems and Solutions." In *Seas at the Millennium*, ed. C. Sheppard. Amsterdam: Elsevier.

Hannigan, P.K., J.R. Dietrich, P.J. Lee, and K.G. Osadetz. 2001. "Petroleum Resource Potential of Sedimentary Basins on the Pacific Margin of Canada." *Geological Survey of Canada, Bulletin* 564.

Haraway, Donna J. 1991. "Situated Knowledges: The Science Question in Feminism and the Privilege of Partial Perspective." In *Simians, Cyborgs, and Women: The Reinvention of Nature*, chapter 9, 183—201. New York: Routledge

Hare, G.M., and D.L. Dunn. 1993. "A Retrospective Analysis of the Gulf of St Lawrence Snow Crab (*Chionoecetes opilio*) Fishery." *Can. Bull. Fish. Aquat. Sci.* 226:177–92.

Hargreaves, A., L. Earl, and J. Ryan. 1996. *Schooling for Change: Reinventing Education for Early Adolescence.* Washington, DC: Falmer Press.

Harris, Carol E. 2002. "Community Schools Fulfil Different Needs." *Times Colonist*, 11 February, A7.

– 1998. *A Sense of Themselves: Elizabeth Murray's Leadership in School and Community.* Halifax: Fernwood.

Harris, L. 1990. *Independent Review of the State of the Northern Cod Stock.* Ottawa: Communication Directorate, DFO.

Harris, M. 1998. *Lament for an Ocean: The Collapse of the Atlantic Cod Fishery: A True Crime Story.* Toronto: McLelland and Stewart.

Hart, G.S.L. 1971. *Report of the Royal Commission on Pollution of Canadian Waters by Oil and Formal Investigation into Grounding of the Steam Tanker Arrow.* Ottawa: Information Canada.

Harter, S. 1999. *The Construction of the Self: The Developmental Perspective.* New York: The Guildford Press.

Hartup, W.W. 1992. "Peer Relations in Early and Middle Childhood." In *Handbook of social Development: A Lifespan Perspective*, ed. Vincent B. Van Hasselt, and Michel Hersen, , 257–81. New York: Plenum Press.

Haughey, Margaret. 2002. "Foucault and Educational Administration." Paper presented at the Canadian Association for the Study of Educational Administration, 28–30 May, Toronto. margaret.haughey@ualberta.ca.

Hayles, N. Katherine. 1984. *The Cosmic Web: Scientific Field Models and Literary Strategies in the Twentieth Century.* Ithaca, NY: Cornell University Press.

Hayter, R. 2001. "Forest Re-regulation and Industrial Restructuring: Reflections on the NDP's Forest Policy for British Columbia, 1991–2001." Paper presented at Canadian Association of Geographers' Annual Meeting.

Health Canada. 2004. *Towards a Healthy Future: Second Report on the Health of Canadians.*

Hébert, M., A. Hébert, E. Wade, T. Surette, D. Girard, P. DeGrâce, M. Biron, and M. Moriyasu. 2000. "The 1999 Assessment of Snow Crab, *Chionoecetes opilio,* Stock in the Southwestern Gulf of St Lawrence (Areas 12–25/26, E and F)." DFO CSAS Res. Doc.2000/014.

Hessing, M., and M. Howlett. 1997. *Canadian Natural Resource and Environmental Policy.* Vancouver: UBC Press.

Hilborn, R., T.A. Branch, B. Ernst, A. Magnusson, C.V. Minte-Vera, M. Scheuerell, and J. Valero. 2003. "State of the World's Fisheries." *Annual Review of Environmental Resources* 28: 15.1–15.40.

Hill, Cam, and Eva-Ann Hill. 2003. Letter to J. Thompson.

Hill, L. 1997. "Traditional Knowledge in Science." Paper presented at the 1997 Waigani Seminars, University of Papua New Guinea, August.

Holling, C.S. 2003. "Command and Control and the Pathology of Natural Resources Management." *Conservation Biology* 10:328–37.

– 1973. "Resilience and Stability of Ecological Systems." *Annual Review of Ecology and Systematics* 4:1–23.

Hollis, T.I. 2004. "Stewardship of Local Wetlands: Environmental Ethics and Traditional Ecological Knowledge in Four Rural Newfoundland Communities." Master's thesis, Memorial University of Newfoundland, St John's.

Holm, P. 2003. "Crossing the Border: On the Relationship between Science and Fishermen's Knowledge in a Resource Management Context." *MAST* 2(1):5–33.

– 2001. "The Invisible Revolution: The Construction of Institutional Change in the Fisheries." Unpublished doctoral dissertation, Norway, Tromso University, Norwegian College of Fisheries Science.

– 1996. "Fisheries Management and the Domestication of Nature." *Sociologia Ruralis* 36(2):177–88.

Homer-Dixon, T. 2001. *The Ingenuity Gap. Can We Solve the Problems of the Future?* Toronto: Vintage Canada.

Hourston A.S., and R. Chaulk. 1968. *Herring Landings and Catches in Newfoundland and Their Implications concerning the Distribution and Abundance of the Stocks.* Fisheries Research Board of Canada Technical Report No. 58.

Hunn, E. 1999. "The Value of Subsistence for the Future of the World." In *Ethnoecology: Situated Knowledge/Located Lives,* ed. Virginia D. Nazarea, chap. 2, 23–36. Tucson: University of Arizona Press.

Hunter, Heather. 2000. "In the Face of Poverty: What a Community School Can Do." In *Solutions That Work: Fighting Poverty in Winnipeg*, ed. J. Silver. Halifax: Fernwood.

Hutchings, J.A. 1996. "Spatial and Temporal Variation in the Density of Northern Cod and a Review of Hypotheses for the Stock Collapse. *Canadian Journal of Fisheries and Aquatic Sciences* 53: 943–62.

Hutchings, J., and M. Ferguson. 2000. "Temporal Changes in Harvesting Dynamics of Canadian Inshore Fisheries for Northern Atlantic Cod, *Gadus morhua*. *Canadian Journal of Fisheries and Aquatic Sciences* 57: 805–14.

Hutchings, J., and R. Myers. 1995. "The Biological Collapse of Atlantic Cod off Newfoundland and Labrador: An Exploration of Historical Changes in Exploitation, Harvesting Technology, and Management." In *The North Atlantic Fishery: Strengths, Weaknesses and Challenges*, ed. R. Arnason and L. Felt. Charlottetown, PEI: The Institute of Island Studies, 37–93.

Hutchins, R.M. 1970. *The Learning Society*. Harmondsworth, England: Penguin.

Hyndman, R.D., C.J. Yorath, R.M. Clowes, and E.E. Davis. 1990. "The Northern Cascadia Subduction Zone at Vancouver Island: Seismic Structure and Tectonic History." *Canadian Journal of Earth Sciences* 27(3):313–29.

Ife, Jim. 2002. *Community Development: Community-Based Alternatives in an Age of Globalization* 2d ed. New South Wales: Longman.

Iles, T.D. 1993. "The Management of the Canadian Atlantic Herring Fisheries." *Canadian Bulletin of Fisheries and Aquatic Sciences* 226: 123–50.

Industry Canada. 2002a. *Canada's Innovation Strategy – Achieving Excellence: Investing in People, Knowledge and Opportunity*. Ottawa: Industry Canada.

– 2002b. *Canada's Innovation Strategy – Knowledge Matters: Skills and Learning for Canadians*. Ottawa: Industry Canada.

Internet Weekly Report. 2003. "IWR Summary – Science and Doubt." http://www.internetweekly.org/iwr/scientific_knowledge.html.

Irving, E., P.J. Wynne, D.J. Thorkelson, and P. Schiarizza. 1996. "Large (1000 to 4000 km) northward Movements of Tectonic Domains in the Northern Cordillera, 83 to 45 Ma." *Journal of Geophysical Research* 101:17901–16.

IUCN (International Union for the Conservation of Nature); UNEP (United Nations Environment Program); and WWF (World Wildlife Fund). 1991. *Caring for the Earth: A Strategy for Sustainable Living*. Gland, Switzerland: IUCN.

Jackson, L., S. Tirone, C. Dovovan, and R. Hood. 2004. "Restructuring and Youth's Perspectives on Future Job Opportunities: A Study of Youth in Northern Newfoundland (Canada)." Eleventh World Congress of Rural Sociology, Trondheim, Norway, July.

- 2003. "Youth in a Coastal Community in Northern Newfoundland: What Are Their Perceptions of Their Educational Experiences and Career Opportunities?" Canadian Society for the Study of Education, Halifax, Nova Scotia. May.
Jacques Whitford. 2006. *Star Lake Reservoir: 2005 Habitat Compensation Year-End Report.* JWEL Project no. FS 10253.
- 1998. *Trans Labrador Highway (Red Bay to Cartwright) Environmental Assessment.* JWEL Project no. 1152.
Jeletzky, J.A. 1973. "Age and Depositional Environments of Tertiary Rocks of Nootka Island, British Columbia (92-E): Mollusks versus Foraminifers. *Canadian Journal of Earth Sciences* 10:331–65.
Jensen, F., and N. Vestergaard. 2002. "Moral Hazard Problems in Fisheries Regulation: The Case of Illegal Landings and Discard." *Resources and Energy Economics* 24:281–99.
Johannes, R. 1981. *Words of the Lagoon: Fishing and Marine Lore in the Palau District of Micronesia.* Berkeley: University of California Press.
Johnsen, J.P. 2005. "The Evolution of the "Harvest Machinery": Why Capture Capacity Has Continued to Expand in Norwegian Fisheries." *Marine Policy* 29 (6): 481–93.
Johnson, J.L. 2004. "Crossing the Line: Adolescents' Experience of Controlling Their Tobacco Use." *Qualitative Health Research* 14(9):1276–91.
Johnson, M., ed. 1992. *Lore: Capturing Traditional Environmental Knowledge.* Ottawa: International Development Research Centre, and Hay River, NWT: Dene Cultural Institute.
Keats, D., J. Steele, and D. Green. 1986. *A Review of the Recent Status of the Northern Cod Stock (NAFO Div. 2J, 3K and 3L) and the Declining Inshore Fishery.* Report of Memorial University of Newfoundland, St John's.
Keith, L.H., W. Crummett, W. Deegan Jr, R.A. Libby, J.K. Taylor, and G. Wentler. 1983. "Principles of Environmental Analysis." *Analytical Chemistry* 55:2210–18.
Kennedy, J.C. 1995. *People of the Bays and Headlands: Anthropological History and the Fate of Communities in the Unknown Labrador.* Toronto: University of Toronto Press.
King, A., W. Boyce, and M. King. 1999. *Trends in the Health of Canadian Youth.* Ottawa: Health Canada.
Kirby, M.J.L. (chairman). 1983. *Navigating Troubled Waters. Report of the Task Force on Atlantic Fisheries.* Ottawa: Supply and Services.
Knorr Cetina, Karin. 1999. *Epistemic Cultures: How the Sciences Make Knowledge.* Cambridge, MA. Harvard University Press.
Kooiman, Jan, and Maarten Bavinck. 2005. "The Governance Perspective." In *Fish for Life: Interactive Governance for Fisheries,* eds. Jan Kooiman, Maarten

Bavinck, Svein Jentoft, and Roger Pullin, 11–24. Amsterdam: Amsterdam University Press.

Kort, B., and R. Reilly. 2002. "Theories for Deep Change in Affect-Sensitive Cognitive Machines: A Constructivist Model." *International Forum of Educational Technology and Society* 5(4):1–13.

Krause, H. 1993. "Environmental Consciousness: An Empirical Study." *Environment and Behaviour* 25:126–42.

Kretzmann, John P., and John McKnight. 1993. *Building Communities from the Inside Out: A Path toward Finding and Mobilizing a Community's Assets.* Institute for Policy Research, and Northwestern University (Evanston, IL). Chicago: The Asset-Based Community Development Institute, Institute for Policy Research. Distributed by ACTA Publications.

Kuhn, T.S. 1970. *The Structure of Scientific Revolutions.* 2d ed. Chicago: The University of Chicago Press.

Kulka, D. 1986. "Estimates of Discarding by the Newfoundland Offshore Fleet in 1984 with Reference to Trends over the Past Four Years." NAFO SCR Doc. 86/12. Serial no. N1120.

– 1984. "Estimates of Discarding by the Newfoundland Offshore Fleet in 1982." NAFO SCR Document, vol.84/VI/86, 1–16.

– 1982. "Estimates of Discarding by Newfoundland Offshore Vessels in 1981." CAFSAC, Res. Doc. 82/34.

Kurlansky, M. 1997. *Cod: A Biography of the Fish That Changed the World.* New York: Walker Publishing.

Landry, R., M. Lamari, and N. Amara. 2003. "The Extent and Determinants of the Utilization of University Research in Government Agencies." *Public Administration Review* 63(2): 192–205.

Langer, S.K. 1948. *Philosophy in a New Key.* New York: Mentor.

Latour, B. 2004. *Politics of Nature: How to Bring the Sciences into Democracy.* Boston: Harvard University Press.

– 1987. *Science in Action.* Cambridge, MA: Harvard University Press.

Lear, W.H., and L.S. Parsons. 1993. "History and Management of the Fishery for Northern Cod in NAFO Divisions 2J, 3K and 3L." *Canadian Bulletin of Fisheries and Aquatic Sciences* 226: 55–89.

Leiss, W. 2001. *In the Chamber of Risks: Understanding Risk Controversies.* Montreal and Kingston: McGill-Queen's University Press.

Lerner, S.C. 1993. "The Importance of Active Earthkeeping." In *Environmental Stewardship: Studies in Active Earthkeeping,* ed. S.C. Lerner, 3–8. Waterloo: University of Waterloo, Department of Geography Publication.

Levin, S.A. 1999. *Fragile Dominion: Complexity and the Commons.* Reading, MA: Perseus Books.

Leslie, P.M., and D.H.S. Davis. 1939. "An Attempt to Determine the Absolute Number of Rats in a Given Area." *Journal of Animal Ecology* 8:94–113.

Lieberwitz, R. 2000. "Academic Freedom vs Corporatization: Rediscovering a Collective Faculty Identity." Paper presented at the Law and Society Association 2000 Annual Meeting.

Lilly, G.R., P.A. Shelton, J. Brattey, N.G. Cadigan, B.P. Healey, E.F. Murphy, D.E. Stansbury, and N. Chen. 2003. "A Summary of the February 2003 Assessment of the Divisions 2J+3KL Stock of Atlantic Cod (*Gadus morhua*)" NAFO SCR Doc. 03/62 Serial no. N4881.

Loch, J.S., M. Moriyasu, and J.B. Jones. 1994. "An Improved Link between Industry, Management and Science: A Case History – The Southern Gulf of St Lawrence Snow Crab Fishery." ICES CM 1994/T: 46.

Longino, Helen E. 1990. *Science as Social Knowledge*. Princeton: Princeton University Press.

Lopes, C.S., L.C. Rodrigues, and R. Sichieri. 1996. "The Lack of Selection Bias in a Snowball Sampled Case-Control Study on Drug Abuse." *International Journal of Epidemiology* 25:1267–70.

Luhmann, Niklas. 1989. *Ecological Communication*. Trans. J. Bednarz, Jr. Chicago: University of Chicago Press.

M'Gonigle, M. 1999. "The Political Economy of Precaution." In *Protecting Public Health and the Environment: Implementing the Precautionary Principle*, ed. Carolyn Raffensperger and Joel A. Tickner, 123–47. Washington, DC: Island Press.

– 1986. "The Tribune and the Tribe: Toward a Natural Law of the Market/Legal State." *Ecological Law Quarterly* 13:233–310.

MA (Millennium Ecosystem Assessment). 2005. *Ecosystems and Human Well-being: Synthesis*. Washington, DC: Island Press. http://www.millenniumassessment.org/.

Mackenzie, A.R. 1936. "Standard Oil Company of British Columbia, Ltd. Survey of the Consumption of Petroleum Products on the Coast of British Columbia." Manuscript, Royal British Columbia Museum.

Mailhot, J. 1993. *Traditional Ecological Knowledge: The Diversity of Knowledge Systems and Their Study*. Montreal: The Great Whale Public Review Support Office.

Mallet, P., R. Campbell, and M. Moriyasu. 1993. "Assessment of the 1992 Snow Crab (*Chionoecetes opilio*) Exploratory Fishery in Bay of Islands, Western Coast of Newfoundland." *Canadian Manuscript Report of Fisheries and Aquatic Sciences* No. 2189.

Malone, T.F. 1994. "A Defining Moment." *EOS* 75:313–18.

Bibliography

Marcia, James E. 1994. "Identity and Psychotherapy." In *Interventions for Adolescent Identity Development*, ed. Sally L. Archer, 29–46. Sage Publications.

Markey, S., J. Pierce, K. Vodden, and M. Roseland. 2004. *Second Growth: Community Economic Development in Rural and Small Town British Columbia.* Vancouver: UBC Press.

Markus, H., and P. Nurius. 1986. "Possible Selves." *American Psychologist* 41, 954–69.

Marshall, A. 2002. "Life-Career Counselling Issues for Youth in Coastal and Rural Communities: The Impact of Economic, Social and Environmental Restructuring." *International Journal for the Advancement of Counselling* 24: 69–87.

Marshall, A., and S. Batten. 2004. "Participatory Action Research: Projects with Ethnic and Marginalized Youth." Proceedings of the Fourth International Conference on Education, Honolulu, Hawaii.

Marshall, J.M. 1990. "Report of the Working Group on the 4R, 3Pn Cod Fishery." Moncton, NB: DFO, unpublished Report.

Martin, D. 1990. Report of the Special Committee on the Conservation and Protection of the Gulf of St Lawrence Groundfish Stocks. DFO, Quebec Region.

Martin, Jane Roland. 1994. *Changing the Educational Landscape: Philosophy, Women, and Curriculum.* New York and London: Routledge.

Martínez Murillo, Maria de las Nieves. 2003. "Size-Based Dynamics of a Demersal Fish Community: Modeling Fish-Fisheries Interactions." PhD dissertation, Memorial University of Newfoundland, St John's.

– 2001. "Size Structure and Production in a Demersal Fish Community." NAFO SCR Doc. No. 134, Serial no. N4529.

Mason, F. 2002. "Newfoundland Cod Stock Collapse: A Review and Analysis of Social Factors." School of Kinesiology, University of Western Ontario. http://egj.lib.uidaho.edu/egj17/mason1.html.

Maxwell, Lani. 2003. "Teachers Speak: Impact of Restructuring on the Daily Lives of Elementary Educators." University of Victoria, Victoria

McCambridge, J., and J. Strang. 2004. "The Efficacy of Single- Session Motivational Interviewing in Reducing Drug Consumption and Perceptions of Drug-Related Risk and Harm among Young People: Results from a Multi-site Cluster Randomized Trial." *Addiction* 99(1): 39–52.

McCreary Society. 2004. *Healthy Youth Development: Finding From the 2003 Adolescent Health Survey.* Vancouver, BC: McCreary Centre Society.

McEvoy, A.F. 1986. *The Fisherman's Problem: Ecology and Law in the California Fisheries, 1850–1980.* Cambridge: Cambridge University Press.

McLearn, F.H. 1929. "Contributions to the Stratigraphy and Palaeontology of Skidegate Inlet, Queen Charlotte Islands." BC Canada Department of Mines, National Museum of Canada, *Contributions to Palaeontology*, Bulletin no. 54, 1–68.

McNeill, Captain R.W. 1980. "Interview with Captain of the *B.C. Standard*" by Allen Specht. Chevron Canada Limited History Project Interviews, transcript, Royal British Columbia Museum.

McNeill, Desmond. 1999. "On Interdisciplinary Research: With Particular Reference to the Field of Environment and Development." *Higher Education Quarterly*, 0951–5224, 53(4): 312–32.

McQuinn, I.H., M. Hammill, and L. Lefebvre. 1999. "An Assessment and Risk Projections of the West Coast of Newfoundland (NAFO division 4R) Herring Stocks (1965 to 2000)." DFO CSAS Res. Doc. 99/119.

McQuinn, I.H., and L. Lefebvre. 1997. "An Assessment of the West Coast of Newfoundland (NAFO Division 4R) Herring Stocks (1973 to 1994). DFO Atlantic Fisheries Research Document 97/116.

– 1995. "A Review of the West Coast of Newfoundland (NAFO division 4R) Herring Fishery Data (1973 to 1994)." DFO Atl. Fish. Res. Doc 95/56.

Meidinger, E.E. 1998. "Laws and Institutions in Cross-Boundary Stewardship." In *Stewardship Across Boundaries*, ed. R.L. Knight and P.B. Landres, 87–110. Washington, DC: Island Press.

Metuzals K.I., C.M. Wernerheim, R.L. Haedrich, P. Copes, and A. Murrin. 2006. "Data Fouling in Marine Fisheries: Findings and a Model for Newfoundland." In *2005 North American Fisheries Economists' Forum Proceedings*, ed. U.R. Sumaila and A. Dale Marsden. Fisheries Center Research Reports 2006, vol. 14, no. 1, 87–104. University of British Columbia Fisheries Centre.

Miller, Bruce. 1995. *The Role of Rural Schools in Community Development: Policy Issues and Implications*. Northwest Regional Educational Laboratory 1995 [cited 2005]. http//www.nwrel.org/ruraled/Role.html.

Miller, K., J. Chopyak, and R. Blair. 1999. *What Works, What Doesn't?: Community-Based Research and Strategies for Change*. Report on the 1999 Annual Community Research Network Conference, Amherst, MA. Washington, DC: The Loka Institute.

Mills, C. Wright. 1959. *The Sociological Imagination*. New York: Oxford University Press.

Mishra, Pankaj. 2004. *An End to Suffering: The Buddha in the World*. New Delhi: Picador.

Monger, J.W.H., J.G. Souther, and H. Gabrielse. 1972. "Evolution of the Canadian Cordillera: A Plate-Tectonic Model." *American Journal of Science* 272:577–602.

Moores, J.A., and G.H .Winters. 1984. "Migration Patterns of Newfoundland West Coast Herring, *Clupea harengus*, As Shown by Tagging Studies." *Journal of Northwest Atlantic Fisheries Science* 5:17–22.

Muller, J.E., B.E.B. Cameron, and K.E. Northcote. 1981. *Geology and Mineral Deposits of Nootka Sound Map-Area, Vancouver Island, British Columbia*. Geological Survey of Canada, Paper 80–16.

Murray, G.D., B. Neis, and D. Bavington. "Local Ecological Knowledge, Science, and Fisheries Management in Newfoundland and Labrador: A Complex, Contested, and Changing Relationship." In *Participation in Fisheries Governance*, ed. T.S. Gray, 269–90. Dordrecht, Netherlands: Springer Publications.

Murray, G.D., B. Neis, and J.P. Johnsen. "Lessons Learned from Reconstructing Interactions between Local Ecological Knowledge, Fisheries Science and Fisheries Management in the Commercial Fisheries of Newfoundland and Labrador, Canada." *Human Ecology* 34(4):549–72.

Murray, G.D., B. Neis, C. Palmer, and DC. Schneider. Accepted. "Mapping Cod: Fisheries Science, Fish Harvesters' Ecological Knowledge and Cod Migrations in the Northern Gulf of St Lawrence." *Human Ecology*.

Murray, G.D., B. Neis, and DC. Schneider. 2008. "The Importance of Scale and a Multi-Method Approach in Reconstructing Socio-Ecological System Change in the Newfoundland Inshore Fishery." *Coastal Management* 36(1):1–28.

Murrin, A. 2003. "Data Fouling Activities and Poor Management: Major Factors Contributing to the North Atlantic Cod Collapse." Master's thesis, Memorial University of Newfoundland, St John's.

Myers, D.G. 1990. *Social Psychology*. Toronto: McGraw-Hill.

Myers, R.A., J. Hutchings and N. Barrowman. 1997. "Why Do Fish Stocks Collapse?" *Ecological Applications* 7(1): 91–106.

Myers, R.A., S.A. Levin, R. Lande, F.C. James, W.W. Murdoch, and R.T. Paine. 2004. "Hatcheries and Endangered Salmon." *Science* 303: 1980.

Nadasdy, P. 2006. "The Case of the Missing Sheep: Time, Space, and the Politics of "Trust" in Co-management Practice." In *Traditional Ecological Knowledge and Natural Resource Management*. Lincoln, NE: University of Nebraska Press.

Nameth, Tammy Lynn. 1977. "Pat Carney and the Dismantling of the National Energy Program." Master's thesis, University of Alberta.

NASA (National Aeronautics and Space Administration). 1988. *Earth System Science: A Program for Global Change*. Report of the Earth System Sciences Committee, NASA Advisory Council.

Nazarea, V.D., ed. 1999. *Ethnoecology: Situated Knowledge/Located Lives*. Tucson: University of Arizona Press.

Neis, B. 2003. "Signposts at the Border: A Comment on Holm.: MAST 2(1): 35–8.

Neis, B., and L. Felt, eds. 2000. *Finding Our Sea Legs: Linking Fishery People and Their Knowledge with Science and Management*. St John's, NL: ISER Books.

Neis, B., L.F. Felt, R.L. Haedrich, and D.C. Schneider. 1999. "An Interdisciplinary Method for Collecting and Integrating Fishers' Ecological Knowledge into Resource Management." In *Fishing Places, Fishing People: Traditions and Issues in Canadian Small-Scale Fisheries*, ed. D. Newell and R.E. Ommer. Toronto: University of Toronto Press.

Neis, B., L. Felt, D.C. Schneider, R.L. Haedrich, and J. Fischer. 1996. "Northern Cod Stock Assessment: What Can Be Learned from Interviewing Resource Users?" DFO Atlantic Fisheries Research Document. SCR 96/45.

Neis, B., and R. Kean. 2003. "Why Fish Stocks Collapse: An Interdisciplinary Approach to Understanding the Dynamics of 'Fishing Up.'" In *Retrenchment and Regeneration in Rural Newfoundland*, ed. R. Byron. Toronto: University of Toronto Press.

Neis, B., D.C. Schneider, L.F. Felt, R.L. Haedrich, J. Fisher, and J. Hutchings. 1999. "Fisheries Assessment: What Can Be Learned from Interviewing Resource Users?" *Canadian Journal of Fisheries and Aquatic Sciences* 56: 1949–63.

Nemec, T.F. 1993. "The Newfoundland Coast: Prehistoric and Historic Cultural Adaptations." In *Through a Mirror Dimly: Essays on Newfoundland Society and Culture*, ed. M. Hanrahan, 17–66. St John's: Breakwater.

Newfoundland and Prince Edward Island Reports: Digest and Consolidated Indexes. 1976–. Eric B. Appleby and David C.R. Olmstead, eds. Fredericton: Maritime Law Book.

Newson J. 1998. "The Corporate-Linked University: From Social Project to Market Force." *Canadian Journal of Communication* 23(1). http://www.cjc-online.ca/viewarticle.php?id=449&layout=html.

Nielsen, J.R., and C. Mathiesen. 2000. "Incentives for Compliance Behaviour: Lessons from Danish Fisheries." Paper presented at IIFET Conference, 11–14 July, Corvalis OR.

Nowotny, H., P. Scott, and M. Gibbons. 2001. *Re-thinking Science*. Oxford: Blackwell.

NRC (National Research Council). 2000. *Improving the Collection, Management and Use of Marine Fisheries Data.*, Washington, DC: National Academy Press.
– 1993. *Solid Earth Sciences and Society: Committee on the Status and Research Opportunities in the Solid Earth Sciences.* Washington, DC: National Academy Press.
– 1992. *Oceanography in the Next Decade: Building New Partnerships.* Ocean Studies Board, Commission on Geosciences, Environment, and Resources. Washington, DC: National Academy Press.
Ohmagari, K., and F. Berkes 1997. "Transmission of Indigenous Knowledge and Bush Skills among the Western James Bay Cree Women of Subarctic Canada.: *Human Ecology* 25: 197–222.
Okihiro, N.R. 1997. *Mounties, Moose and Moonshine: The Patterns and Context of Outport Crime.* Toronto: University of Toronto Press.
Ommer, R.E., ed. 2002. *The Resilient Outport* St John's, NL: ISER Books.
Ommer, R.E. and the Coasts Under Stress research project team. 2007. *Coasts Under Stress: Restructuring and Social-Ecological Health.* Montreal: McGill-Queen's University Press.
Omohundro, J.T. 1994. *Rough Food: The Seasons of Subsistence in Northern Newfoundland.* St John's, NL: ISER Books.
Overton, J. 1980. "Tourism Development, Conservation, and Conflict: Game Laws for Caribou Protection in Newfoundland." *Canadian Geographer* 24:40–9.
Paavola, Jouni, and W. Neil Adger. 2004. "Knowledge or Participation for Sustainability? Science and Justice in Adaptation to Climate Change." In *Proceedings of the 2002 Berlin Conference on the Human Dimensions of Global Environmental Change, "Knowledge for the Sustainability Transition: The Challenge for Social Science,"* eds. Frank Biermann, Sabine Campe, and Klaus Jacod, 175–83. Amsterdam, Berlin, Potsdam, and Oldenburg: Global Governance Project.
PAGSE. 2000 *Setting Priorities for Research in Canada.* Ottawa: Partnership Group for Science and Engineering.
Pal, L. 1992. *Public Policy Analysis: An Introduction.* 2d ed. Scarborough, ON: Nelson Canada.
Palmer, C.T., and P.R. Sinclair. 1997. *When the Fish Are Gone. Ecological Disaster and Fisheries in Newfoundland.* Halifax: Fernwood Books.
Pálsson, G. 2000. "Finding One's Sea Legs: Learning, the Process of Enskilment, and Integrating Fishers and their Knowledge into Fisheries Science and Management." In *Finding Our Sea Legs: Linking Fishery People and Their Knowledge with Science and Management,* ed. B. Neis and L. Felt. St John's, NL: ISER Books.

Park, P. 2001. "Knowledge and Participatory Research." In *Handbook of Action Research: Participative Inquiry and Practice*, ed. P. Reason and H. Bradbury, 81–90. London: Sage.

Parrish, C.C., N.J. Turner, and S.M. Solberg, eds. 2007. *Resetting the Kitchen Table: Food Security in Canadian Coastal Communities.* New York: Nova Science Publishers.

Pascoe, S., I. Herrero, and S. Mardle. 2001. "Identifying Misreporting in Fisheries Output Data Using DEA." Paper presented at the seventh EU productivity and efficiency workshop, Oviedo, Spain, September.

Pauly, D. 1995. "Anecdotes and the Shifting Baseline Syndrome of Fisheries." *Trends in Ecology and Evolution* 10(10):430.

– 1994. *On the Sex of Fish and the Gender of Scientists: Essays in Fisheries Science.* London: Chapman & Hall.

Pauly, D., V. Christensen, J. Dalsgaard, R. Froese and F. Torres. 1998. "Fishing Down Marine Food Webs." Science 279: 860–3.

Pepall, J. 1998. "Putting a Price on Indigenous Knowledge." In *Biodiversity, Equity and the Environment: A Review of Research and Development.* Ottawa: International Development Research Centre (IDRC).

Perry, I., and R. Ommer. 2003. "Scale Issues in Marine Ecosystem and Human Interactions." *Fisheries Oceanography* 12 (4/5): 513–22.

Philbrook, T. 1968. *Fisherman, Logger, Merchant, Miner: Social Change and Industrialism in Three Newfoundland Communities.* St John's, NL: ISER.

Pimm, S.L. 1991. *The Balance of Nature? Ecological Issues in the Conservation of Species and Communities.* Chicago: University of Chicago Press.

Pitcher, T.J., and R. Watson. 2000. "The Basis for Change: Estimating Total Fishery Extractions from Marine Ecosystems of the North Atlantic." In *Methods for Assessing the Impact of Fisheries on Marine Ecosystems of the North Atlantic*, ed. D. Pauly and T.J. Pitcher. Fisheries Centre Research Reports 8(2).

Pitcher, T.J., R. Watson, R. Forrest, H. Valtysson, and S. Guenette 2002. "Estimating Illegal and Unreported Catches from Marine Ecosystems: A Basis for Change." *Fish and Fisheries* 3:317–39.

Port Simpson Curriculum Committee. 1983. "Port Simpson Foods: A Curriculum Development Project." The People of Port Simpson and School District no. 52 (Prince Rupert).

Portelli, J.P., and R. Patrick Solomon. 2001. *The Erosion of Democracy in Education: Critique to Possibilities.* Calgary, AB: Detselig Enterprises.

Portelli, J.P., and A.B. Vibert. 2001. "Beyond Common Educational Standards: Towards a Curriculum of Life." In *The Erosion of Democracy in*

Education: From Critique to Possibilities, ed. J.P. Portelli and R.P. Solomon. Calgary: Detselig.

Power, M.J., and R.L. Stephenson. 1990. "Logbook Analysis for the 4WX Herring Purse Seine Fishery, 1985–1989." DFO CAFSAC Res. Doc. 90/53.

– 1987. "An Analysis of Logs from the 4X Summer Purse Seine Fishery." DFO CAFSAC Res. Doc. 87/77.

Power, W. 1997. "Rebuilding Trouters' Heaven. *Newfoundland Sportsman* 7 (4, July/August): 26–31.

Preikshot, D. 2001. "Observation and Inspection Data: Determining Catch and Bycatch by Foreign Fisheries on the Grand Bank outside the Canadian EEZ." In *The Sea Around Us*. Vancouver: University of British Columbia.

Puskar, K., K. Tusaie-Mumford, S. Sereika, and J. Lamb. 1999. "Health Concerns and Risk Behaviors of Rural Adolescents." *Journal of Community Health Nursing* 16 (2): 109–19.

Quinlan, Allyson. 2003. "Resilience and Adaptive Capacity: Key Components of Sustainable Social-Ecological Systems. *IHDP Update: Newsletter of the International Human Dimensions Programme on Global Environmental Change*, vol. 2, 4–5. Footnotes in http://www.ihdp.uni-bonn.de/html/publications/publications.html.

Rabinow, Paul. 1999. *French DNA: Trouble in Purgatory*. Chicago: University of Chicago Press.

Raff, A.D., and D.G. Mason. 1961. "Magnetic Survey off the West Coast of North America, 40° N. latitude to 52° N. latitude." *Geological Society of America Bulletin* 72:1267–70.

Raffensperger, C., S. Peters, F. Kirschenmann, T. Schettler, K. Barrett, M. Hendrickson, D. Jackson, R. Voland, K. Leval, and D. Butcher. 1999. *Defining Public Interest Research*. A white paper written for the Science and Environmental Health Network, the Centre for Rural Affairs, and the Consortium for Sustainable Agriculture, Research and Education. http://www.loka.org/alerts/loka.6.3.htm

Raphael, D. 2003. "Addressing the Social Determinants of Health in Canada: Bridging the Gap between Research Findings and Public Policy." *Policy Options* 24(3):35–44.

– 1996. "Determinants of Health of North American Adolescents: Evolving Definitions, Recent Findings, and Proposed Research Agenda." *Journal of Adolescent Health* 19: 6–16.

Reason, P. 1994. "Three Approaches to Participative Inquiry." In *Handbook of Qualitative Research*, ed. N.K. Denizen and Y.S. Lincoln, 324–39. Thousands Oaks, CA: SAGE Publications.

Ristock, J.L., and J. Pennell. 1996. *Community Research as Empowerment: Feminist Links, Postmodern Interruptions.* Toronto: Oxford University Press.

Roach, C.M. 2000. "Stewards of the Sea: A Model for Justice?" *Just Fish: Ethics and Canadian Marine Fisheries,* ed. H. Coward, R. Ommer, and T. Pitcher, 67–82. St John's, NL: ISER Books.

Robinson, Leah. 2003. "Restructuring and Coastal Community Health: A Case Study of Teachers' Work." Unpublished MED thesis, University of Victoria, Victoria.

Rolston, H. 1995. "Does Aesthetic Appreciation of Landscapes Need To Be Science-Based? *British Journal of Aesthetics* 35(4):374–86.

Royal Society of Canada. 2004. *Report of the Expert Panel on Science Issues Related to Oil and Gas Activities, Offshore British Columbia.* Ottawa.

Ryle, Gilbert. 1990. *The Concept of Mind.* Middlesex, England: Penguin Books.

Saila, S. 1983. *Importance and Assessment of Discards in Commercial Fisheries.* FAO Fisheries Circular no. 765.

Savickas, M. 1995. "Constructivist Counseling for Career Indecision." *Career Development Quarterly* 43 (4): 363–74.

Schindler, D.W. 2001. "The Cumulative Effects of Climate Warming and Other Human Stresses on Canadian Freshwaters in the New Millennium. *Canadian Journal of Fisheries and Aquatic Sciences* 58:18–29.

Schneider, D.C. 2001. "The Rise of the Concept of Scale in Ecology." *BioScience* 51:545–53.

Schneider, D.C., P. Hennebury, D.A. Methven, D.W. Ings, and D. Pinsent. 1997. "Fleming Survey of Demersal Juvenile Cod in the Coastal Areas of eastern Newfoundland." *NAFO Scientific Council Studies* 29: 13–21.

Schön, D.A. 1983. *The Reflective Practitioner: How Professionals Think in Action.* London: Temple Smith.

– 1973. *Beyond the Stable State: Public and Private Learning in a Changing Society.* Harmondsworth, England: Penguin.

Schroeder, P. 1997. "A Public Participation Approach to Charting Information Spaces." Paper presented at Auto-Carto 13, Seattle WA, April.

Scoones, I. 1999. "New Ecology and the Social Sciences." *Annual Review of Anthropology* 28:479–507.

Scott, James C. 1998. *Seeing like a State: How Certain Schemes to Improve the Human Condition Have Failed.* New Haven and London: Yale University Press.

Seife, Charles. 2003. *Alpha and Omega: The Search for the Beginning and End of the Universe.* New York: Viking.

Serres, Michel. 1997. *The Troubadour of Knowledge.* Trans. Sheila Faria Glaser with William Paulson. Ann Arbor, MI. The University of Michigan Press.

- 1995a. *The Natural Contract.* Trans. Elizabeth MacArthur and William Paulson. Ann Arbor, MI. The University of Michigan Press.
- 1995b. *Angels: A Modern Myth.* Trans. Francis Cowper. New York: Flammarion.

Shapin, Stephen. 1998. *The Scientific Revolution.* Chicago: University of Chicago Press.

Sheehan, G. 2001. "'Hearing' the People of a Subsistence Culture: Traditional Knowledge and Environmental Impacts on Alaska's North Slope." In *Traditional Knowledge,* ed. G. Sheehan and R. Glenn.

Shepard, B., and A. Marshall. 2000. "Career Development and Planning Issues for Rural Adolescent Girls." *Canadian Journal of Counselling* 34(3): 155–71.

- 1999. "Possible Selves Mapping: Life-Career Exploration with Young Adolescents." *Canadian Journal of Counselling* 33:37–54.

Shouldice, D.H. 1971. "Geology of the Western Canadian Continental Shelf." *Bulletin of Canadian Petroleum Geology* 19(2):405–36.

Shucksmith, S., and L. Hendry. 1998. *Health Issues and Adolescents: Growing up, Speaking Out.* London: Routledge,

Simon, Roger I. 2001. "Now's the Time: Foreword." In *The Erosion of Democracy in Education: From Critique to Possibilities,* ed. J.P. Portelli and R.P. Solomon. Calgary: Detselig.

Sinclair, Peter R., and Rosemary E. Ommer, eds. 2006. *Power and Restructuring: Canada's Coastal Society and Environment.* St. John's, NL: ISER Books.

Small, S. 1995. "Enhancing Contexts of Adolescent Development: The Role of Community-Based Action Research." In *Pathways through Adolescence: Individual Development in Relation to Social Contexts,* ed. L.J. Crockett and A.C. Crouter, 211–33. Mahwah, NJ: Lawrence Erlbaum.

Smith, B.D., P.S. Maitland, and S.M. Pennock. 1987. "A Comparative Study of Water Level Regimes and Littoral Benthic Communities in Scottish Lochs." *Biological Conservation* 39: 291–316.

Smith, L.T. 1999. *Decolonizing Methodologies: Research and Indigenous Peoples.* London: Zed Books.

Smith, M.K. 2001. "Donald Schön: Learning, Reflection and Change. The Encyclopedia of Informal Education." http://www.infed.org/thinkers/et-schon.htm.

Smith, R. 1998. "Hishuk ish Ts'awalk – All Things Are One: Traditional Ecological Knowledge and Forest Practices in Ahousaht First Nation's Traditional Territory, Clayoquot Sound, BC. MA thesis, Canadian Heritage and Development Studies, Trent University, Peterborough, ON.

SSHRC (Social Sciences and Humanities Research Council of Canada). 2003. *From Granting Council to Knowledge Council: Renewing the Social Sciences and Humanities in Canada.* Ottawa: SSHRC.

St Denis, V. 1992. "Community-Based Participatory Research: Aspects of the Concept Relevant for Practice." *Native Studies Review* 8(2): 51–74.

Stanley, R.D., and J. Rice. 2007. "Fisher Knowledge? Why Not Add Their Scientific Skills to the Mix While You Are At It?" In *Fisheries and Science Management,* ed. N. Haggan, B. Neis and I. Baird. Paris: UNESCO Publishing.

Statistics Canada 2006. Community Profiles. http://www12.statcan.ca/english/profilo1/.

Stengers, Isabelle. 1997. *Power and Invention: Situating Science.* Trans. Paul Bains. Minneapolis, MN. University of Minnesota Press.

Stenmark, M. 2002. *Environmental Ethics and Policy Making.* Aldershot, England: Ashgate.

Stephenson, R.L, M.J. Power, K.J. Clark, G.D. Melvin, F.J. Fife, and S.D. Paul. 1998. "1998 Evaluation of 4VWX Herring." DFO CSAS Res. Doc. 98/52.

Stephenson, R.L., M.J. Power, and W.H. Dougherty. 1990. "Assessment of the 1989 Herring Fishery." DFO CAFSAC Res. Doc. 90/50.

Stephenson R.L., K. Rodman, D.G. Aldous and D.E. Lane. 1999. "An Inseason Approach to Management under Uncertainty: The Case of the SW Nova Scotia Herring Fishery. *Journal of Marine Science* 56:1005–13.

Stocker, M. 1993. "The Management of the Pacific Herring Fishery. *Canadian Bulletin of Fisheries and Aquatic Sciences* 226. p. 267–93.

Stockner, J.G., E. Rydin, and P. Hyenstrand. 2000. "Cultural Oligotrophication: Causes and Consequences for Fisheries Resources." *Fisheries* 25 (5): 7–14.

Stringer, E. 1996. *Action Research: A Handbook for Practitioners.* Thousand Oaks, CA: Sage Books.

Super, D.E., M.L. Savickas, and C.M. Super. 1996. "The Life-Span, Life-Space Approach to Careers." In *Career Choice and Development,* ed. D. Brown and L. Brooks, 121–78. San Francisco: Jossey-Bass.

Sutherland-Brown, A. 1968. *Geology of the Queen Charlotte Islands British Columbia.* British Columbia Department of Mines and Petroleum Resources, Bulletin no. 54.

Sutton, Stephen G. 2000. "Local Knowledge of a Unique Population of Atlantic Salmon: Implications for Community-Based Management of Recreational Fisheries in Newfoundland and Labrador." In *Finding Our Sea Legs: Linking Fishery People and Their Knowledge with Science and Management,* eds. Barbara Neis and Lawrence Felt. St John's, NL: ISER Books.

- 1997. "The Mystery Fish of Bonavista North: A Multidisciplinary Approach to Research and Management of a Unique Recreational Salmonid Fishery in Newfoundland.' MSC thesis, Memorial University of Newfoundland.
Tainter, Joseph A. 1988. *The Collapse of Complex Societies*. Cambridge: Cambridge University Press.
Task Group on Newfoundland Inshore Fisheries. 1987. A Study of trends of Cod Stocks off Newfoundland and Factors Influencing Their Abundance and Availability to the Inshore Fishery." A Report to the Hon. Tom Siddon, Minister, Fisheries, Canada.
Taylor, D., and P.G. O'Keefe. 1999. "Assessment of the 1998 Newfoundland and Labrador Snow Crab Fishery." DFO CSAS Res. Doc. 99/143.
- 1998. "Assessment of the 1997 Newfoundland and Labrador Snow Crab Fishery. DFO CSAS Res. Doc. 98/140.
- 1989. "Assessment of the Newfoundland Snow Crab, *Chionoecetes opilio*, Fishery." 1988. CAFSAC Res. Doc. 89/69.
Taylor, D., P.G. O'Keef, and C. Fitzpatrick. 1994. "A Snow Crab, *Chionoecetes opilio* (Decapoda, Majidae), Fishery Collapse in Newfoundland.: Fishery Bulletin 92: 412–19.
Telegram. 2003a. "Councilors Attack Environmental Concerns." 15 April, St John's, NL.
- 2003b. 14 November, St John's, NL.
Thompson, Andrew R. 1978. "Statement of Proceedings, West Coast Oil Ports Inquiry, Commissioner Dr Andrew R. Thompson, February 1978." West Coast Oil Ports Inquiry, Vancouver.
Thompson, J.C. 2004. "Gitga'at Plant Project: The Intergenerational Transmission of Traditional Ecological Knowledge Using School Science Curricula." Master's thesis, University of Victoria.
- 2003. "Unit 2: Traditional Plant Knowledge of the Tsimshian." Department of Anthropology and Sociology, University of British Columbia, Vancouver.
Tillich, P. 1961. "The Religious Symbol." In *Religious Experience and Truth*, ed. S. Hook. New York: New York University Press.
- 1958. *The Dynamics of Faith*. New York: Harper.
Tirone, S., A. Marshall, B. Sheppard, N. Turner, and J. Thompson. 2007. "Celebrating with Food. Food and Cultural Identity: Feasts, Ceremonies and Celebrations." In *Resetting the Kitchen Table: Food Security, Culture, Health and Resilience in Coastal Communities*, ed. Chris Parrish, Nancy Turner, and Shirley Solberg, chap. 10. Hauppauge, NY: Nova Science.

Tobias, T. 2000. *Chief Kerry's Moose: A Guidebook to Land Use and Occupancy Mapping, Research Design and Data Collection.*, Vancouver BC: Union of BC Indian Chiefs and Ecotrust Canada.

Todorov, Tzvetan. 1984. *Mikhail Bakhtin: The Dialogical Principle.* Minneapolis, MN: University of Minnesota.

Tracy, A.P., and S. Oskamp. 1983. "Relationship among Ecologically Responsible Behaviours." *Journal of Environmental Systems,* 13(2):115–26.

Tremblay, M.J., M.D. Eagles, and R.W. Elner. 1994. *Catch, Effort and Population Structure in the Snow Crab Fishery off Eastern Cape Breton, 1978–1993: A Retrospective.* Canadian Technical Report of Fisheries and Aquatic Science 2021.

Tress, Bärbel, Gunther Tress, and Gary Fry. 2005. "Integrative Studies on Rural Landscapes: Policy Expectations and Research Practice." *Landscape and Urban Planning* 70:177–91.

Turner, M.A. 1997. "Quota-Induced Discarding in Heterogeneous Fisheries." *Journal of Environmental Economics and Management* 33 (2): 186–96.

Turner, N.J. 2003a. "'Passing on the News': Women's Work, Traditional Knowledge and Plant Resource Management in Indigenous Societies of Northwest North America." In *Women and Plants: Case Studies on Gender Relations in Local Plant Genetic Resource Management,* ed. Dr P. Howard, 133–49. London: Zed Books.

– 2003b. "The Dynamics of People-Plant Relationships: Examples from the Gitga'at First Nation of Hartley Bay, British Columbia." Paper presented to the Society of Ethnobiology annual meetings, University of Washington, Seattle, March.

– 2003c. "The Ethnobotany of 'Edible Seaweed' (*Porphyra abbottiae* and Related Species; Rhodophyta: Bangiales) and Its Use by First Nations on the Pacific Coast of Canada." *Canadian Journal of Botany* 81(2): 283–93.

Turner, N.J., and E.R. Atleo (Chief Umeek). 1998. "Pacific North American First Peoples and the Environment." In *Traditional and Modern Approaches to the Environment on the Pacific Rim: Tensions and Values,* ed. Harold Coward, 105–24. Albany, NY: State University of New York.

Turner, N.J. and F. Berkes. 2006. "Coming to Understanding: Developing Conservation through Incremental Learning in the Pacific Northwest." *Human Ecology* (August).

Turner, N.J., and H. Clifton. 2006. "'The Forest and the Seaweed': Gitga'at Seaweed, Traditional Ecological Knowledge and Natural Resource Management." In: *Integrating Local Level Ecological Knowledge with Natural Resource Management: Exploring the Possibilities and the Obstacles,* ed. Charles

Menzies. Lincoln. NE: University of Nebraska. Also to be published in *Eating and Healing: Traditional Food as Medicine*, ed. Andrea Pieroni and Lisa Leimar Price. Haworth Press (USA).

Turner, N.J., A. Marshall, and R.J. Hood. 2001. "Gitga'at Plant Project: Proposal to School and Community." Unpublished manuscript, University of Victoria, Coasts Under Stress Project.

Turner, N.J., and R.E. Ommer. 2004. "The Informal Economy in Historical Perspective." *Labour/Le Travail* 53 (spring 2004): 127–57.

Turner, N.J., and J.C. Thompson, eds. 2006. *Nwana'a lax Yuup: Plants of the Gitga'at People*. Hartley Bay, BC: Gitga'at Nation and Coasts Under Stress Research Project (R. Ommer, Project Director). Victoria, BC: Cortex Consulting Inc.

Umeek (E. Richard Atleo). 2004. *Tsawalk: A Nuu-chah-nulth Worldview*. Vancouver: UBC Press, and Seattle: University of Washington Press.

Usher, J.L. 1952. "Ammonite Faunas of the Upper Cretaceous Rocks of Vancouver Island, British Columbia." *Geological Survey of Canada*. Bulletin 21.

van Zyll de Jong, M.C., R.J. Gibson, and I.G. Cowx. 2004. "Impacts of Stocking and Introductions on Freshwater Fisheries of Newfoundland and Labrador, Canada. *Fisheries Management and Ecology* 11:183–93.

van Zyll de Jong, M.C., N.P. Lester, R.M. Korver, W. Norris, and B.L. Wicks. 2002. "Managing the Exploitation of Brook Trout, *Salvelinus fontinalis* (Mitchill), Populations in Newfoundland Lakes." In *Management and Ecology of Lake and Reservoir Fisheries*, ed. I.G. Cowx, 268–83. Fishing News Books, Blackwell Publishing.

Vine, F.J., and J.T. Wilson. 1965. "Magnetic Anomalies over a Young Oceanic Ridge off Vancouver Island." *Science* 150:485–9.

Vining, J., and A. Ebreo. 1990. "What Makes a recycler? A comparison of Recyclers and Non-recyclers." *Environment and Behaviour* 22:55–73.

Visser, Leontine E. 2004. "Reflections on Transdisciplinarity, Integrated Coastal Development, and Governance." In *Challenging Coasts: Transdisciplinary Excursions into Integrated Coastal Zone Development*, ed. Leontine E. Visser, pp. 12–23. Amsterdam: Amsterdam University Press.

Vodden, K. 2004a. "Knowledge Sharing and Collaborative Watershed Governance – Coast to Coast." Paper presented to the Canadian Water Resources Association Conference, Regina, SK, November.

– 2004b. "Watershed Management in Canada: Lessons and Implications for Institutional Design." Paper presented to UN Environment Program Hilltops Two Oceans Partnership Conference, Cairns, Australia, May.

- 2003. "Cape Breton (Unama'ki) Mi'kmaq Communities and University College of Cape Breton Work Together to Recognize Traditional Knowledge and Protect Canada's Inland Sea." *Coastal Bulletin. Newsletter of the Ocean Management Research Network Linking Science and Local Knowledge*. Node 1 (3): 9–10.
- 1999. "Nanwakola: Co-management and Sustainable Community Economic Development in a BC Fishing Village." Master's thesis, Simon Fraser University. http://www.sfu.ca/coastalstudies.

Vodden, K., R. Ommer, and D. Schneider. 2005. "A Comparative Analysis of Three Models of Collaborative Learning in Fisheries Governance: Hierarchy, Networks and Community." In T.S. Gray, ed. *Participation in Fisheries Governance*. Dordrecht, Netherlands: Springer/Kluwer Academic Publishers.

Vøllestad, L.A. and T. Hesthagan. 2001. "Standing Stock of Freshwater Fish in Norway: Management Goals and Effects." *Nordic Journal of Freshwater Research* 75:143–52.

Voumard, J. (Inquiry Chair). 2000. *Commonwealth Public Inquiry into Access to Biological Resources in Commonwealth Areas*. Commonwealth of Australia.

Walsh, C.M. 2001. "Commercial and Non-commercial Fish Species in Newfoundland's Southern Coast Ecosystem: An Examination of Trends in Abundance and Landings with a Consideration of Ecosystem Health." Master's thesis, Memorial University of Newfoundland, St John's.

Wangersky, P.J. 2000. "Intercomparisons and Intercalibrations." In *Marine Chemistry*, ed. P.J. Wangersky. Berlin: Springer-Verlag.

Watson, R., and D. Pauly. 2001. "Systematic Distortions in World Fisheries Catch Trends." *Nature* 414 (6863): 534–6.

WCED (World Commission on Environment and Development). 1987. *Our Common Future*. Oxford: Oxford University Press.

Webster, D.C. 1999. *Nestucca: An Oil Spill Turns Creative*. Olympia, WA: Malamalama Press.

Weigel, R., and J. Weigel. 1978. "Environmental Concern: The Development of a Measure." *Environment and Behaviour* 10:3–15.

Weinstein, M. 1998. "Sharing Information or Captured Heritage: Access to Community Geographic Knowledge and the State's Responsibility to Protect Aboriginal Rights in British Columbia." Paper presented to the Seventh Annual International Association for the Study of Common Property Conference, Vancouver, June.

Wellman, J. 2004. "Time for Caution: The 2004 Science of Crab in Newfoundland and Labrador." *The Navigator*. 7 (5, May).

Wernerheim, C.M., and R.L. Haedrich. 2007. "A Simple Empirical Model of Data Fouling by High-Grading in Capture Fisheries." *Land Economics* 83(1): 74–85.

West Coast Offshore Exploration Environmental Assessment Panel. 1986. *Report and Recommendations of the West Coast Offshore Exploration Environmental Assessment Panel.* April. Ministry of Energy and Mines, Province of British Columbia. http://www.offshoreoilandgas.gov.bc.ca/reports/environmental-assessment/default.htm.

Whalen, J. 2005. "Using Harvesters Knowledge to Develop an Individual-Based Computer Simulation Model of the St John Bay, Newfoundland, Lobster (*Homarus americanus*) Fishery." Master's thesis, Memorial University of Newfoundland, St John's.

Wheeler, J.P., and R. Chaulk. 1987. "Newfoundland East and Southeast Coast Herring: 1986 Assessment." DFO CAFSAC Res. Doc. 87/60.

Wheeler, J.P., B. Squires, and P. Williams. 1999. "Newfoundland East and Southeast Coast Herring: An Assessment of Stocks to the Spring of 1998." DFO CSAS Res. Doc. 99/13.

Wheeler, J.P., G.H. Winters, and R. Chaulk. 1988. "Newfoundland East and Southeast Coast Herring: 1987 Assessment." DFO CAFSAC Res. Doc. 88/74.

Winters, G.H., and J.A Moores. 1977. "Assessment of Yield Potential of Eastern Newfoundland Herring Stocks." DFO CAFSAC Res. Doc. 77/12.

Wiseman, I. 1972. "The Politics of Fish Dumping: Torbay Fisherman Protest Ineffective." *Alternate Press* 2(5, July): 8.

Wolfe, L. 2000. "Patterns of Equivocality in Decision Making for Marine and Terrestrial Ecosystems: Towards the Design of Equivocality-Reducing Management Systems." PHD dissertation, Simon Fraser University.

Woodsworth, G.J., ed. 1991. *Evolution and hydrocarbon potential of the Queen Charlotte Basin, British Columbia.* Geological Survey of Canada, Paper 90–10.

Wright, Ronald. 2004. *A Short History of Progress.* Toronto: Anansi.

Wright, Will. 1991. *Wild Knowledge: Science, Language, and Social Life in a Fragile Environment.* Minneapolis, MN: University of Minnesota Press.

Wroblewski, J. 2000. "The Colour of Cod: Fishers and Scientists Identify a Local Cod Stock in Gilbert Bay, Southern Labrador." In *Finding Our Sea Legs: Linking Fishery People and Their Knowledge with Science and Management*, ed. B. Neis and L. Felt. St John's, NL: ISER Books.

Yorath, C.J., A. Sutherland Brown and N.W.D. Massey. 1999. *Lithoprobe, Southern Vancouver Island, British Columbia: Geology.* Geological Survey of Canada, Bulletin 498.

Young, R.A., L. Valach, and A. Collin. 1996. "A Contextual Explanation in Career." In *Career Choice and Development*, ed. D. Brown and L. Brooks, 477–512. San Francisco: Jossey-Bass.

Zobeck, M.L. 2001. "Grand Challenges in Earth and Environmental Sciences: Science, Stewardship, and Service for the Twenty-first Century." *GSA Today*, December, 41–7.

Index

abalone, 51, 52
Aboriginal Research Pilot Program, 246
Aboriginal People, 9, 37, 39, 45–8, 156, 166, 211, 246, 264, 269. *See also* First Nations; name of specific First Nation
Aboriginal title, un-extinguished, 209, 211
abstract knowledge. *See* knowledge, abstract
adolescent health determinants. *See* youth, health determinants
Alert Bay, BC, 254–7. *See also* Namgis First Nation
Alert Bay Economic Development Commission, 254
Alert Bay Marine Research Society, 257
Alexis River, NL, 169
Anderson, David, 209
anthropocentric approach, 184, 193
Anyox, BC, 25
Arctic char, 167, 171–3
Arrow (oil spill), 206, 208
Atlantic cod, 11, 21. *See also* cod fishery

Atlantic crab association, 91
Atlantic groundfish biomass, 23, 126
Atlantic groundfish stocks, 96
Atlantic Herring Management Committee, 163, 167
Atlantic salmon, 89–92. *See also* salmon
Atlantic snow crab, 87, 89–92, 132. *See also* crab
avoidance behaviour, 122

Bakhtin, Mikhail, 17
Barkley Sound, BC, 17, 249–53
bay stocks, 113
benthic organisms, 105, 172
benthic stream habitat, 167
berrypicking, 183, 188
big bang theory, 23
big science, 15, 222–3, 272–4
biodiversity loss, 221
biomedical discourse, 139, 151
biomedical model, 139
biophysical environment restructuring, 5, 272
black boxes, 12, 100–7, 130
blueberries, 55
Boethius, 27

Index

Bonavista Bay, NL, 160, 258
Bonavista North, 258
bottom-up approach, 164
Bourdieu, Pierre, 224–5, 238
Bras d'Or Lakes, NS, 264; watershed, 17, 249
British Columbia Knowledge Development Fund, 217
British Columbia moratoria on oil and gas exploration, 198, 202–20
British Columbia oil and gas development, 15, 39, 197–213, 219–21
brook trout, 157, 161–3, 167, 171–3
Buddha, 36
Burrard Inlet, BC, 205
by-catch dumping, 13, 123, 125, 129. *See also* data fouling

California sardine, 85
Canadian Atlantic Fisheries Scientific Advisory Committee (CAFSAC), 91
Canadian Code of Conduct for Responsible Fishing Operations, 133
Canadian Council of Professional Geoscientists, 216
Canadian Foundation for Innovation, 216–17
Cape Freels and Gambo-Indian Bay Development Association, 161
capelin, 128
Cartwright, NL, 14, 157, 166
catch per unit effort (CPUE), 85–7, 91, 108, 173
Centre for Coastal Studies, 256
Centre for Cooperative Ecosystem Studies, 259
Centre for Public Sector Studies, 249–50
Centres for Research in Youth, Science Teaching and Learning (CRYSTAL), 246
chaotic systems, 33
citizen control, 184
Clayoquot Alliance for Research, Education, and Training (CLARET), 249, 262–3
Clayoquot Biosphere Trust (CBT), 249
Clayoquot Sound, BC, 17, 249–50, 254
Clifton, Johnny (Chief), 46, 50, 52–3, 57–61
climate change, 3, 22, 30, 194, 218, 221
climatology, 49
Coast Tsimshian [Ts'msyen]. *See* Tsimshian
coastal communities, xii, 5, 17–20, 32–5, 39, 79, 81, 141–6, 153, 202, 220–1, 237
Coasts Under Stress project, 4–6, 15–20, 29, 32, 41, 50, 54, 61, 157, 179, 224, 232, 240, 243–6, 271
cod by-catch, 129
cod fishery, 87–8, 96, 98, 116, 124, 127–8. *See also* Atlantic cod; golden cod
cod migrations, 109, 112
cod poaching, 134
Code of Responsible Fishing, 127
co-governance, 275
collaborative partnerships, 247, 253, 269
community adaptation, 9, 46
Community Alliances for Health Research (CAHR), 246
community as curriculum, 65, 80

Community Futures, 74; Community Futures Development Corporation, 257
community health, 78, 147, 176–7, 212, 253; promoters, 10, 78, 140
community resilience, 9, 10, 46
community-university collaboration, 17, 247–51, 253–69
community-university-government cooperation, 160
Community-University Research Alliance (CURA), 246
complex adaptive systems theory, 33–4, 38
complexity theory, 37
conservatism, 37, 278
continuing studies departments, 256, 348
crab, 51, 87, 91, 98, 116, 127–34. *See also* Atlantic snow crab
crab pots (size of mesh), 129
critical participatory writing, 242
cross-cultural interaction, 7, 11, 16, 252, 264
cross-disciplinary collaboration, 11, 236. *See also* interdisciplinarity

data fouling, 13, 121–38. *See also* by-catch dumping; illegal, unreported, unregulated fishing
decolonizing methodologies, 60–1
Department of Fisheries and Aquaculture (NL), 108
Department of Fisheries and Oceans Canada (DFO), 23, 68, 78, 102, 162
Department of Regional Economic Expansion (DREE), 165
Department of Transportation and Works (NL), 166

Diamond, Jared, 3
discarding of catch, 91, 105, 123–8, 130–4. *See also* by-catch dumping
disciplinary silos, 6, 15
disciplinary values, 15, 202
dockside monitoring, 91–2
dockside sampling, 92
drug and alcohol use. *See* youth
ducks, 51, 189, 191
Ducks Unlimited, 184
dumping of catch. *See* discarding of catch

earth system science, 15, 198, 212, 215–21
Eastern Habitat Joint Ventures (EHJV), 179
ecosystem change, 33, 105
educational restructuring, 10, 78. *See also* headings under *schools*
El Niño, 33
Eliot, T.S., 27
environmental change, 4, 25, 33, 61, 101, 118
environmental degradation, xii, 3, 24, 159, 221
environmental health, 38, 143
environmental impact assessment (EIA), 172–3
environmental-human impact studies, 15, 215
equilibrium democracy, 81
ethics: environmental, 186, 192; research, 241, 247
ethnographic filmmaking, 58
ethnographic participant observation, 225, 238
ethnography, 16
eulachon (oolichan), 51

Exclusive Economic Zone (EEZ), 126
experiential learning, 153
extension services, 248, 261, 265
Exxon Valdez, 206, 208–10

feedback loops, 159, 160
First Nations, 67, 251, 254; communities, 37, 39, 50, 67, 250, 254; cultural programs (in schools), 66, 67, 70–80; fishing, 205, 209; reserves, 69, 67, 72, 77; studies (in schools), 60–80; wisdom of, 252, 264; youth, 53–6, 66, 69–80. *See also* traditional ecological knowledge; Aboriginal People; names of individual First Nations
First Nations elders, 38, 207, 267; committees, 264
fish canneries, 206
fish farms, 100
Fish, Food and Allied Workers Union, 127
fish landings, 12, 115, 128
fish migration, 167. *See also* cod migration
fish morphology, 86
fishbowl effect, 150
fisheries. *See* individual species fisheries
fisheries biologists, 12, 95, 259
folk knowledge. *See* local and traditional ecological knowledge
food web, xii, 5, 170, 272
Forest Renewal BC, 255
forestry, 5, 6, 28, 250, 254, 259
four-quadrant model of learning, 214
Frontier Geoscience Program, 214

Galbraith, John Kenneth, 30

Gander, NL, 179, 183
gatekeepers, 141, 148–9
geohazards, 215
Geological Survey of Canada, 214
geoscience, 15, 212–20
Gilbert Bay, NL, 105, 114
Gitga'at First Nation, 9, 46–63; Cultural Centre, 59; Plant Project, 53–7. *See also* Hartley Bay
Gitga'at Spring Harvest film, 57–60
Gitxsan First Nation, 50
global warming. *See* climate change
globalization, 5
Glovertown, NL, 183, 185
Gold River, BC, 210
golden cod, 105, 114. *See also* cod
Goose Bay CFB, 16
Goose Bay, NL, 166
governance, 4, 251, 264, 275–8
Government of Canada Habitat Stewardship Program for Species at Risk, 179
Graham Island, BC, 207
Grand Banks of Newfoundland, 31
granting councils. *See* Natural Science and Engineering Research Council; Multi-Council Research Initiative; Social Sciences and Humanities Research Council
Greenpeace seal campaign, 187, 208
grey literature, 252, 269
ground truthing, 106–7
groundfish. *See* Atlantic groundfish

halibut, 47, 51, 57–8
Happy Valley Goose Bay, NL, 166
harm reduction approach, 147
Hartley Bay, BC, 45–6, 50, 53–9. *See also* Gitga'at First Nation

health, 139–54, 224, 241, 276–8; challenges, 4; of communities, 77–81, 101, 139–54, 176, 200, 210, 237, 253; of ecosystems, 23, 174, 176, 189, 200; of First Nations, 51–2, 73; holistic, 143; multiple dimensions of, 151; sciences, 12, 227; social-ecological, 22, 28–34; promotion, 139, 142. *See also* community health; environmental health; mental health; public health

Hecate Strait, 25, 39, 207

herring 87, 89, 93–8; catch rates, 128; fisheries, 87, 93–8; roe, 51. *See also* Pacific herring, Atlantic herring

Hibernia oilfield, 203

high grading, 122–4, 130–1, 135–6

holistic health, 143

Holling, C.S., 33

Homer-Dixon, Thomas, 30–2

humanities research, xi, 221, 228, 242, 272

identity development. *See* youth

illegal, unreported, unregulated fishing (IUU fishing), 123. *See also* data fouling; under-the-table sales

Imperial Oil, 205

index fishery, 94–5, 128. *See also* sentinel fishery

Indian Bay Centre for Cooperative Ecological Studies (ICCES), 163

Indian Bay Ecosystem Committee, 160–2

Indian Bay Ecosystem Corporation, 258, 262–3

Indian Bay, NL, 14, 17, 157, 160–5, 171, 175–7, 258–9

Indian Bay/Cape Freels Ecosystem Committee, 161

Indigenous People. *See* Aboriginal People; First Nations

individual quotas, 92, 132

individual transferable quotas, 132–5

informal learning contexts, 51, 71–2, 119, 151–2

Inner Coast Natural Resource Center (ICNRC), Alert Bay, BC, 254, 262–3

inshore fleet, 10, 86–7, 91, 116, 125–7, 133

institutional structures, 5, 6, 17–8, 22, 245

intellectual modernization, 186, 194

interactive processes, 4, 6, 11, 101, 274

interdisciplinarity, 6, 15–16, 29, 34–5, 104, 222–43, 273–4. *See also* multidisciplinarity

interdisciplinary work, methodology of, 29, 35, 231, 241

intergenerational knowledge transfer, 9, 47, 48, 54

International Commission of the Northwest Atlantic Fisheries (ICNAF), 104

inter-sectoral collaboration, 34, 221

introduced species, 52, 194

Juan de Fuca Marine Park, BC, 210, 214

K'yel (Kiel) spring camp, 46, 52, 57–61

Kittiwake shore, 258. *See also* Bonavista North

knowledge: abstract, 11, 31, 143; accumulation, 18, 46, 66, 103,

149, 155, 278; acquisition, 9, 14, 45, 48, 225; assembly, 89, 98, 118–19; bi-directional, 8, 20, 40, 80; blockages, 171; bundle, 200–1, 220, 274; circularized flows of, 18, 266–7; combining, 114, 117; common, 52, 150; ecological: *see* traditional ecological knowledge and local ecological knowledge; efficiency of transfer, 197, 221; erosion, 46, 53; exchange, 6–17, 92, 119, 189, 201, 211, 249, 274; expert, 102, 107, 139, 192, 229, 236, 246; fisher's, 10, 12, 86, 103–4, 106; flows, 7–10, 14–18, 66–7, 77, 98, 118, 154, 159, 171–7, 180–3, 200–7, 215, 247, 266–78; generators of, 18; grounding of, 153; humanistic, 26, 28, 29, 40; hunter's, 11, 180, 182, 185–8; indigenous, 8, 46–51, 60–3, 272; integrated, 6, 49; local: *see* local ecological knowledge; moving, 12, 18, 176, 204, 236, 275; pathways, 13, 19, 202, 220; practical, 6, 11, 98; production, 4–16, 36, 111, 156, 176, 197, 228, 254, 267, 273–6; providers, 149; reconstruction, 101, 103; reflexive, 224; scientific, 15, 20, 25, 49, 103, 119, 155–6, 158–60, 170, 176, 180, 228, 236, 245; societal, 7; transfer, 67, 80, 153, 164, 197–8, 211, 221; transdisciplinary, 6, 272; translation, 4, 18, 142, 157, 268; transmission, 6, 9, 11, 18, 20, 45, 48, 54, 63; traps, 3; uptake, 13, 140, 150, 154, vernacular, 11, 272, 274
Kwakwaka'wakw peoples, 254
Kyle Scow Memorial Park, 151

L'Anse au Clair, NL, 165
Labrador Métis Nation, 158, 166, 170
Labrador Road, 14, 168
landings data, 97, 104, 105, 114, 117, 122, 124
Leslie analysis, 92
Leslie-based models, 98
Leslie Harris Centre of Regional Policy and Developments, 261
littoral zones, 6, 171–2
lobster catch rates, 116, 130
local ecological knowledge (LEK), 86, 101–8, 112–20, 173, 211. *See also* traditional ecological knowledge
longitudinal information, 87

Major Collaborative Research Initiative (MCRI), 4, 246, 272
managerial ecology, 191
marine social-ecological systems, 100–1
Marine Stewardship Council, 133, 179
Mary's Harbour, NL, 166, 169
maximum sustainable yield, 190
mega-school districts, 64
mental health, 146, 152
mercury content (in fish), 172
methodological design, 107, 232, 243
micro-level heterogeneity, 115
mining, 5, 28
Ministry of Energy and Mines (BC), 214
misreporting, 89, 105, 122–36. *See also* data fouling
mitigation (hatchery), 171
moratorium (cod), 86, 126–9

Index

moratorium on hydrocarbon development, 198, 208–10
multidisciplinarity, 12, 231. *See also* interdisciplinarity; transdisciplinarity
Municipal Wetlands Stewardship, 14, 178

Namgis First Nation, 16, 255–7, 263, 264; research protocol, 255. *See also* Alert Bay
Nanaimo, BC (coal miner's strike), 205
natural authority, 182
Natural Science and Engineering Research Council (NSERC), 4, 214, 224, 246, 272
NEPTUNE Project, 217–21
Newfoundland and Labrador Municipal Wetland Stewardship Program, 14
Nisga'a First Nation, 50
non-consumptive nature activities, 180
North American Waterfowl Management Plan, 184–90
northern cod, 10, 125, 128; collapse of, 276–7. *See also* cod
Northwest Atlantic Fisheries Organization (NAFO), 104
Nutrition, poor, 73, 80, 143, 148
Nuu-chah-nulth Central Region Language Group, 253, 264
Nuu-chah-nulth First Nation, 250
Nuu-chah-nulth language revitalization project, 253, 264

observer programs, 125–6
Ocean Drilling Program, 213–14
Ocean Falls, BC, 205
offshore oil and gas reserves, 198–204, 209–15, 219
offshore research vessel, 102
oil economy (BC coast), 204
oil spills, 194, 202, 207–8, 220
oligotrophication process, 172–3
oolichen (oulachan), 51
out-migration, 5, 10, 64, 146
over-estimation, of fish stocks, 106, 126. *See also* data fouling
overfishing, 13, 123, 129–34, 170
over-reporting, of fish stocks, 124

Pacific Accord, 209
Pacific herring, 95. *See also* herring
Pacific Rim National Park, 210
panarchy (def.), 34
Parent Advisory Council (PAC), 79. *See also* school councils
Parent Teacher Associations (PTA), 79. *See also* school councils
Parsons Pond, NL, 183, 191, 193
participatory decision-making, 153
Pesticide Environmental Stewardship Program, 179
Petroleum and Natural Gas Act, 210
photo-assisted interviewing techniques, 141
physical systems, 33, 198
physico-chemical environment, 155
place identity, 147
population structure, 114, 155
Port Alberni, BC, 211
Port Alice, BC, 205
Port Hope Simpson, NL, 166
power differentials, 159
power relations, 7, 9, 78, 238, 240
practical knowledge. *See* knowledge, practical

precautionary principle, 31, 37, 89, 278
predator prey relations, 155
Prince Rupert, BC, 50, 78, 206
Ptolemy, 23, 27
public health initiatives, 7, 147
Puget Sound, WA, 208

Queen Charlotte Basin, 67, 207, 210, 215
quota busting, 123
quotas (fish), 13, 89, 92, 94–7, 116, 121–7, 132, 180

rational evaluation approach, 157
raven (trickster), 38
reflection in action, 160
reflexive mandate, 238
reflexive methodology, 224, 238
relationship building, 142, 265, 268
research community, 236–7, 252
Resilience Alliance, 34
resource degradation, 5
resource extraction, 25, 213, 219
resource scarcity, 5
riparian habitats, 167

salmon, 51, 58, 68, 147, 157, 163–74, 205, 258. *See also* Atlantic salmon
salmonberries, 55
sardine. *See* California sardine
scholarly knowledge, 67–9
school as community centre, 65
school-based enterprise, 65
school-community interactions, 66–9, 77–80
school councils, 79. *See also* Parent Teacher Committees and Parent Advisory Councils

science-industry collaborations, 213
scientific competition, 213, 257
scientific methodology, 231
scientist/elder talking circle, 264
selective dumping, 123, 126, 131
self-esteem, 51, 56, 146, 193
Sentinel fishery, 89, 128
serial dependence, 114
Shell (oil company), 207
shifting-baseline syndrome, 101
Skeena River, 50
Sm'algyax language, 53, 54, 59
Small Pelagics Advisory Committees, 96
snowball sampling, 126
snow crab, 89–92, 132. *See also* Atlantic snow crab
social change, 29
social construction, 229
social determinism, 33
social networks, 147
social restructuring, 5, 146, 197, 272
social sciences, 7, 12–29, 33, 101, 119, 152, 221, 223, 226–31, 272
Social Sciences and Humanities Research Council of Canada (SSHRC), 4, 245, 272
social scientific research, 242
social systems analysis, 33
social-ecological change, 101
social-ecological health, 22, 28, 31, 34, 38
social-ecological system, 31, 35, 39, 101–6, 112, 118, 261, 273
sociologists, 6, 13, 19, 29, 60, 86, 276
socio-political restructuring, 141
St John Bay, NL, lobster fishery, 115–17

Standard of Conduct for Research in the Northern Barkley and Clayoquot Sound Communities, 252, 265
Standard Oil, 205
Star Lake, NL, 14, 158, 171–7
Star Lake hydro dam, 14
steady state theory, 23
Stephenville Crossing, NL, 183, 186, 194
stewardship, 14, 60, 179–94
stewardship arrangement, 190
stickleback, 172
stochastic variables, 179, 192
stock assessment, 11, 24, 87–93, 95–7, 104, 276. See also trawl survey
Strait of Belle Isle, 101, 112, 165
stream remediation, 168
subsistence hunting, 183, 186
subsistence resource value, 193
sustainable exploitation, 155
sustainable relationship, 197
symbolic capital, 234
symbolic thinking, 26

talking circles, 71, 264
techno-hubris (def.), 30–2, 35
tectonic displacements, 212
Tillich, Paul, 26–9
Tilt Cove, NL, 25
tipping points, 3
Tofino Basin, 210
Torrey Canyon spill, 208
total allowable catch (TAC), 85, 93, 95
tourism, 5, 73, 202, 210–11, 220, 251, 253, 259, 260
traditional ecological knowledge, 8–9, 45–51, 53, 54, 60–3, 179, 186, 187, 272, 274. See also local ecological knowledge

traditional rights, alienation of, 188
traditional stewardship ethic, 186, 187, 193
Trans Labrador highway, 159, 165, 166
transdisciplinarity, 6, 7, 12, 16, 231, 274. See also multidisciplinarity; interdisciplinarity
transdisciplinary team writing, 7
trawl survey, 92, 102, 105, 117
trophic levels, 105, 115
trout. See brook trout
Tsimshian [Ts'msyen], 9, 45, 50, 54, 59, 61–2. See also Sm'algyax language; individual First Nations
turbot, 128

U'mista Cultural Centre, Alert Bay, BC, 257
Ucluelet, BC, 210, 250
Unama'ki Institute of Natural Resources, 266
under-the-table sales, 125
UNESCO biosphere reserve, 249–50
Unilever, 133
Union Oil Barges, 205, 208
United Nations, 3, 31
un-mandated catch, 123

value conflicts, 186
Vancouver Foundation, 256
VENUS Project, 217
volunteer burnout, 256

Waterford River, 175
West Coast Oil Ports Inquiry, 209
West Coast Vancouver Island Aquatic Management Board, 252
wetland protection, 183, 189
Wildlife Habitat Canada, 184

wisdom, 28–32, 36–41, 56, 59, 63, 149, 153, 165, 187–91; formation of, 4–19, 277–8

Wright, Ronald, 3

yew wood, 55

youth: aboriginal, 53, 56, 71; alcohol consumption, 144–5; drug use, 144–5, 150; health determinants, 143; identity development, 140; knowledge of, 13, 139–54; participation in community, 45, 74, 246